"Born in a Mighty Bad Land"

"Born in a Mighty Bad Land"

The Violent Man in African American Folklore and Fiction

Jerry H. Bryant

INDIANA
University Press

Bloomington & Indianapolis

This book is a publication of
Indiana University Press
601 North Morton Street
Bloomington, IN 47404-3797 USA

http://iupress.indiana.edu

Telephone orders   800-842-6796
Fax orders   812-855-7931
Orders by e-mail   iuporder@indiana.edu

Library of Congress Cataloging-in-Publication Data

Bryant, Jerry H., date
   "Born in a mighty bad land" : the violent man in African American
folklore and fiction / Jerry H. Bryant.
       p. cm. — (Blacks in the diaspora)
   Includes bibliographical references and index.
   ISBN 0-253-34206-6 (cloth : alk. paper) — ISBN 0-253-21578-1
(pbk. : alk. paper)
       1. American fiction—African American authors—History and criticism.
2. Violence in literature. 3. Literature and folklore—United States.
4. African American men in literature. 5. African Americans—Folklore.
6. Violence—Folklore. 7. Men in literature. 8. Men—Folklore. I. Title.
II. Series.
   PS374.V58B79 2003
   813.009'355—dc21

                                                    2002011578

1 2 3 4 5 08 07 06 05 04 03

For Betty

CONTENTS

ACKNOWLEDGMENTS

Over the thirty or so years that I've taught, thought, and written about this material, I've developed a fondness for the African American badman that I've heard novelists express for the characters they have created. For sure, I didn't invent Stagolee, Devil Winston, John Hardy, Dupree, Railroad Bill, or any of the other actors in the badman drama. For that I'm indebted not only to the anonymous black musicians who gave such complexity to the personality of the badman, but also to the collectors who recorded the ballads, however imperfectly, before the badman lore drowned in the sea of commerce that became the grave of folk expression. I am a passive and grateful beneficiary of their labors.

This book is the second (and final) part of a project of many years' duration. The first part, *Victims and Heroes: Racial Violence in the African American Novel,* dealt mainly with the way black novelists depicted the violence that whites have committed against blacks in this country and black attitudes toward retaliation. *"Born in a Mighty Bad Land"* focuses on violence between African Americans, specifically with the type of man who becomes identified by his angry, defiant, and violent behavior within the black community.

Both books took many shapes before they emerged in their present form, and several friends and colleagues read parts and tentative wholes. Jacob Fuchs and George Cuomo, Cal State Hayward colleagues, read dauntingly long versions before I chopped what was once one unwieldy book into two. And Michel Fabre, of the University of Paris, read segments on Richard Wright and Chester Himes. I want especially to remember the late Norman Grabo, whose advice and encouragement meant more to me than I was ever able to tell him. I value the patient and tactful help of all of these generous spirits too much to hold them accountable for its inevitable imperfections. Those are inescapably mine. In addition, I owe to George Cuomo some very canny suggestions about the title. My son, Craig Bryant, opened the doors to rap music for me, making available albums and tapes I would otherwise never have known about. I must also acknowledge various kinds of assistance from California State University, Hayward: sabbaticals, paid quarters off, and the mere opportunity to teach what I came to write about. And I can't say enough in praise of the Cal State library staff, especially its interlibrary loan department led by Lynn LaFleur, all of whom gave me invaluable assistance in tracking down and then getting into my hands books I could not have done without. Finally, I raise my glass to Robert J. Sloan and Jane Lyle, of Indiana University Press, for greasing the wheels of a publishing process that is too often slowed by varieties of bureaucratic impediments, and to Shoshanna Green, the most indefatigably meticulous copyeditor I have ever encountered.

"Born in a Mighty Bad Land"

Introduction

I was bohn in a mighty bad lan',
For my name is Bad-Lan' Stone.
Well, I want all you coons fer to understan',
I am dangerous wid my licker on.

Bad-Lan' Stone is one of a distinct type in the African American imagination: the "bad nigger," the "badman," the "bully." He is a violent man: a killer, a creator of mayhem, a sower of disorder. He lives to "break up the jamboree," to put down opponents, build a reputation, create awe in the timid and fear in competitors. Black historian L. D. Reddick suggests that this personage and his opposite, the Uncle Tom, constitute

> the two extreme and opposite reactions to the hostile forces that bear down upon the Negro. . . . The [Uncle Tom] accepts his inferior status passively, or for internal peace or special favors actively cooperates in the subjection of himself and his people. The ["bad nigger"] fights all the way—with his fist, knife, or gun—boisterously aggressive or sullenly silent, in either case violently protecting himself and family against "anything white" that crosses. He has no respect for a law not made by or for him. He expects no justice from the courts. The police are his natural enemies. Between these two poles may be found the intermediate types, mixtures in varying proportions of the extremes.[1]

When given a choice, many African Americans prefer the "bad nigger" to the Uncle Tom, like a "young stenographer" in Chicago interviewed in the mid-1940s by sociologist Samuel M. Strong. She understood perfectly which side she came down on and what doing so meant:

The "bad nigger" [she said] refuses to accept the place given to Negroes. He does not fight intelligently [like the trickster or "smart nigger"]. It is a blind and reckless kind of fight. Many Negroes admire the "bad nigger" but are afraid to follow him. I admire the "bad nigger" and would rather see him fight desperately and furiously than crawling on his knees. I appreciate that more than the bowing and scraping that some Negroes are doing. Illiterate people who have independence of character admire the "bad nigger." He is usually one of that class.[2]

One can see the attraction of the figure. For the white man, says folklorist and literary critic H. Nigel Thomas, the "bad nigger" suggested defiance of white rules, "situations or individuals diametrically opposed to white control of black existence."[3] The "bad nigger" was the white man's worst dream: the slave or (after Emancipation) the laborer who refused to knuckle under, who repeatedly ran away, who deliberately slowed down work, surreptitiously or openly throwing sand into the master's machines. He was the out-of-control black man, the surly slacker, the belligerent troublemaker, and occasionally the killer of whites. For one postbellum southerner, "A bad negro is the most horrible human creature upon the earth, the most brutal and merciless."[4]

Such thinking helps account for the way African Americans came to revise the language of the white value system. "Signifying" upon the adjective, the young Chicago stenographer inverts the normal (that is, "white") meaning of *bad,* overturning "the normative moral structure of the oppressing society. Bad becomes good, and vice versa."[5] What is negative for whites becomes positive for blacks. This special denotation of "bad" was encoded in its special pronunciation, the prolonged rather than the short "a," as in "ba-ad." "Thus transformed," as historian Lawrence Levine puts it, "the term has been used to describe those who were admired because they had the strength, courage, and ability to flout the limitations imposed by white society,"[6] and thus gain a point for racial pride and self-esteem.

The badman falls into two principal types. Boxers like Jack Johnson and Muhammad Ali, political leaders like Malcolm X and Huey Newton, and musicians like rapper Tupac Shakur are the kind of "bad niggers" who revolt mainly against whites within the white system. They gain their victories not, as Levine says, by preying "upon their own people" or "breaking the laws of the larger society but by smashing its expectations and stereotypes, by insisting that their lives transcend the traditional models and roles established for them and their people by the white majority." Moreover, "They defeated white society on *its* own territory and by *its* own rules," providing "models of action and emulation for other black people."[7] Basketball star Dennis Rodman invoked this kind of badness in the title of his autobiography, *Bad As I Wanna Be.* The "ba-adness" of these figures contains a strong element of politics and social protest, and it is in this sense that the warriors of the Black Power and Black Arts movements appropriated "ba-ad" as their own, investing it with unprecedented political force and using it as an epithet of their bravura revolt against the long years of humiliation suffered under white prejudice. Sonia Sanchez's *We A BaddDDD People* is one of the best examples of the practice. But these groups employed a usage that had probably been in existence for a couple of centuries in the black community. Levine calls this rebel figure a "*moral* hard man," opposing him to a considerably larger and less political group.[8]

The second qualifying type falls under the rubric of what folklorist Roger D. Abrahams simply calls "hard-men."[9] Their violence is unqualified by morality or protest. Unlike Levine's "moral hard man," this figure breaks the laws of mainstream society and turns his violence and surliness not only upon whites who get in his way, but also against the people in his own black community. In the slave quarters he might deliberately seduce other slaves' wives just to achieve dominance, beat his own wife and children, pugnaciously strut around the shacks looking for a fight, challenge less irascible slaves to mortal encounters, and possibly kill others in the field. In the post-Emancipation world, he might terrorize the work camp, his black neighborhood, the church social, the crossroads tavern.

The "moral hard man" was often a racial warrior with a political agenda. His type erupted especially in the late 1960s as a fomenter of the Black Power movement. The simple "hard man" scorned social action. He was a fierce individualist, a scourge in his own community, introducing disorder and arousing fear, disapproval, and alarm as well as a reluctant admiration. He was known for his viciousness, and his excesses were material for stories around a slave-cabin fire or, later, at the barber shop or pool hall and the springboard for exaggerated tales of boundless priapic feats, triumphs over the devil, incomparable cruelties, and a cool style that young studs sought to emulate. In the black community, this "bad nigger" was the king of the street corner, the terror of the roadside honky-tonk, the superbly self-confident and solitary operator.[10]

Except for the famed "moral hard man" John Henry, it is Abrahams's style of "bad nigger"—together with the figure's two other incarnations, the badman and the bully—who is the more involved in the day-to-day African American experience and the powerful subject of the imaginative life of the people. As psychologists Price M. Cobbs and William H. Grier say, the "bad nigger" is "one of the constant themes in black folklore. . . . It seems that every community has had one or was afraid of having one."[11] He demands his own place in the scheme of things and belligerently sets the standard for manhood. Some call the badman a permanent fixture in the collective black male character, a virtual archetype in the Jungian sense. "[E]very black man harbors a potential bad nigger inside him," Cobbs and Grier write. His value to the African American male, though, is ambiguous. He is "a reminder of what manhood could be," to be sure. Yet, if they are to survive, black men "must ignore this inner man." First, because he calls forth the limitless power and hostility of whites, and second, because he violates "the American ideal of respectability."[12] And respectable is definitely what the classic folk badman is not. This is what makes him such a tar baby for black middle-class strivers. Traditionally, though perhaps less so today, whites have insisted on identifying the respectable middle class with the most disreputable types among blacks. So those African Americans of all classes who lived perfectly respectable lives too often found it impossible to disengage themselves from this infamous and, in some circles, contemptible type. They seemed stuck with him, sometimes for better, sometimes worse. Ralph Ellison points out that in a massive defense mechanism against the brutal racial violence of the South, black families worked to suppress in the Negro man those "unknown forces *within himself* which might urge him to reach out for that social and human equality which the white South says he cannot have," an equality the "bad nigger" by definition fights for. James Baldwin saw Ellison's inner "unknown forces" as a syndrome, a Jungian "shadow" dwelling deep in the black psyche: a "dark and dangerous and unloved stranger," a permanence that every African American must accept as "part of himself forever."[13]

Baldwin makes this statement in his discussion of Richard Wright's *Native Son* (1940), whose protagonist, Bigger Thomas, is doubtless the best-known instance of the "bad nigger" literary type. Wright uses the figure as a warning to whites of the dangers that could grow out of a permanently suppressed class. In his essay "How 'Bigger' Was Born," he describes the five different forms of the single metatype of the "bad nigger" which he had personally observed and out of which he sculpted Bigger Thomas as a composite. Acting out of both terror of being caught in a white girl's bedroom and frustrated rage at his stifled life, Bigger, playing the role of the white man's "bad nigger," kills his would-be benefactress, the daughter of a wealthy Chicago businessman. More characteristic of the folk badman, though, Bigger also kills his own black sweetheart and bullies and intimidates his friends and his family, injecting the kind of disorder into the neighborhood of South Side Chicago's Indiana Avenue that typifies "bad nigger" behavior. While claiming that Bigger is a stereotype, Baldwin at the same time acknowledges the accuracy of Wright's portrait and Bigger's ubiquity as a type among blacks, claiming that "no American Negro exists who does not have his private Bigger Thomas living in the skull."[14] Both Wright and Baldwin emphasize a powerful feature of the badman, the social and psychological dangers he poses for blacks in a white society. As Cobbs and Grier say, he is a force that must be suppressed and controlled if African Americans are to make any progress in mainstream culture. Yet his meaning for black culture lies precisely in his defiant individualism, in the fear he strikes not only among blacks but among whites, too. He is the pride of the black community ("You should see that dude operate: he is *ba-ad!*"); he is the despair of the black community ("We can get nothing constructive done with that man around!"). He is the violent outlet for anger and frustration, an example of fearlessness and autonomy. But he is a threat to communal stability and achievement. The uneducated folk are inclined to accept the badman in all his disorderliness and to grasp the tragic implications of his impulsive violence. Activists in the middle class attempt to reform him and then use him to improve their lives and expand their potential. The folk write ballads to express their perceptions, the middle class writes novels. What do they make of the traditional badman and how do they relate to each other?

Black artists of all classes and genres have understood the badman's iconic value. His lineage goes back well into slavery and continues today in the imagery of the "gangsta" rapper. Stories about him appear in the badman ballads of the late nineteenth century and the later "toasts," whose doggerel testifies to the street popularity of Dolomite, the Great MacDaddy, and the always priapic Stagolee. And at least since the Harlem Renaissance, literate artists have mined the oral folk tradition for their themes and values in the same way that composers turned for inspiration to ethnic musical forms. Black authors from Rudolph Fisher to Toni Morrison have used the badman type for their own purposes. They have poked, punched, pinched, and shaken him in every conceivable way to see what he is made of. They have embraced him whole, broken him down and reassembled him, placed him against myriad backdrops and foils to bring out his seemingly infinite qualities. In doing so, along with their folk artist cousins, they confirm the badman as one of the central mythic elements in the African American experience. Over a couple of centuries of development, the man of violence changes forms and functions according to the use to which the author puts him and the social class in whose terms the author thinks. He is nearly as prevalent as the trickster and in many cases shares features with that universal being.

I speak of the violent *man* in African American folklore and fiction. To be sure, there have been violent women, but they are the exception; there has never been a "badwoman" type. Only a couple of the badman ballads are about women killing men. And even then, a character like Frankie kills Albert (or Johnny, depending on the version you choose to sing) out of jealousy rather than a "ba-ad" temperament.[15] I should say here, though, that I do not want to pick a fight with Hazel Carby on this matter. Speaking for a large and articulate contingent of black women, she argues that black intellectual life has been controlled by black men at least since W. E. B. Du Bois's *The Souls of Black Folk* (1903). Black men, she says, have rejected the ideas and contributions of black women as irrelevant to the true issue of race in America. They assume that the important concern of black life is the status of black men with respect to white men and see the winning of power and authority by black men as the key to the race question. Black men consider the issues relevant to the subject of race and nation to be defined and limited by their masculinity.[16] My study is no brief for or against Professor Carby's argument. It is true that one of the features of the badman type, especially in its later incarnations, is a pronounced misogyny. But as an observer, I do not contend that the badman figure embodies either the most important dimension of the history of the African American man or the defining feature of black life. The badman is worth studying because he appears so often in the products of black men's and women's imaginations. He is one of many vehicles the African American community employs to deal with many issues that concern its members.

But if the creation of a violent type that is all but exclusively male reflects reality, it evokes an old question: are men genetically wired for violence? It seems to go without saying that it is men who commit the great bulk of the world's violence, in wars, gang fights, shootings, stabbings, beatings, rapes. "Ninety percent of known murderers are men," says political commentator Joshua Shenk.

"The FBI estimates that in the United States a man rapes a woman about once a minute." Many students of the phenomenon still profess to find evidence that "violence lurks deep in the male soul" and go on asking questions about the "laws" of male violence.[17] Is it genetic or cultural? Are men born to the gunfight and the duel or do they absorb the practice from the world around them? Whether violence "is a primal male instinct," used to solve problems of control and gain personal or cultural status, or a learned behavior, its ubiquity among males continues to plague and fascinate us. For the African American male the issue is complicated by race and its unique role in American culture. The rate of violence between blacks, historically, has been higher than the average in the population as a whole. The African American badman plays a role in that phenomenon.

In the oral folk tradition, the violent man evolves through three distinct stages, all embodied in storytelling or song. The slave tale produces no clear badman figure, but violence is endemic in the forest of the animal characters, reflecting the harsh world of slavery and the slave quarters. By the end of the nineteenth century, the black balladeer gives a distinct shape to the type. The badman is the central figure who pumps bullets into a gambling companion or shoots his woman down in the street. His birth accompanies the proliferation of vice districts in cities burgeoning after the Civil War; the honky-tonks and roadhouses of the rural South; the work camps of itinerant laborers; and myriad other places where forms of shady street life became options for the most daring, defiant, and restless blacks in the years after Reconstruction. By the twenties or thirties, the gun-toting badman of the ballads has become a sexual superman in the "toasts," long poems of widely varying quality, generally recited by black convicts or young black men on street corners and in the bars and poolrooms of the urban scene. Violence is in his blood. Frequently he is caught in the net of white law and imprisoned or executed. Less often he triumphs and brassily flaunts his victory. But the folk do not probe his mind or his morals, nor do they protest the consequences of his behavior. He is as natural and common a part of their experience as thunder or lightning, rainstorms, floods, or fires. The badman may be the product of a suppressed collective rage, his violence a displacement of his anger from the white oppressor to the less dangerous targets of other blacks. But he is seldom formulated in those terms. For the most part he seems relatively unconcerned with white presence, with which middle-class writing is so preoccupied. He is therefore an unusual window upon the inner life of the unlettered African American community.

The badman enters the African American novel in the 1920s and 1930s, particularly in the fiction of Rudolph Fisher, Arna Bontemps, and Zora Neale Hurston. Between then and the present, he appears in a wide array of roles: as a pimp, a hit man, a ghetto hard man, a youth gang leader and "corner boy," a murderer, a wanderer, a private investigator, even a jockey and a furniture mover. Whatever form he takes, his literate creators are much more self-conscious about his behavior and his psychological makeup than are the folk artists. His violence, for them, is an issue. They analyze him sociologically, psychologically, morally.

They make him a man who has mastered the violent methods of the conventional "bad nigger" but who has graduated to bourgeois self-control and renounced violence for the rewards that middle-class conformity gives him. He becomes a mixture of rebel and social climber. The novelists produce plenty of the old-style badmen, but they tend to paint them in disapproving colors, sometimes depicting their chief characteristics as cowardice and deceit. The fundamental middle-class bias of the novelist is reflected in this treatment of the badman figure, and it determines the great difference in tone between the badman narrative of the oral folk tradition and that of the written novelistic tradition. Neither group has a monopoly on literary merit or historical importance. Both contain gems that no reader would wish to discard, as well as flaws most readers would prefer expunged.

I must say a word about the violence that beset the inner cities of America particularly during the 1980s. The crack epidemic of those years, even though it increased the murder rate among young black men, did not receive a great deal of attention from makers of the badman image. Killing by itself did not gain one admission into the fraternity. There seems to have been something in the violence of those years that put off the artists who might have explored it imaginatively. Rap did make its contributions, but crack, for the rappers, was seen as a source not (or rarely) of ambivalently admired badness but of social and psychological destruction caused by white racism. The young black men who shot each other seem to have lacked the particular characteristics necessary for them to qualify for legendary status, however much they might have been adulated and looked up to by some of the neighborhood youth.

An unavoidable sense that he is fated to die hangs over the classic badman figure. He even carries with him a hint of redemption for African Americans, not from their sins but from their oppression. It may have been this element of the redemptive potential of death that was lacking in the crack wars of the 1980s. Those deaths, sordid, useless, and destructive, may have disqualified the gun-toting crack dealers as models for the ambiguously honored badman of legend. It is the legendary figure and his later forms that I focus on in this study. Their individual badness had hardly any political or social agenda, nor did it link them with groups or movements. Instead, it brought nonracial violence to their too often isolated communities.

1

The Classic Badman and the Ballad

While "bad niggers" doubtless prowled the paths of the slave quarters and picked fights in free black taverns in southern cities, the full lineaments of the classic bad-man were not drawn until after the Civil War, when the slave society was re-configured as a quasi-free one. De facto slavery replaced the "peculiar institution" in the form of Jim Crow, sharecropping, and a carefully controlled labor market that forced black men and women into the worst and lowest-paid jobs. But op-tions opened that had been closed in slavery, options that replaced such sources of slave folk expression as the spiritual, the animal tale, and the stories about the witty trickster-slave High John the Conqueror. Former slaves and their children could migrate north or go west, and did so in increasing numbers. Escape, though difficult for the impoverished freedperson, became accessible in more than dreams, fantasies, and the words and music of the spirituals. Working conditions did resemble those of slavery, but the slyness and cunning of Brer Rabbit and High John, which had provided psychological satisfaction under slave conditions, ceased to be quite as relevant with the disappearance of Ol' Massa and the grow-ing importance of money and fairness rather than legal bondage.

As the black slave community disappeared, the new freedom, even though constrained, saw change in communal structures. Old slave quarters became the homes of laborers who could come and go much as they pleased—restricted, perhaps, by the ubiquitous "paterollers," but far less so than in slave conditions. In the last decades of the nineteenth century, self-contained black enclaves grew up: neighborhoods in small towns and scattered districts in the growing cities of the North and South. The new African Americans sought entertainment with greater freedom in the vice districts of the cities, at crossroads barrelhouses, village honky-tonks, backyard picnics. New artistic forms emerged reflecting the new sensibilities that accompanied these changed arrangements, exploring new feelings and new types of people. From an elaboration of old field hollers and risqué party songs to nonsense verses, material intended for performance, rather than group participation as the spirituals had been, provided a more individualistic vehicle and a transition from folk to more professional and commercial art. The blues turned attention from Christian soldiers fighting sin and John tricking Ol' Massa to the inner experience of individual black men and women in laments over an unfaithful mate, rehearsals of the universal pain of loss, and a general sense of melancholy, all leavened with a rich irony and humor.

The ballad became one of the vehicles of the folk imagination exploring these new conditions, and the violent badman became the ballad's central actor. He pumped "rockets" into a gambling adversary who annoyed him, or "blew away" the woman who cheated on him, or gunned down a white sheriff who had broken the rules of engagement in the black quarter. He became a familiar figure in the turpentine and logging camps, among the river levee roustabouts, in gambling dens, brothels, pool halls. He represented all that the educated elite and the church-going classes sought to leave behind them. Yet in this period he became emblematic for large segments of the African American community, in both the North and South.

THE BADMAN BOASTER

Over the forty or fifty years in which the ballad badman took shape, from about 1880 to 1930, some thirty separate characters appear in as many prototype songs.[1] Some of these prototypes occur in dozens, even scores, of different variants that amateur and professional folklorists have collected and edited over the years.[2] Except for one or two women murderers, their protagonists are all men of violence, and the ballads and songs about them recount a particular exploit or set of qualities that, for one reason or another, had special significance for composers, singers, and audiences. As song collector John Wesley Work says, "The life and death of notorious characters fired the imagination of many song-makers. The individual flaunting [sic] the law served to appeal much more to the creators than did those of better social status."[3]

The protagonist of these pieces was the imaginative embodiment of the real-life "bully" and "bad nigger," the id to the more genteel black superego, a man who lived on the margins, who was familiar with violence and death, and who reacted impulsively to any perceived personal injury, from friend or foe, man or woman. The genre had the distinction of being the only art form whose defining purpose was to explore and interpret the violence of the black folk, a fact suggested by folklorist G. Malcolm Laws's comment that "More than half the Negro ballads are based on murder, a percentage far higher than that of the white ballads." And of the five "traditional Negro ballads" in print that do *not* deal with violent crime, four are of doubtful authenticity.[4] For the most part, the ballads and songs are not expressions of racial protest or polemical demonstrations of racial injustice. They largely confine themselves to conflict between blacks. White functionaries of the law are ubiquitous in them, to be sure, but in all but a few cases, such as "Po' Laz'us" and "Duncan and Brady," the motivating forces arise from intraracial, not interracial, relationships.

Ten of the thirty badman prototypes involve boasters and braggarts, suggesting how central to the art of the badman song is the *rhetoric* of badness. The boasting song is a compilation of the qualities that make the braggart special. What makes him rejected among respectable people is a virtue for him. "Ba-ad-ness" is the *sine qua non* of his self-respect, the essence of his identity, and it is largely measured by the assurance with which he *says* he is bad. Bad-Lan' Stone, for example, whose boast I quote at the beginning of this book, glories in the description of his own and others' orneriness and his ability to strike fear in other badmen. He concludes

> You may bring all yo' guns from de battleship,
> I make a coon climb a tree.
> Don't you never dare slight my repertatin,
> Or I'll break up this jamberee.
>
> Well, well, I wus bohn in a mighty bad lan',
> For my name—name—is Bad-Man Stone.[5]

He cherishes the most important badman possession, a "repertatin" for badness. No "jamberee," picnic, party, or gambling room, in the city or in the country, is safe from the wreckage a true badman might cause over an affront.

The boasting songs are not the most popular badman songs. They seem not to have been as widely dispersed as ballads like "Stagolee" or "Railroad Bill," since they exist in very few variants. The pieces in this group, moreover, are lyrics rather than ballads, for they do not tell stories about an act of violence and its consequences. They are the arias of "devil" music, pugnacious reflections on the central figure's inflammable toughness, spoken either by the protagonist himself or by some other first-person observer. Disentangled from the interests of a narrative, the boasting songs are the archives of the black version of manliness in these years of the installation of Jim Crow. They reveal the core standard by which the badman lives and the qualities he and presumably his audience esteem, and express what the audience deems "boastworthy," as Alan Dundes aptly puts it. "The values of a society or of a segment of a society," says Dundes, "could in theory be extrapolated by analyzing the content of the 'boasts' of that society."[6] In the black boasting song badness and manliness are synonymous, and the badman's badness is measured by his ability to evoke fear wherever he goes. In the outrageousness of his behavior the singers and the audience recognize kin, and, while perhaps not unconditionally approving, nevertheless they take some pride in what the badman forces them to deal with.

Bolin Jones, Buffalo Bill, Joe Turner, Roscoe Bill are all boasters, bullies, and badmen who advertise their badness or have it advertised for them. They reflect, interpret, and comment on the environment in which they compete for dominance and reputation, asserting their power over other blacks in their own black community. The example of Bolin Jones will illustrate the type:

> Bolin Jones wuz
> A man of might,
> He worked all day
> And he fit all night.
>
> O Lawsy, Lawsy,
> He's a rough nigger,
> Han' to his hip,
> Fingers on de trigger.
>
> Lay 'em low,
> Lay 'em low,
> When Bolin's 'round,
> Mind whar you go.[7]

The childlike shortness of line masks an authentic metrical sophistication. The wit of the rhyme, with meaning and sound conforming so exactly to each other, shows how vastly far from doggerel and self-parody this black minstrel has traveled. His song is epigrammatic, almost gnomic, in its pithiness, calling up the whole environment in which Bolin Jones operates, the bluff terseness of men more used to acting than talking, to whom any kind of literary refinement is foreign. And yet the text is not without its own kind of eloquence.

The lack of any defining geographical background forces all our attention upon Bolin Jones himself. We cannot even tell where it is that he fights "all night"—in the streets and dives of a city like Memphis, the country juke joints, or a camp gambling room? But Bolin Jones is a composite of the typical black laborer. His life has no domestic content or personal intimacy. It is made up of a daytime of hard labor and a nighttime of blowing off steam by fighting, and illustrates how being respected and feared by others is more important than friendship, community, or racial solidarity. His is a limited and self-absorbed life, without expansive horizons or any thoughtful self-examination. Any ideas concerning racial improvement, working to enfranchise blacks, or securing a better life seem utterly alien to the sphere in which Bolin Jones moves.

The laconic lines and repetitions of these songs express the volcanic psyches of their protagonists, poised constantly on the edge of violence, as well as their physical strength, their recklessness, and their indifference to public opinion and community values. Conventional respectability is reversed. The respectable man honors women and avoids the low life of fighting, gambling, drinking, killing. The pious sing of God and heaven as the source of their grace and comfort. The badman takes pains to evoke imagery that aligns him with quite the other side of the battle. He is the quintessential black man living in a quintessential black world. He readily, *eagerly,* seeks other black men against whom to test himself, to kill if necessary, rejecting with gusto the nonviolent propriety of the respectable community.

THE FACES OF STAGOLEE

The boaster, though, is a one-dimensional figure, at times verging on the ridiculous. It is the ballad that provides the nuances in the delineation of the classic badman. While Bolin Jones and Bad-Lan' Stone and the rest of their boasting-song companions all seem very much alike, each of the thirty figures who are the protagonists of their own ballad "protonarratives" possesses his own personality. But they evade most of the easy generalizations that have often been made about the group. Roger Abrahams calls them "murderers and thieves, sadistic in their motivation, badmen looking for a fight just to prove their own strength and virility."[8] In similar language, Lawrence Levine characterizes the ballad badmen as "pure force, pure vengeance; explosions of fury and futility," anarchical and lawless, preying "upon the weak as well as the strong, women as well as men," and killing "not merely in self-defense but from sadistic need and sheer joy." They are "hard, unyielding, remorseless."[9] They represent, says another commentator, "a misanthropic perception of society."[10]

To be sure, nearly all of them are killers. Stagolee and John Hardy shoot other black men over trivialities like Stagolee's Stetson hat and Hardy's twenty-five-cent bet. But words like "remorseless" and "sadistic" do not apply consistently or universally. Dupree is what later black men might call "pussy-whipped." He is driven by his irresistible lust for his girlfriend's "jelly roll" to rob a jewelry store, and in doing so he inadvertently kills a policeman. Po' Laz'us is celebrated for his badness, but his death at the hands of a posse in the mountains is full of pathos. Railroad Bill becomes a feared train robber, but by the time another posse tracks him down and kills him, he is nothing but rags and desperation. Devil Winston, a psychopath; Bill Martin, a meek man who suddenly turns violent; and Bad Lee Brown, insulted at being punished for his crime, are all motivated by insecurity and jealousy when they kill their women. They flee, they are caught, they are taken to court, and they are jailed or executed. Some badmen engage white police and win, like Duncan in Leadbelly's "Duncan and Brady" and Danny Major in "Bugger Burns." But for the most part, they are bound inescapably by a white law, and are figures of awe and pity rather than of sadism and remorselessness.

Even the variants of a single protonarrative contain varying portraits of the eponymous protagonist. Stagolee—a.k.a. Stacker Lee, Staggerlee, Stackalee, Stackolee, Stack-O-Lee, Staggalee, Stack-O, and Stack Lee—is the star of the badmen. The several forms his name takes suggest the numerousness of the versions of his story, and those versions reflect a range of attitudes toward this most famous of the badmen: the exaggeratedly bombastic, the boastful, the tragic, the pathetic, the heroic. They do not all add up to the Stagolee Greil Marcus speaks of, "an archetype that speaks to fantasies of casual violence and violent sex, lust and hatred, ease and mastery, a fantasy of style and steppin' high . . . [of] no-limits for a people who live within a labyrinth of limits every day of their lives, and who can transgress them only among themselves. It is both a portrait of that tough and vital character that everyone would like to be, and just another pointless, tawdry dance of death."[11] Marcus's figure is more the superstud of the later "toasts," celebrated by young street men for the size and virility of his penis, than the Stagolee of the earlier ballads. Many of those ballads are precisely about the limits of black life, about what black men can and cannot get away with, about their power (or powerlessness) over women. It is this that gives them their depth and substance.

In most ballad variants Stagolee does mercilessly shoot Billy Lyons merely for abusing his Stetson hat, sneeringly indifferent to Billy's plea for his life because of his wife and children.

> "Don't care nothin' about your chillun,
> And nothin' about your wife,
> You done mistreated me, Billy,
> And I'm bound to take your life."[12]

But Stagolee does not kill with impunity. Sometimes the deputies the sheriff attempts to form into a posse are so intimidated by the famous badman they refuse to help with his arrest. But almost universally the sheriff kills Stagolee or apprehends him. He is taken to court and sentenced to death. At this point the variants show the greatest difference in their treatment of Stagolee. In the most ribald, the scene moves to hell, where Stagolee overwhelms the devil himself, a clear demonstration of the ultimate badman's incorrigibility. The aim is clear enough, but the devil episodes often twist the ironic-realistic ballad into the form of the exaggerated tall tale. Indeed, some, in which the hijinks are cartoonishly violent, approach farce:

> Stagolee, he told the Devil,
> Says, "Come on and have some fun—
> You stick me with your pitchfork,
> I'll shoot you with my forty-one."[13]

Other times they are merely bumptious:

> Stagolee say, "Now, now, Mister Devil, ef me an' you gonna have some fun,
> You play de cornet, Black Betty beat de drum."[14]

Such puffery is designed to show Stagolee eluding the serious punishment of the mortal courts that have sent him to his death for killing Billy Lyons. The ribaldry does work as a literary effect, and Stagolee maintains his reputation for being equal to any situation, but it surrenders the tone of menace that gives the badman his real power.

The prose tale of Stagolee provides a gloss on the question of Stagolee's Stetson hat and the scene in hell. In it, Stagolee was not only born with a "veil" over his face and hence was capable of seeing ghosts and raising "41 kinds of hell," he sold his soul to the devil in return for a special "oxblood magic hat." It was the key to Stagolee's fate, for "the devil fixed it so when Stack did lose it he would lose his head, and kill a good citizen, and run right smack into his doom."[15] In the half-ahundred ballad variants of "Stagolee" I have seen, a few refer to Stagolee's "magic" hat. But nowhere have I seen the supernatural side of the Stagolee story in such detail as in the folk tale. Yet we might surmise that the balladeers assumed that most of their audience knew of the magic oxblood hat and how Stack got it, which would support a view that Stagolee killed because of other influences besides his natural badness. Stack cannot help himself. He has been fated by the devil himself to kill any man who is foolish enough to fool with his hat, a spine-tingling feature for an audience that probably saw much of life through a lens of superstition.[16]

Stagolee is, thus, sometimes a pitiless killer, sometimes an intrepid conqueror of the devil, and sometimes a childlike joker. At other times, though, he is a man of dark somberness, a figure of high romance, even tragedy, boxed into his fate as he is in the folk tale. In these cases, he is no swaggerer but a great sufferer who is as intense in his anguish as he is in his heartless arrogance. Some variants create an atmosphere that recalls the romantic English and American novel of gothic horror. In fact, Stagolee's chronicler might almost have been reading Bulwer-Lytton himself:

> It was on a dark
> And cold stormy night
> That Billy Lyons and Stackolee
> They had that awful fight.[17]

Some versions are even more explicit about the bad weather and the related lawlessness of the venue in which Stagolee commits his crime:

> The night was dark and stormy
> And the rain came pouring down;
> There was nary a police
> In that part of town,
> That bad, that bad man Stackalee.[18]

The dreariness of the rain and the dismal cold in these variants establish a wonderful ominousness, an atmosphere of foreboding nearly as powerful as in some of their literary betters, like the gray marshes of *Great Expectations* or the blasted oak of *Jane Eyre*.

Some of these uneducated poets have a feel for the great themes. They know that great emotion does not occur in the clowning of a farcically triumphant Stagolee tearing hell apart, but in the defeat of the strong, the entrapment of the defiant spirit. They understand to the core the psychology of a violent man like Stagolee, know that he is capable of guilt and superstitious anguish. In these variants, Stagolee prowls his cell in feral desperation after being imprisoned for murder. Awaiting execution, he suffers from a spiritual anxiety that borders on psychosis. Sometimes the ghost of his victim eerily appears in his visions and makes it impossible to sleep:

> Stackalee said to the jailer, "Jailer, I can't sleep,
> From my bedside Billy Lyons began to creep."[19]

Other times Stagolee faces the door of hell itself, but now he takes no pratfalls, nor does he engage in slapstick with a comically bewildered devil:

> Now late at night you can hear him in his cell,
> Arguin with the devil to keep from goin to hell.
> And the other convicts whisper, whatcha know about that?
> Gonna burn in hell forever over an old Stetson hat![20]

The uncanny late-night atmosphere, the listening from a distance to this doomed man on the verge of madness, the whispering of the other convicts in their awed respect for some mystic thing happening—all this suggests in Stagolee the same fear of the supernatural, the same fear of endless punishment, as Faustus feels awaiting the devil's minions. Stagolee is, indeed, in some variants, not an embodiment of "fantasies of casual violence and violent sex, lust and hatred, ease and mastery, a fantasy of style and steppin' high," but a black badman Faustus, who, having sold his soul to the devil for a magical hat, suffers the tremendous metaphysical anguish of fearing that "no end is limited to damnèd souls."[21] And the other prisoners, who also know this, conclude that neither saving his Stetson hat by killing Billy nor creating a reputation for hardness that will last for years is worth Stagolee's terrifying fate: "Gonna burn in hell forever."

It is the many-sidedness of Stagolee's composite portrait that most strikes one here, surprising us with the variety of tints, tones, and textures that one imaginary figure can stimulate in a people's singers. Any folk minstrel who ever sang a Stagolee song was part of the creative process, in the barrelhouse, in the field, at a picnic or backyard party, on the porch of the crossroads store. Professional or amateur, single or in groups, those who enacted the musical story were not historians seeking some objective truth or sociologists trying to explain their culture. They were not out to locate the "true" Stagolee, only to create one, with greater or lesser effectiveness, from the legendary material available to them at the moment of their singing. Nor do the variants express any final attitude toward Stagolee's violence, moral or otherwise, but a shifting kaleidoscope that sometimes brings up farce, sometimes tragedy. The community out of which these various faces grow was no monolith, nor is its badman confined to a single shape.

For all their differences, these badmen form a variegated profile for the times, a projection of anger, frustration, and isolation under Jim Crow, of a simultaneous helplessness and power. They enact the fate of the black male: to be pursued, caught, and punished. One of the most striking and oft-repeated plot motifs of the John Hardy prototype is his attempt to escape arrest after killing a man during a gambling game: "And you ought to have seen Johnny getting away, / Poor boy, and to have seen poor Johnny getting away." Though this couplet appears in several different forms, it is all but universal in John Hardy variants. In several cases, a whole stanza is devoted to his flight:

> John Hardy had ten miles to go,
> And half of that he run;
> He ran till he came to the broad river bank.
> He fell to his breast and swum.
> Lord, Lord! he fell to his breast and swum.[22]

But John Hardy is not fated to escape:

He went to the end of the East Stone Bridge,
There he thought he would be free,
But up stepped a man and took him by the arm,
Saying Johnny, come and walk with me.[23]

How the emphasized line resonates to the black male's condition under the restrictions of Jim Crow and lynch law. No amount of running, no amount of cleverness or speed, enables him to elude white punishment. Like Stagolee, John Hardy may be desperate; he may be mean, brave, tough, unequaled with a gun. But his condition is "caughtness." Indeed, he may have amazed onlookers by the sheer brass of his act and the shrewd quickness of his flight, but his toughness comes to nothing against the implacable mechanism of white law. This is the core drama of the badman ballad, fraught with fatalism and an austere sense of the inescapable. It is at the same time a hard-edged suggestion that a system of rough justice does operate in the badman's world. The laws of the court and the laws of event form the mechanism of punishment. Once that mechanism is triggered by the violence and arrogance of the badman, it cannot be switched off. To be a black badman is in itself a crime, and its punishment is inescapable.

This is not to say that the men who are tracked down and punished are innocent victims of an unfair justice system. They do commit crimes for which they must be punished. That is part of the frustration. And sometimes they deny their own badness. Pleadingly, Dupree tells the judge, "I am not so brave and bol'." It may be that, as Dupree avers, he has "quit" his pursuit of life's jelly rolls, but the judge answers with the implacability of the machinery of punishment:

. . . you quit too late,
Because it is
Already your fate.

He goes inevitably to his death.[24]

Fate and necessity preside over these narratives. Jail or execution: they are the end stops of the iron rails upon which the badman's life runs. The badman ballad rides these rails again and again, tirelessly, repetitively, showing its audience the territory with which its members, too, are all too familiar, for being "caught" is surely one of the dominant motifs in the lives of the levee roustabout and itinerant laborer, of, if most studies are to be credited, the black man in general. In most of the "fugitive" and "betrayal" ballads,[25] this is the image that rules, rather than the crimes themselves or examples of an unfair justice system, however unfair that system may have actually been. The theme the balladeers and their audience are most preoccupied with is the all-engulfing reality of their predicament.

In many of the ballads, we are flooded with the feelings and reactions of the badman himself, and their psychological power lies in the deep understanding the poet shows of the killer. In the most affecting pieces, the poet leaves us, in the end, with the badman's sense of a total loss of identity and of being cut off from any supportive world. In one of the most evocative stanzas in all the ballad literature, the imprisoned murderer of "The Coon-Can Game," who has killed his unfaithful girlfriend, drooping in his gloomy cell awaiting his death, laments that

> The night was dark and stormy, boys,
> It sure did look like rain;
> Not a friend in all this wide, wide world,
> Nobody knowed my name.[26]

This stanza not only sounds natural and unforced, it has few rivals in the ballads for expressing the isolation, loneliness, and anonymity that come with crime and the jail time it brings. It explores what James Baldwin half a century later called "the graver questions of the self" in *Nobody Knows My Name.* Who am I, asks Baldwin, behind the mask of the "Negro" I am forced by whites to wear? Once in the court of the white judge, the "Coon-Can" narrator's only identity is the mask the judge and his society force him to wear. And when he steps into that prison or dons the stripes and chains of the prison work gang, he loses all signs of self, becomes, as Orlando Patterson has put it, socially dead.[27] It is only in the killing of his sweetheart that he is somebody with feelings strong enough to draw a distinct outline around himself, and the outcome of that is his destruction. If murder is an act of agency, it also leads to agency's loss.

The conclusion of "The Coon-Can Game" shows us the moral and social web in which this class of African American was often caught. The narrator is not the swaggering, boasting badman, independent, defiant, self-sufficient, admired for his prison experience by the local small fry and resident street loafers. He is a gambling man whose luck has run out, hurt by the betrayal of his woman, and now cut off from his world. His cry of profound isolation speaks for the guilty and the condemned in all the ballads. These men *are* guilty, and that is what gives pathos to their plight. They are caught in a system of justice that convicts and punishes. Their guilt, though, the balladeers seem to say, does not efface their pain. That is the humanity that the badman ballad teaches with the understanding of those who know that pain firsthand. At their best, the ballads do not render any kind of moral verdict or purport to teach any moral lesson. They reproduce a vital experience of pain for which there is no balm. This is what makes these folk poets the true chroniclers of their world and their protagonists powerful symbols of a trammeled people.

2

Postbellum Violence and Its Causes

"Displaced Rage" in a Preindustrial Culture

What accounts for this genre of folk song? To what extent did such men exist in the real black world in these years? How widespread *was* the kind of intraracial violence that these men committed and the songs tell us about? There was, in fact, an unusually high homicide rate among lower-class African Americans in the years between the Civil War and World War I. Both North and South were afflicted, with violence among blacks increasing in both regions in the last several decades of the century.

While the statistics recent scholars have turned up apply to blacks in both the North and the South,[1] it is the South that is most relevant to the early development of the image of the violent man, in part because ninety percent of the black population still lived in the South in these years and in part because it is the southern, not the northern, badman mostly memorialized in the ballads. In his study of Mississippi's Parchman State Prison in the early Jim Crow years, David Oshinsky found that "blacks comprised about 67 percent of the killers in Mississippi and 80 percent of the victims."[2] Another scholar, citing "court, prison, and arrest records," says that in Memphis, in more or less the same period, "the great proportion of violent crimes by Negroes were . . . committed against other Negroes, including repeated cases of gambling altercations, barroom brawls, and domestic fights."[3] City historian William D. Miller turns up truly breathtaking numbers for Memphis in 1916, which led "the 31 large American cities" that were surveyed with 89.9 murders per 100,000 as compared, for example, with

Atlanta's thirty-one. Moreover, the homicide rate seems to have increased exponentially in the first years of the twentieth century, jumping from twenty-four arrests for murder in 1902 to 134 in 1917. Most of the murders were committed by blacks. Miller reports that "70 per cent of the homicides in the years 1920–1925 were committed by Negroes," and while the evidence is sketchy for the years before World War I, he speculates that the figures for those years were proportionately the same.[4] The situation in Memphis seems to have been merely a heightened version of what was going on in other southern African American communities in the years before World War I. Atlanta, Shreveport, St. Louis, Jacksonville, New Orleans, Kansas City—all saw their black neighborhoods grow, and along with the law-abiding came others more prone to crime and disruption. Atlanta had a large population of black pimps who "controlled much of the sporting action and barrooms on Decatur Street. Rowdiness, violence, and gangsterism were common occurrences." Razor fights were common. Deaths were frequent.[5] Jim Crow cars on trains, as black contemporaries complained, were also sites of cursing, fighting, shooting, cutting, and murder.[6]

Most observers tacitly assume that this real-world violence needs explaining, since it seems to occur in greater abundance between blacks than between the members of most other groups in the America of these years. What's *wrong* with these people? That is the unspoken question. How is it that so many black men (and even women) incline toward violence? Surely something has gone wrong with the cultural psyche. It is illuminating, for two reasons, to examine the attempts to explain these questions. They reveal how scholars think about this group of African Americans, and they fill in many of the details of the period's socio-economic background. Unfortunately, these details do not change materially over the decades, but simply get worse. The badman grows out of them.

So common had alarm in the African American community over this violence become that in 1904, W. E. B. Du Bois's think tank on black social problems at Atlanta University did a study of southern Negro crime. The study found that while African Americans made up about one-eighth of the population in the South, they accounted for about one-fifth of the crime. A quarter of Negro prisoners had been confined for "fighting and quarreling, ending at times in homicide, and also the crime of rape."[7] Even before the Atlanta study was made, Du Bois readily conceded that "There can be no doubt that crime among Negroes has sensibly increased in the last thirty years, and that there has appeared in the slums of great cities a distinct criminal class among the blacks."[8]

In spite of its often scolding tone, the Atlanta report attributes the high incidence of violence among blacks to what has been done to them in America, adducing virtually every one of the explanations later presented by more modern opinion and research. Du Bois's investigators, citing the whole system of racism and economic exclusion and exploitation, trace black violence back to slavery itself, and the white attitudes slavery engendered. Blacks existed for the profit and service of whites and had no rights whites were bound to respect. Whites also thought, complained the researchers, that freed Negroes would not work and needed sharp oversight on the job and strict punishments for even the smallest infractions. Since whites owned the judiciary system, they could enforce these prejudices against powerless blacks, arresting and imprisoning them for the most minor of crimes, while whites got away with less stringent punishment for more serious crimes. These attitudes accounted for the growth in southern states of the convict lease system, which encouraged imprisonment of blacks so they could be hired by wealthy whites at slave wages. This in turn stimulated the invention of more crimes for blacks to be guilty of. More and more blacks were convicted and sent to prison, there to be educated in even greater crimes and conditioned to think in a criminal way. Southern blacks, in other words, did commit crimes at a rate disproportionate to their numbers in the population, but that disproportion, the Atlanta report concludes, could be blamed on poverty and the way blacks were treated by the southern white judiciary.

Later commentators add little new to the findings of the Atlanta report. Black violence emerged from the social conditions in which blacks were forced to live by Jim Crow.[9] In 1927, sociologist E. B. Reuter concluded that black delinquency and violence arose from the same causes as white, except that the problems were greater and more intense among blacks because of their lower educational levels, their greater poverty and unemployment rates, their suffering under greater social and industrial discrimination, and their greater abuse by the police and unfair treatment by the courts.[10] More recent research concurs: the incidence of homicide in populations reflects employment rates and education. For example, as the Irish became absorbed into the industrial economy and more fully employed, their early excessive homicide rate declined. Many scholars believe that the lower homicide rates among white groups were due to the increasing industrialization of the work force, whose members were educated, in both the schoolroom and the workplace, to practice cooperation, regularity, and self-restraint, and to delay gratification.[11] White workers, women as well as men, learned to arrive on time at their jobs, to take lunch breaks when the clock and their managers told them to, and to quit at a precise hour. They learned to wait for their paycheck, to save for purchases. As the American public education system grew, it became a partner in this industrial education.

The experience of blacks was precisely the reverse. They were excluded from the industrial system and their murder rates increased. They continued to live in a preindustrial world, according to seasonal rhythms, with long periods of leisure time, which reinforced the tendency to drift from one job to another. Turpentine sap ran from the trees only between March and November. The sugar harvest and processing season and cotton gin operation usually lasted just three months, and sawmills were in operation mainly in the spring, when the rivers were high and could carry large volumes of logs. Thus field laborers would go to work in the sawmill after the crops were harvested, or cut ties for the railroad, or take up temporary residence in a logging or turpentine camp. They would float from job to job as the season dictated and as work became available. This pattern prevailed in the towns as well as the rural communities, powerfully disrupting not only the black labor force but the black family. Moreover, even when there was work, black laborers seemed to prefer the preindustrial rhythms, however unprofitable they were. In Appalachian coal mines, "the routine of factory work" characteristic of Northern manufacturing plants contrasted "with the 'free lance' nature of coal digging. . . . Paid by the ton, a man might reach a self-imposed quota by midday . . . and then head for home; 'early quits' were routine." Black workers sought to maintain control over their own work time, preferring "that work assignments be parceled out by tasks and not by time."[12]

The great majority of blacks, preserving a rural culture, timed their days by the sun and their years by the seasons.[13] Herbert Gutman writes that first slavery, then their exclusion from the modernizing work force, kept blacks "preindustrial for more than merely two or three generations" and separated the huge majority of black laboring people "from all immigrant and native white workers."[14] Those who failed to internalize self-control and restrain impulsive behavior with the help of school or factory training were more likely to be involved in violent crimes. The group whose rate of violence increased, African Americans, "was the one least touched directly by the industrial revolution, the one left farthest behind."[15]

In his frequently cited study of small-town southern life in the 1920s and 1930s, *Caste and Class in a Small Southern Town* (1937), John Dollard accounts for the high rates of black violence with the thesis of "displaced rage," the "frustration-aggression hypothesis." Dollard contends that their isolation from mainstream work and social worlds created in blacks a unique psychology that resulted in a relative passivity in their relations with whites and a compensating aggressiveness in their dealings with each other.[16] The whites' hold on all aspects of social and economic power created tremendous frustration for any black person seeking dignity or higher achievement. "The usual human response to frustration," says Dollard, "is aggression against the frustrating object," in this case the white man. But when the frustrating object is too powerful to overcome and threatens any challenge with immediate and painful death, members of the lower caste must, if they are to survive, submit and divert their frustration "from the provoking object to some other object," here "the Negro group itself." The advantage of this diverted aggression, Dollard speculates, is that it gives the Negro a biologically satisfying outlet, and does so without bringing down on the whole community the overwhelming power of the whites in retaliation. Because of the hopelessness of success in any violent conflict with whites, blacks seemed to choose "conflict within the group and peace without," because they did not have the strength to make an "out-group" of the whites. Under such conditions "Strong in-group loyalties are impossible,"[17] and violence within the group becomes a means of siphoning off the pressures of frustration, though at the same time this "only succeed[s] in perpetuating discord among themselves."[18]

Subsequent scholars tend either to agree with Dollard[19] or, like anthropologist Hortense Powdermaker, to use his thesis as a starting point. She wonders if the "displaced rage" theory might help account for the abnormally high rate of violence she finds among the blacks of the small southern town she studies. Perhaps, she speculates, a black man might "vent against another Negro the rage he is unable to direct against the white men who have wronged him."[20] But she advances the idea as an adjunct of another way of explaining black violence. The premise she starts from is that southern courts seldom tried, much less convicted, one black man for killing or assaulting another. This, she reasons, might lead a black man "unconsciously" to take out his anger on another black person because he can do so with little fear of punishment. The theory shifts the problem of constraint from the psychic inner world of uncontrolled impulse to the outer world of the legal structure.

In the South the law provided little recourse to African Americans injured by others, black or white. Nor did it punish them consistently or rationally for crimes committed. No one has grasped the situation, then or now, with greater acuteness than Du Bois. The abnormally high rate of black southern crime, he says in *The Souls of Black Folk* (1903), derived from the "double system of justice" that was established in slavery and maintained after Emancipation, that made every white man a member of the police force and exposed every black man to criminal accusation. After slavery, the courts became the means by which blacks were reenslaved. "It was not then a question of crime, but rather one of color, that settled a man's conviction on almost any charge. Thus Negroes came to look upon courts as instruments of injustice and oppression, and upon those convicted in them as martyrs and victims." This had a detrimental effect upon the entire black community in the postslavery years, for when the real criminal—a murderer or rapist, a robber or a burglar—was brought before the legal system, so distrustful were most blacks of the system that accused, tried, and punished him that he was turned into a mistreated victim. Thus "the greatest deterrent to crime, the public opinion of one's own social caste, was lost, and the criminal was looked upon as crucified rather than hanged."[21]

With the whites holding legal power and applying it to the two races with a double standard, African Americans fell "outside the law." Their estrangement from and distrust of the white justice system and its courts, this theory holds, was one of the principal sources of intrablack violence, for when a black man considered himself unjustly treated he might kill his antagonist rather than turning to the white law, from which he could expect little relief. Indeed, as H. C. Brearley says, "In some Negro groups it is not quite honorable to appeal to the courts for redress of an affront that seriously affects one's status in the community. Unless the difficulty can be settled by the intervention of friends or church officials, fighting it out may be the only recourse."[22] Such conditions, says Powdermaker, encourage "the Negro to take the law into his own hands when his difficulties involve other Negroes. Since he can hope for no justice and no defense from our legal institutions, he must settle his own difficulties, and often he knows only one way. He is the more ready to use it, since the same court which would crush him if he accused a white man of cheating him will probably let him off if he is accused of killing a black man."[23]

In such a culture the "bully" and the "bad nigger" thrive. This is hardly surprising, given an inadequate justice system and a weak central authority. For a bullying or violent man in such a system, personal conflict is not only unexceptional, it is the natural mode of problem solving. Powdermaker conjectured that in the small black southern community she studied, "physical violence is a more *familiar* pattern than [in other communities] . . . where it might be regarded as an aberration." She means not that the African Americans she observed were more inherently violent than whites, but that there were in the structure of their environment forces different from those in the environment of most whites, and this difference explained the difference in the way blacks reacted to each other. If this was so, she concluded, it would have "implications quite different from those which" one would draw from theories that regarded social violence as deviant or pathological.[24] Much of the violence in black communities, therefore, can be seen not as necessarily pathological, a deviance from a more healthy nonviolent norm, but as a rational way of behaving for those living in preindustrial conditions. This viewpoint bears directly upon how we explain and respond to the badman songs and African American novels that interpret violence in the black community. That is, in some cases violence can be a rational response to certain conditions, like those in a "subculture of violence" in which *not* using violence may be a frustrating, ego-deflating, even guilt-ridden experience.[25]

The historical real-life badman was a creature of these conditions: a laborer with a preindustrial temperament that gave free rein to violent impulses; a black man whom, according to most researchers, white law ignored for such violence. He lacked both internal and external constraints. He was "outside the law" in the sense that he could commit with relative immunity any mayhem among blacks. But here we need to introduce a caveat. This black man *was* subject to the law and to punishment. His abnormally frequent presence in southern jails, in the convict lease system, and on the chain gang proved it. In other words, black men were not "outside the law" in the sense that the white law left them alone; rather, the laws they were most often imprisoned for breaking were laws peculiarly designed for them to break. Most of the time they went to jail for alleged crimes against whites, or petty victimless crimes like vagrancy, not having proof of employment, or public disorderliness. Prison became a normal part of life for many black families. The ex-cons came back from prison heroes at once feared and admired, looked up to by the young fry who would follow them. Jail time was a sign of badness. And being bad came to carry a powerful cachet.[26] It indicated a defiance of white law and an individual strength in a community where few had the courage to fight back. Those who did fight back and were sent to prison were regarded with a combination of fear and admiration when they got out.[27]

Such values, of course, from the viewpoint of respectable society, were upside down. What would bring shame to a law-abiding black man was worn by the ex-convict cohort as a badge of honor. Not all members of the badman type were ex-convicts, but the general sense of being "outside the [white] law" was a major source of the image of the badman. As a subject first of the black folk oral tradition and then of black fiction, he became a vehicle for exploring one of the more frustrating conditions of the African American experience and the response to that condition in the black imagination.

3

Between the Wars

The Genteel Novel, Counterstereotypes, and Initial Probes

RELIGION, ROMANCE, AND RACE

Before the Harlem Renaissance of the 1920s only the folk seem to have made anything of the violent side of black life. Black novelists avoided the subjects of intrablack violence and the violent man. The four novels known to have been written by blacks before Emancipation—William Wells Brown's *Clotel; or The President's Daughter* (1853), Martin Delany's *Blake; or The Huts of America* (1859–62), Frank J. Webb's *The Garies and Their Friends* (1857), and Harriet E. Wilson's *"Our Nig"; or Sketches from the Life of a Free Black* (1859)—were far more concerned with violence done to blacks by whites than with that which they did to each other. As for sheer violence, Brown and Delany depict a good deal of whipping and Brown recounts the horrific burning of a slave at the stake. At the heart of Webb's novel, a race riot erupts in Philadelphia when a mob of unruly Irish immigrants, egged on by an envious white real estate lawyer, attacks a group of upright and stalwart blacks who give as good as they get in protecting their own. And in *"Our Nig"* the strident, hateful shrew of a New England mistress works the black heroine from dawn to night and beats her repeatedly when the girl displeases her. Similarly, the authors of the antebellum slave narratives focused upon interracial rather than intraracial violence, with slaveowners and their deputies turning the lash into a fiendish instrument of abuse and employing everything from sharp fingernails to bonfires for torturing, maiming, and killing disobedient slaves. But there is little mention of blacks attacking each other.

William Wells Brown presents the first fictionalization of Nat Turner's revolt in his first version of *Clotel; or The President's Daughter* (1853), but Nat receives only a couple of pages and is a distinctively minor note in the main story, about Clotel and her daughter. Brown comes close to a depiction of the violent "bad nigger" in Nat Turner's lieutenant, the fictional bloodthirsty Picquilo. He is a "full-blooded Negro," an African prince enslaved by whites, treasuring his home-made sword and drenching "his hands in the blood of all the whites he could meet." But Picquilo is more an "avenger" than a "bad nigger," for he uses Nat's liberation crusade to retaliate against whites as an equal. As African royalty, he does not need to assert his self-respect.[1] Martin Delany's Henry Blake, in the course of his failed attempt to arouse the southern slaves to rebellion, kills a pack of slave-chasing bloodhounds, a cruel black overseer, and a white cracker who attempts to capture him. But Blake is far too aristocratic (and political) to bear any resemblance to the conventional badman.[2]

In the sixty-six years between the appearance of the last known chapter of *Blake* in 1862 and Claude McKay's *Home to Harlem* (1928), some eighty or so novels were published by African Americans, and of these just three depict intra-black violence. Oddly, when 90 percent of African Americans still lived a rural life in the South, the violence of all three was set in northern cities.[3] There are plenty of reasons so few novelists wrote of intraracial violence or of the badmen who committed it in these years. For one thing, not many blacks could read and write well enough to produce a novel, and those who could tended to gravitate toward the city. For another, the class to which literate blacks belonged had its own interests and agenda, and by and large those did not include exploring the black demimonde. The concerns this group expressed in its novels were enormously various. Half of the eighty works I refer to defy all classifying. They are eccentric and individualistic, and show little storytelling ability or understanding of novelistic technique. This is perfectly understandable, since most of these writers were not novelists as we understand the term, but earnest advocates of racial uplift, active in organizations working to educate lower-class African Americans and advance the fortunes of the race, or just people with a single story to tell. Writing a novel or two for them was a way of carrying out their agenda. Mrs. A. E. Johnson, for example, the wife of the Reverend Harvey Johnson of Baltimore and a frequent contributor to black journals, wrote two novels, *Clarence and Corinne; or God's Way* (1890) and *The Hazeley Family* (1894), both raceless and focusing upon two of Mrs. Johnson's preoccupations, temperance and Christian propriety.[4] Emma Dunham Kelley wrote similar nonracial narratives emphasizing Christian piety: *Megda* (1891) and *Four Girls at Cottage City* (1898).[5] Since many of what Du Bois called the Talented Tenth of the black population had been educated as ministers, a good portion of these novels did focus on Christian themes. The Reverend Thomas H. B. Walker wrote *Bebbly; or The Victorious Preacher* (1910), an autobiographical narrative; *Revelation, Trial, and Exile of John in Epics* (1912); and *J. Johnson; or "The Unknown Man"* (1915), an "answer" to the southern racist writer Thomas Dixon's *The Sins of the Father*. The Reverend H. N. Brown's *The Necromancer; or Voo-Doo*

Doctor (1904) is a bizarre but intriguing little allegory in imitation of *The Pilgrim's Progress,* celebrating the victory of Christianity over Haitian Voodoo.

Other novels are wildly improbable tales of romance in which all the characters are white, with unbelievable plot twists, murderous spouses, and amazing happy endings.[6] They are, like the sentimental popular novel of the period and the dime novels published by Adams and Beadle in the last third of the century, packed with action, intricate plots that are all but impossible to follow, and exotic settings. They show almost no concern with racial or social issues. Only Oscar Micheaux, the prince of the black romancers, makes any gesture toward such issues. His men are outsized heroes, always black and devoted to the race, displaying extravagant abilities and achieving great feats, the total opposite of black badmen or bullies.[7]

The more polemical novels of these years deal with race as a problem, with white prejudice, economic and political discrimination, lynching and riots, violent retaliation, and mixed bloodlines. Sutton Elbert Griggs, Frances Ellen Watkins Harper, and Pauline Hopkins grapple with the problems that weigh most heavily upon the "aristocracy of color": miscegenation, their white ancestry, the personal indignities and financial obstacles imposed by racial discrimination. They put the race's best foot forward, advancing what scholar Arlene Elder calls "counterstereotypes" of respectable and educated Negroes against the vicious stereotypes of white propaganda.[8] Culture, manners, sobriety, respectability, and, especially, Christian piety: these were the values and topics upon which the genteel novelists dwelt. The violence they did depict flowed almost exclusively from white to black, and their novels made vehement arguments against lynching and race riots. But they expostulated most on the fact that whites tended to discriminate by race rather than class, lumping socially advanced blacks in the same group as the crude and uneducated "nigger." "It is nonsense to my mind," says one character, "to say [whites] cannot distinguish between the educated and the ignorant among the colored people just the same as you do among the white." Blacks should be considered "men in so far as they are fitted by education and integrity to be so considered."[9]

Charles Waddell Chesnutt was the most accomplished novelist of this period. He wrote three novels and numerous short stories before he gave up trying to make a living with his pen after the cool reception of his last novel, *The Colonel's Dream* (1905).[10] It is in *The Marrow of Tradition* (1901), though, that Chesnutt most commands our attention. Josh Green, the proud and independent stevedore on the docks of the fictional southern port city of Wellington, speaks eloquently in a plausible black dialect about his rights as a man without a hint of authorial condescension. But he must be warned against overstating his claim to respect and fairness. Such behavior red-flags him as a "bad man," as the educated Dr. William Miller calls him. Chesnutt thus acknowledges the existence of the type and is the first African American novelist to explore the type's implications for the race. Josh is indeed inclined to violence, but it is the violence of the "moral hard man," justifiably deployed as a defense of his racial dignity and self-respect. His determination to kill a crude cracker Ku Kluxer is inspired not by his own ruthlessness but by the vicious and intolerable racism of the redneck.

Chesnutt's focus, though, is not the inevitable fate of the violent man, as the badman ballad's is, but the dilemma posed by Josh for the middle class. Dr. Miller is no coward. He responds sympathetically to what, in a white person, would be praiseworthy but in a "bad man" like black Josh Green, or himself, is "taken as the marks of savagery." Indeed, "every manly instinct urged him to go forward" and join Josh's little band of black defenders against the rampaging whites during the riot at the center of the novel. But Miller's class values dictate that he be "wise" rather than "heroic," and his "wisdom" tells him that the overwhelming superiority of whites makes resistance futile. "Our time will come," he tells Josh. "Good may come of this [riot], after all."[11] It is the nonviolent stand of the respectable black man, committed to white values, that marks him as a member of civilized society, though it deprives him of rights claimed by whites for themselves. Chesnutt has appropriated the folklore figure of the "bad nigger" for his own use and has tamed him, cleaned him up, made him sympathetic. But in Chesnutt's value system, for all his admirableness, Josh must be rejected as an example of improper and ineffective racial action. The violence even of the "moral bad man" does not reside comfortably in the thinking of respectable blacks.

PAUL LAURENCE DUNBAR: SOUTHERN INNOCENCE, NORTHERN SIN

Chesnutt's novels are set in the South, but two other exceptions to the standard genteel novel are set in New York City and a third in Chicago. Paul Laurence Dunbar's *Sport of the Gods* (1902), James Weldon Johnson's *Autobiography of an Ex-Colored Man* (1912), and James D. Corrothers's *The Black Cat Club* (1902) are all very different books. In them we get a portrait not of the full-blown man of violence, but rather of the milieu in which the type flourishes and several figures that only distantly resemble the badman being drawn in the ballads produced in these same years. Dunbar and Johnson explore what Johnson called the "flourishing black Bohemia" in New York's upper Twenties and lower Thirties west of Sixth Avenue, the "old Tenderloin," where black life thrived at one stage in its slow migration north toward Harlem. This was "the business and social centre" of the sporting set, the entertainers, gamblers, pimps, and prostitutes frequenting the nightclubs and pool halls of turn-of-the-century black New York.[12] It is the seamier side of this neighborhood that nurtures the black badman and cultivates the loose behavior that morally destroys the innocent blacks pouring northward from the South.

Or so Dunbar sees it in *The Sport of the Gods*. From its title to its conclusion, it is explicitly a sober, pessimistic study of the toxic effects of lingering southern racism and the soul-killing evils of the wicked northern city. The novel's single act of violence, Joe Hamilton's murder of his sweetheart, Hattie Sterling, is the novel's climax, the point toward which all the action inclines and which illustrates the ultimate sickness of urban life. This is not a racial issue, nor a complaint about ghettoization or the economic and social exclusion of African

Americans in the North. Color-neutral, the book demonstrates that it is the pleasures of the flesh, the gaming table, and the ravages of drink that are spiritually
destructive. These are the pursuits that ensnare Joe Hamilton, who has come
with his mother and sister from pious respectability in the South to reside in a
city whose blandishments he is too morally weak to withstand. Hattie, the
warm-hearted prostitute highly respected by the worldly street culture, accepts
him as her lover, acting as his teacher and protector. When, because of his uncontrollable drinking, she decides to wash her hands of him, Joe kills her in
drunken desperation. This is the ballad archetype with a twist.

Dunbar turns the ballad badman into a moral weakling (thinking, perhaps, of his own alcoholism, which resulted in his premature death in 1906[13])
toward whose destruction he directs middle-class, finger-pointing platitudes and
sentimentalizing clichés. Joe kills in drunken hysteria and then retreats from his
deed in a kind of escapist catatonia. He is jailed and the Hamilton family's disintegration is complete. Joe's fate illustrates the paradox in much black thinking at
the turn of the century. The Jim Crow South, where black poverty reigned and
lynching had become the white method of controlling the black population, was
nevertheless the seat of black religious piety and virtuous simplicity. The northern city was dangerous to the simple goodness of blacks not because it forced the
migrants from the South into segregated enclaves that prevented them from enjoying the opportunities of mainstream America but because it seduced them
into sin. This is not a paradox Dunbar acknowledges or attempts to solve with
his melodrama. He focuses instead upon the didactic use to which he puts the violent man, moralizing and sentimentalizing him in his progress toward murder.
Had Dunbar imitated some of his naturalistic contemporaries, like Stephen
Crane or Theodore Dreiser, he might have dramatized how powerless blacks are
caught between a racist South and the stultifying cities of the North. Instead, he
preaches a sermon whose conclusion is that when everything is added up, the
South is preferable to the North, that even the South's faults are "better than
what awaited [the simple southern blacks] in the great alleys of New York."[14]

JAMES WELDON JOHNSON: MURDER IN RAGTIME

As in *The Sport of the Gods,* the most important scene of black violence in James
Weldon Johnson's *Autobiography of an Ex-Colored Man* (1912) is set in New
York City sometime around 1900, before Harlem became the black capital of
America. Johnson sees much the same thing in the great metropolis as Dunbar:
the excitement of its crowds, the glowing allure of its lights, the sybaritic pleasures of its entertainments. Dunbar sardonically warns his innocent away from
these irresistible temptations, advising him to go anywhere else, "if he be wise,"
yes, even "to Jersey" (p. 71). Johnson's imagery is slightly more extravagant, but
contains something of the same understated humor. To his unnamed narrator,
the city, as he enters it, appears "fatally fascinating," like "a great witch" disguised as an "alluring," "enticing," and "tempting" beauty who seduces her victims with lethal ease and treats them with utter caprice:

> Some she at once crushes beneath her cruel feet; others she condemns to a fate like that of galley-slaves; a few she favours and fondles, riding them high on the bubbles of fortune; then with a sudden breath she blows the bubbles out and laughs mockingly as she watches them fall.

For Dunbar, New York is an intoxicating wine, for Johnson opium. For both it has powerful addictive qualities, so dangerous that its users make any sacrifice rather than separate from its enticements. The important difference is that Johnson's unnamed ("ex-colored") narrator is much more self-aware than Dunbar's Joe Hamilton. He can describe what is happening to him as he enters the city's mesmerizing turmoil and encounters its arousing stimuli:

> . . . as I walked about that evening, I began to feel the dread power of the city; the crowds, the lights, the excitement, the gaiety, and all its subtler stimulating influences began to take effect upon me. My blood ran quicker and I felt that I was just beginning to live. (p. 442)

Johnson's narrator is an observer of and commentator upon the city scene, not a blind participant and ultimate victim. But this does not give him immunity from the effects of the sporting world he begins to frequent, a world whose natural fauna include violent badmen. The narrator's encounter with one of those badmen is fleeting but significant. Johnson leads his reader to the violent moment with the skillful care of a born realist. In the course of several pages, the narrator takes us on a tour of black Manhattan, its gaming parlors and dance halls, its restaurants and brothels. All the actors in the great show move before us: dice throwers and card players, dancing girls and bar shills, jockeys, boxers, pimps, pickpockets, and streetwalkers. We are introduced to the techniques of craps, the undulations of slow drag dancing, and the routines practiced by the professional entertainers. It is a spectacle of exotica, animated, glittering, carnal.

It is also dangerous, especially for outsiders. In the club where the narrator plays ragtime piano, his fame attracts the attentions of the beautiful "rich widow," a cultured white woman who has taken to slumming in the black dives and supports a handsome but sinister black gigolo. She invites him to her table, but the narrator realizes that the woman is only using him in a lovers' quarrel with her boyfriend, the "surly black despot who held sway over her deepest emotions" (p. 460). The dangers of the situation are great, for the gigolo, as the narrator has been warned, "was generally known as a 'bad man.'" This is recognizable ballad material, but for Johnson's readers, by definition literate, it is the stuff of *Police Gazette* stories, sexual jealousy intensified by interracial taboo. Avoiding Dunbar's melodrama, Johnson conveys the scene with ballad-like understatement:

> I saw the black fellow approaching; he walked directly to our table and leaned over. The "widow" evidently feared he was going to strike her, and she threw back her head. Instead of striking her he whipped out a revolver and fired; the first shot went straight into her throat. There were other shots fired, but how many I do not know. (p. 461)

He does not know because, understandably, he finds himself "rushing . . . into the street," only vaguely aware of his "surroundings and actions" (p. 461). This is not his world. He is a visitor in an environment for which he is utterly unprepared.

The narrator is rescued by his millionaire white patron who has, over the past months, hired him as a piano player for his private parties. Light-skinned enough to pass for white, the narrator leaves the black and enters the white world, abruptly going to Europe with his white patron and retreating permanently from the city. The shooting, though, continues to disturb his mind, for "still I could see that beautiful white throat with the ugly wound. The jet of blood pulsing from it had placed an indelible red stain on my memory" (p. 461). The narrator finds in this image a symbol of black Manhattan, a fusion of beauty and ugliness, of vitality and violence. It is in the nature of the city's dynamism to contain these contradictions, a vigorous and inventive popular art thriving amidst violent feelings and vicious acts. Music, dancing, gambling, drinking, public display all infuse the players of the game with spirit and energy. At the same time they lead to spiritual and moral enervation and the kind of extreme passion that incites impulsive and deadly violence. Johnson is the first literary artist to subject this world to serious analysis. He sees that the ugly acts of the badman occur in the midst of stimulating excitement and musical creativity. The best of this world can be embodied in the ragtime music that the narrator believes is the foundation of great formal art, which always comes "from the hearts of the people" (p. 448). To this part of black Manhattan the narrator is strongly drawn. But the worst of it is its dark underside, and the eruption of that underside sets him on a path toward his most fateful decision, to become an *ex*-colored man. Johnson's black gigolo flashes across the fictive screen only for a moment, but in his creation, Johnson demonstrated his own deep understanding of a figure that had already emerged in black folk culture as a type. It was a type that was alien to cultivated middle-class or lower-working-class respectability.

JAMES D. CORROTHERS AND THE BLACK CAT CLUB

James D. Corrothers's *The Black Cat Club* is the most unusual but the least known of the three works I have mentioned. It is a collection of vignettes, dialogues, and dialect poems that falls somewhere between Charles Dickens's *The Pickwick Papers*, Finley Peter Dunne's Mr. Dooley articles in the late nineteenth century, and Langston Hughes's later series in the *Chicago Defender* starring Jesse B. Semple. And like all three of these collections, the fifteen chapters of *The Black Cat Club* first appeared as articles in a periodical, the *Chicago Journal*, at the turn of the century. They were not a journalist's reports of actual events and real people, but inventions drawn from what Corrothers knew of Chicago's black community. The Black Cat Club was purportedly founded by one Sandy Jenkins, whom Corrothers "discovered" among the "denizens" of the Chicago "levee" district.[15] Corrothers quite knowingly chose the most disreputable section of Chicago. According to one account, this area, extending a short distance south of the Loop, contained, in the years around the turn of the century, "thirty-seven houses of prostitution . . . forty-six saloons, eleven pawn brokers, an obscene book store, and a shooting gallery."[16] Although most of Chicago's black population lived along the north-south avenues down into the thirties, the black presence in the levee district itself was relatively insignificant. Blacks made up just slightly less than 2 percent of Chicago's overall population in 1900, but were most heavily concentrated in the Second and Third Wards, between 16th Street on the north and 35th Street on the south, where they constituted 16.6 percent and 22.8 percent of the population. The main part of the levee district, and the oldest, was contained in the First Ward, in which blacks made up just 6.3 percent of the population.[17]

Though fashionable sections like Prairie and Calumet Avenues were just a block or two away, the levee was not a pretty place to be. Crime flourished here and life was hard. Bums were thrown on the stone floors of the jailhouse and toilets in the cells consisted only of a single open gutter. Streetwalkers and pickpockets, homeless children and the insane, gamblers, whores' johns, dandies, and Democratic Party functionaries scrounging up votes for the city council—all these populated the streets of the unsavory levee.[18]

We see none of the levee hard life in the sketches that make up *The Black Cat Club*. Corrothers explains in his preface that in writing the pieces for the *Journal* he intended to compile "a series of character studies of Negro life as it may be observed in the great cities of the North," with Chicago as the representative city where one can find "every type of the American Negro and nearly every phase of his social life." His aim was "to paint the Negro as he is," neither apologizing for nor exaggerating his "shortcomings," but rendering especially "the humorous side of Negro life, as I have observed it" (p. 7). But Sandy Jenkins and the other club members were hardly realistic, unexaggerated renderings of typical black levee residents. Looking at these late-nineteenth-century characters from the viewpoint of the twenty-first century, we can see that they were intended to correct the conventional image of the Sambo, Jim Crow, Zip Coon that dictated the way most of the white public looked at African Americans. That is, writing for the *Journal* with his very first by-line, Corrothers surely wanted neither to offend the editors, who had surprised him by taking his first submissions and then asking for more, nor challenge his mostly white readers with a confrontational, revolutionary version of blacks they were not prepared to accept. He seems to have tried to meet them halfway.

Corrothers plays upon the convention that all blacks are superstitious. Every Club member carries his own rabbit's foot and a quarter in his shoe for good luck. The very name of the club derives from the most basic superstition of them all, "that black cats are the children of his Satanic majesty, and that all kinds of bad luck await the unfortunate individual whose luck is crossed by one of these sable disturbers of the midnight peace." Sandy, whose fame rests upon his poetry and his position as the accepted colored "poet laureate" of the levee, has acquired "a big black cat with which to hoodoo a dozen literary rivals" (p. 18). But this is fun, not seriousness or ridicule. Corrothers claimed to see value in the lore of the black folk, especially its humorous side, believing it "worthy of preservation" and useful for giving readers "a clearer insight into certain phases of Negro life and character" (p. 8). Thus, at least for these *Journal* pieces, Corrothers used a romping, playful style to correct what he takes to be an inaccurate image of blacks. For example, he attacks by implication the black elite, who rejected as shameful and disreputable the oral tradition of slaves and contemporary urban folk, by making Sandy a burlesque "doctor" of folklore. Collecting it is part of the club's purpose, for "the club members are expected to learn all they can concerning cats, witches, ghosts, quaint Negro sayings and plantation stories and melodies, and to impart them in an original manner at the meetings of the club" (p. 17).

Just as blacks were supposed to be superstitious, they were also expected to speak dialect. Corrothers satisfies this expectation as well. He is perfectly aware of the potential entertainment power of the "Many quaint Negro expressions, droll sayings, and peculiar bywords, used by Negroes universally." He is also aware that people from different parts of the country speak English in different ways, and takes care to inform his readers, like Mark Twain in his "Explanatory" note to *Huckleberry Finn,* that "since in Chicago are Negroes from all portions of the South, the dialect spoken in the 'Black Cat Club' naturally embraces and commingles nearly all of the Negro dialects in Dixieland" (p. 9).[19]

Black dialect, though, was more than just a matter of accurately recording how people from different areas spoke. Of all the conventions governing the representation of blacks in the public sphere, the use of dialect was probably the most basic. Black dialect had been largely created by whites, not only by the blackface stage minstrels acting out the Jim Crow and Zip Coon stereotypes of the antebellum period, but by such professed admirers of the old slave culture as plantation-tradition poets Irwin Russell, Thomas Nelson Page, and Ruth McEnery Stuart. The blackface minstrel routine, the racial vaudeville act, and the "coon song" employed an ersatz oral "black" dialect to convey the buffoonish image of the African American that passed for reality in much of the public discourse. The plantation poets, thinking they were capturing the true American Negro, created a written dialect that depended more on spelling than on any fidelity to authentic pronunciation to convey their stereotype, usually an old uncle who looked back longingly to slavery days and the loving treatment he received from generous masters and mistresses. The connection between the caricatured slave and ex-slave and his speech made black dialect a sign for the inherent inferiority of blacks.[20]

After Emancipation, even as black performers began using dialect, playing on the minstrel stage and mounting full-scale musicals in the 1890s, dialect was the means by which blacks were confined in the image of the subcivilized slave. It was for this reason that Corrothers did not, at first, support its use. He boasted that, having gone to school with white children, he had "never talked Negro dialect, nor done plantation antics." It smacked "too much of '*niggerism*' which all intelligent coloured people detest."[21] But any attempt to represent blacks more realistically was ignored by the mainstream entertainment industry and rejected by the white public. Therefore, the "coon song," also largely a white creation, became a medium for some black songwriters, and a whole platoon of African American poets began attempting to seize control of the black image in dialect verse, a trend ultimately made both profitable and respectable by Paul Laurence Dunbar. And by the mid-nineties the dialect bandwagon had become crowded with black poets and performers, many, as Dickson Bruce aptly puts it, trying to "rescue folk Negroes from caricature" by appropriating the white minstrel and plantation dialect and putting it to black use as a means for establishing a racial identity.[22] The respectability Paul Laurence Dunbar in particular gained for the form gave his own folk characters a modicum of dignity and authenticity seldom conveyed by the "coon song" or plantation tradition. Indeed, it seems to have been Dunbar who changed Corrothers's mind about the use of dialect, for after reading Dunbar's early dialect poetry, he came to feel that there were some thoughts that only dialect could express.[23] He must have felt the occasion was right in the pieces he wrote for *The Black Cat Club,* for in his preface he suggests that he is going to provide "a clearer insight" into blacks "as they appeared on Southern plantations in ante-bellum times," a clear challenge to the validity of the white-created plantation tradition (p. 8).

Like any black writer using dialect, Corrothers was taking a chance, for if he satisfied the popular white expectation that all blacks spoke dialect, he risked having to satisfy the other expectations that went with it: that all blacks shared the features of the minstrel, plantation, and "coon song" stereotypes. Sandy Jenkins and his friends are, indeed, characterized by the dialect they speak. Yet they are not like the figures in the usual dialect poems and stories. There is nothing soft or sentimental about them, as there is about so many of Dunbar's characters. They make us laugh, but they are not minstrel buffoons. We sense that there is something about them not explained by the black dialect tradition alone. And indeed, there is plenty of reason to believe that Corrothers was also trying to cash in on the whole popular fad of dialect, from James Russell Lowell's creation of Yankee cracker-barrel philosopher Hosea Biglow in the 1840s to the Hoosier poetry of James Whitcomb Riley. And right in his own back yard was Finley Peter Dunne, cranking out his Mr. Dooley sketches first in the Chicago *Evening Post,* then in the same paper that published Corrothers, the *Chicago Journal.*[24] Over at the *Chicago Record,* where Corrothers wrote occasional filler articles, George Ade was becoming famous for his "Stories of the Streets and the Town," followed by his "Fables in Slang" and then his series on black shoeshine boy Pink Marsh.[25]

If whites could get mileage out of their dialects, why not blacks out of theirs? If Mr. Dooley and Hosea Biglow could use just-folks talk to puncture the pretensions and affectations of "educated" high-class speech, why not Sandy Jenkins and his Black Cat Club fellows? Much of the club's program is, in fact, aimed at ridiculing "de eddicated colored man" and "de high-tone' dahkies dat hab forgot dey mothers, an' is tryin' to prove dey ain't got no slave blood in 'em" (p. 124). In their speech, the club members are boisterously contra-bourgeois, as they are in their entire book of etiquette. They cultivate a misbehaving stance that subverts the image of a striving middle class of cultured, educated, mannerly black people, especially those counterstereotypes in the genteel novel. The club members pride themselves on their ability to eat and drink large quantities and on their distance from advanced learning. No one with a college education is admitted to the club, and too great a familiarity "with the classics" is forbidden (p. 17).

These are the features that supposedly define the authentic "negroness" of Sandy Jenkins and his club members, in something of the same way that the simple uneducated speech of Hosea Biglow and Mr. Dooley suggests a truer "Americanness." But it is their unthinking subscription to violence with which Corrothers finally pins down their African American identity and meets the final expectations of his mainly white audience. In addition to their appetites for food and drink, their superstition and simple-minded view of the world, they display a pronounced inability to control their anger and an irresistible impulse to physically attack the objects of that anger. Corrothers had himself known men like this as a fifteen-year-old lad. They were black roustabouts on Lake Michigan. On their bodies they wore trophies of their violent lives, "great, ugly razor cuts—raw, sickening gashes into which a finger could have been laid." Though as a strapping young man he held his own with this crew, these badmen disgusted him, and he speaks critically of how they "profanely joked" about their scars, "sometimes with the very fellow who had done the cutting. Wallowing about on the floor of the 'flicker,' every night these dusky gamblers shot dice, and excitedly threatened one another with murder in every degree." They seemed to revel in their degradation, while the better-educated Corrothers followed a "decent" life, avoiding drinking, gambling, and dancing.[26]

To Sandy Jenkins and his fellows' badness, Corrothers gives a considerably more forgiving spin, making them comic versions of the roustabouts he had known on Lake Michigan. There is something infectiously joyous in their readiness to fight, and for Corrothers's readers, their weapon of choice, the razor, links them definitively to their special quality as "Negroes." At their meetings, the members eat, drink, give speeches, tell old stories they have collected, and read their own original poetry, applauding each other with little discrimination. But they also routinely get into arguments that they try to settle by fighting. Indeed, in the levee district they *expect* to fight. Thus, along with a rabbit's foot, a silver spoon, and a quarter in the toe of his shoe to ward off negative influences, each also carries "a newly sharpened razor," which, like a soldier with his rifle, he often "presents" for inspection. Corrothers thus uses the already well-established badman tradition for laughs, making sure that he introduces interesting variety into their badness. "Bad Bob Sampson" at one time was "a special detective," apparently on the Chicago police force, and gained "the reputation of being exceedingly 'bad.'" But "his associations with levee highwaymen" led to his dishonorable discharge. Saskatchewan Jones loves to fight, "to mutilate human countenances with his razor" (p. 29). And while he is warm and generous with his friends, "He would carve that friend or foe on the slightest provocation. He would even 'hunt trouble,' and his joy at finding it was equaled only by his ability to consume large quantities of liquor and 'good eatin's'" (p. 29). All the members are exceedingly touchy about their reputation and take offense easily. When they do, they pull their razors and threaten each other. They are full-blown but comic examples of the first literary badmen in African American prose fiction.

This is not the serious violence Corrothers experienced as a young man working on Lake Michigan steamboats, but rather a part of the whole comic picture: stylized, conventionalized, exaggerated in the same way that a caricature picks out the characteristic features to be overdrawn. It is presented not as a grim and destructive reality but as an invention. In his review of the book, William Stanley Braithwaite, himself a respected member of the American literary establishment who had edited several well-received anthologies of current poetry, puts his finger exactly on the pulse of the Black Cat Club's violent men:

> The club-men are lovable. There is so much good nature behind the actual impression of their doings in moments of bad feelings and unreasonable temper, one cannot somehow ally them with the typical Negro of the same stamp. No fracas they indulge in seems real. The best good intention seems to prevail even when razors are drawn and a bitter injury is imminent.[27]

At their first meeting, Sandy Jenkins sets the scene for future gatherings when he reads his poem "De Cahvin.'" This is a hyperbolically bloody piece about two young men, Jim Johnson and Sambo Brown, who get into a fight over a girl. The featured element of the fight is the men's use of their razors; indeed, how their razors virtually survive them. Their fortunes during the fight swing back and forth. First Johnson seems to be on the verge of victory, having "like to cut de coon to deff!" But then Sambo recovers, "draws a bran' new razah out," and gives Johnson as good as he got, cutting "out Johnson's bes'es eye," in fact, nearly cutting "his tongue out," until the narrator "thought Jim's time had come!" (p. 24). Then it is Johnson's turn to rally and the two fill the air with their razors,

> Slashin' one 'nother all to slashes,
> An' gashin' each other all to gashes. (p. 25)

Soon they are "mincemeat." But now the picture turns surreal, for

> . . . in de midst ob dat brown hash,
> De razahs still contrived to clash,
> As ef de souls ob dem two shades
> Still struggled in de razah blades! (p. 25)

This is a splendid image, capturing, as few of the "coon songs" current at the time do, the preeminence of the razor in the mythic stereotype of the black tough. Such resonant imagery sets Corrothers's poetic treatment of the levee class apart from the other dialect verse of the age. "De Cahvin" ultimately turns into a highly original fantasy, for the observers of the fight attempt to glue the parts of the two cut-up men back together again. Their failure to do so sets up the marvelously grotesque denouement:

All we could do wuz git a broom,
An' sweep 'em bofe out ob de room. (p. 25)

Corrothers's interest in these sketches lay at least as much in literary form as in purveying the "real" image of levee blacks. "De Cahvin'" is the "coon song" *reductio ad absurdam,* a rhetorically hyperbolic image of a literary stereotype. It conveys a happy receptiveness to the magical and the zany. And if "De Cahvin'" is a *reductio ad absurdam* of the "coon song," so are the boisterous fisticuffs and razor fights elsewhere in Corrothers's chronicle. They are jokes he seeks to share with his audience, black and white, laughing at his own exaggerations of the cliché of the "nigger" and his razor.

It is not only the dialect poem that is exaggerated in these sketches, but also the speech and the behavior of the members themselves. They talk and act like characters out of Sandy's poem. Sandy, for example, irritated by the three-hundred-pound Roustabout Thompson, threatens to "cahve you long's I kin fine a piece uv you" (p. 44). When the club visits Herr Shake Schneider's saloon on the North Side, Sandy lines the members up in single file and they march into the place with their razors drawn (p. 67). Roughhouse is the order of the day. Robert's Rules of Order are routinely broken by shouts and outcries. Members throw chairs at each other and smash tables, doors, windows. No debate can be concluded peacefully, since someone must lose, and none of the pugnacious bunch accepts loss readily. When the debate judges find in favor of Slippery Simon against Saskatchewan Jones, Jones goes after Simon, brandishing his razor. The action is described in standard English by the newspaper reporter allegedly observing the proceedings.

> Round and round the room fled Simon, panting and straining his utmost, his coat cut in tatters, and the crimson on his back showing plainly that Saskatchewan's deadly razor had several times gone home. In vain did Sandy call for order; in vain he pounded his desk; in vain did he and the rest of the club endeavor to head off the flying combatants! Even Bad Bob failed. Fear had given Simon wings, and desperation, long pent up, had maddened Saskatchewan. Around they swept like a hurricane, smashing chairs and leaving ruin in their wake—a wake like the trail of enraged buffaloes. (p. 200)

But Simon finds a window and plunges through it headfirst to the pavement twenty feet below, and Jones follows him, pushed out by Bad Bob. Both lie unconscious, Jones's nose "bleeding and apparently broken, and the blood . . . trickling slowly from his mouth and ears." Both are taken to the hospital, where they later are found by Sandy to be "a good deal mo' skeert den hu't" (p. 201). In this cartoonish action, no one is badly hurt, and when all is over and the men are comically bandaged and lying next to each other in the hospital, they "made up friends" (p. 203), as do the rest of the members at the next meeting. As a truly sly commentary on what is happening in this sketch, Corrothers includes a white blackface minstrel performer in the audience watching the debate and the ensuing free-for-all. At the height of the turmoil, he takes notes to use in his own show (p. 190). Sandy and his friends are the models for the minstrel stereotypes, not the stereotypes themselves, and therefore, for all their stylized exaggeration, they have a certain solid reality about them.

Perhaps their most conspicuous feature is their aggressive confidence in their own habits and pursuits. They make no concessions to either the genteel propriety of the black upper classes or the condescensions of a racist white public. They never raise the question of racism nor question the value of who they are or what they do. Nor do they see any resemblance between themselves and those blacks struggling in poverty and hopelessness. They expect to advance, to become somebody.[28] Not for them the inevitable fate of the ballad badman. They have a strong sense of their own dignity and self-worth. Nor does Corrothers ever invite his reader to mock them or laugh derogatorily. In the end, Corrothers brings them down solidly in the center of the successful bourgeoisie. There is Sandy's wedding to a Terre Haute belle, featuring Mendelssohn's "Wedding March" and "a quadroon girl in white" carrying a bouquet of lilies of the valley, a socially acceptable reception line, a fashionable departure in a carriage, and above all a future of proper and prosperous business dealings (p. 256). But we get the feeling that, instead of being tamed by middle-class propriety, they will bring their levee vitality *to* middle-class propriety.

Corrothers feels no need to account for the rambunctious, razorous violence of his Black Cat Club members. He does not suggest that these characters taint the black community or threaten the respectable classes. In fact, their violence is not an "issue" for Corrothers, except as a source of the humor he hopes will attract readers. It is simply one of the characteristics of this lively group and, by implication, other black men who belong to the same rather indistinct class. We get no suggestion, therefore, that a deep social impetus is at work or a ghetto is in the making. Their behavior does not consign them to the back alleys or the gutters of the levee streets. Indeed, Sandy Jenkins leads his club colleagues into a reconciliation with the snooty Mrs. Woodby-Jenkins and a promising future in the catering business as he sashays off to domestic bliss with his young lady from Terre Haute. They are incorrigibles who, for all their anti–middle class behavior, can in the end be accepted into respectability.

In none of these three novels do we see any suggestion of the difficult social and economic problems that are developing among blacks in the North. No one in the Black Cat Club, no one Johnson's narrator knows, and not even Joe Hamilton and his friends at the Brannan Club have trouble with employment. All can find jobs if they choose to do so. This is not the northern urban picture that many blacks were familiar with at the time these books came out. J. Saunders Redding, tracking the movement of southern blacks to the cities before the Great Migration and the segregation patterns into which they were forced, quotes Dr. W. S. Montgomery, assistant superintendent of schools in Washington, D.C., speaking in 1904:

> The poverty and prejudice everywhere encountered, and the fierce competition, constrain these [Negro] people to settle in unsanitary localities, in the al-

leys, closes, and courts where thousands are rotting and festering in the slums and tenements. . . . Diseases to which they have heretofore been immune claim them as victims, and they become a menace to the general health of the community. The brutal battle for existence develops a violent spirit, cheapens human life, creates a cunning which seeks to win by fair or foul means, producing the thief and sharper who live by their wits. Lack of steady employment does not call out the sterner qualities of patience, honesty, honor, duty and self-control. Competition pushes to the wall, and the man, despised and rejected, turns an Ishmaelite—a law breaker, and swells the criminal list. Politically he is lost as an individual or unit of society, swallowed up into the mass.[29]

Civic leaders in all the northern cities struggle to clean up the sorts of neighborhoods Corrothers finds humorous and Dunbar and Johnson see as a fertile soil for murder. All three of these authors are more preoccupied with class than with race. Success is not necessarily moving into a nicer neighborhood, as it becomes later in Lorraine Hansberry's *Raisin in the Sun* (1959), but moving up a notch or two in the ranks of the "refined" respectables, as Sandy Jenkins and his friends do. Johnson's narrator makes the racial leap into the white world, but is able to do so only because of his light color and good manners. To fail to rise is to fall into degradation or disintegration, like the Hamiltons. These novels, therefore, for all the explosive social potential of their violent subject matter, show a greater concern for the moral quality of urban life than its racial, social, and economic demographics. Neither Corrothers, Dunbar, nor Johnson sees the violent act as a result of racial injustice. It is rather a feature of the northern city and the result of the moral weakness of a new type of violent man.

chapter **4**

From the Genteel to the Primitive

The Twenties and Thirties

THE "NEW NEGRO" FINDS THE FOLK

The "new Negroes" of the 1920s Harlem Renaissance belonged to the generation raised in the first couple of decades of the twentieth century. Their parents were proper, upward-striving members of the growing black bourgeoisie. The "new Negroes" had the same sense of confidence in their status and abilities that members of the Black Cat Club had, though with considerably more education and much less levee crudeness. They quickly revolted against the generation that had brought them up and sent them to school. One of the major items on their revolutionary agenda was the establishment of folk life and its oral expression as legitimate subjects for respectable *written* literature. Their parents and grandparents had considered the "folk" a drag on the race's upward movement in the years after Emancipation. Illiterate, loud, misbehaving, and often violent, the lower classes were an embarrassment to respectable "right-thinking Negroes." And so were the songs, the stories, the dances, and the pleasure-palaces of those classes. The younger generation was going to change all that.

In part, their work had already been done for them, for the product of the folk had gradually become more acceptable to many in the respectable classes. James Weldon Johnson found that even the most upscale black churches were admitting the old slave songs into their Sunday services.[1] Of course, those old songs had been properly cleansed and, ironically, as Robert Hemenway points out, transformed from "low" into "high" art, as when Paul Robeson donned a black tie to sing spirituals to an audience equally formally dressed. No matter that these concert-goers believed they were listening to the outpouring of rugged "peasant" expression and failed to "grasp the full possibilities of black folklore."[2] Their receptivity to the once-avoided "sorrow songs" made it possible to revisit them.

It was just such possibilities that many of the educated children of upward-striving blacks, both genteel and working-class, searched for in what they felt to be the most authentic forms of African American culture. They became students of the racial past and advocates of the black masses. Langston Hughes, great-nephew of light-skinned John Mercer Langston, epitome of the old elite, found the "folk culture of the black masses . . . preferable [to] and richer than the superficial culture of the city's aristocrats of color."[3] More important to the artist, Hughes believed that the folk furnished "a wealth of colorful, distinctive material for any artist because they still hold their own individuality in the face of American standardizations."[4] No one explains the changes of the twenties better than *Opportunity* editor and sociologist Charles S. Johnson. It is understandable, says Johnson, that the older generation, so near to slavery and its aftermath, would

> rule out the Sorrow Songs as the product of ignorant slaves, taboo dialect as incorrect English, and the priceless folk lore as the uncultured expression of illiterates,—an utterly conscious effort to forget the past, and take over, suddenly, the symbols of that culture which had so long ground their bodies and spirits in the dirt. The new voices, at a more comfortable distance, are beginning to find a new beauty in these heritages, and new values in their own lives.[5]

Thus, against "an utterly conscious effort to forget the past" many young Renaissance artists made an equally conscious effort to recover it, to embrace it, to affirm all that a previous generation found so distasteful and harmful. They received plenty of encouragement from the trends of Europe and America. Cutting-edge painters like Picasso, Matisse, Vlaminck, and Modigliani found inspiration in primitive imagery that was coming out of colonialized Africa and the ancient Iberian stone heads on display in the Louvre.[6] J. M. Synge turned to Irish peasants to reinvigorate the language and narrative lines of his revolutionary theater.[7] And in America, Eugene O'Neill, Waldo Frank, Vachel Lindsay, Dubose Heyward, and a dozen other white writers found original rhythms and characters in the underclasses of the American Negro and featured black folk and their African sources in their novels, plays, and poetry.

This whole cultural movement was part of the larger revolt against the tight gentility of the Victorian age, a determination to show that the primitive had not been refined out of the European and his American cousin. Freud's theory of the unconscious and the id, Joseph Conrad's psychological journey into the Congo River's savage *Heart of Darkness* (1902), James Fraser's study of primitive myth in *The Golden Bough* (1890–1915), as well as the resurgence of interest in the folk ballad stimulated by Francis James Child's monumental collection *English and Scottish Popular Ballads* (1883–98)—all reflected a definable shift of interest to the remnant of the primitive in the civilized mind. The march of Western culture, thought to be approaching its apogee in the Victorian Age, now seemed exhausted and false. An injection of the less civilized might rejuvenate a spent force.

Among the novelists of the Harlem Renaissance, Claude McKay, Rudolph Fisher, Arna Bontemps, and Zora Neale Hurston most conspicuously turned toward the vernacular of the lower class.[8] And there, growing out of the same admired spontaneity as the unstructured spirituals and work songs, the improvisatorial jazz and blues, the untrammeled dance, they found what might be called a "vernacular" character type. He lived in a world of impulsive, unpremeditated violence, similar to the kind that had been chronicled in the badman ballad and the narratives of Corrothers, Dunbar, and James Weldon Johnson: knife fights, shootings, razor slashings, hair-pullings, sweetmen beating their girlfriends and girlfriends shooting their boyfriends. But conditioned by the cultural changes that occurred between 1910 and 1930, these novelists brought new sensibilities to bear upon the man of violence in the folk communities they explored, ranging over a variety of the old types, and forging a new one who was a cousin to the turn-of-the-century Stagolees, Bad Lee Browns, John Hardys, and Roscoe Bills but somewhat softened and, ironically, made more acceptable to a middle-class reading public. The badman from the oral tradition becomes a figure in the literate tradition, presented through the prism of the middle class's respectability and its ambition to make a place for itself in American culture.

The writers who went after the folk were, so to speak, "intellectual mulattos": truly comfortable in neither the world of the white artist, to which their tastes were educated, nor that of the black folk, to which they traced their own heritage. But their own sensibilities, their sense of ethical and moral behavior and of what makes relationships valid and genuine, were all shaped by the very bourgeois world they now criticized.

The educated black intellectual, therefore, had to ride into the midst of the black folk in the same vehicle as whites. Langston Hughes, for example, says that hearing Paul Robeson sing the spirituals made it easier for him to understand and feel the sensibility of the southern folk.[9] Claude McKay, educated in Jamaica by his schoolteacher brother and with free access to a sympathetic white man's library, insists upon his affinity with the "unskilled Negro worker" through "working with him as a porter and longshoreman and as waiter on the railroad," and living "in the same quarters" and drinking and carousing "together in bars and at rent parties." Even so, he laments, "My damned white education has robbed me of much of the primitive vitality, the pure stamina, the simple unswaggering strength of the Jakes of the Negro race."[10]

Rudolph Fisher was probably one of the best educated of the Renaissance writers. Born in Washington, D.C., and raised in Providence, Rhode Island, largely among white children, he excelled at Brown University, where he earned a B.A. and M.A., and went on to get a medical degree from Howard University and become a specialist in roentgenology. In Harlem, where he practiced, he was the sort of writer-observer "on whom nothing is lost." With amused hyperbole, Robert Bone sees Fisher as a tour guide conducting expeditions through Harlem "for a party of visitors from downtown. The name of the tour is 'Adventures in Exotic Harlem,' and it includes observations on the quaint customs of the country, helpful hints for fraternizing with the natives, and a Berlitz phrase-book for the comprehension of contemporary Harlemese."[11]

Bontemps, too, as a youth went to school with white students, then taught at a Seventh Day Adventist academy in Harlem and finally at black Fisk University, where he finished his career as the university librarian. He composed his novel *God Sends Sunday* (1931) largely from the stories his Uncle Buddy told him when the older man came to visit. Zora Neale Hurston did grow up in all-black Eatonville, Florida, but as the daughter of an educated family. She studied at Barnard, Howard, and Columbia, returning to Eatonville and other southern sites in the thirties to study the folklore as an anthropologist under the direction of Columbia professor Franz Boaz. As Hurston biographer Robert Hemenway puts it, she was "an educated innocent whose memory of the village folklore has been diminished by her urban experience and academic study; she must renew community ties."[12]

All four of these "primitivist" novelists do the same thing, in different ways, with their lower-class characters. They write about them realistically, capturing their manners, their language, their violent milieu. But when compared with the badmen of the ballads, these characters seem sometimes more and sometimes less laundered versions of the originals, intended for a literate audience. Now that enough historical distance was established, the educated writers of the Renaissance could clean up the violent man and make him more acceptable and sympathetic to readers. They rounded off his sharp corners and softened his violent temperament. For all their determination to break free of middle-class morality, that morality lies at the heart of their representation of the violent environments of black communities. The revolutionary primitivists are linked with the educated middle class as allies. Where the folk pronounced no moral judgment on the men and women who fight with and kill each other, the writers of the Harlem Renaissance view them through a subtle lens of bourgeois values, using words like "primal," "primitive," "strange," and "barbaric," words that would have been incomprehensible to the balladeers. A key to the novelists' point of view is that they make their most ruthlessly and irrationally violent badmen secondary characters, and the least sympathetic. The protagonists tend to transcend that ruthlessness and redeem themselves, sometimes as bringers of social order through a commitment to nonviolence and middle-class institutions like marriage and sexual loyalty that give coherence to society. In some cases, their transformation is accomplished through the influence of a good woman, and the result of the badman's reform is a domestic pairing off. We get, in any case, a distinction something like that between Roger Abrahams's "hard-man" and Lawrence Levine's "*moral* hard man," which I discussed in the introduction. The former is an unredeemed "bad nigger," the latter is a badman who agrees to live within the law.

RUDOLPH FISHER'S HARLEM TOUR

This narrative pattern appears most explicitly in the work of Rudolph Fisher and Claude McKay, who people the streets of Harlem with men of violence. Indeed, Rudolph Fisher is the premier bourgeois portrait artist of the badman in Harlem. To use Robert Bone's metaphor, as tour guide Fisher can take the most timid readers into this dangerous region, evoking shudders and exposing them to that "distinct group of Negroes, mentioned even by their own as 'bad,'" without subjecting the tourists to real peril.[13] It is this dangerous potential for violence that makes these dark Harlem places so alluring to the "party of visitors from downtown," who wish to approach that threat without actually being exposed to it. Fisher hyperbolizes the sinister here, the "tameless corner of Negro Harlem" where at night "*strange* songs ring, and *queer* cries sound, and life stumbles blindly toward death" (p. 119, emphasis added). In the dire shadows of these Harlem badlands stands "The Club," where black men play pool, "men in vests and silk-striped shirtsleeves; big men with brown felts pushed back from their brows, small men with caps yanked down over one eye; mostly young men, war vets, consciously hard, the most worldly-wise and the most heedless Negroes on earth" (p. 120). Where Corrothers emphasized the playfully comic, Fisher projects the artificially menacing.

These are familiar figures, evolved from the dives of Memphis's Beale Street and New Orleans's Garden District, but while they may occupy Harlem's "tameless" corners, decency always holds the four-ace hand over hard ruthlessness in Fisher's Harlem. The tone is more Paul Laurence Dunbar or O. Henry than "Stagolee" or "John Hardy." For example, in Fisher's short story "Blades of Steel" two men of the street become locked in a powerful enmity. Dirty Cozzens, whose name denotes his character, has become deeply jealous of Eight-Ball Eddy Boyd. They represent the moral poles of Harlem's badland. Dirty is devious, sneaking, and sly, with a reputation for bullying lesser foes and leaving them scarred by his ready razor or knife, a true "bad nigger." Eddy Boyd is respected by even the shadiest denizens of the sporting life, liked by Pop Overton, the best barber on 135th, and admired by attractive beauty parlor operator Effie Wright. These connections rankle Dirty and he finds an occasion to challenge Eddy in Pop's barber shop. It is a typical Dirty Cozzens move, for he holds a razor and Eddy does not. Bloodshed is momentarily averted by the sudden entrance of Effie, but only momentarily.

Later, after the Annual Barbers' Ball, during which Effie and Eddy deliver a well-deserved rebuff to Dirty on the dance floor, Dirty draws his knife on Eddy in a cabaret, believing that Eddy is unarmed. But Eddy, though smaller than Dirty, is unafraid. In the fight that follows, the reason for Eddy's fearlessness soon becomes clear: "Regularly in the ensuing scuffle Eight-Ball's right hand landed open-palmed against Dirty's face—landed again and again with a sounding smack; and for every time that it landed presently there appeared a short red line, slowly widening into a crimson wheal" (p. 105). Eddy has palmed a razor blade slipped to him earlier by Effie. The result is poetic, but bloody, justice. Straightshooter Eddy does not kill Dirty. He simply teaches him a lesson in Dirty's own language, reinforces his own approval rating among Harlem's solid citizens, and walks off with the most attractive girl on the block. He exposes badman Dirty Cozzens as the "craven" coward he is and sends the whimpering bully out to a hospital for treatment, with the implication that Dirty's bullying days are over.

This is clearly a tough crowd. Effie is no petal of fragile womanhood who cannot bear the sight of blood. And Eddy does not draw back from giving Dirty a lesson in viciousness. Yet the sharp images of Dirty's rent face are muffled in sentimental morality. The victor is appropriately the good guy. And Fisher works deliberately upon the reader's reactions with emotionally charged words, slanted against the villain.

In the introduction to her edition of Fisher's short stories, Margaret Perry remarks that "Fisher stresses the significance of the old-time values that need not become lost in the big city; indeed, these values are the link with the past, with the South that sustains and nourishes the transplanted Negro" (p. 15). My own feeling is that the values Fisher sees at work in his characters belong less to the old-time South than to the new-time middle class, both white and black. Certainly his stories do not grow out of either the new blues or the folk tradition of the hard-hearted animal-trickster tales and the violent badman ballads. They derive from the tradition of sentiment that pervaded much of the popular moralistic literature of the nineteenth century, certainly not from the naturalistic pessimism of contemporaries like Ernest Hemingway and Theodore Dreiser.

What Fisher does bring to the badman type is a divertingly quick wit and a polished literary style. It is that literary style, indeed, by which he changes the way the badman is presented. One of the minor figures in his novel *The Conjure-Man Dies* (1932) is Tiger Shade, a badman very much in the tradition of Stagolee and John Hardy. Tiger "was by a fair margin the tallest, widest, and thickest man in Harlem," and he "was as bad as he was big." Moreover,

> the Tiger simply enjoyed a congenital absence of sympathy. . . . His reputation was known, and his history of destruction was the more terrible because it was so impersonal. He proceeded in combat as methodically as a machine; was quite as effective when acting for someone else as when acting for himself, and in neither case did he ever exhibit any profound emotion. True, he had a light sense of humor. For example, he had once held an adversary's head in the crook of his elbow and with his free hand torn one of the unfortunate fellow's ears off. He was given to such little drolleries; they amused him much as it amuses a small boy to pull off the wings of a fly; but it was quite as impersonally innocent.[14]

Like those back at the turn of the century who told stories about the neighborhood badman over their beer in the alley barrelhouse or sang about him at backyard parties, Fisher takes a certain pride in Tiger Shade's excesses. Affectionate but condescending, taking the point of view of a slickly confident minstrel interlocutor toward his end-men, he clothes the coarse roughness of the badman in the formal attire of elegant language, allying himself, not with the violent men of the tameless Harlem streets, but with his educated audience, who can appreciate and be amused by his symmetrical locutions and intimations of the mock epic. Fisher was a shrewd and interested observer of the Harlem scene, witty in conversation and fluent in the argot of the low-life. If he did give his readers a cross-section of the Harlem community, from the pimps, streetwalkers, and badmen to the grand dames of high society, he did so more for spectacle and entertainment than in a serious effort to probe the social dimensions and growing problems of the alienated and the violent.

In *The Walls of Jericho* (1928), Fisher turns the narrative of the old ballad into a superficial psychological drama in which a new type of badman, who uses his size and strength to protect himself from the pains and weakness of real emotion, is transformed into a proper member of the middle class, able to admit that he has feelings and ready to abandon the dives and gambling rooms for marriage, that most basic of all middle-class institutions. To be sure, we like Joshua "Shine" Jones from the start. There is something attractively vulnerable about this great strong furniture mover who works harder than everyone else and whose special expertise is pianos. But everything that Fisher's narrator tells us about him suggests that he belongs to that class of "'bad' Negro" that Fisher outlines in his short stories. He is a gambler, and when he walks into the card room of Henry Patmore's club, he behaves with the unmannerly ruthlessness of Stagolee. Big enough to bully almost anyone, if all the chairs were taken he simply "lifted some player out by the collar, thanked him with a grin, and assumed his place." He is, in fact, "the hardest boogy in Harlem," who, like "his associates," sees compassion as an "unpardonable" weakness.[15]

But instead of following Shine's hardness to its logical consequences (John Hardy is hanged, Stagolee goes to hell), Fisher changes the badman paradigm. Shine can speak the language of the street and accept the values of the middle class at the same time.[16] In the first place, the narrator tells us, Shine "had never found it necessary to be nasty as well as bad" (pp. 18–19). And unlike other antecedents like Dupree and Bad Lee Brown, Shine falls hard but nonviolently for a pretty girl, Linda Young. She takes him to an Episcopal sermon, during which he experiences a kind of epiphany that stimulates him to pull down the wall he has built around himself. Dupree's infatuation with a pretty girl, or, to put it more coarsely, with her "jelly roll," leads to violence, arrest, and execution. Fisher's story is far too respectable to allow any taint of actual sex to embarrass its readers. It is the bourgeois measure of Joshua Jones that his infatuation with Linda Young is not overtly sexual and leads in the other direction from Dupree's tragedy, toward redemption rather than murder and its consequences. His kindness, compassion, and gentleness are now set free by the respectable morality of a pretty girl and her church, enabling him to discover his true self. In two subsequent encounters, he pulls back from the violent vengeance his previous self-deluding hardness would have demanded. Employing the gambit of inverted values, Fisher plays upon his audience's taste for the cliché. Shine passes up his chance to avenge himself upon one of the characters he has mistaken for an enemy and feels the shame of the badman for violating his code, like Huckleberry Finn resigning himself to Hell for protecting the slave Jim. However, *we* know where true virtue lies, whether Shine does or not: right there in the truly gentle heart of this huge man. Fisher's conclusion, though, is more Horatio Alger (or James Corrothers) than Mark Twain. Shine not only gets the girl, he is also set up in his own business by the wealthy patron he came close to killing. Huck Finn's decision marks a profound revolt against the racist conventions of an America sympathetic to slavery. Joshua Jones embraces the middle-class values of his day: industry, reliability, domesticity.

Just as explicitly, the "paired stock 'folk' characters,"[17] Jinx Jenkins and Bubber Brown, reflect a realignment of attitudes toward the traditional badman type. They maintain throughout *The Walls of Jericho* a running verbal competition in which they insult each other with the standard street-lingo put-downs. They preserve these minstrel-style combative façades, however, not because they dislike each other but "to suppress the mutual affection that their class considers unmanly and unnatural."[18] And when it comes to actual fighting, they find an escape. Toward the end of the novel, the dozens (the competitive game of rhyming insults) they slip into becomes too serious, and they are sent into the basement of Henry Patmore's poolroom to fight it out. But they emerge drunk rather than battered, with Bubber murmuring in a drowsy stupor, "Ain' nuthin' to fight about, boogy. Ain't you my boy?" (pp. 201–14). Such boozy camaraderie is the sentiment of the popular magazine. It substitutes the middle-class desire for reconciliation and harmony for the unflinching folk vision of a street-world reality.

The metaphor for the walls Jinx and Bubber, and Joshua too, raise around themselves is the "walls of Jericho," made famous in the rousing spiritual that Fisher uses as an epigraph to the novel. Fisher puts his explanation of the image into the mouth of Episcopal minister Tod Bruce, as educated and verbal as Fisher himself. In the key sermon, Bruce uses the biblical tale to picture the way people cut themselves off from others, deluding themselves with misjudgments about their strengths and weaknesses (p. 184). The Episcopal church of which the Reverend Bruce is pastor is surely the most conservative and sedate of all black churches.[19] And we know that his congregation is made up of bourgeois strivers, so concerned with rejecting any identification with the unmannered and expressive classes that they have to go to other venues in order to hear spirituals. Yet Bruce addresses his sermon not only to the class attending his church but to the badman as well. The motto "of the ruffian on the street," he says, "is 'Don't kid yourself.'" This is good advice, but we all too often do not take it. We do "kid ourselves," especially "about our Self. And what is our Self, our knowledge of ourself, if not Jericho—chief city of every man's spiritual Canaan?" Stripping away our illusions about ourselves is like the battle Joshua fought for Jericho. And we cannot know ourselves until we have fought that battle and breached those walls of illusion successfully. The unstated assumption here is that self-knowledge, not status and reputation, is the goal of life, the means for the self-fulfillment we all seek. Even the "ruffian on the street" is inherently bourgeois. He deludes himself into thinking that he is fulfilled by the values of his class, boasting "that he is evil and merciless and hard when all this is but a crust, shielding and hiding a spirit that is kindly, compassionate, and gentle" (p. 185).

These are Fisher's key values: kindness, compassion, gentleness. Fisher makes us recognize the essential goodness of his moral badmen so that we do not give up on them as unredeemable characters. He wants us to believe that their true selves are their good selves. More than that, it is not simply that Fisher's "badman" is actually kind, compassionate, and gentle rather than hard, relentless, and merciless, but that the point of his stories is to turn those dynamic qualities to good use. Once the character discovers and accepts these qualities in himself, the story can end, for they establish the ideal life. Nothing else needs to be resolved.

CLAUDE MCKAY'S *HOME TO HARLEM*

When Claude McKay's Jake Brown returns to Harlem after World War I, from a reader's standpoint it seems not much different from St. Louis's Targee Street, Atlanta's Decatur, Memphis's Beale back at the turn of the century. The cabarets McKay describes boom with dancing, gambling, drinking, and prostitution. Immigrants from the South and from the old black neighborhoods in lower Manhattan "colonize" the new black city and crowd into its "buffet flats," drinking gin, playing cards, dancing to the new jazz records blaring from the Victrolas. In dance halls like the Sheba Palace, men and women of all shades and shapes drag dance to the new blues. Uncle Doc's small bar entertains the local streetmen, who signify on each other and argue.[20]

Woven into this atmosphere is endemic violence. At the rent parties, in the cabarets, on the streets, men and women go at each other with a frantic viciousness. Two Caribbean harridans fight naked over a cocky little bantam of a man who enjoys their tear. A jealous woman knocks down cabaret singer Congo Rose and stomps her. In the Baltimore nightclub a "mulatress" smashes the ribs of her rival and spits in her face. Men's fights are bloodier, but like the women's, they are usually for status in sexual competition; either that or money, gambling winnings or loans owed. One pimp, egged on by his newly acquired whore, smashes a rival with a broken whisky bottle until "blood bubbled from his nose and his mouth." Zeddy Plummer wrestles Nije Gridley to the floor and would cut his throat if Jake did not stop him. The fight is over money Zeddy owes Nije. There is an animal savagery to these combats. Without warning a "light-brown" strikes the "chocolate" dealer of a card game at Gin-Head Susy's buffet flat over a throw-in to the pot. "The chocolate leaped up like a tiger-cat at his assailant. . . . Like an enraged ram, he held and butted the light-brown boy twice, straight on the forehead. The victim crumpled with a thud to the floor."[21]

McKay presents these scenes with the unjudgmental voice of the literary naturalist, but he is far from indifferent to his characters or their acts. Indeed, McKay is too much of a romantic not to suggest that the violence is at least part of what is so compelling about Harlem, the yeast of the cabaret life whose artificial interiors play to the Negro's love of "the pageantry of life," with their "Soft, barbaric, burning, savage, clashing, planless colors—all rioting together in wonderful harmony" (pp. 319, 320). Ray, the self-conscious intellectual, articulates the somber clash that lies somewhere beneath the surface in the "low-life" fiction of the Renaissance. It is between the moral repugnance at the sometimes brutal behavior of the Harlem folk and the need to see them as the source of what is authentic and true in the race:

> How terribly Ray could hate [Harlem] sometimes. Its brutality, gang rowdyism, promiscuous thickness. Its hot desires. But, oh, the rich blood-red color of it! (p. 267)

McKay appears to be much more aware of this conflict than Fisher. He certainly brings it out more explicitly. The Baltimore cabaret epitomizes the dynamic forces that charge Harlem with its tremendous but ambiguous energies:

> Haunting rhythm, mingling of naïve wistfulness and charming gayety, now sheering over into mad riotous joy, now, like a jungle mask, strange, unfamiliar, disturbing, now plunging headlong into the far, dim depths of profundity and rising out as suddenly with a simple, childish grin. And the white visitors laugh. They see the grin only. Here are none of the well-patterned, well-made emotions of the respectable world. A laugh might finish in a sob. A moan end in hilarity. That gorilla type wriggling there with his hands so strangely hugging his mate, may strangle her tonight. But he has not thought of that now. He loves the warm wriggle and is lost in it. (p. 337)

McKay deeply inscribes his portrait of Harlem with these contradictions. The blood, the rage are elemental to the unconstrained life of the folk, frightening, perhaps, painful and uncivilized, but part of the heritage. The intense emotions they signal are derived from a past that is close to the rhythms of basic existence; they are symptoms of spontaneity and freedom from overcivilized cynicism. The "new Negro" uses his art to help the reader experience this richness. He frames the violence for us and teaches us its ambiguous value without forcing a moral judgment that would turn an account of it into an instrument of disapproval.

One wonders, though, if the reader is to take as ironical the fact that Ray, the representative of "civilization," and Jake, the embodiment of the uninhibited primitive, both feel flaws in themselves and wish for the attributes of the other. While Ray yearns for the simple feelings and responses of the unpolished and more primal Jake, Jake both in his private reflections and in his talk with Ray wishes he had Ray's education so that he could better himself in the world. "I wish I was edjucated mahself," he tells Ray. "Ef I was edjucated, I could understand things better and be proper-speaking like you is." And while Ray, like any promiscuous street man, flees a permanent domestic relationship with Agatha, Jake's ideal is not to pursue a new woman every night but to "settle down" with Felice, his "little brown" (pp. 272, 273). Ray's education makes him dissatisfied in a way that he thinks Jake is not. But after he himself is involved in a nearly fatal fight, Jake feels the same depression Ray feels and says with the weariness of a disappointed romantic, "I'm jest sick and tiah'd a everything" (p. 329).[22]

Sensitive, aware, moved by nesting instincts that might even be called monogamously bourgeois, Jake, like Joshua "Shine" Jones in Fisher's *Walls of Jeri-*

cho, is a cleaned-up badman. He is uneducated, like his antecedents in the bad-man ballad. And he plies the dangerous depths of the black community's low-life, its gambling rooms and cabarets, its buffet flats and whorehouses. But at heart he is a morally decent man, who avoids violence when he can. In fact, McKay shows us that Jake and some of his friends are increasingly uncomfort-able with Harlem. Even as Harlem offers rich experience in its music and dance and food, it is also becoming a place of ever more irrational and purposeless vi-olence. His friend Billy Biasse tells Jake about seeing a harmless man walk by a pool room "when a bad nigger jest lunges out and socks him bif! in the jaw." The man did not retaliate, but Billy does, smashing the "bad nigger" in the eye and then pulling his gun and running the bully off the street. "I tell you, boh, Harlem is lousy with crazy-bad niggers, as tough as Hell's Kitchen, and I always travel with mah gun ready" (p. 286). If everyone carried a gun, says Jake, there would be social chaos. Yet later he reflects on "Niggers fixing to slice one another's throats. Always fighting." The old type, then, is still around, but it is presented to us from a different angle than in the ballad, one that is quite unsympathetic. Even so, the old code still prevails in some sense. "Got to fight if youse a man," says Jake. And while he does not like the idea of carrying a gun, for his own safety he finally accepts the gun Billy offers him, since "I gambles mahself and you nevah know when niggers am gwineta git crazy-mad" (p. 287).

Just such an irrational encounter brings the action of the novel to its cli-max. Reunited with Felice, the "little brown" he finds then loses in the first pages of the novel, Jake has to fight his old friend Zeddy, who claims her for his own. In his attack on Jake, Zeddy is reduced to animal rage, which transcends the civil loyalties of friendship. He advances on Jake "like a terrible bear," his razor poised for cutting (p. 326). But Jake's cool head and his rational, though reluc-tant, decision to carry a gun enable him to control Zeddy. His set-to with Zeddy resembles the fight between Eight-Ball Eddy Boyd and Dirty Cozzens in Fisher's "Blades of Steel." When Jake pulls the gun, Zeddy, like Dirty Cozzens, is stopped "like a cowed brute" (p. 326). And Jake behaves with the same cool courage as Eddy Boyd does in facing the attack of the hyped-up Dirty. For both Fisher and McKay, Harlem's irrational violence may have its forbidden attrac-tions, but it also has a bestial sleaziness beneath the dignity of inherently decent men like Jake and Joshua Jones. In their fictions the violence is ultimately brought under control by the forces of rational restraint within the irrational world itself. Like Eddy Boyd, Jake, in courageous control of the methods of the street, employs them with perfect effectiveness, avoiding the outcome he most dreads, somebody's death. The white legal system has nothing to do with it. And Jake's influence is salutary, for Zeddy later apologizes.[23] A "civilized" harmony is restored.

That harmony is reinforced when Jake and Felice decide together to leave Harlem for Chicago to make sure Jake is not apprehended for going AWOL back in France. They are, for all intents and purposes, married, though they dis-regard the book rules of the wedding ceremony. Indeed, in the whole final epi-sode Jake transcends the "primitive" and the "spontaneous" of Harlem. McKay presents Jake as a man of Harlem low-life inherently qualified to rise out of that low-life. This tacitly assumes that he moves in the most desirable direction, out and away from the Zeddys, the Obadiahs, and the Yaller Princes who represent the new, disapproved incarnations of the Stagolees and John Hardys, into a monogamous, nonviolent life with his "little brown."

ARNA BONTEMPS'S "DON'T-CARE FOLK"

Some Renaissance novelists, whose proper and upward-striving families had attempted to shield them from the debased world of the loud, unmannerly, and immoral, felt they had been kept from the richest and most interesting aspects of their racial heritage. "Don't go up there acting colored," Arna Bontemps's father instructs him before he heads off to a white boarding school.[24] But why should he *not* act colored? Bontemps asks himself resentfully. Why should he deny who he is when whites have been acting colored for years: in their blackface minstrel shows, in their theft of black music, whenever they step onto a dance floor. In these reflections, Bontemps is the perfect exemplar of the cultural and generational conflict that gave the Renaissance "new Negro" his energy and momentum.

Paul Bontemps moved his family from Louisiana to Los Angeles when Arna was just three years old, partly to escape from violent whites and partly to avoid the stigma of being "colored." But "colored" followed them several years later in the person of Uncle Buddy, the younger brother of Bontemps's grandmother. He beckoned the young Arna in precisely the direction that Paul had sought to close off, toward the superstitions of the black folk, the ribald songs and stories, the vignettes of his youthful reprobate behavior. Paul thought him a "baneful influence" and tried to protect his children. But Arna was fascinated. With the literary self-consciousness of his generation, Bontemps in retrospect saw clearly the symbolic importance of these two men in his life. The conflict between "their opposing attitudes toward roots," he wrote, reflected an argument in which all blacks "must somehow take sides. By implication at least, one group advocates embracing the riches of the folk heritage; their opposites demand a clean break with the past and all it represents." As Bontemps put it, Buddy, and the friends he took up with in Los Angeles, "were sometimes below the level of polite respect. They were not bad people. They were what my father described as don't-care folk."[25]

God Sends Sunday (1931), Bontemps's first extended work of fiction, is an "acting colored" novel about such "don't-care folk." His sees them, though, not as one of them but as an affectionate, not quite condescending observer, a man with a college degree and a job in an academic institution. His protagonist, Li'l Augie, is a feisty, diminutive jockey from Louisiana with the energy, ambition, and wanderlust that Bontemps saw in his Uncle Buddy. As he achieves jockey fame on the southern race track circuit, he takes up the recreations of his type. He gambles, drinks, dances, parties with the best prostitutes, and presents himself as a tough "nigger."

Augie's size is a constant problem for him. It is the impetus, in fact, for his conviction that it is more important to be "ba-ad" than successful with the horses. Augie thinks badness secures status, frightens off contenders, compels respect, and bullies women into faithfulness. Thus when he meets the San Antonio whore Parthenia, he "tried to give a big impression of himself. He had to keep fighting off the fear that she would laugh at him, that she would think him childish; for he was no more than half her size." Her affectionate description of Augie as a "putty lil papa" is more insult than compliment. Augie wants to be known as something tougher: "Wha, wha! Well, I's jes' as bad as I is putty," and he commands her to "Po' anuther drink." He proves his badness by getting drunk, quarreling with her, and blacking "both her eyes." He views himself, now, as one with the "macks, pimps, gamblers, prize-fighters, and other jockeys like himself." To sustain his manliness, he turns to equalizing weapons like pistols and knives, through which he protects his right to possess those women. "I may be lil," he tells Della Green, but in any confrontation he might have with a competitor, "I's loud as a six-gun. An' I wants anybody whut don't think so to try me a barrel."[26]

Augie's world of the 1880s resembles the one frequented by the old ballad heroes. Joe Baily and Tom Wright, for example, are "notoriously dangerous" young men, who carry the "fighting-tools" of the traditional badman: "knives, brass knuckles, razors, and, in some cases, pistols" (p. 27). We learn that half a dozen of Joe Baily's siblings have been killed in fights and an equal number have been in jail (p. 28), and the rumor is that his father had "kilt seben o' eight white mens" (p. 32). "There was no doubt that Joe Baily was a bad nigger," Bontemps's narrator tells us. "Tom Wright, a more subdued, consumptive fellow, was equally dangerous," for "he had already killed a man" (p. 28). The men who hang out at that clearinghouse of community information, the barber shop, describe Joe Baily with a certain local pride as "one mo' bad nigger," whose "people was bad niggers," too (p. 32). And the loungers all agree that Tom Wright was also "a bad young one" (p. 33).[27]

Like the figures described by folklorist Howard Odum, ne'er-do-wells who love "breaking up the jamboree," "Church meetings and picnics,"[28] Baily and Wright deign to put in an appearance at a church picnic, and they get into a typical badman fight. Bontemps's account of what happens when they set their cap for the same girl reads like an art version of an old ballad variant. When Baily insults Wright "in the presence of" the girl, Wright gets furious. Fumblingly, he searches his coat pocket for his pistol.

> "I'm gonna shoot you, Joe Baily," he said.
> "I'll be damned if you do, Tom Wright."
> Joe whipped his own [gun] from his pocket and fired while Tom continued to fumble. The bullet went into the consumptive boy's belly. Still Tom kept fishing into the coat pocket. Joe banged again . . . then again.
> "You betta keep shootin', Joe Baily, 'cause if I ever get ma hands on mine, I gonna kill you."
> "You kilt Jimmy Hines, Tom Wright, but I'll be goddamned if ever you kills me." He banged two more into Tom's belly.

Tom dropped to his knees. As he fell, the pistol slid from his coat pocket to the ground. He reached forward feebly and picked it out of the grass.

"I'm gonna kill you, Joe Baily."

He fired once. Then his strength failed. But it was enough; the bullet whizzed through Joe's teeth. Joe pitched face forward. Tom curled into a knot, still holding his belly with one hand, and died in that position. (p. 30)

These are familiar badmen, impulsively violent, indifferent to death. And just as the typical ballad would shift from the death of the badman's victim to the chorus of women dressing in red and sounding the alarm or expressing grief or joy, Bontemps moves from the fight to the choral group of the local barber shop, where the drama is reported and a post mortem of the event is conducted. Here, though, the similarity ends. The old balladeer would most typically have had his badman kill one man and then flee. He would have been captured, tried, and punished for his crime. Bontemps's agenda calls for a different treatment. His aim is assuredly to bring to his readers this little-known cast of black characters. But it is also to explore the psychological mechanics of a cultural code that makes a matter of life and death out of a trivial affront and to pass judgment on the moral and social implications of that code. For the two badmen the stakes are the highest possible, their male honor. But Bontemps shows the reader that protecting this honor is self-defeating folly. He puts this critique in the mouth of one of the barber-shop loungers during their commentary on the shooting the next day. Mississippi Davis criticizes the two men for shooting each other while the whites look on in approval: "Niggers is crazy to shoot up one anuther dat-a-way. Dat's jes' whut white folks likes to see. Meantime they is doin'-up niggers right an' lef' an' nobody says boo" (p. 33). But what really highlights the folly of the deaths of Tom and Joe is that the girl over whom they had killed each other was, in Mississippi's words, "nuthin' but a white man's strumpet," and she "ain't studyin' no niggers." She is the concubine of Mr. Woody, Augie's boss, and far out of the dead men's reach (p. 34).

Like both Fisher and McKay, Bontemps is interested in what might lie behind the cruel hardness of the traditional badman type. There is the futility and folly of Tom Wright and Joe Baily, to be sure. But more broadly, there is the insecurity that Augie feels about his size. We can take his smallness as a metaphor explaining not only Augie's behavior but figuratively that of the hard men that he seeks to compete with. Augie affects all the characteristics of the badman to countervail his sense of personal inadequacy, but they are a loose fit for his real personality.

The essence of Bontemps's characterization of Augie is that Augie is no Joe Baily or Tom Wright. We are given too much knowledge of him—his desperate desire to appear to *be* a badman, his childlike vulnerability—to be convinced that he has the proper ruthlessness to be a Stagolee or a Railroad Bill. It is true that Augie blacks the eyes of the whore Parthenia and finally beats his St. Louis sweetheart Della Green. But Bontemps always manages to suggest that his violence against women is a pose, that he is a naturally loving little man compensating for his size by doing what badmen are expected to do. This conflict between what the code calls on him to do and his real character emerges especially in his discord with Biglow Brown, a St. Louis pimp and a true badman. Riding high as a winning jockey, Augie steals the attractive young prostitute Della Green from the pimp, setting up a hostility that results in Augie's eventually stalking the bigger and more dangerous man outside a Targee Street pool hall. The badman code requires him to protect his manly honor against the arrogant pimp. But he obeys that code without the calm panache of the traditional badman. As he waits for the swaggering Brown to come out on the street, Augie is "assailed by fears" and "aware of his own trembling." At the critical moment, as Brown appears, one of his old whores unexpectedly approaches the pimp with a grievance. As Brown is distracted, Augie leaps from the shadows and shoots him. But instead of strutting in pride over his victory and declaring his badness to the street, Augie stands in a trance, everything seeming "unreal" to him. He reverts to his true childlike self, more like the paralyzed Joe Hamilton than John Hardy. The police take him, without resistance, to jail. This is the climax of Augie's career as a badman, and it illustrates how unfit the ebullient little man is for the role he has tried to play.

Augie's childlike quality reflects how blacks are treated by those white institutions that intrude into the black community. Taken into custody, Augie falls under the control of the white court, and his experience with it is quite different from the typical ballad badman's. "In those days," Bontemps's narrator tells us, referring to the 1880s or 1890s, "red-light murders were so commonplace they evoked but slight interest from court authorities. Condemnations were rare. Almost anything passed for self-defense. Consequently the impression got about that the state did not wish to bother with crimes committed by Negroes against Negroes" (p. 87). As in many actual cases, Mr. Woody, the white man, vouches for "his nigger, [as] a fine well-behaved sort and an excellent jockey." The judge releases him with an admonition "to avoid the company of bad niggers like Biglow in the future" (p. 88). Instead of meting out the justice Augie's crime calls for, the court demonstrates its power and its indifference to intrablack violence by freeing him. The court and Mr. Woody treat Augie as if he were merely a wayward child, "irresponsible, volatile, unaccountable," whose naughtiness may be forgiven because it lacks real criminal gravity. In the conventional pattern of the badman ballad, the killer is at least given the dignity of being taken seriously by the system. Bontemps, observing the crime from the periphery of the badman's world, is influenced by the sensibilities of his class, however sympathetic he might be to Augie. Augie's crime is for Bontemps an occasion for commenting upon white racism rather than dramatizing the serious consequences of violence in the black community. The badman balladeer tends to see the upshot of violence from the viewpoint of the badman himself and from inside the "low-life" world in which the badman lives, and from the inside, the badman is no child. For Bontemps the badman is one of "them" while the more appealing Augie is one of "us." And while there is a certain glitter in the St. Louis playground where Augie kills Biglow, Bontemps makes sure that we see the decay underneath.

This world is at least partly an outgrowth of the court's treatment of Augie and other "outside-the-law" blacks. It exemplifies, Bontemps effectively demonstrates, one of the main social problems of the black community, the failure of law enforcement. Into the vacuum that results from weak state authority step the aggressive, the proud, the desperate. With no stable institutional way to redress grievances available, the social structure collapses into destructive collisions between the frustrated and the strong. Dominance is at the top of the badman's agenda and he achieves it by force. Relationships are mediated by violence. Self-restraint and reason lose out to impulse and rage or one's hypersensitivity to perceived insult. These emotions rule the players on Targee Street and take a fearful toll. Prostitution is ostensibly illegal, but the white law essentially turns a blind eye to it, and the industry thrives. Its regulation is thus a free-for-all.

Bontemps also makes clear in ways that the folk artist does not that in this world violence is fundamental to the customs of gender relations. Like some kind of extreme Victorian patriarch, Biglow Brown uses "his great physical power" to keep his ladies in line. Indeed, in his business, beating his whores is not only legitimate but necessary. The macks believe "that the nature of women requires a certain modicum of brutality," and that "It was a man's duty" to administer whatever blows were called for (p. 63). In this male-dominated world, it does not take much for such a self-serving code to be adapted to other kinds of male-female relationships, even loving ones. On Targee Street, the narrator says, "A beating was an act of singular intimacy between a gal and her man" (p. 94). Even after they start living together in a love relationship, Augie has no compunction about Della's continuing her activities as a prostitute. That is business. Beating is love, a more intimate act than sexual intercourse. It is only when Biglow Brown attempts to take back the sexual heights and beats Della that Augie feels honor-bound to kill him. Practices which are scandalous and immoral for the middle class are normal for the culture in which Augie moves, and the violence of that culture is part of its protocol for regulating relationships. The badman must preserve his honor by beating up his woman and killing any competitor who tries to move into this sacrosanct territory.

The middle-class writer in Bontemps suggests that these relationships are deviant, not normative, and he finds it necessary to account for their deviancy. The cause is largely the power of the white man. The white court refuses to enforce conventional middle-class order at the social level. And the individual white man exerts limitless rights over black women with even less sense of responsibility to them than the black man assumes. Mr. Woody, by taking the very willing young beauty Florence Dessau for his concubine, not only shows the centuries-old white disrespect for the idea that blacks might observe the conventional standards of sexual chastity, he also forecloses the possibility of Augie's abiding by those standards as well, for Augie falls for Florence as the ideal woman. Instead of entering into what might have been a permanent relationship with the woman of his dreams, Augie is forced to take up one with Della that he knows will be impermanent and await the availability of Florence. She does indeed become available, but her code directs her to abandon Augie when he ceases to supply her with the material comforts she has been trained to expect. In making Augie a sort of child—diminutive, self-centered, explosive—even though he is an endearing one, Bontemps suggests that this whole world is childlike, a play-space in which impulse and immediate self-gratification reign. White refusal to grant African Americans maturity and reasonableness, when whites dominate every institution in which those are required qualities, simply reinforces the preindustrial impulsiveness of those in the black low-life. Though the white world makes direct contact with the black one only at the edges in *God Sends Sunday,* its power is godlike and is exerted in institutions like the courts and in relationship like concubinage. It is Mr. Woody's taking Florence as his concubine that determines the whole subsequent structure of Augie's life.

The last act of that life occurs at his sister Leah's house in Los Angeles years after Florence leaves him for a more prosperous man. In his pathetic figure, we see what happens to the high-rollers of the old sporting set. Leah offers him the rocklike sanctuary of family, but Augie has not been bred to the tame life of Mudtown. He tries to trade on his former status as a glamorous city boy, but even the hicks he tries to impress easily see that he is a has-been and treat him accordingly. He gets into trouble when he stabs a younger sexual rival and must once again take to the road. This time, though, he has no future, only a past, and that gives him no help now. As he heads down the railroad track that carried so many black men from one pointless experience to another, he has a moment of painful self-knowledge: "I ain't nobody. I ain't nuthin'. . . . I's jes' a po' picked sparrow. I ain't big as a dime, an' I don't worth [*sic*] a nickel" (p. 196). Yet, in the back of the truck on which he hitches a ride, he gets a "feeling of exhilaration, an illusion that came with speed" (p. 199). We know indeed that this is an illusion, that Augie is not the hero he fancies himself, and that he is headed, probably, for his final adventure. Yet his irrepressibility leaves us with a sort of joy in his refusal to admit defeat.

In a conclusion quite different from most ballads', Bontemps makes us sympathize with the little man whose life drags him down but who loves every minute of it and refuses to succumb to discouragement. When we track the line of Augie's life back to its origins, violence plays its role. But at the crucial points it is the social and psychological issues that dominate, the fatal way in which indifferent white power and authority shatter all permanence, order, and security and rob Augie of the chance for fulfillment. We know Augie better than Stagolee or Dupree or Bad Lee Brown. Our relationship with him carries more feeling, more sentiment, suggesting the difference between the viewpoint of those chroniclers who lived alongside the badman and shared his vicissitudes and that of the next-generation middle-class artist whose temporal and class distance from the events he reports inevitably tinge them with a subtle though no doubt unintended condescension. It is a condescension, though, softened with a deliberate tenderness. It is the method of the discursive novel rather than the pithy ballad.

ZORA NEALE HURSTON: COUNTRY MEN AND WOMEN

No Renaissance writer went further than Zora Neale Hurston in the search for the authentic expression of the folk. Nor is any Renaissance writer better known now than this once grossly under-appreciated woman. She has become, in the last thirty years, the worshipped icon of the black feminist movement. Reclaimed from the dustbin of literary history by Alice Walker (who, in 1973, famously placed a gravestone for the forgotten writer in a remote cemetery in Fort Pierce, Florida) and by Robert Hemenway in his excellent biography, Hurston now is as well known as almost any writer from the pre–World War II era. She is remembered as one of the spark plugs of the Harlem Renaissance, a buoyant teller of side-splitting race tales, a falsifier of her birth date, an anthropologist who did field work among the very people with whom she had grown up, and the author of what is now perhaps the most revered novel by any African American woman—*Their Eyes Were Watching God* (1937).

It might be that Hurston was more qualified than any other writer of the twenties and thirties to translate the sensibility and the style of the black folk into the studied "higher" (and more commercial) forms of the novel and the short story. At the same time she was probably more deeply conflicted than others over how that should be done. She spent her childhood as the daughter of a southern Baptist minister known for his powerful preaching and she had hung upon the conversation of the men telling "lies" on the porch of Joe Clarke's country store, which was the center of the all-black town of Eatonville, Florida.[29] She devoted her late teens and early adulthood to getting a college education at Howard, Barnard, and Columbia. Her angle on the world was thus a mix of the "folk" and the "educated." But it was the division between the artist and the anthropologist rather than the literate and the oral in her background that lay at the root of her ambivalence toward her subject. Should she limit herself to being, as Hemenway puts it, an anthropologist whose "cultural imperialism" tacitly assumed the inferiority of the lore she set out to study? Or should she roam freely as an artist, meeting the folk style on its own ground and accepting its equality to any other cultural mode?[30] The main body of her work—the folklore of *Mules and Men* (1935), her autobiography *Dust Tracks on a Road* (1942), and her two novels, *Jonah's Gourd Vine* (1934) and *Their Eyes Were Watching God*—suggests that the artist won out over the anthropologist hands down. She brings to the treatment of the folk world a gusto and respect all her own, combining her firsthand experience as a child with the results of her anthropological field studies in the South and her college training in literature and research.[31]

In both her fiction and nonfiction, her communities are packed with hypocrites and cowards, spiteful women and mean-minded men, vicious violence and irrepressible fun. In *Moses: Man of the Mountain* (1939), the princely Moses tries to help the lowly Hebrew slaves being held in Egypt by Pharaoh. But when they become suspicious and accuse him of wanting to "boss" everyone, he reflects that "the will to humble a man more powerful than themselves was stronger than the emotion of gratitude. It was stronger than the wish for the common brotherhood of man. It was the cruelty of chickens—fleeing with great clamor before superior force but merciless towards the helpless."[32] Hurston is famous for her seeming indifference to the white racial prejudice that angered so many of her black contemporaries in the Harlem movement. She directs her contempt upon the petty vanities, the small revenges, the paltry jealousies of the working as well as the malingering black folk. Relentlessly, she ridicules their intolerance of those who behave differently, criticizes the lowly who hypocritically put themselves forward as superior or are resentful of their betters, who are cowardly in their treatment of the less powerful, who are full of trivial thoughts about flashy clothes and special food, who are lazy and ungrateful, and especially who make a fuss over color. Her love for the uneducated people of the South whose lore she collects as an anthropologist does not blind her to their faults. But in painting those faults with a broad brush, she spreads her disapproval equally across class and race, for the black lower classes she so assiduously criticizes belong to the same human family as the black and white middle and upper classes who puff themselves up with their own petty intolerances and frauds.

Hurston's take on the violent badman is one with her take on the black culture she writes about. She cuts her violent men—and women—from the same cloth as the other members of their communities. They appear in many forms in Hurston's portraits, like the figures in a Brueghel painting, teeming with motion and variety. They act out of spite, envy, insecurity. The boasters advertising themselves as the baddest of the bunch are often simply covering up their cowardice. These, Hurston guilefully suggests, must be ancient types, because she sees them even in the camel drivers in an Arab caravan that Moses attaches himself to. Like a couple of anachronistic Harlem streetmen, Hurston's desert camel drivers signify on each other with taunting threats they are too cowardly to back up. "I don't beat up bums like you," says one. "I pass you up and call you lucky. I'm bad! and if you hit me they'll give you four names—Nubby, Peggy, Bad-eyed and Shorty, cause you'll look like all of them." Hurston's narrator derides the two loudmouths: "They had everything for a good fight except the courage." Then, like the comic characters in a movie short, "They imitated a frenzy to rush upon each other so successfully that they actually did. The shock of actually having to do what they had threatened to do was too much. They sprang apart and ran several yards in opposite directions before they went back into character." When they have exhausted themselves in their posturing, "they returned to the circle about the fire and drank together as if not a word had passed between them. When they turned in to sleep they rolled themselves in their separate blankets and slept side by side" (pp. 107–108), just like Jinx Jenkins and Bubber Brown in Henry Patmore's basement. Moses provides the gloss: "Here it is just like it is in Egypt [or Eatonville or Harlem]—the scared people do all of the biggest talk" (p. 108).

As extraterrestrial bodies cannot exist without space, the badman and badwoman in Hurston's work cannot exist without the community. It is the social context that gives significance and identity to the small and the mean. Sometimes the "scared people" who do so much boasting and threatening are the community's most emotionally vulnerable ones. The overweight Good Breath pulls her knife angrily when others in her work gang bait her about her poundage. But when they simply laugh at her, she flounces off in irate frustration. In this culture, psychological pain does not excuse public anger. Those who explode not only lose in the game of signifying, they also draw the disapproval of the group. One of the men says of Good Breath, "She always pickin' fights and gittin beat. Dat 'oman hates peace and agreement."[33]

Hurston's view of what she calls badmen is that they conduct their business by cheating and deceit. Their signature method is stealth, their favorite direction of assault is from the rear, and their favorite target is those smaller or weaker than they. In *Jonah's Gourd Vine*, John Pearson calls one version of the type "woman-jessie[s]. Beat up women and run from mens," like the jealous Duke who is afraid to confront John directly. John Pearson's stepfather beats him until he is big enough to defend himself against the older man's bullying.[34]

In her contribution to the evolution of the literary badman, Hurston pays much attention to these contemptible features of the type, a public enemy rather than an awesome monument, marked by smallness of behavior rather than real badness. But there is more than enough room for the straightforward man or woman who does things in jumbo-sized gestures, who gets drunk and lets the neighborhood know it, who will fight for his game or his friend. But if his excesses are to be counted virtues, he must at the same time work hard, take care of his family, handle all personal difficulties himself, and fight fair and face-to-face. In fact, the respectable success, the "accumulating man," the "good provider," who "paid his debts and told the truth": this man is even more admirable if he is "hard-riding, hard-drinking, hard-cussing." Not only is being "powerful hot under the collar" no impediment to being "a useful citizen," it tends to raise the value of a man's stock. "Nobody found any fault with a man like that in a country where personal strength and courage were the highest virtues. People were supposed to take care of themselves without whining." Hurston's example of how this code worked is the "two men who came before the justice of the peace," the defendant having "hit the plaintiff three times with his fist and kicked him four times. The justice of the peace fined him seven dollars—a dollar a lick." He paid his fine with a smile. When the justice then fined the plaintiff *ten* dollars, the latter was stunned and aggrieved. "Why Mr. Justice," he complained, "that man knocked me down and kicked me, and I never raised my hand." The justice answered, "That is just what I'm fining you for, you yellow-bellied coudar [tortoise]! Nobody with any guts would have come into court to settle a fist fight." This is why we know that John Pearson's brother-in-law is a sniveler for taking John to court over the fight he loses. "Decency was plumb outraged at a man taking a beating and then swearing out a warrant about it," says Hurston in her autobiography. As for signifying between two boasters, a person cannot win a fight by calling the enemy names. "You can call 'em all the names you want to, after the fight. That's the best time to do it, anyhow."[35]

Hurston's is a colorless, raceless, classless code. The man who taught it to her was a wise white man who became her model of strength, courage, and honor, and who advised her not to "be a nigger" when it came to making her own way in the world (p. 30). For Hurston this is not a racist remark. Such a man, she implies, does not see race, only class, or, rather, the *classiness* of admirable behavior no matter where one stands on the economic, social, or ethnic ladder. And in Hurston's projection of the various types of violent men, it is this classiness she is thinking of, the esteem that comes from great character, not from economic or social privilege. The princely Moses, the vagabond Tea Cake of *Their Eyes Were Watching God,* the philandering preacher John Pearson of *Jonah's Gourd Vine,* even the wise white man all have the same genes. They are men of expansive character, capable of great emotion, genuine sexual love, and (except for John Pearson) fidelity.[36] They are loyal to friends, and above all they are unparalleled fighters. Boasting is not their game. Courage, seriousness of purpose, and indifference to status, convention, and the opinion of the masses: these are their guides.

As a self-reliant individualist, Hurston's wise white man conforms to the value system of his culture, reinforced by the vigilant local justice system. But Hurston's other heroes all have an element of the rebel in them. Moses challenges the tremendous power of the Egyptian crown prince and places himself in extreme jeopardy. He finally must go into exile for siding with the enslaved Hebrews. John Pearson, driven by his sexual appetites, cheats on his wife Lucy and blunders defiantly against her outraged respectable and influential family. Tea Cake Woods is a free spirit who liberates Hurston's heroine, Janie Mae Starks, from the starchy propriety of Eatonville's moral watchdogs and himself takes on the color-struck tavern owner Mrs. Turner, who regards herself as superior to "common niggers" (p. 134).

Their resolute individuality and fighting skills give these characters the specialness of the leading man, the actor singled out at stage front for the focus of the audience's attention, the one the audience sympathizes with and roots for in his conflict with the forces of rigid convention, hypocrisy, small-mindedness. Their rebelliousness, in other words, reflects the way the readers would like to think of themselves. Hurston's good badmen, far more numerous than her heroines, champion in their own characters the spontaneity and freedom of spirit that Hurston herself celebrates. Tea Cake brings these qualities into Janie's life, helping her to break free of the puritanically respectable working class composed of people like her grandmother, who tries to launch her along a rigidly planned track as protection from injury and pain. Tea Cake's "commitment to a life of chance," as Addison Gayle aptly puts it, "to living by the roll of the dice, to moving outside of conventional values" is what frees Janie from the "better-thinking" suffocation of Eatonville.[37] Indeed, Tea Cake's gambling success does seem to be Hurston's metaphor for his entire approach to life. Janie resents the prudes who disapprove of Tea Cake's gambling. "Tea Cake wasn't doing a bit more harm trying to win hisself a little money than they was always doing with their lying tongues. Tea Cake had more good nature in his toe-nails than they had in their so-called Christian hearts" (p. 120).

Nor are these free spirits forces of social disorder. They are feared by the sour and the shrunken, like Mrs. Turner in *Their Eyes,* John Pearson's brother-in-law Bud Potts in *Jonah's Gourd Vine,* the crown prince in *Moses.* They use the courts to try to immobilize the hardy badmen in the belief that such middle-class institutions are on their side. But Hurston's courts are often on the side of spontaneity and open-heartedness. The judge releases John Pearson into the custody of a sympathetic white man when Bud Potts takes him to court. And the Everglades all-white jury acquits Janie of killing her beloved Tea Cake in self-defense when nearly the entire black community, willfully misunderstanding, speaks out against her. Later, the division is healed, but the initial impulse of the folk is to disapprove, and Hurston's point is that thoughtless impulse too often guides the worst inclinations of the people. Hurston's Egyptian allegory takes a slightly different route. Moses' enemies enlist the Egyptian state against him with lies and manipulated half-truths. Their plan backfires, though, for they succeed only in inspiring his temporary flight from Egypt and creating conditions that allow him to free the Hebrews, the one thing they are trying to prevent.

These men thus may be rebels against the suffocating status quo, but for Hurston that status quo is not always identical with established authority. In their individual strength and fearlessness, unlike the badmen of the ballads, they bring order to a world in which petty jealousy and vindictiveness too often weaken the social structure and enable the cowardly to browbeat and exploit the weak. These men have a largeness about them, as well as a massive, self-destructive flaw, that makes inevitable a major sacrifice or catastrophe but also enhances their admirableness. Moses, instead of living the life of the mind as his natural intellectual curiosity inclines him to do, gives himself to the service of the enslaved Hebrews in order to lead them out of Egypt to freedom. The attractive recklessness of Hurston's wise white man leads to his death in a riding accident. John Pearson's uncontrollable larger-than-life sexual appetite ends in a fatal automobile accident. Tea Cake's heroic fight with a mad dog to save Janie in the aftermath of the great Okechobee storm results in his contracting incurable hydrophobia and the final tragedy of the novel.

Hurston's baddest man is a woman, a real one, who, though given relatively little space, is a star of Hurston's two main autobiographical works. Her name is Big Sweet and Hurston meets her on one of her anthropological expeditions into Florida for folk material. She is a female version of the good badman, for, like the other literary badmen of the Renaissance, she protects the values of the educated classes. She has a personality of epic size and a well-earned reputation among the work-camp personnel. Hurston's landlady tells her about Big Sweet's courage, her fighting skills, her strength, the respect she commands from everyone, including "Dat Cracker Quarters Boss." To be sure, she commits the violence of the type: "She done kilt two men on this job and they said she kilt some before she ever come here." But like Hurston's other good badmen, she is free of the cruel ruthlessness associated with the ballad heroes. "She ain't mean," says the landlady. "She don't bother nobody. She just don't stand for no foolishness, dat's all."[38] And in true badman style, Big Sweet herself "didn't mind fighting; didn't mind killing and didn't too much mind dying." But she understands that Hurston is from another way of life and "ain't got dat kind of a sense."[39] Intrigued by Hurston's mission as a folklorist and amused by the shiny new car in which Hurston gives her rides, Big Sweet becomes Hurston's patron, protector, friend, and companion.

Hurston needs such a protector, for the territory she has entered is not universally friendly to outsiders. Big Sweet has enemies, Lucy in particular, who sees in the inexperienced outsider a way that she can get at Big Sweet, whom she is afraid to attack straight-on. This drama takes place in the atmosphere of the "jook" joints in Polk County, Florida, where lumber camp laborers go to play.

Hurston's account gives them archetypal shape. They vibrate with potential and kinetic violence, which Hurston describes in rich detail. Dice players brandish switchblades, warning each other against cheating. Women taunt each other and square off like men, knives drawn. People are bloodied, killed. Paydays are especially volatile, often with "two or three killings" in a single evening. But such action is so common that even death cannot stop the "dancing and singing and buying of drinks, parched peanuts, fried rabbit."[40]

Hurston plays up the menace to which she is dangerously vulnerable. She clearly relishes telling the story to a wide-eyed middle-class audience. Like Claude McKay, she sees this as a "primeval" world, peopled by "primitive minds," who can move from love to murder as quickly as a sigh or the wrong expression of a mouth. Its exoticism offers to educated readers the appeal of vicarious thrills. "My life," says Hurston, "was in danger several times. If I had not learned how to take care of myself in these circumstances, I could have been maimed or killed on most any day of the several years of my research work."[41]

As it happens it is Big Sweet who saves her, not her own knowledge of how to handle herself. The showdown comes when Lucy catches Hurston at a party supposedly without her protector. It is a splendid scene, full of the noise of people having a good time, card players shouting above the din, songs coming to Hurston from the guitar player and his friends. Suddenly Lucy appears, demands quiet and attention, and walks "hippily" toward Hurston. Hurston is "sick and weak," terrified. But at the last moment, Big Sweet leaps from nowhere into the fray, "a flash from the corner." Lucy, revealing herself to be one of Hurston's generic cowards, tries to flee. Big Sweet trips her up and the fight is on. *Mules and Men* and *Dust Tracks* contain different details of the fight, but in both accounts Hurston escapes from what promises to be a deadly battle. She leaves us with the sound of combat in our ears, with virtually the entire group of party-goers lined up on one side or the other. It is a powerful expression of the tremendous abyss between the outsider in pursuit of the Rhinegold of folklore and the natural custodians of it. It is also an effective statement of what the educated observer perceives in this atmosphere, how bloody, ugly violence is the natural setting of a folk art that has, in its music and stories and sheer vernacular expression, its own intrinsic beauty.

Those of us who live outside the world of the "folk" can, of course, never know the residents of that world as they themselves do. We can never know the badmen of the ballads as the balladmakers did. We can be grateful to these Renaissance novelists for attempting to build a bridge between the two worlds. In doing so, they essentially create a mutation of the original type with its own genuineness and plausibility. Joshua "Shine" Jones, Eight-Ball Eddy Boyd, Jake Brown, Li'l Augie, John Pearson, and even Big Sweet share many of the characteristics that defined the ballad badman, perhaps the most important being a mastery of personal combat and a willingness to engage in it. If the later badman mutations are sometimes more inclined to the values of middle-class readers and show virtues like fairness and feeling, it is no more than we expect from authors writing for middle-class readers.

5

The Ghetto Bildungsroman

From the Forties to the Seventies

> The ghetto is ferment, paradox, conflict, and dilemma. Yet within its pervasive pathology exists a surprising human resilience. The ghetto is hope, it is despair, it is churches and bars. It is aspiration for change, and it is apathy. It is vibrancy, it is stagnation. It is courage, and it is defeatism. It is cooperation and concern, and it is suspicion, competitiveness, and rejection. It is the surge toward assimilation, and it is alienation and withdrawal within the protective walls of the ghetto.
> — Kenneth Clark[1]

RICHARD WRIGHT: BIGGER THOMAS AND A NEW CONSCIOUSNESS

In Richard Wright's *Native Son* (1940), his protagonist, Bigger Thomas, becomes enraged with his friend Gus for arriving late at Doc's pool hall in Chicago's South Side. Now, raves Bigger, the robbery of Blum's delicatessen they had planned will have to be scratched. With Doc and Bigger's two other friends, Jack and G.H., watching, Bigger pulls his switchblade, holds it to Gus's throat, and forces him to lick the knife blade in an act of humiliating submission. When Bigger finally lets him up, in his own helpless fury Gus flings a pool ball at him, then flees. Doc, observing it all, laughs. Bigger glares at the proprietor "with speechless hate," walks deliberately to a billiard table, and, challenging Doc with angry defiance, begins "to cut the green cloth on the table with long sweeping strokes," never taking "his eyes from Doc's face." As Doc, now brandishing a pistol, furiously orders him from the pool hall, forbidding him ever to return, Bigger disdainfully closes his knife, slips it into his pocket, and swaggers out the door.[2] This is a "bad nigger" in action circa 1940. He is a different breed from his predecessors: the cool killers of the turn-of-the-century ballad, the "crazy-bad niggers" shooting off their weapons that Billy Biasse complains about in *Home to Harlem,* or the shadowy pool players and gamblers that Rudolph Fisher plants on 135th Street. With the proper opportunities and guidance, Bigger might have followed the upwardly mobile path of such bourgeois badmen as Fisher's Joshua Jones or McKay's Jake Brown. The Renaissance authors tend to offer their badmen a way out. But Wright's point is that Bigger is closed off from such opportunities and guidance and therefore his fate is virtually preordained.

In Wright's hands Bigger, as his name suggests, is the mid-century culmination of the badman type, a composite of five versions of the "bad nigger" that Wright says he knew as a child and young man in the South and now saw emerging in the northern cities. They swaggered, they bullied other black youngsters, they cheated whites as well as blacks, they pulled knives on streetcar conductors rather than move to a rear seat, they pushed to the limits against the rigid boundaries erected by whites. But for them there was "no exit" and they paid a "terrible price" for their defiance. "They were shot, hanged, maimed, lynched, and generally hounded until they were either dead or their spirits broken." But they were the only blacks Wright ever saw rebelling against the South's oppression.[3]

The pithily laconic ballad form allowed no psychological or social analysis, and the artists sought no mitigation or explanation of the badman's behavior. For Wright the psychological and social analysis is everything. He advances the psychological interest of the Harlem Renaissance writers another several degrees. Above all, he endows Bigger with a self-consciousness that enables him to see how his violence can bring him metaphysical and psychological freedom.

Bigger is a South Side Chicagoan who has come with his mother and two siblings from the South. He and his buddies seem younger than the knowing players that frequented the Baltimore cabaret and Gin-Head Susy's buffet flat in the 1920s, and more affected by the seedy character of their ghetto. Aimless and adrift, out of school and work, they loiter about the streets, keeping their eyes open for opportunities to steal from the area's small black businesses. They play pool, but they do not gamble or patronize the prostitutes or take in the jazz and blues scene for which Chicago has by now become famous. This Chicago is strangely empty of the animated night life that we know existed there. Wright's Windy City is a social wasteland, not a blues musician's heaven. Its streets are choked with refuse. Where offices and shops used to teem with customers and workers strolled the sidewalks, now the buildings stare bleakly out through broken windows that reveal vacant interiors. Bigger has spent time in a "reform school," and on the day that the novel opens, he worries about the robbery he and his friends have planned for Blum's delicatessen—their first job on a white man— and faces an interview with a rich white man for employment as the family's limousine driver. These are the tensions that move him to attack Gus, seeking relief through violence.

Bigger's bullying of Gus is only preparation for what he goes on to do. He murders Mary Dalton, the clumsily well-meaning daughter of the wealthy white man who hires him as a chauffeur, and his own black girlfriend, Bessie Mears. Earlier badmen murdered or beat their women out of jealousy or according to the male code. Bigger's violence is a violence of horror, which Wright intensifies by a multitude of naturalistic details both of the crime and of Bigger's emotions. Having assisted the drunkenly immobile Mary Dalton to her room and thought the sexual thoughts about her that are forbidden to black men, Bigger smothers her to death with her own pillow so that she cannot tell her blind mother that he is in her room. To hide his crime, he decides to burn her body in the mansion's huge furnace, decapitating her to fit her into the burner. Later, once he reveals to his girlfriend Bessie what he has done, he knows that he must kill her too for his own protection. In an empty room in a vacant South Side building, he forces her to have sex, then, as she sleeps, he crushes her head with a brick (p. 222).

The gruesomeness of Bigger's crimes has no precedent in the literature of the African American badman.[4] Only Devil Winston, who carries a piece of his murdered girlfriend's shoulder in his suitcase, comes close. Wright has his reasons for resorting to such tactics. He wants to avoid making Bigger out to be the kind of victim that, in his well-known and much-parsed phrasing, "bankers' daughters could read and weep over and feel good about."[5] What he does want to do is to show how Bigger's violence—his terrorizing Gus, his dismembering Mary, his smashing Bessie's skull—all rises from what Eldridge Cleaver called a "profound political, economic, and social reference."[6] With full explicitness, Wright shows Bigger's badness to be the result of the conditions produced by white racism. It is possible, against the background of these details, to see Bigger's terrible murders as revolt and show the use to which Wright decided to put the "bad nigger" as a literary type.

Just as the violent act of the old ballad gave way to pursuit and ended in capture and punishment, Bigger's murder of Mary activates a huge police dragnet, which finally traps him on the top of a water tower in the icy cold. He is taken to court and put through a trial. And as in some versions of Stagolee, the narrative closes on him in his cell, reflecting on his crime and waiting for his execution. Sometimes earlier badmen are transformed. John Hardy undergoes contrition and conversion. Joshua Jones tears down his psychic wall and lets his street hardness be softened by pretty Linda Young. Bigger, too, is transformed, but in a way no proper Baptist or bourgeois Episcopal churchgoer would find comfortable. In a unique twist of the violence that was the source of the old badman's self-esteem and social identity, Wright shows how Bigger's murders give him dignity and his life significance. The murders he commits were "act[s] of *creation!*" as his attorney, Boris Max, says in his famous court summation. "What I killed for must've been good!" Bigger cries in the last minutes in his cell. "I didn't know I was really alive in this world until I felt things hard enough to kill for 'em" (p. 392). His crimes are a source of his best self and the vehicle of personal fulfillment. It is a deep penetration of the violent man's mind and with it, Wright discovers a quite new aspect of the badman type. Bigger explicitly demonstrates the rage against whites previous badmen were said to have expressed in their own violence against black competitors. But more than that, the fulfillment which he finally, vividly feels no predecessor ever experienced in quite the same way. For the bourgeois world, his acts are unforgivably criminal. For Bigger they are an awakening.

Bigger swells far beyond the bounds of the traditional "bad nigger." Wright makes him clearly the result "of the forces that molded the urban Negro's body and soul." In *Black Metropolis* (1945), for which Wright wrote these words in an introduction, St. Clair Drake and Horace Cayton, two University of Chicago sociologists, apply these sociological principles to Chicago's Black Belt. Drake and Cayton lay out the details of the comparative death rates, demographics, real estate covenants, employment limitations, and economic exploitation that are the sociological basis for *Native Son;* they also point out that the "stirrings of revolt" to be seen in Chicago are part of a world-wide movement among peoples of color in China, Africa, India, and Asia no longer willing to tolerate the colonial oppression of the white European.[7] The sociopathic rage that drives Bigger is thus not confined to the African American male. It is a world-wide phenomenon. Like the masses in Nazi Germany and Communist Russia, Bigger "is a product of a dislocated society . . . a dispossessed and disinherited man," groping through violence toward dignity and meaning.[8] What Bigger does to Gus and Doc and then to Mary Dalton and Bessie Mears is a psychosocial issue, to be studied and understood like a laboratory specimen, with Wright working "like a scientist" inventing "test-tube situations" for Bigger in order to work out the "resolution of this problem" (p. xxi). This attitude connects him with the Zola-Dreiser school of literary naturalism, whose quasi-scientific method of dealing with character and event assumes that the ambient background is at least as important as the figures whose actions and fate are determined by that background. "[A]n understanding of Negro expression," says Wright, "cannot be arrived at without a constant reference to the environment which cradles it."[9]

Moreover, just as Shakespeare used the literary conventions of the braggart soldier (the *miles gloriosus*) to produce Falstaff and of the grasping, usurious Jew to produce Shylock, Wright used the badman type in the creation of Bigger Thomas. And, like Shakespeare, he takes Bigger far beyond the traditional figure, using him to represent not only the black victim of American racism but also the participant in the larger class struggle between workers and capitalists he thought was transpiring in the rest of the world. Sounding the Marxist predilections that made him a social writer, Wright declares that "there were literally millions of [Biggers] everywhere" (p. xiv), all part "of a complex struggle for life going on in my country, a struggle in which I was involved. I sensed, too, that the Southern scheme of oppression was but an appendage of a far vaster and in many respects more ruthless and impersonal commodity-profit machine" (p. xv).

Literature's role is to project this struggle through the concrete behavior of characters caught up in it. No one before Wright had gone so deeply into the social dynamics of the badman or located him so centrally in the collective black experience. Nor had anyone gazed so directly into the molten center of the violent man's psychic interior.

But Bigger Thomas was one of a kind in the saga of the African American badman. He was both more and less than the traditional type as black artists had previously portrayed it. Bigger does not go up to Mary's room intending violence. He is maneuvered into it by the thoughtlessness of the white woman herself and her white boyfriend. But once he has done the killing, he decides that he will appropriate the white myth for his own uses. The important point is that he takes an independent attitude toward a crime that only a black man could have stumbled into committing, and in doing so, as Bernard Bell cogently remarks, becomes "an outsider or marginal man, a person living apart from the values of both black and white cultures," and hence "a synthesis of white and black myths of the Bad Nigger."[10]

Ultimately, it was not Bigger as a character that influenced black writers who followed in the wake of *Native Son,* but Wright's treatment of the ghetto and the larger social background. For the artists of the Harlem Renaissance, the Harlem scene radiated creative energy. Jazz, dance, the blues were expressions of black joy, of African exhilaration, and of folk inventiveness brought to commercial success. The imagery of visual artists like painters Archibald Motley and Aaron Douglas and photographer James Van Der Zee shows a prosperous, exuberant black urban community. Motley, like Wright, grew up in Chicago, but his "Bronzeville" series shows a Chicago totally different from the one in which Bigger feels suffocated. *Black and Tan Cabaret* (1921), *Syncopation* (1924), and *Stomp* (1927) reverberate with the rhythms of blaring jazz bands and bright dancing figures. *Syncopation* especially could be an illustration for McKay's Baltimore café in *Home to Harlem,* with its whirling bodies, gleaming lights, and high bandstand. Aaron Douglas's mural *Aspects of Negro Life* (1934) celebrates in geometrical monumentality the climb from slavery to the post-Reconstruction industrial age. *Aspiration* (1936) rejoices in the triumphant achievement of black engineers and artists, all heroically gazing up at a "city on a hill." The most expressive of all, though, is Van Der Zee's black and white photograph *Couple, Harlem, 1932.* Standing beside a classy roadster with white sidewalls and a sparkling chrome spare tire case, a young mulatto woman wears a cloche hat and a luxuriant fur coat. A darker young man, also ensconced in furs, sports a felt hat, rakishly fitted and brimmed, and regards the camera with a sardonic, self-confident smile. The only discordant note in this icon of black prosperity is the brownstones in the background. Their imitation classical facades are subtly starting to go to seed.

By 1940, this subtle process had become painfully evident in its dark and squalid fruit, the northern black ghetto. The Harlem party of the Renaissance years had come to a sad and shabby end, a victim of the Depression and the accelerated economic deterioration of the inner cities of the North. Arna Bontemps even questioned whether Harlem had *ever* been the black Camelot suggested in the iconography of Motley, Douglas, and Van Der Zee, and in Alain Locke's collection of literary manifestoes in *The New Negro* (1925). Returning to the city in 1942, Bontemps wonders what happened to the former black playground. "To me," he says, "there seemed only one explanation. No matter what else one might see there, Harlem remained what it had always been in essence, a black ghetto and slum, a clot in the American bloodstream."[11] By the years of World War II and after, Harlem had ceased to be the throbbing, barbaric party that played to the reputation of darktown's marvelous spontaneity. Tom-toms sound, but only in the movie that Bigger goes to for escape, *Trader Horn,* in which black Africans are portrayed by white filmmakers as half-animal wild men (p. 36).[12] The rhythms that seemed so exhilarating in the Harlem of the twenties are now the cacophony of Bedlam. "All Harlem," writes James Baldwin in 1948, "is pervaded by a sense of congestion, rather like the insistent, maddening, claustrophobic pounding in the skull that comes from trying to breathe in a very small room with all the windows shut."[13]

Richard Wright, besides showing black urban squalor in *Native Son,* also helped convey the new visual representation that projected the changed perception of the northern city, recalling the tenement images of Jacob Riis at the turn of the century. The text he wrote for *12,000,000 Black Voices* (1941) was accompanied by photographs selected by Edwin Rosskam.[14] To be sure, there are pictures of black city youth having fun at the roller rink and dance hall (pp. 126–29). But the images that predominate are of garbage-cluttered streets (pp. 138–39), antiquated tenements with sagging walls and stairways (pp. 114–15), filthy toilets whose floors are thick with muck and whose walls have lost their plaster (p. 106), and three dirty children sleeping on a small greasy mattress covered by a single grimy blanket (p. 107). The worst thing is what happens to the children:

> We watch strange moods fill our children [says Wright], and our hearts swell with pain. The streets, with their noise and flaring lights, the taverns, the automobiles, and the poolrooms claim them, and no voice of ours can call them back. They spend their nights away from home; they forget our ways of life, our language, our God. Their swift speech and impatient eyes make us feel weak and foolish. . . . The city has beaten us, evaded us; but they, with young bodies filled with warm blood, feel bitter and frustrated at the sight of the alluring hopes and prizes denied them. It is not their eagerness to fight that makes us afraid, but that they go to death on the city pavements faster than even disease and starvation can take them. As the courts and the morgues become crowded with our lost children, the hearts of the officials of the city grow cold toward us. (p. 136)

This is the form the ghetto takes in most of the fiction of the forties, fifties, and sixties. The children about which Wright worries are at constant risk in this fiction. The issue he focuses on is not the strut and style of new Stagolees, but the danger of the young falling prey to the corrupted streets and *becoming* predatory badmen.

JAMES BALDWIN: ESCAPING FROM VIOLENCE

Besides Wright, the other two major writers of the three-decade period I am now focusing on are James Baldwin and Ralph Ellison. They do not make their major characters badmen. But they employ their own forms of the traditional type as part of the central experience of their protagonists, using that type with the tacit assumption that any black reader, and perhaps some whites, will recognize it and understand its significance. It becomes for them a sort of shorthand, an emblem of what has gone wrong in the northern urban black community and a warning of what black youth should avoid.

Baldwin, like Wright, fears that the young are vulnerable to the destructive potential of the northern ghetto streets. "All over Harlem," he writes, "Negro boys and girls are growing into stunted maturity, trying desperately to find a place to stand; and the wonder is not that so many are ruined but that so many survive."[15] In *Go Tell It on the Mountain* (1953), John Grimes is one of those youngsters at risk. Like Bigger Thomas, he is subject to all the new forces at work upon young African Americans in the northern city: the northern migration of blacks, the cultural shock of the encounter between the old southern moral system and the new urban society, and the way in which family, religion, and the street shape the lives of this transitional generation. John's problem, though, is a nature not too violent, but too sensitive. His foe is the father he hates and the deadly bitterness his father arouses in him.[16] It is not the balking of his ambitions by the oppressive conditions of Harlem that enrages John and thereby hampers his emotional and spiritual development. It is the suffocating authority of his puritanical father, the self-righteous deacon of the Temple of the Fire Baptized.

John's transcendence of his father's false and loveless piety as well as the bleak and ugly streets of Harlem comes only through his own triumphant conversion on the "threshing floor" of his father's storefront church. This is a mystical embrace of his family and a reenactment of their racial past. In that past John finds a version of the badman figure, and it plays an important, though secondary, role in the same kind of self-discovery to which Bigger Thomas came by a different route. Like Wright's, Baldwin's use of the badman is deeply imaginative and wholly unconventional. Wright sees the badman through the lens of the psycho-social, Baldwin the psycho-religious. Wright takes Bigger Thomas through the naturalism of his mental processes and the civil law and courts. Baldwin makes his badman's badness a matter of sin and God. Gabriel Grimes, John's father, as a "ba-ad" young man is suffused with moral guilt and spiritual anxiety. In his young southern years, Gabriel drank, fought, fornicated. He pained his pious mother and he wallowed in sin (pp. 120–21). Gabriel took no joy in his excess. He felt imprisoned by the demons of his appetite, and "hated the evil that lived in his body, and feared it, as he feared and hated the lions of lust and longing that prowled the defenseless city of his mind" (p. 120). Under the guilt-inducing eyes of his gentle, all-forgiving mother, he finally underwent a powerful conversion. In Gabriel's ensuing pursuit of the religious life, Baldwin shows us something that the ballads occasionally shrewdly touched on, the closeness of the violent and sybaritic zealot and the pretentiously pious religious zealot, each driven to excess by powerful unconscious forces.

In the religious atmosphere of the novel, Gabriel as "bad nigger" is a fallen man who is raised up by God's intervention. But because his conversion simply replaces one form of excess with another, it does not erase the pride that had impelled his corruption. The badman pride becomes the spiritual pride of the converted. Gabriel is convinced he has been selected for special treatment by God.

Stern, cold, self-righteous, he retains the hatefulness, anger, and resentment that motivated him before conversion and at the same time is swollen with the sense of his own virtue and sacrifice. The violence that marked his preconversion behavior remains in his beating his sons for defying his authority and for breaking the laws of God as he interprets them. His vanity persuades him that his reward will be a son, for "the line of the faithful was a royal line—his son would be a royal child" (p. 186). He gives up his old ways and waits all these "bitter years to see the promise of the Lord fulfilled" (p. 151), punitive and unforgiving to the end.

But the two sons Gabriel sires refuse to accept the role of the "royal child." The first, named Royal, is born of a carnal affair, after Gabriel's conversion. As angry and mutinous as the father he does not know, Royal gets himself killed in a seedy Chicago gambling fracas, stabbed in the throat by one "of them northern niggers" and left to die "right there on the floor in that barroom" (p. 197). Closer to John Grimes is his half-brother, Roy, about twelve and already on a course for the violence of the streets. He has taken up with a local gang and is stabbed in a fight with some white boys, a fight he and his buddies went looking for. Like Gabriel, Roy is incorrigible and defiant, but he is also contemptuous of the religion by which his father lives. Where does a badman come from? Baldwin's answer: from youngsters like Roy, who find in the ghetto streets something undefined they cannot find at home. It is not that Roy languishes in abject poverty in a dysfunctional home. His father may be an unloving authoritarian, but he provides adequate food, clothing, and shelter. Nor is his mother, Elizabeth, a permissive, unconditionally loving mammy. She has had her fling with revolt in an affair that produces the illegitimate John. No, Roy's inclination to badness cannot be easily explained by Harlem's social conditions alone, but rather by a combination of psychological, genetic, and social factors. "I can't stop him," says Elizabeth to Gabriel, "and you can't stop him neither." Roy's personality lies beyond easy blame-fixing or some sort of authoritarian solution. "Ain't nobody to blame, Gabriel. You just better pray to God to stop him before somebody puts another knife in him and puts him in his grave" (p. 56).

Roy is only a bit player in Baldwin's drama, to be sure. But as John's principal foil, he is used by Baldwin to throw John's psychological conflict into sharp relief. Roy's Harlem—those seductive, condom-littered, action-packed streets—frightens John. It is a "pit" of smoldering brimstone, just one of the black holes gapingly awaiting sinners, full of indefinable terrors. It reinforces John's sense of his own "sinful body," of which he has been puritanically warned by his mother, his father, and the "saints" he scorned as they cried out their faith on the "threshing floor" of the Temple of the Fire Baptized. In their menu of sins, masturbation is, along with any other sexual expression, an unspeakable crime. John, vulnerable to the dire admonitions of the church, broods agonizingly over the sin "of which he would never dare to speak" (p. 14). Baldwin does not laugh at this adolescent anxiety. Instead, he links it with the blasphemous rebelliousness of Roy, for in John's mind, "the darkness of [his] sin . . . was like Roy's curses, like the echoes these curses raised in John." He recalls Roy "cursing in the house of God, and making obscene gestures before the eyes of Jesus" (pp. 14–15). John conflates the rebellious discoveries of the "sinful" pleasures of his own body with an even deeper and more sinful revolt against his father and the church. John's problem is believing that the two are one, that in order to "bow before the throne of grace" he must kneel before his father, and he resists that with all the strength of the overtly more defiant Roy.

Baldwin suggests that in order to find himself, John must somehow separate the unchristian anger and vindictiveness of his stepfather from the supportive body of the church itself. He does that in the mystical experience that he finally has on the threshing floor. That is John's coming of age on his fourteenth birthday, his embracing of the racial past that has hitherto repelled him, the first stepping stone out of the repellent Harlem streets. As he says in the novel's final lines, "I'm coming. I'm on my way" (p. 303).

The answer to the quagmire of the ghetto or of the oppressiveness of the small southern town is neither the enraged violence of the badman nor the vengeful piety of the unforgiving convert, but genuine emotional acceptance of the pain of all who have gone before, who shape those who come after them. Baldwin excels in making this experience profoundly real and fundamentally important, a milestone in the family history. After his exhausting but transformative experience in the storefront church on that stormy Saturday night, John's demanding aunt and loving mother are newly responsive, his father still coldly distant. The key figure, the sensitive counterpoint to the rebellious Roy and the loving opposite to the unloving Gabriel, is Elisha, the seventeen-year-old nephew of the temple's pastor, precociously "saved" and now a "preacher." Elisha has had his own brush with sin by "walking disorderly" with pretty Ella Mae, but he accepts the public chastisement of his uncle and meekly submits to church discipline. Yet he never seems to lose his own strength and dignity. John looks up to Elisha with adoration. It is Elisha—his biblical name means "God has granted salvation"—who sees John through his climactic and tumultuous night of conversion. In Elisha John gains a brother. Roy is his brother "in the flesh," in the word's familial and carnal senses. Elisha embodies a more profound brotherhood, for, modifying the biblical story, Baldwin gives Elisha the role of Elijah and John that of Elisha. As Elijah, rising to heaven upon the "chariot of Israel" (2 Kings 2.12), laid his own mantle upon Elisha, so Elisha figuratively lays his mantle upon John. He bestows upon the younger boy "a holy kiss," and as he walks away from John in the early Harlem morning, the rising sun "fell over Elisha like a golden robe, and struck John's forehead, where Elisha had kissed him, like a seal ineffaceable forever" (p. 302).

Given Baldwin's own sexual preferences, it is difficult not to see this as an early affirmation of the homosexual bond, employed here as a metaphor of understanding between sufferers, whose vehicle in this case Baldwin makes the religious experience. Roy, the nascent badman, lies outside this brotherhood. But only through his presence can Roy's failure of John (and of Baldwin) be meaningful, fusing John's deliverance and his union with Elisha. In Baldwin's view, the figure of the man of violence leads only to the dead end of self-destruction. This gives the victory to the ghetto. Grace lies in the secular priesthood of male love and the overcoming of the terrors of "this dark and dangerous and unloved stranger" which is the essence of every black man.[17]

RALPH ELLISON'S RINEHART

Harlem, and by extension the northern urban black ghetto, had by the decade of the thirties become pathological for Wright and Baldwin. Ralph Ellison joins them: "Harlem is a ruin—many of its ordinary aspects (its crimes, its casual violence, its crumbling buildings with littered area-ways, ill-smelling halls and vermin-invaded rooms) are indistinguishable from the distorted images that appear in dreams, and which, like muggers haunting a lonely hall, quiver in the waking mind with hidden and threatening significance." Harlem is permeated with "the frustrations of Negro life," out of which grows a general "free-floating hostility," creating what some call "evil Negroes" who "become enraged with the world."[18] Ellison writes in a time when the Stagolees and the John Hardys would more probably be sent to Harlem's Lafargue Psychiatric Clinic than be memorialized in songs sung by itinerant guitarists and work gangs, when rage is a psychiatric problem rather than a motive for the violent defense of a man's reputation. The viewpoint marks the difference between the folk grasp of the world and the educated perspective. Like his contemporaries and his predecessors, Ellison, while remarking that the novel is "a form which has absorbed folk tradition into its thematic structures," also understands that the black writer is heir as much to an American literary tradition as he is to a "folk tradition," and the former "might well be more important to him" than the latter. Indeed, "novelists in our time are more likely to be inspired by reading other novels than by their acquaintance with any folk tradition. I use folklore in my work not because I am Negro, but because writers like Eliot and Joyce made me conscious of the literary value of my folk inheritance. My cultural background, like that of most Americans, is dual."[19] It is a statement that could apply to all those who incorporate the badman figure of the folk oral tradition into the literate form of the novel.

Typically Ellison presents his badmen with sly sophistication. Tod Clifton is cool, graceful, and handsome, an admirable young man in every way. He is "leader of the youth" in the quasi-Communist organization The Brotherhood, which the unnamed narrator joins in Harlem. Tod holds in his one image a combination of the trendy and the old-fashioned, looking "somehow like a hipster, a zoot suiter, a sharpie—except his head of Persian lamb's wool had never known a straightener." Tod is an experienced street fighter who likes the violence, but is admired and respected by friends and enemies alike.[20] It is Tod's role to revolt against both the self-serving restrictions of the Brotherhood and the silly restrictions of New York's street vending laws. When he breaks the latter, he comes under the authority of the New York City police department. The encounter is fatal, for Tod strikes the policeman who arrests him for illegally selling demeaning Sambo dolls on the street. In response, the lawman shoots Tod dead. It is a Quixotic revolt, deliberately self-destructive but admirable even in its callow pointlessness.[21]

The meaning of Tod's death (nothing is meaningless in *Invisible Man*) is expressed by three young black zoot suiters the narrator observes in the subway, swaying slowly along the platform in their high collars, broad-shouldered hip-length coats, and ballooning trousers, communicating with each other enigmatically. They are ahistorical forces unaccounted for by the Brotherhood's logic, a trifle sinister, "the stewards of something uncomfortable, burdensome" (p. 431). They are the essence of post-Renaissance Harlem, potently radiating a latent violence, badmen cocked and ready to fire. Their importance, though, is their effect upon the narrator, who sees them as extensions of Tod Clifton and signs of a Harlem ghetto from which he has until now hidden behind the false philosophy of the Brotherhood. They flash through Ellison's cloud chamber like atomic particles, symptoms of an old reality in, literally, new dress, exuding badness looking for an occasion to explode.

It is in the figure of Rinehart, though, that Ellison shows just how far he brings us from the traditional badman figure and just how clever he is in using that figure to explore his own interests. The badman type is just one of the roles Rinehart plays in his Harlem drama, donning multiple costumes as the lord of chaos.[22] Fleeing Ras's thugs, the Invisible Man puts on the dark glasses and broad-brimmed white hat of some of the streetmen he sees, not realizing that in this costume he resembles the many-sided Rinehart. Harlemites from all classes and categories think they recognize him, and the narrator realizes that Rinehart is a whole multitude of types: a numbers runner, a lover, a pimp, a briber of the police, the minister of a religious cult. Given Rinehart, wonders the narrator, what is identity? "What on earth was hiding behind the face of things?" (p. 482). Rinehart both raises and solves the ontological problem, for he teaches the Invisible Man his final lesson: "The world in which we lived was without boundaries. A vast seething, hot world of fluidity, and Rine the rascal was at home. Perhaps *only* Rine the rascal was at home in it" (pp. 486–87). The world is not the "scientifically" predictable unfolding of history whose course can be tracked by the Brotherhood or the nationalist home of activist blacks intent on ridding the world of whites. It is the multiple possibilities demonstrated by Rinehart.

Like John Grimes, the Invisible Man learns from, but does not identify with, an updated form of the traditional badman, for that is precisely what Rinehart is. He is a brother in "a fraternity" whose members are recognized "at a glance—not by features, but by clothes, by uniform, by gait" (p. 474). To qualify as a member of this fraternity—that is, to be Rinehart—"You got to have a smooth tongue, a heartless heart and be ready to do anything," as one loiterer tells the narrator (p. 482). People the narrator knows in the Jolly Dollar, a bar he has frequented at other times as himself, react to the narrator's costume. Those in the fraternity are expected to behave in a certain way and to be equipped with certain weapons. "Somebody say something you don't like and you kinda fellows pull your switch blades," says the narrator's friend Brother Maceo, thinking he is talking to Rinehart (p. 476). And when Barrelhouse, the

Jolly Dollar's bartender, orders Rinehart out of the tavern when his presence threatens the peace, he warns Rinehart, as if he expected him to use it, not "to pull no pistol neither, 'cause this here one is loaded and I got a permit" (p. 478). But Ellison is not interested in Rinehart's violence, only in his multiplicity, seeing him as a token of the real material world that cannot be pinned down with reductive labels. He appears in the novel as an absence, existing only in the expectations of those Harlemites for whom the signs of the fraternity are sometimes as real as the actuality. And in those signs, even though he is one of many, the badman is a vividly recognizable type.

THE GHETTO SETTING

Inherent in the expansion of the northern ghetto is its deterioration, and its deterioration expands racism and injustice to include a geographical locale, specific neighborhoods whose streets and buildings can be described and whose effects upon their inhabitants, especially their young, are added to the old concerns of prejudice, disfranchisement, economic exploitation, and various forms of violence. Wright, Baldwin, and Ellison, whose fiction sets the tone for the lesser artists of the forties, fifties, and sixties, concentrate upon the education of their youthful protagonists. As Bigger Thomas, John Grimes, and the Invisible Man discover themselves, they escape the psychological and emotional confinements of the ghetto, though perhaps not the physical ones. Each comes to see himself and his world in a new way.

Those writers who use new forms of the badman during these decades in order to address the new issues tend to follow the lead of these three major figures and regard the education and growth of their leading characters as the most important of their concerns. Their violent protagonists are usually youths involved in a gang who engage in rituals of status maintenance, wielding the traditional weapons: fists, knives, guns. From gangs they graduate to be the street soldiers of the syndicate, the numbers racket, or the protection organization. Alongside these figures, the ghetto itself evolves and becomes much more explicitly a player in the badman saga: the source of both the young streetman's destructive violence and the strength that enables him to transcend the tough neighborhoods. As the staging area for the badman's action, it contains the sociology of the new folk life that develops with the migration of so many thousands of blacks to the northern city.

The ghetto's increasingly substandard living conditions create a street life that incubates gang fights, criminal killings over drug and gambling turf, fatal quarrels between family members and friends. The picture of the ghetto that comes out in the novels of these decades is one in which the young protagonists, almost always male, move between the streets and home. It is not the conflict between these two sets of values that is now played up, though. The main focus is the street, which for some kids is home, school, playground, and family. The groups they belong to, whether formally organized or simply created out of continually shifting loyalties, set values and standards, enforce the street code, and approve or censure their members.

The ghetto is the setting of a core black experience, significant culturally because of its sheer size and widespread manifestation. The authors of the stories about this experience were ghetto kids themselves, often the first generation to be born and bred in the ghetto, their parents among those who surged northward in the hundreds of thousands in a vast migration that began in the years before World War I and continued until just after World War II. In the foreword to his groundbreaking novelistic autobiography, *Manchild in the Promised Land* (1965), Claude Brown explains the aim of his book: "I want to talk about the first Northern urban generation of Negroes. I want to talk about the experiences of a misplaced generation, of a misplaced people in an extremely complex, confused society."[23] Ronald Fair prefaces his autobiographical novel, *We Can't Breathe* (1972), with an "Author's Note" in the same vein:

> This is a narrative of what it was like for those of us born in the thirties. Our parents had come from Mississippi, Louisiana, Tennessee, Georgia, Alabama, and many other southern states. . . . But mostly they came from Mississippi. . . . They came north, and we were the children born in the place they had escaped to—Chicago.[24]

The authors in this group write about the ghettos of the thirties, forties, and fifties, the world of their childhood, where they fought for their identity and survival, came to puberty, grew into adults. These are retrospective novels, the best ones written without sentimentality but infused with the nostalgia that most feel about their childhood, even a childhood in which violence was a part of the atmosphere.

These novelists do not suggest that whites had disappeared. Racist white policemen still patrol black neighborhoods. White gangs still threaten from the edges. But their characters fight the white gangs on a level field and always hold their own if they do not actually defeat them. And the attacks from white police occur as much because the victims live in the ghetto as because they are black. Indeed, whites as well as blacks complain of "police brutality." Violence was brought on by inner-city demography as much as by ownership of a black skin. The ghetto novelists show an acute awareness of the white world that surrounds and determines much of what goes on in the ghetto. For some it continues to unjustly restrict the opportunities of those who live in the ghetto and brutalize them, making criminals of them for living where they have been forced to live. For others, that white world deserves only a few sentences. The ghetto for them is where black life happens, and that becomes the topic of their novels. They may treat injustice, but they do not seek to arouse indignation, prove the worthiness of blacks, or show them as sympathetic victims of racism. They write about how their young characters grow up, as if the increased negatives of the ghetto stimulate a compensatory increase in the need to achieve personal identity.

Many of the novelists of the fifties and sixties are ambivalent about the ghetto. Its increasing shabbiness and isolation can thwart one's development, but it is also a place where one can live a challenging life and find and affirm an identity. Certainly, the pervasive violence is not to be condoned. The point is to rise above it. Maturity comes when the swaggering stance is abandoned. But taken as a whole, the reality of the ghetto contains nourishment for a full self and a sharp personal awareness, even though personal progress sometimes requires breaking free of its pull. That is why it seems valid to call the ghetto novel, in its first stages, a kind of bildungsroman, the story of the protagonist's development from childhood to maturity in the environment of the inner city, with an emphasis upon how that environment helps to shape his growth. The sympathetic "good" badmen of the Harlem Renaissance, like Joshua Jones, Jake Brown, and Tea Cake Woods, are recast as youngsters who struggle to transcend the dangers that confront them and discover their true manhood, or, in the saddest cases, fail in the effort.[25]

For all its ambivalence, the bildungsroman does present the ghetto as the source of its characters' problems, and is thus related to the work of social protest writers like Wright and his disciple Ann Petry (*The Street* [1946]) as well as that of Willard Motley (*Knock on Any Door* [1947]) and William Attaway (*Blood on the Forge* [1941]). But in its interest in the quest for identity, it is nearer kin to the novel of search and self-discovery on both sides of the race line. In addition to Baldwin's *Go Tell It on the Mountain* and Ellison's *Invisible Man*, there are Carson McCullers's *Member of the Wedding* (1946), Saul Bellow's *The Adventures of Augie March* (1953), J. D. Salinger's *The Catcher in the Rye* (1951), and Jean Stafford's *The Mountain Lion* (1947), to name just a few of the most conspicuous examples. After the great convulsion of World War II, nearly every group in the nation had set out on a new course. Identity and self had become major areas of interest, as Freud, psychoanalysis, and social psychology flooded the popular consciousness. An era of prosperity began and made possible the substitution of self-reflection for economic worries and class warfare. The ghetto bildungsroman illustrates that African American writers were an active part of this movement. For them identity was an affirmation of where they had been—the ghetto—and where they hoped to go—into middle-class life. The bildungsroman declares not only loyalty to the tradition of which the ghetto was now the conservator but also the sense of promise in the air, as the novel runs parallel to such fundamental shifts as President Truman's 1948 integration of the armed forces; the Supreme Court's 1954 decision to integrate the schools; the success of the Montgomery, Alabama, bus boycott in 1955–56; the integration of the Little Rock, Arkansas, schools in 1957.

These novels pick up the same middle-class concerns that appeared in the work of many Renaissance writers. Here, though, the middle-class value system is much more explicitly and unapologetically invoked. In its general pattern, the bildungsroman depicts the conflict between the aspiration to rise out of the ghetto and find a life in the materially prosperous world of clean, white-dominated neighborhoods and the implacable drag of the ghetto, which pulls its young men into its destructive depths.

THE NURTURING GHETTO I
(MARK KENNEDY AND HERBERT SIMMONS)

Philip Kaye's *Taffy* (1950) contains one of the sad cases. It is a transitional work between protest novels like *Native Son* and *The Street* and the more autobiographical novels.[26] Kaye's streets are pernicious results of white racism that smother, balk, and kill. Into their destructive environment Taffy goes for satisfaction, and, with the rest of the young crowd, vies for attention and status. On the edges of Taffy's neighborhood, like guards, stand all the symbols of white authority. But within that circle, he and his companions live lives of implicit and overt violence. Sarcasm, put-downs, threats of physical harm are the texture of the world in which Taffy conducts his futile search for personal importance. In these depths, the strongest, the most fearless, and the most indifferent to the pain of others hold the highest positions in the street hierarchy. Thinking to increase his stature, Taffy pointlessly kills a helpless insurance collector and then is himself shot by the police. Whatever the causes of the anger that drives him to violence, and they are complex, the important thing is that Kaye's picture of Harlem street life shows how competitive violence pervades all relationships between the young people who live there. It shows, too, the determination this violence symbolizes, the need to participate, to strive, to contest one's status. These youngsters may be desperate, but they are not resigned, have not given up.

Taffy reflects the pathology of the ghetto as later sociologists describe it. Writing a decade after the publication of *Taffy*, Lewis Yablonsky remarks that the gangs that develop in the inner city after World War II lack the friendships and camaraderie of earlier groups. One of Taffy's problems is that he does not belong, can find no fulfilling relationship. Fat little Billy McIntosh, himself an outcast from the Brooklyn crowd because of his dumpy appearance, tries to get close to Taffy. But while Taffy allows him to come along on his trips to Harlem, he never gives him friendship. Similarly, Taffy suffers from what Yablonsky calls a "low self-estimate," which drives him to look "for a quick, almost magical way of achieving power and prestige, and in a single act of unpremeditated intensity he at once establishes a sense of his own existence and impresses this existence on others."[27] This, says Yablonsky, is characteristic of the new kind of gang member. He uses violence to prove he is alive and worthy to be part of the gang. Membership in the group has become Taffy's goal and he seeks it through violence, in contrast to the original badman who scornfully rejected such relationships.

As the ghetto novel develops and black novelists abate their judgment of the ghetto as a diseased environment that fatally contaminates all who live in it, the perception of violence as a pathology disappears and a more adaptive perception emerges. This comes out particularly in Mark Kennedy's *The Pecking Order* (1953) and Herbert Simmons's *Corner Boy* (1957) and *Man Walking on Eggshells* (1962).[28] The settings of these novels are controlled by whites. A white police force and white ownership of business and housing make the ghetto subservient to the majority culture. But Kennedy and Simmons do not focus on the oppression of blacks by whites as the cause of their characters' behavior and fate. Their ghetto has its own culture which conditions the growth of their characters. Kennedy's Bruce Ashford Freeman, an eleven-year-old growing up on Chicago's South Side, joins the Warriors, takes a girlfriend, and participates in "The Life" of the South Side streets. Jake Adams, the "corner boy" of Simmons's first novel, is hip, sells drugs for the "organization," and takes pleasure in the street life of his unnamed ghetto (probably in St. Louis, where Simmons grew up). Both youngsters are bright and tough. They learn the dangers of the streets and how to meet them as a hunter does those of the forest. Indeed, the ghetto is inhabited by beasts of all sorts, which pose a constant threat to those we like.

The violence that is part of the contour of their lives is not restricted to clashes between gangs and their individual members in the constant struggle for supremacy. One youngster "who did not have any limits" steals a car and smashes it up, impaling a younger passenger on the gearshift rod. Drunken men beat their wives. Criminals who run prostitutes, dope, and numbers protect their businesses with guns. The ghetto continues to experience violence from whites, too. White police shoot youths who run from them in fear or defy them in anger, but such encounters seem like extensions of the rest of the ghetto violence, not the kind of ritual killing performed in the race riot, the lynching, or even the prosecution of Bigger Thomas.

These environments are home to an energetic, though dangerous, life process. They are not, to be sure, models of a middle-class community of the fifties' "silent generation," whose ideal was corporate advancement and a peaceful suburban home to hold their ever more numerous material acquisitions. In the ghetto, sons fall out with their fathers. Hip streetmen go on the nod with heroin. Those who are "with it" listen not to the piously safe Pat Boone but to the transgressive "Pres and Bird, Miles, Ventura, Diz, Kenton." People are "square" and good musicians are "tough." At soda fountains youths listen to records and gang leaders organize and plan challenges and revenge. They have access to several kinds of dope—"pod for the light heads, boy and girl for the mainliners and now snow for the sniffers."[29]

Bruce Freeman and Jake Adams traverse these streets with finesse and, finally, satisfaction. They do more than survive. They undergo the archetypal initiation, a rite of passage to individuality and awareness and even freedom. Thus, while not advocating violence, Kennedy presents it as an initiatory test. It contributes to Bruce's toughness. The main danger in The Pecking Order is that Bruce will succumb to the gang mentality that destroyed Taffy, surrender his individuality to what Ralph Ellison might call the "strait jacket" of group demands. Bruce's friend B.J., a Warrior chieftain, has lost his identity to the streets in the same way others lose it to dope. He depends totally upon the gang, not, however, as a healthy urban family of social redemption, but as a protection against the open seas of personal freedom. He lives in constant fear that he will be sent back to reform school, and this breeds a desperation that makes him incapable of loyalty or love, to gang members or anyone else.

Bruce, helped by his girlfriend Evelyn, has the strength to reject The Life, which B.J. would force him into. In order to grow, he has to sever himself from the buddies he knew on the street, who have been carried off by the law or death or drugs. But he does not deny them. They have helped to shape him, and he acknowledges, as Baldwin's John Grimes acknowledges his own past, that he is as much a part of them as they are of him. This acknowledgment brings him a liberating self-knowledge: "They were his inheritance . . . given to him all at once in this fullness of his time. And he knew himself a little now—he was a small, sturdy creature, hopeful in his growth." Not in spite of, but because of his experience in the violent streets, he has found himself: "I am Bruce Ashford Freeman . . . I am me—for real."[30] Bruce paradoxically escapes from the ghetto mindset by affirming himself as its product, becoming psychologically free.

Jake Adams also wins through to a strong sense of self and a feeling of identification with the streets in which he has grown up. When he is threatened with jail for selling drugs as a "corner boy," he remains steadfastly loyal to the street code, refusing to inform on the major drug dealer the police are really after. He has not been broken. The "corner" is in his blood, and he determines to return to it when he gets out of jail, get the things money can buy. His approaching prison term seems like not an ending but a beginning, the episode which tells him who he is, and he affirms his discovery in full and conscious awareness. He may face prison with a grim fatalism, but he vows that not even it can keep him from "the harbor from which he had been exiled" (p. 266).

We are, however, ambivalent about Jake's materialistic goal, so palpably derived from the selfish mainstream society for which acquisition is the sole purpose of existence, and exaggerated in the circumscribed ghetto. On the one hand, we deplore the environment that has shaped him and the shape he has acquired. At the same time, we give respect to a world that requires such toughness to survive. And we unambivalently admire the integrity with which Jake meets that world and the hardiness with which he makes his choice. Bad things do happen. Young toughs face off against each other with fists and knives. Jake tragically kills his girlfriend in a car accident. A friend must give up a basketball scholarship when his mother is paralyzed and he must go to work to support her. But Jake's choice of the ghetto need not be seen as an abdication of moral behavior. In his ghetto parents do care about their children. Youngsters shoot marbles in backyards, fly kites, play Superman and Captain Marvel, and speed through the neighborhood on homemade "skate trucks."

In *Man Walking on Eggshells* (1962), Simmons's Raymond Douglas, a gang member in good standing, a tough youngster respected by other tough youngsters, even goes to college, and then takes up music. He is not closed off from a better life, unless by his own weakness, and he is not weak. Raymond acknowledges his debt to his background, gaining success and fame as a musician by incorporating that background into a hit song. Though his record expresses the negative side of the ghetto, the frustrations of being black in America, and the black determination to be free, he could not have produced it had he not been shaped as he was by that particular life. By not denying the ghetto, he gains true freedom, symbolized by the "new jazz" in which he replays the ghetto experience. In this period of civil rights activity, however, Simmons is careful to separate Raymond from the ideological constraints that strait-jacket later artists. Raymond retains his autonomy, going his own way, following his own artistic vision, and playing his own music for esthetic rather than ideological reasons.

THE NURTURING GHETTO II: THE AUTOBIOGRAPHICAL VISION (CLAUDE BROWN)

In the sixties, Claude Brown turns the ghetto story into autobiography and identifies the story with the storyteller. Claude Brown the author of *Manchild in the Promised Land* is also Claude Brown the central actor in the drama of his narrative. He belongs to the new breed of post–World War II black men, strong and confident but searching, individualistic shareholders in the ghetto experience, but not its prisoners. With the autobiographical *Manchild,* however, Brown creates a new and distinctive vehicle for expressing that experience. It is a clear product of the 1960s civil rights movement, during which the audience for the "experiences" of blacks grew exponentially. It reads like a novel, with a mix of dialogue, action, and interpretation of the events it describes. In it, Brown gives us a richly detailed account of the post–World War II inner city and reflects upon its nature with convincing insight, upon its social implications, its historical currents and changes. He looks back upon his childhood in Harlem with a combination of softening nostalgia and hard-edged realism, while explaining the complex and contradictory feelings that the ghetto evokes. The retrospective tone deepens; the ghetto experience becomes personal history.

Brown's revisitation of the scenes of his childhood and adolescence is a bittersweet experience. The social degradation in which his narrator lives those years does not become clear to him until he begins to understand that his behavior leads to jail, a shortened life, and a lowered quality of experience. But even then, he refuses to deny the ghetto world. Home, to the young Claude Brown, was the streets. He loved their excitement, their variety, their danger. He sought to live by their code and accepted the need to fight for a position. "[M]ost of the cats I swung with were more afraid of not fighting than they were of fighting. This was how it was supposed to be." Everyone "lived by the concept that a man was supposed to fight." "The little boys in the neighborhood whom the adults respected were the little boys who didn't let anybody mess with them" (pp. 263, 267). Fighting, in fact, carried no more emotional and moral charge than stealing. The young Brown did both frequently, and because of it he was in and out of the Warwick and Wiltwyck state schools for boys.

But his adolescent street fights change colors as he enters his mid-teens and moves toward young adulthood. He gains a reputation for fighting, and people admire him for his pugnacity. But, says Claude, "I had to keep living up to it every day that I came out of the house" (p. 269). Worse, he has to increase the viciousness of his fighting as he and his opponents grow up, has to turn from safe fists to lethal knives, even guns. This is the street code. It is expected of him. He can retain the respect of the street only by killing someone. And that respect is the only support he feels he has. But that support will be no help to him in the electric chair. Chance frees him once, but he realizes that next time he might not be so fortunate, and he decides to escape the streets by going to school.

In 1954, when he makes this decision, going back to school seems a fairly natural possibility. Claude Brown has a freedom we do not now normally associate with the grim prison of the ghetto. Not that it is easy for Claude. He knows that he will have to change his life. But the change is a matter of relationships. He ceases to be a street kid. He now occupies a different world from the one in which old friends are already, at seventeen, "in jail or dead or strung out on drugs" (p. 183).

At this point, the interest of *Manchild* begins to turn on the psychological conflict in Claude between "the street life and the school life" (p. 183). To get away from the street, he makes a symbolic move to Greenwich Village, and from that distance Claude can observe his old world with a new objectivity. No longer having to maintain his front with a gun, he feels freed, and he likes returning to Harlem for brief visits. What attracts him reflects the spirit of his autobiography. He loves "meeting old people and old things," revisiting his past, connecting with people out of his childhood and youth. From this perspective he begins to grasp what has happened to the Harlem he knew as a youngster, which he continually tries to recover in his visits. But that Harlem has disappeared. In the old Harlem, manhood was a matter of physical force. One defended it with a knife or fists. By the late fifties, Harlem has become "less vicious" (p. 269) but more imprisoning. Drugs have replaced fighting as the measure of manhood. The youngsters seek place by imitating the "junkie drag," the slur in the talk and the harshness of the junkie voice. Everyone believes that they will eventually, inevitably, become junkies. Junk is the new violence, and everyone can see that it is much more self-destructive than the old.

From his position outside of the new Harlem, Claude perceives "a generation of new niggers" taking shape in reaction to the "plague" of heroin. They are not the docile rule-observers their southern-born parents were, frightened of the white man and fearfully staying in "their place." Nor are they badmen, killers, or drug addicts. These "new niggers" are "something that nobody understood and that nobody was ready for" (p. 298). They grew up in the ghetto and live its life, but resist its worst influences. They are particularly strong because they do not reject Harlem life, only suicide. "They were dynamic and beautiful cats. They all stood out, ten feet tall, because they had the strength of character not to be swallowed up in vice and crime." Claude plays down his own strength. He fled, he says. He is only part "new nigger." But going back to Harlem and mixing with this group of young men makes Claude feel "strong . . . even though I knew in my heart that I hadn't achieved what these guys had. I had run away, I had hidden. That's how I'd gotten away from it. Still," he concludes, "I felt good. I just wanted to be around them, as though some of their strength might rub off on me" (p. 368).

Fulfillment does not require escape from the ghetto. But it does require strength, and that only a few of the most heroic have. But even in his admiration for the young musicians of the "new Harlem," Claude retains his respect for his old friends and the harsh life he lived among them. He refuses to think of himself as better morally or psychologically than his close buddy Reno. In their last talk, they discuss the issue that Claude has struggled with for so long, leaving Harlem permanently. It is clear to Claude by the time he completes this tour of his past that it is not a matter of escape but of choice. For Reno, the streets continue to be home, and when he goes to jail it is like visiting "family" (p. 425). In choosing the ghetto, Claude decides, Reno "had managed to become one of the happiest people in Harlem" (p. 426).

The rich world in which Reno and Claude matured is passing, not only because they are getting older but because the ghetto is changing along with the rest of the world. Reno, though, is not growing with the new world. Claude is, and he feels at the end of his account not joy over his departure or grief over Reno's deciding to stay, but a Wordsworthian regret that they have to part, that his family is disintegrating, that the excitement of the streets is no longer his. He does not attack the ghetto, demand its eradication, or angrily call for our indignation. He only laments that he has to lose it as his own need to grow propels him beyond childhood and puts the old Harlem behind him.

THE STRUGGLE FOR MORAL CHARACTER (RONALD FAIR AND GEORGE CAIN)

When the sixties end, the autobiographical vision of the ghetto continues to be intense but becomes considerably more skeptical. It is a vision that coincides with the growing evidence that the ghetto is locking some of its inhabitants into a prison of violence and drugs. Two novels show a modification of the critical but ultimately affectionate picture of the ghetto drawn in the fifties and sixties: Ronald Fair's *We Can't Breathe* (1972) and George Cain's *Blueschild Baby* (1970). Of the two, Fair's novel more resembles in tone and temper *Manchild in the Promised Land,* but his account of the Chicago South Side where he grew up in the thirties and forties has a sharper edge than Brown's book, more criticism and protest, and his images are seamier, his streets more run-down, his youngsters more violence-prone. Even so, like Kennedy and Simmons, he preserves the possibility that moral character can grow there, even out of the family brutality and the internecine warfare of the gangs.

The ghetto of *We Can't Breathe* abounds with rats, alleys littered with smashed wine bottles, apartment walls covered with decades of accumulated and unattended filth. Because of white oppression, black adults have little more power than their children and can offer them no protection. White prejudice relegates them to inferior jobs; or they are killed by careless white civilians who are never punished or forced to make restitution; or they are dealt with by capricious cops, "the beaters of black men," who "robbed even the pimps and whores" and "roughed up the pushers and even the black numbers runners—the police were the assassins for white society" (p. 67).

But the South Side residents fight back—against condescending white clerks, against the white gangs that dominate adjacent neighborhoods. The youngsters also fight each other, using knives to protect themselves, show their courage, and establish their status. "The more strength we showed to others," says Ernie, the narrator, "the better protected we were" (p. 62). Stabbing a threatening opponent on the street may provide protection, but it also reflects the rage the ghetto produces, the fear of each other, the anger over ghetto conditions. And such violence is a reflection outside the home of what goes on inside: the father who beats his children, Ernie's uncles who lose all control when they immigrate north and start beating their wives. Beating up members of rival gangs and assaulting pedestrians and store owners is simply retaliation for domestic abuse, as well as a practical defense against the menace of the alleys.

Yet Ernie looks back on his boyhood in this Chicago with a muted pleasure, remembering the games, the gangs, the exciting forays into the streets, the coolness of the ice trucks in the summertime. No social worker tells Ernie and his friends that they lead a deprived existence, nor would they believe it if they were told. But as they grow into early adulthood, the ghetto begins having its effect. Ernie's friend Willie becomes a junkie, his friend George is shot by a policeman during a robbery. Without sentimentalizing or romanticizing it, Fair recalls Ernie's childhood with moving nostalgia. He appreciates the strength of the black ghetto people and their power to transcend impossible conditions, neither inflating nor exaggerating. Some surrender to the ruinous temptations of the street or collapse under the weight of the ghetto's negations. Some do not. In the end, he sees it all through Sterling Brown's poem "Strong Men," in which the "strong men" keep "comin' on" and "gittin' stronger," persisting, surviving, growing.

Ernie's ambivalence about the ghetto is not mere literary nostalgia. It seems to be part of the experience, and the bildungsroman its embodiment. Members of ghetto gangs express the same mix of feelings about the fights, the killings, the muggings. Cupid, one of R. Lincoln Keiser's informants in his 1969 study of a Chicago gang, implicitly acknowledges the substandard conditions of the slums he lives in. The youngsters in his general vicinity, perhaps four or five thousand of them, "got problems. Half of them are drop-outs, and ain't nobody trying to get no job for them." Ludicrously few caseworkers are funded to help them, and then those few are ineffective. "They might as well not be there—just a lot of expense, just a way to spend money. It's sickening!" Yet he speaks proudly of his experience on the streets, where "you learn what's what." On the one hand, he understands that dropping out of school is a "problem." On the other hand, he contends that school does not teach you what you need to know. Only the ghetto does that. "School put education in you head, but the streets tell you what you goin' to do when you grown. The streets teach you how to live."[31]

George Cain, writing about the Harlem of the sixties, asserts a more negative vision. On the one hand, he does full justice to Harlem as a place whose excitement is undeniable and whose colorfulness compensates for some of its defects. On the other, he sees Harlem as a tremendous drag on those who want more than a life of crime or poverty. His protagonist does not become a victim of the ghetto's violence. He survives, but with an eye irreversibly jaundiced by a difficult experience.

Blueschild Baby is the most anomalously poetic of the bildungsromans. Its surface is a kind of fog, suggesting the state of heroin haziness in which Cain and so many of his Harlemites float. *Blueschild Baby* is Cain's fictionalized account of his own descent into and struggle to climb out of heroin addiction. The "way" of the addicts in Harlem has its own "culture, language and code," and George learns "the strange words and the glorified romances of its heroes and heroines" and is "awed" by them. But it is "all show," "cheap glamour," beneath which is a desperate, sordid effort to survive. Dope is at once a literal weapon and a metaphor for the ghetto's steadfast inclination to self-destruction. "Tragic figures," says Cain, as he surveys the Harlem sidewalks crowded with nodding shapes. The addicts' "lifeless eyes" show they are already figuratively dead and are "impatient to be gone about their self-destruction . . . their killing." The toll is immense. An entire generation, thinks Cain, has been "sacrificed" and its members are "dropping like flies."[32]

Like Ronald Fair, Cain places much of the blame for the drug generation's wasting itself in Harlem on the white world. To be sure, the junkies become addicts partly through personal weakness, but it is a weakness conditioned by a white world aiming to keep blacks segregated and spiritually weak. "[T]hey're killing all of us," Cain says. "We've got to stop it and warn the others" (p. 115). White police do kill blacks. But Cain sees a larger, more indirect, but effective white control of the ghetto. The dope that all the young men are using, that even girls are into now in 1967, is "part of the Man's scheme, a way to keep a large part of the people helpless, an excuse for jailing and abusing them" (pp. 115–16).

Dope is the self-destructive version of the more literal violence blacks inflict on each other. A sidewalk crowd goads two men arguing over a gambling point into a knife fight merely for the spectacle it affords them, excitement in a dull existence. Some black kids rob a bar, then kill the bartender when he fails to hand over the money fast enough. But to leave the ghetto is to renounce one's own nourishment and die in another way. Not only does Cain remember his time in the ghetto as a child living with his great-grandmother as "warm and golden," but the Harlem streets themselves are as great an addiction as heroin. The companionship of the streets, the "sacrament" of sharing wine with a street gang, even the fraternity of the addicts recall his childhood feeling in church of being "an integral part of the community of man" (p. 39). Yet "The air of [that community] is charged with a suppressed urgency, making you feel that at any moment all hell must break loose, a brawl, killing, anything." The ghetto atmosphere "is dynamic," with "a presence of its own" (p. 21); it is the glitter of the light for the eager moth.

When he is taken away from that and set in a white world, George loses his soul. And though he becomes a prep basketball star at the white high school into which his parents put him in New Jersey, he finds himself drifting back to Harlem. Even the old bartender's warning to "stay away" cannot dilute the attraction. The mythic hero who hears the siren voices and is tempted, who sees his companions turned into swine and sails to Hades to summon the spirits of the dead, must himself undergo the experience of hell. Cain takes his first fix, rejoining the ghetto culture, falling "from grace," and losing the soul he came to find.

Cain's, however, is the ancient "fortunate fall," for only in his own addiction can he tell us about the paradox of ghetto life, explain those walking corpses. Only when we understand the powerful contradictions of Harlem can we understand its effects upon its victims. Sometimes it is warm and full of life, but that swarm of people as if on holiday can become like maggots on a decaying corpse. It gratifies and excites, but it also devours. It is a harbor that shelters but also a prison that dries up one's heart. Its streets exude a "festive air," but turning into one of them "is like entering Hell." Lively children who have not yet lost their innocence play in a circle of light ringed by junkies standing in the shadows, "stalking" and nodding. Harlemites are drawn together by a deep "love bond," but they betray, deceive, and kill one another. The paradox, however, also suggests the inevitable outcome of addiction to the ghetto streets and their dope. The hipness of the junkies "is only a new way of dying" (p. 156). To take up dope is not to reject the white murderers by turning authentically ghetto-black. It is to collaborate with them in their scheme. Cain's marriage to white Nichole reinforces his addiction. For the short time he is married to her he is as much imprisoned by his infatuation with her white skin as he is by his habit.

To free himself he must get rid of both and return to his blackness. The help of his black girlfriend Nandy is therefore indispensable. She becomes the midwife in the agony of his withdrawal, the labor pain of his rebirth. Cain does not rise from the dead and lead the way out of hell, however. There is no glory in the hours of pain he undergoes as he tries to kick. The chronicle of his experience, "the file on myself," traces "all those dead wasted years from which I recall nothing but the pain" (p. 184). But if Cain does not prevail, he does survive. In the end, he lies exhausted and in fragments, but the monkey is off his back, and he is ready to reassemble the pieces.

"Everybody wants to live decent," says Vice Lord Cupid to sociologist R. Lincoln Keiser. "We not going to be young savages all our life . . . everybody in a club got to change and go through a different way of life. You not going to be a gangfighter all your life."[33] The growing process that Cupid describes, like the gang members' ambivalence toward the ghetto experience itself, threads its way consistently through the vision of these novelists. The badman stalks their characters in the urban streets, and they see him not as a cool or awesome transgressor but as a threat to the growing self. And here sounds a note that virtually defines much African American writing: the protagonists of the bildungsromans, even when caught in the deepest trails of the maze of competitive violence or the self-destruction of dope, believe in themselves, and know they will triumph. Triumph does not require escape from the ghetto, either. It does require transcendence of its destructive conditions. Returning to Harlem from prison on a dope charge, Cain acknowledges he is still alive only in "bits and pieces," and there is no "me." But as Nandy brings him through the cure, he knows he can "begin anew." He reenters Harlem, recovers the soul he had lost, and prepares to undergo his final stage of growth. That "process is nearly complete," he says. "Someday soon, I shall emerge as Georgie Cain" (p. 6). *Blueschild Baby* is the evidence of that emergence.

Back in 1953, this same process produced a "me" out of Bruce Ashford Freeman, in Mark Kennedy's *The Pecking Order,* and though Cain arrives at his "me" with greater difficulty out of a tougher ghetto, both Kennedy and Cain illustrate what happens when these African American writers return to the scenes of their childhood. They mix nostalgia with criticism. Their vantage point, though, is the same as that of the Harlem Renaissance writers, not of the folk composers of the badman ballad. From the middle-class system into which their education has moved them, they look into the badman's world in which they once lived and in retrospect see the gang fights and muggings and murders as wreckers, not venues for a determined and boasting badness. Yet they have paid their dues and have the right to record at the same time the attraction of the streets, the tough and unforgiving stringency that required good reflexes and quick wits. And they tell their stories with pride in themselves and their companions, just as a fighting man tells his war stories and hints at a mystical brotherhood of combat. In *Native Son* Richard Wright introduced the "black metropolis" as a new setting for the experience of black travail in America. The novelists that follow him, after World War II, find in the ghetto the same travail, but it is a travail that tests the strength of their young characters consigned to its mean streets. In these novels, those youths are not found wanting, but are the vehicle for the literary affirmation of black life lived under the severest conditions.

THE CODE OF THE STREET: THE BILDUNGSROMAN WORLD UPDATED

In his 1990s studies of Philadelphia's black Germantown Avenue neighborhood, sociologist Elijah Anderson investigates the society of the northern inner city from the viewpoint of the social sciences. It turns out to be surprisingly similar to the inner city that the bildungsroman novelists, some thirty years earlier, had explored in fiction. Giving ethnographic and social science labels to the street culture that Herbert Simmons, Claude Brown, and Ronald Fair saw as first-person participants, Anderson analyzes the "code of the street" and, not surprisingly, concludes that it developed out of an inner-city culture created by a white racist majority. That culture grew in response to its increasing exclusion from the mainstream economic, law enforcement, and judicial systems. Anderson sees, in other words, what Hortense Powdermaker and John Dollard saw in small southern towns in the 1930s, the condition of being "outside the law." The inhabitants of the inner city substitute for the established mainstream judicial system their own code of behavior, with its own "set of prescriptions and proscriptions, or informal rules." These rules are adopted to protect one of their most precious possessions, pride and respect, the revised version of the old badman's reputation. At the core of the code is "the credible threat of retaliation,"

> promising an "eye for an eye," or a certain "payback" for transgressions. In service to this ethic, repeated displays of "nerve" and "heart" build or reinforce a credible reputation for vengeance that works to deter aggression and disrespect, which are sources of great anxiety on the inner-city street.[34]

The principle of "respect" dominates the street code. It is the "juice" or "capital" of a community in which real capital is brutally scant and in which the mainstream sources of self-esteem are absent. Respect is essentially the assurance of a dominant place in the group, neighborhood, or community and is achieved by fighting, by quickness and intelligence, or both, and by making sure that one is never *dis*respected, or "dissed." This code replaces the mainstream criminal justice system, from which the inner-city street people feel so alienated.[35]

A more recent firsthand account of the psychological conflicts of the street is Nathan McCall's autobiographical *Makes Me Wanna Holler* (1994). McCall spent his young years in the segregated black neighborhood of Portsmouth, Virginia. His neighborhood, if not affluent, at least enjoyed a modicum of middle-class prosperity. Cavalier Manor was no Beverly Hills, but it was a pleasant residential community. Its main weakness for McCall was that it was segregated, sitting cheek by jowl against the equally segregated white development Academy Park. His separation from the Academy Park world, enforced by Virginia's entrenched customs, created a marrow-deep anger which drove his behavior within his own black world, whose law was the "code of the street." Beating up whites gave him and his gang-buddies enormous satisfaction. Violence within his group bought respect, protection, and the euphoria of power that countered the universal scorn he felt emanating from the whites he saw only at a distance. When a rival gang member, Plaz, insults him and his girlfriend at a carnival, he reacts as the code requires: he gets his gun, follows his enemy, and shoots him. As McCall looks into the eyes of the fallen Plaz and sees "terror," he "felt like God . . . so good and powerful that I wanted to do it again . . . until I emptied the gun."[36]

McCall's straight-arrow parents stand solidly by him in the ensuing criminal trial, getting him one of Portsmouth's best defense attorneys. He himself begins thinking like them. And though he relishes the reverence of his old street buddies, who think him "a bona fide crazy nigger," and falls briefly back into his old habits, a subsequent stint in jail brings him back to his senses (p. 117). He realizes that most of the "bloods" in prison had "misguided ideas about manhood." They aren't killers, says McCall, striking the same note as Rudolph Fisher's Episcopalian minister in the 1920s. They simply want to appear to be tough and hard. Most of them are really afraid, and not "as confident of [their] manhood as [they] pretended to be" (p. 202).

One is tempted to call this a case of *plus ça change, plus la même chose*. With this insight, McCall comes to appreciate that violence is irrelevant, even contradictory, to real manhood, something his stepfather and his gym teacher had been trying to tell him all along. If he is to survive and grow, he must cut himself off from his homeboys. He wins a place in the prison printing program and is freed by the parole board. College follows and then his string of successes in journalism. He has made it into the mainstream.

6

chapter

Toasts

Tales of the "Bad Nigger"

People who are in the fast life or underground, you know. Or it be somebody that's superstrength, you know . . . doing something as far as pimping or hustling or shooting up some people, being a gangster or something. Or it's about some other kind of dealing, all dealing in a illegal thing. Usually if he's not a pimp he's a hustler, if he's not a hustler, it might be a jive bartender, or it just might be a guy that thinks he's bad, that throw his weight around. . . . Usually at the time I heard them, when I was young, that was like a insight on being big personally. Say, 'Yeah, I like that. Wow, he was bad!' . . . Seemed like everybody would like to be whoever that guy was.[1]

Nathan McCall and the bildungsroman novelists write from the viewpoint of those who have left violent badness behind and entered the nonviolent world. As is only natural, they apply the measurements of the respectable and law-abiding to the street culture of the community which they fled. Even if the bildungsroman protagonist is to the ghetto born, and most of them are, his escape moves him into a different frame of reference whose judgments are set by a different, nonviolent moral code. But those who remain citizens of the street community calibrate their behavior to that community, not the straight one outside. And for them, the American streetmen who develop in the urban landscape of the thirties, forties, fifties, and sixties, violence is not a pathology but a way of preserving order in their social structure. As folklorist Anthony Reynolds puts it, "In the Darwinian environment of the ghetto streets, physical prowess is a quality to be admired and emulated."[2]

Those who reside in the inner city and help build a violent and criminal brotherhood have their own bards, street poets who create a virtual mythology that embodies the attitudes and values of the street society. Their genre is the "toast," a narrative poem, usually cast in a sort of pre-rap rhythm, designed for oral delivery by a single performer to an informal or casual audience of other street people, usually young men. The toast chronicles the heroes of the street; defines, celebrates, exaggerates, and often ridicules them; exemplifies behavior to be avoided or emulated; lays out the rules for pimps and whores; shows the rise and fall of con men; dramatizes the accumulation and loss of wealth; and recounts the transformation of brilliantly clothed macks into threadbare tramps. It is a mirror into which the streetman gazes to see himself, to analyze his lifeways, to find reasons to laugh at and praise himself, to express his understanding of the world into which he is sealed so hermetically that escape is not even thinkable. Its purpose is the opposite of that of the ghetto bildungsroman. The novel is a lesson in a destructive experience escaped. The toast is a statement of stoical, sometimes joyful, explicit or implicit acceptance of the inescapable given.[3]

THE TOAST AND ITS MYSTERIES

The origin of the term "toast" is unclear. Toast collector Bruce Jackson says that he has "never met anyone who knows why these poems are called toasts" or when they came into being. His own knowledge of the form dates from 1961, when he listened to black convicts perform them at the Indiana State Penitentiary.[4] Other scholars trace their origins back to the beginning of the century.[5] One of the earliest students of the toast, Roger D. Abrahams, tracks the general toast form to a Scottish tradition of secret drinking societies, a tradition sustained by college fraternities in America. In some cases, says Abrahams, the exchanges between the old blackface minstrel end men and the interlocutor sound a good deal like the later toasts. A simultaneous influence could have been "the custom of the dedicatory speeches or verse toasts pledged with a drink, some of which were quite long and flamboyant. We know that this custom was taken over by the Negro at least as early as the beginning of this [the twentieth] century."[6]

There are many fewer toast collections than ballad collections, so we have considerably less to work with than in the case of the badman ballad. Nearly all of the collections, furthermore, were made by white men in the fifties and sixties. Bruce Jackson claims that most of these pieces derive from an earlier creative period and were kept alive by young black men, especially those who went to jail, where they heard the poems and performed them in their own segregated cell blocks. Collectors "now rarely discover any texts that weren't in the tradition twenty years ago, and only rarely are their informants young men." Nor do all its practitioners call the form a "toast." Some call it "stories," others (like Zora Neale Hurston does in the thirties) "lies."[7]

The toast is an apt parallel to the bildungsroman novel. It covers the inner-city sensibilities that the novel excludes and provides the reader unfamiliar with this aspect of the African American community evidence of the attitudes toward violence held by those who lived closest to the action. I base my discussion mainly on seven toast collections, those by Roger D. Abrahams, Bruce Jackson, Anthony Reynolds, Dennis Wepman and colleagues, William Labov and colleagues, and Seymour Fiddle.[8] Most of these collectors agree that three figures dominate the toasts they collect: Stagolee, the Signifying Monkey, and Shine.[9]

Shine is a laborer on the *Titanic* and the only black aboard. By swimming through the cold sea, ignoring the pleas of pampered whites to help them, and arriving back at his favorite bar on the mainland ahead of the news of the ship's

catastrophe, Shine confirms not only the physical superiority of the black phy-
sique but the social superiority of the fellowship of the street, spotlighting white
selfishness and weakness. "The Signifying Monkey" descends from the old slave
animal tales, with the monkey playing the role of trickster Rabbit, stirring up
trouble amongst the larger animals just for the hell of it. He maneuvers Lion into
challenging Elephant, and then watches happily as the "king of the jungle" is
pulverized by Elephant. Then, by deploying the same wit and knowledge of psychology, he escapes from Lion's anger. The toast is a classic example of the smart
weak getting the best of the dumb strong.[10]

RETURN TO STAGOLEE

Of the three major toast prototypes, only Stagolee descends directly from the
tradition of the badman ballad. He is, in fact, the only figure from the ballads
preserved in the toasts, at least those that have been published. No toast that I
have seen tells of Bill Martin, Devil Winston, Duncan and Brady, or any other of
the murderous badmen of the old ballads. But there are more printed toast variants of the Stagolee story than for any other single toast figure.[11] It is a tribute to
Stagolee's reputation as a badman that the black urban poets use him as the archetype of the "bad nigger." As Julius Lester says in his own retelling of black
folk tales, "Stagolee was, undoubtedly and without question, the baddest nigger
that ever lived."[12]

The variants of "Stagolee" are remarkably uniform in content and style.[13]
Stagolee, who narrates his own story, establishes himself as an outlaw from the
beginning, sometimes with "a sawed off shot-gun," but nearly always with "a
crooked [sometimes marked] deck of cards." His dress varies between run-down
seedy and pimp-style snazzy, and sometimes he has "a T-model Ford," even if
the setting is as late as 1941. Enraged over his eviction by his woman and insulted by the sea of mud he has to struggle through on this very nasty night to get
to it,[14] Stagolee wreaks mayhem in the Bucket of Blood saloon. When the bartender disrespects him, Stagolee "pump[s] six a my rockets in his motherfucken
chest."[15] Then he sneers at the bartender's grief-stricken mother, pointing to the
"hole in the ugly motherfucker's head" as proof of his death. All are reduced to
powerlessness by the implacable badman. When one of the bar's whores challenges him to combat ("Come on upstairs, I'ma set you straight"), Stagolee is
more than equal to her dare. Even on her own turf, or, more precisely, her bed,
Stagolee is the master, throwing "nine inches of dick into that bitch before she
could move her gristle."[16]

In toasts like the Stagolee prototype, sex is empty of erotic pleasure. The
point is to establish dominance, to overwhelm, to display a total lack of sensitivity or affection. As in the old badman ballads, the penis is employed as a weapon,
identical with the bullets that blast from the badman's .38s and .44s. It is as if all
womanhood deserves punishment for its disrespect of black manhood. The satisfaction found in blasting away with guns is echoed in the pleasure taken in
ramming penises up the vaginas and rectums of the "ho's."[17]

The badman protects himself by needing no one and never showing sympathy. He wins status and rep by leaving a trail of dead competitors and exhausted "ho's" in his wake. Billy Lyon enters the scene to avenge his brother the bartender's death, and he demonstrates a similar male ruthlessness. He shoots two innocent bystanders simply because one nervously calls out for the "law," and another, a diffident prostitute, begs him to be merciful. This done, the two badmen face off, like a pair of old boasters, bragging of their respective meanness. Billy does not beg for his life because he has a wife and children, as in the old ballads. Instead, we get melodrama: the lights go out, shots ring out, and when the lights return they disclose a dead Billy, the victim of a quick and crackshot Stagolee.

Stagolee's encounter with the court after he kills Billy clarifies the qualities that must appeal to the toaster and his audience. The episode should complete the audience's identification with Stagolee, since by all accounts being arrested and going to court is one of the more common experiences among young black males. Standing before the court, Stagolee is isolated not only from the mainstream, embodied in the remote white man who is going to judge him, but also from members of his own black community who resent him and want him punished and have come to court to see him brought down. This is where badman Stagolee must exercise his hardest hardness. He has deliberately aroused the animosity of other blacks by flouting their own code of order and now he must stand up before their contempt. In the peculiarly surreal atmosphere of the toast, the judge, both avuncular ("Well, son") and maliciously vindictive ("I'm gonna give you a little old sixty-year sentence"), asks what the charges are against Stagolee and what his punishment should be. From the unidentified background, black voices erupt with accusations of rape, murder, theft. Notably, the accusing voices are women's. They express a violent bitterness against the badman that suggests a powerful misogyny on the part of the performer. He presents women as nasty-mouthed harridans who side with the white legal system against their own:

> One say, "Hang him," another say, "Give him gas."
> A snaggle-tooth bitch jumped up and say, "Run that twister through his jivin' ass!"

Ultimately, though, the hags are rendered toothless, for the white judge uniformly ignores their strident and spiteful voices and gives Stagolee a sentence befitting a real badman, one he can courageously defy by sneering at the years he will face. In fact, Stagolee has the satisfaction of throwing one screeching accuser out and watching his own girlfriend appear before the judge to fully restore his sexual power, begging the judge to release him because nobody can "fuck like Stackolee."[18]

Like the ballad, the Stagolee brand of toast is not designed for psychological probing. It is exclusively narrative and its narrative subject is violent action. We do not see what goes on in Stagolee's head, only what he does.[19] Abrahams's Stagolee is "the epitome of virility, of manliness on display." "He does not aim to be a god but rather to be the eternal man in revolt, the devil," rejecting "the

white men's laws," the timidity of the woman-centered home,[20] the slavish respectability of the straight black middle class. The badman expresses himself
through "physical prowess," seeking to remove whatever threatens his "domain" or "ego."[21] Yet, in some cases, even the toaster seems to mock him. When
Stagolee laughs at the "two life terms" and says

> . . . "Judge, . . . that ain't so cold."
> He said, "No, but your black ass will never get on parole."
> He said, "Now laugh at this: case dismissed."[22]

The Stagolee story told in the toasts is also suffused with irony and humor. Its
very exaggerations are the vehicles of self-mockery and satire.[23] After all, it is the
members of the fraternal in-group who are capable of the most ironic laughter
when one of their own is brought down by conditions they all agree are outra-
geous but beyond correction.

Another layer of the toast suggests the archetypal adolescent as much as
the badman. Labov and his colleagues find other evidence that the toast serves as
a staging ground for the adolescent's rejection of the domestic circle where
women rule. "[M]any adolescent boys," they say, "know long toasts" and mem-
orize them easily because of their "structure" and "their great intrinsic interest."[24] With his fixation on sex, pussy, penis size, and loveless intercourse, the
adolescent asserts the dominance of his world over that of the women who have
been disciplining him throughout his childhood.[25] At the same time, the toast
provides a vehicle for the adolescent rebelliousness against all authority.[26] One
of the main instruments for that rebellion is the language of obscenity. It is one
of the first things a reader notices when moving from the badman ballad to the
toast. To be sure, the turn-of-the-century ballad probably comes to us substan-
tially bowdlerized by the prim collectors early in the century, who were guided
by their probably even primmer audience. The collectors of the toast, on the
other hand, have had no such limits on what they might publish. Consequently,
the toasts are flung at us with all stops out, their poetry of obscenity long predat-
ing our public vernacular's current love affair with the four-letter word.[27] If we
wonder, indeed, where the language and attitudes of the current commercial rap
song come from we need only look at the toast. Both are heavily affected by the
adolescent need to swagger and to shock by violating accepted standards of
adult behavior.

There is a spirit of hyperbolic play in these variants of Stagolee that infuses
a number of the other toast prototypes of the traditional badman, and it suggests
a high-spiritedness that is part boyish callowness and part adult sophistication,
though one would not want to overstate the latter. One such toast type creates
its subject out of legendary characters of the Old West and the new urban criminals like Dillinger, in a unique street rendering of American history and white
badmen. In Abrahams's version of "Jesse James," for example, it is Jesse and
Frank James who meet the Dalton Brothers and Geronimo in circumstances very
much like those of "Stagolee," both the toast and the ballad. Here, though, the
action begins in a train that the outlaws are robbing. Jesse is a shooting fool.

First he shoots a man who tries to protect his wife, after which he "fucked her well, / Fucked her till her pussy swelled," right in the midst of the train robbery. He shoots a second man who, like the timid onlooker Billy Lyon kills, calls for the law, but then, as if one deconstructionist text were "talking" to another, Jesse, combining Stagolee and Shine,

> . . . dived out the window, swam through water, swam through mud.
> He was looking for the place they call the "Bucket of Blood,"

where he shoots the bartender for disrespecting him.[28]

But by far the friskiest and the most hyperbolic of the badman toast characters is Dolomite.[29] He is a vicious little wolverine of a badman in the tradition of the bad-from-birth syndrome, informing his father when he emerges from the womb that "From now on, cocksucker, I'm running this place." When he dies, the preacher gives a final prayer of thanks over Dolomite's grave: "I'm glad this here bad motherfucker called Dolomite is no longer here with us." Dolomite is all trouble and irrepressible energy, a threat to men, women, animals, and nature, cheerfully disrupting life on three continents. What seems to charm the toaster most is Dolomite's irresistible and insuppressible phallus, with which he overpowers large animals and top whores.

> He got kicked out of South America for fuckin' steers,
> He fucked a she-elephant till she broke down in tears.

He screws the "boss" of whores, Chi Mabel, to death, and "kept on kickin' asses and fuckin' up the hall." Even "two big rocky mountains" part to let Dolomite's "bad ass through," and special bulletins over the radio warn to "Look out for storms, atomic bombs, and Dolomite."[30] This carries toast hyperbole to new heights while it confirms the role the toast plays in the recreational lives of young black men. This version of "Dolomite" is like a children's story in which all the orderly rules of the adult world are cast asunder, by the Cat in the Hat or by the visiting witch, who turn the house topsy-turvy while mother is away. The more boisterously exaggerated Dolomite's destructive exploits, the more entertaining.

All of these toasts, Abrahams finds, are characterized by a "lack of marriage or any sort of reintegration with society."[31] This does not mean that there is no resolution in the toast, such as death or the incarceration of the hero. It does indicate, though, that the conventional toast vision is a destructive rather than a constructive one. It articulates a code based upon the rejection of the values of the mainstream majority culture, its phony sentimentality as well as its privileged riches.[32] The badness of this badman can best be summed up, perhaps, in a verse used universally in one form or another:

> I've got a tombstone disposition, graveyard mind.
> I know I'm a bad motherfucker, that's why I don't mind dying.[33]

It is the loser's ultimate defiance of ineluctable conditions and the assertion of dignity and personal strength in the face of defeat.

THE PUT-DOWN

The toast story is not a single type. One whole subcategory is devoted to the bad-man's humiliating defeat. It is not the defeat imposed by the overwhelming power of white law, but that administered by The Life itself. This story line seems to be an antidote to the tales of refractory braggarts and their swaggering ways, to which the street crowd can go when the more obstreperous trouble-maker wears out their admiration or overdoes his badness. "Badman Dan and Two-Gun Green" exemplifies this interesting modulation. Bad Dan is con-fronted by Two-Gun Green when he insists on free service from Green's whore. To prove his own badness and frighten Green off, in the best Dolomite tradition, he proceeds to knock down bystanders, defecate, spit, break chairs, and drive the customers out the windows, ending up with his face thrust into that of Two-Gun himself, who in turn undertakes to boast of *his* toughness and then puts "two bullets in [Dan's] motherfucking eye."[34] The count against Bad Dan seems to be that he is a dopehead, vaguely hinting at a weakness not admired by bad-man connoisseurs. Not only does he exercise poor judgment in picking a fight he cannot control, but he allows himself to be controlled by a drug. This is not cool.

The theme is more fully developed in a toast collected in 1971 by Anthony Reynolds from a group of older black men in a back room in Los Angeles. It is a splendid piece titled "One-Lung Joe," an inspired modification of "Buckskin Joe," which John A. Lomax collected around the turn of the century. In both ver-sions, the title character is a consumptive, which makes "one-lung" a most apt adjective. For narrative interest and coherence, as well as for its iconoclastic treatment of the conventional hyperactive badman figure, I have not seen a toast better than this one. Slyly, quietly, ironically, the toaster makes the badman brag-gart, "Master Henry Dean," come off a distinct second to a "pale and . . . stricken stranger" who has inconspicuously entered the saloon where Henry Dean holds forth. Losing at poker, Henry chooses this quiet newcomer as a scapegoat to intimidate, claiming a Dolomite-ish mastery of the elements, of ani-mals, of other humans. The tubercular stranger, though, is calm and quiet, sit-ting in an old chair and toying absently with a deck of cards. Paying no attention to Master Henry Dean, he pulls a five of hearts and tacks it over the door of the tavern. Then

> . . . he stepped back some sixty feet or more.
> He pulled out his six-shooter and fired five rapid shots.
> Each shot a dot was blotted out.
> He said, "I have one more left for you, Master Henry Dean, if you wish to call
>   my play."
> But the bad man merely weakened, and you could see it in his eyes,
> And he had the nerve to try and apologize.

This is truly a fine piece. The traditional qualities of the old badman are rendered buffoonish and ridiculous. Coolness and courage and skill emerge as the admirable qualities by which one deals with false bluster and gains the fame that all badmen long for.[35]

THE FALL

Badmen thus take other shapes in the toast than creators of mayhem like Stagolee and Dolomite. They appear as the hustlers, the pimps, the con men and gamblers who conduct the chief "business" of the street. They are the players in The Life, where money is made and lost in rolls of the dice and according to the acumen and sexual attractiveness of the whore. In The Life, addicts and pushers may reign supreme one day and be cast in the gutter the next. It is a world governed by the inexorable rotation of the wheel of fortune and wild swings of chance (what goes around comes around), by the inevitable aging of the champion prostitute, the encroachment of disease, the moral decay of a value system founded on the insubstantial glitter of material display. It lends itself to the story of success and the melodrama of the fall. The largest group of toasts on this theme has been collected by Dennis Wepman and his colleagues in their book called, fittingly, *The Life: The Lore and Folk Poetry of the Black Hustler*. They recorded their toasts "in shorthand from spontaneous recitations during the 1950's and 60's" in "the prisons of New York—Sing Sing, Clinton, Attica, and Auburn."[36] Most of the toasters come from The Life, and their jail sentence signals that they were the victims of a "fall." The genre requires a "framed" opening in which the narrator addresses an audience, perhaps in jail, more often in a barroom where his listeners have not yet been chastened by failure. Like the ancient mariner, the narrator seems condemned to travel the bars, gambling dens, and pool halls and retell the story of his fall, explain how he came to his sorry state. "Kitty Barrett," for example, opens with this formulaic couplet:

> Say, my man, lend me your ear,
> And I'll put you wise on how I got here [in jail].

Toast heroes fall for a variety of reasons, some, as Wepman and his colleagues point out, because of "outside forces like a narco's trap" or betrayal by a partner or a whore, some through "personal weaknesses," such as carelessness or, worst of all, addiction.[37] Whatever the reason, they recite their story as a caution to their audience. Kitty Barrett is the undercover narco cop who cleverly persuades the narrator to sell her some dope, whereupon she arrests him and he is sent to prison. This is his tale and he concludes with a sigh and a "homiletic"[38] warning:

> Well, baby, I got busted, just like that.
> So I hope this toast helps you when they give you your hat.[39]

Abrahams calls this the "sorry-for-yourself point of view."[40] But if the "fall" toasts get melodramatically cautionary, they also display an unflinching portrait of what happens to the "players" who play the game of The Life. Good-Doing

Wheeler is turned in to the narcos because of his main man's weakness for cheap wine; Toledo Slim, like Dumbo the Junkie, loses his girl to his partner; the Thoroughbred Kid is the betrayer when he tries to run off with his partner's whore and is shot in the process. Broadway Sam takes "a dope fiend whore" into his stable and becomes "a junky" himself. Spending all his money on dope, he is unable to bail out his main source of money, his whore Mabel, and from that point on he degenerates into a male hustler, dies with "garbage under his head," and returns to his old Broadway neighborhood as a "ghost."[41]

"Mexicana Rose" and "Duriella du Fontaine"[42] depict The Life at its extravagant best, reflecting an affectionate respect for the professional whore that one never finds in the hard-man toasts about Stagolee and Dolomite. They chronicle the death of the superb prostitute. Their heroes are not priapic cowboys who crudely pump their bullets and penises into the bodies of their powerless victims. They are smooth operators, princes of the street, who can read a haute cuisine menu and feel manly with clean fingernails. Between them and the women who make them wealthy there is the decidedly unmisogynistic respect and affection of thoroughbreds. Fate, though, intervenes to destroy their success. The cowardly and deceitful Smitty Cocaine, whose submission to drugs is scorned by the street, shoots Mexicana when she chooses the "unflappable" Long Shoe Sam, the "Dean of all mackmen," as her pimp. Duriella du Fontaine dies in an airplane crash as she is arriving in Mexico City with the fortune that would have permitted her and her loyal pimp Andy to have retired from the dangerous Game for life.

A very fine "fall" toast is appropriately titled "The Fall." Dennis Wepman and his colleagues call it "one of the best developed pieces in the literature."[43] Its language and imagery are muscular and robust as well as poetic and imaginative. The toast's ghetto streets are a stage for the Darwinian playing-out of natural forces red in tooth and claw:

> It was Saturday night, and the jungle was bright,
> And the Game was stalking its prey.
> The code was crime in the neon line,
> And the weak were doomed to pay.[44]

The poem's theme is the disintegration of a relationship between a pimp and his whore, and the bitter vindictiveness that suddenly takes over the emotions of a couple when put under pressure. It comments not only upon the universal in all such relationships, but upon the ghetto game itself and the bleakness of the real inner city in which it is played:

> Where belles of vice sell love for a price,
> And even the law is corrupt,
> As you go down trying, you keep on crying,
> "Man, it's a bitter cup!" (ll. 17–28)

The key idea is that the "belles" *sell* love. All relationships in The Life are founded on a raw commercialism. The bottom line governs most behavior, and exploitation of others tends to produce the best bottom line.[45] Thus, when the narrator's "brown-skin moll" inevitably falls sick and can no longer bring in the money he needs to feed his growing drug habit, he brings in another whore. Feeling betrayed, the "brown-skin" goes to the police and her pimp goes to jail. In turning to the white law for redress, she violates the code of the street, the understanding that their relationship is commercial. But this gives the narrator a chance to articulate the more admirable part of that code, the stoical fatalism with which the street players accept the "fall" that must come. Lying in his cell the pimp utters the player's submission to fate:

> Farewell to the night, to the neon light,
> Farewell to you one and all.
> And farewell to the Game; may it still be the same
> When I get done doing this fall. (ll. 265–72)

The "fall" toasts make explicit what is latent in the badman poems, a resignation that ultimately affirms the values of The Life.[46] This is the player's strength, demonstrating, paradoxically, a kind of purity of heart no "lame" can claim. Indeed, there are enough references to "kings" and "thoroughbreds" to suggest a self-conscious insinuation that the street has an aristocracy, and while the victim of the "laws of the system"[47] may not reign like a "king" at the end, he can accept his fate like a "thoroughbred," faithful to the code in failure as well as success. As members of this aristocracy, both the violent badmen and the less violent pimps and drug dealers seem to enjoy a high that more than compensates for the fated fall. Any other mode of life is inconceivable.

chapter **7**

Chester Himes

Harlem Absurd

A MAN OF ANGER

In the late fifties and sixties, during the most active years of the civil rights movement, Chester B. Himes was the African American ghetto novelist par excellence. Nobody wrote about its violent men and women as he did, with such fertile variety, with such knowing and ironic detail. Nobody in Himes's Harlem, though, rises out of the ghetto into the middle class or escapes it by going to college, as do many of the characters in the ghetto bildungsromans. Nor is his Harlem particularly tolerant of young men looking for themselves. He presents Harlem in his ribald and boisterous tales as a community of trickery and deceit, greed and mendacity, and universal violence. Himes develops his version of Harlem in eight novels written between 1957 and 1969, starting with *For Love of Imabelle* and ending with *Blind Man with a Pistol.*[1] In his ghetto no families care enough to worry about their children, and no children grow up to go to college. Instead they enter the world of predatory crime, turning hard-hearted and brutal. They slaughter each other without a second thought. This is the "way of life" in Himes's ghetto, where Harlemites use "any and all means (except work, which is most often denied them) to obtain means, right suspected wrongs, nurture their emotions, afford sex fulfillment or perversions, provide self-respect or at least self-pride, to buy excitement, titillation, leisure and even peace of mind." This is why Himes calls his tales "domestic" rather than "detective" novels, because "the crime and vice" they portray are simply "an integral factor of the domestic life of any ghetto."[2]

This is a badman's world, and Himes himself, in a way no other artist has since the days of the old ballad singers, knows it from the badman's point of view. And not since the days of those balladeers has black expression contained such ire as is in Himes's work (except perhaps for Richard Wright's). Indeed, the signature feature of Himes's domestic novels is anger. This is what makes these eight hard-boiled Harlem detective novels so personal, for Himes himself was a man in a fury and projected it in characters equally angry. It is not an anger of protest, or rather not simply of protest, but a kind of existential rage at the general conditions of living. Only such anger could enable Himes to become the "prose poet"[3] of ghetto violence: its satirist, parodist, savage jokester, vicious clown.

Himes was not born in the ghetto, but in Jefferson City, Missouri, on July 29, 1909. He was thus just a decade short of being a Harlem Renaissance baby. In some ways he resembled the members of that generation. Like them he found a new style and wrote about the black underclass. Like them he was the product of a middle-class home and educated parents, both teachers. And like Claude McKay in particular, he felt alienated from the world itself. He seems to have been as unhappy with black as with white culture. At Ohio State University in Columbus, which he attended for a short time in 1926, he hated its white bigotry and reacted to his white teachers and their assignments with scorn and contempt. He was even more infuriated with the black students' social snobbery, displaying his disdain by seeking out the cruder pleasures of Cleveland's "Bucket of Blood" district,[4] preferring the anti-social types along Scoville and Cedar Avenues, Long Street, Warren Street, 55th Street. He soaked up the black musicals, frolicked with the black prostitutes, gambled, and committed petty crimes. He became, in short, a kind of part-time badman. He found the Columbus ghetto, too, and proceeded to live a double life, joining a fraternity, dating the proper college girls, going to the football games on campus while at the same time making friends with the disreputable citizens of the city's underworld, working hard to shock and puzzle his straight, rigidly proper, and color-struck black classmates.

In the psychic battle between the transgressive ghetto and the stilted middle-class obsessions of the Ohio State campus, the ghetto won easily. Himes found no noses in the air in the inner cities of Cleveland and Columbus, and the danger inherent in The Life attracted him. Before the end of his first academic year he was back in Cleveland. He became, by his often inflated reports, a gambler, a thief, a bootlegger, a pimp, and a possessor of a series of pistols, which he proudly showed to his girlfriends to impress them.[5] Eventually, he bungled an armed robbery, fell into the hands of the police, and found himself in court on a felony charge. The judge gave him twenty to twenty-five years in the state penitentiary. He only served seven and a half, but, he writes in his *Autobiography,* "I grew to manhood in the Ohio State Penitentiary. I became a man, dependent on no one but myself. I learned all the behavior patterns necessary for survival."[6] No writer of the Renaissance generation could claim such credentials.

Some critics have associated Himes with the school of Richard Wright. His first two published novels in particular, *If He Hollers Let Him Go* (1945) and *Lonely Crusade* (1947), do seem to express the standard black protest against white prejudice and injustice. But the domestic novels establish a countercurrent to the Wright school. While they do contain veins of protest, their violence is essentially nonracial, the criminal violence of Harlem's underworld. In them, Himes contributes a unique viewpoint to the decade of the sixties, one which remains free of ideological orthodoxy whether black or white. Himes had always held himself aloof from groups, and as a novelist he never joined any "school" or allowed ideology to taint his own scrupulous vision of the world, even if he spoke another way as a public man.

In some instances, Himes writes in what might be called the "warrior tradition" of black violence, in which black men regard it as their responsibility to retaliate against white oppression. We can assume that Bob Jones, the protagonist of *If He Hollers,* speaks pretty much for Himes when he says that the only solution to the black American's racial problem is violence. "We've got to make white people respect us and the only thing white people have ever respected is force."[7] Nearly twenty-five years later, at the peak of the Black Power movement, Himes is more explicit and expansive on the same topic. In a 1970 interview with John A. Williams, he says, "I think the only way the Negro will ever get accepted as an equal is if he kills whites . . . launches a violent uprising to the point where people will become absolutely sickened, disgusted; to the point where people will realize that they have to do something."[8] In a revolution, he says, echoing Malcolm X in his 1963 speech "Message to the Grass Roots,"[9] "the major objective is to kill as many people as you can, by whatever means you can kill them, because the very fact of killing them and killing them in sufficient number is supposed to help you gain your objectives. It's the only reason why you do so." It may be that Himes felt himself being radicalized by the politics of the day, for he mentions a book he is writing in which he tries to "depict the violence that is necessary so that the white community will also give it a little thought . . . to call to mind what *would* happen, what *should* happen, when black people have an armed uprising, what white people should expect."[10]

But such retributive violence took up very little of the fiction Himes wrote. He knew too much about violence personally not to feel it as an attribute of his own general, race-plus sense of outrage. When he was thirteen, his much-loved brother Joe was blinded in an explosion during a joint chemical experiment. His parents developed a hatred for each other so powerful that they shamed him with their shouting arguments and noisy struggles. Just after he graduated from high school at seventeen, Himes, working as a hotel bus boy, fell into an open hotel elevator shaft, fracturing three vertebrae, an arm, and his jaw, and knocking several teeth out. Against all the doctors' predictions, he walked again, at first with a back brace, which he hated, and then without. Himes, as a self-conscious college student, was humiliated by the brace, and his reaction suggests the mixed nature of his fury. He describes his mother as a "tiny woman who hated all manner of condescension from white people."[11] He inherited this from her, he says, and developed a powerful indignation against condescending whites, and more largely against the power that whites held and exercised over blacks in all aspects of their lives. His injury, though, did not result from white condescension or prejudice. Like his brother's injury, it was a matter of chance, a fluke of existence. Joe patiently bore his own affliction and, doing everything right, became a successful sociologist, with a Ph.D. and all the trappings of accepted academia.[12] Chester did not let the world off so easy. Restive as a black in a white world where he never felt at home, he was angered by life in general, and out of his anger came violence. "I discovered," he writes, "that I had become very violent. I saw a glimmer of fear and caution in the eyes of most people I encountered: squares, hustlers, gamblers, pimps, even whores." When a white waitress refused him service at a restaurant counter, he went berserk, leaping atop the counter, smashing dishes, striking the waitress, and beating the white manager on the head with his "huge, old-fashioned .44 Colt frontier revolver."[13] And he almost committed murder during the robbery that sent him to prison. In prison, his "fits of insensate fury" kept even the other inmates at a distance.[14] When he was a free man, this same "insensate fury" was often directed at his women, whom he often struck, in at least one case engaging in an out-and-out fist fight on a Paris street.[15] Sometimes, like Jesse Robinson in *The Primitive*, he came out of a kind of trance to find that he had actually beaten them and felt remorse at his excess and fear at his loss of control.

Himes's early novels grow directly out of his own complex personality, their protagonists treading a narrow line between explosion and control. Bob Jones, Himes's alter ego in *If He Hollers Let Him Go*, feels like a time bomb in the San Pedro, California, shipyards where he works during World War II, always on the edge of lashing out at the condescending white workers and supervisors who keep the good jobs for themselves and regard Bob with something worse than contempt. Bob drives around Los Angeles with a gun beside him until the police pick him up on weapons possession charges. In *Lonely Crusade* (1947), protagonist Lee Gordon feels anger partly at the way whites treat him and partly at the way his wife treats him. Lee suppresses that anger, though, and lets it out only in fantasy, dreaming of bloody vengeance on the arrogant white man.

Yet the world Himes saw was divided into kaleidoscopic images that did not sort easily into vicious whites and innocent blacks. The urge to strike, to destroy, permeated a reality made of puzzling contradictions. Lee Gordon may have fantasized a gratifying infliction of pain and humiliation on white men, but by the end of his story in *Lonely Crusade* he expresses the same attitude that Himes takes in his Harlem novels: he cannot fall back on his racial identity to account for his failures or his successes. Being a Negro cannot possibly justify "vicious, immoral, criminal behavior." If it could, then the only logical conclusion would be that the Negro is "subnormal" and can "never fit into a normal society." If he is normal, then he must "rise above the connotation America has given to his race. He would have to stand or fall as one other human being in the world."[16]

But violence remains the single most powerful force in Himes's fictive dynamics. In unusual imagery Himes introduces characters that suffer from visionary terrors embodied in nightmarish forces that beset their psychic life. In the most autobiographical of his novels, *The Third Generation* (1954), Charles Taylor, the protagonist, goes into a drunken catatonic trance when his parents are accosted by a violent pimp, and views the physical reality of the awful scene through the images of a terrifying nightmare, in which "bestial faces fought savagely with gleaming knives, cursing in a thousand tongues, gutting each other with inhuman ecstasy, while the screams of women trampled underneath rose from the dark narrow crevices like anguished wails from hell."[17]

Himes gives his pre-Harlem vision of psychotic violence its richest, most complex form in *The Primitive* (1955). Jesse Robinson not only murders his white girlfriend as a surrogate for the white world that has frustrated him, he also symbolically murders himself and other blacks. In killing her, Jesse ceases to be "innocent" and becomes "human," that is, like whites, who live by expedience and self-interest, and coldly destroy even their own kind. The white man need not lynch, beat, or cheat the African American anymore, Jesse reasons, only wait for him to appropriate white behavior and self-destruct.[18]

The tone of *The Primitive* is mocking and bitter, rather than outraged. More importantly, the violence is dream-like, hallucinatory. It is precisely such hallucinatory violence that Himes depicts in his Harlem novels, except that the detective form he adopts for them forces him into another tonal dimension. Perhaps he cannot take the genre completely seriously, and so cannot imbue his action with the angry fatalism of *The Primitive*. Himes's biographer Edward Margolies puts it well. After his five grimly serious socio-psychological novels, Himes, perhaps,

> did not feel so self-conscious about writing the kind of book he did not have to take seriously. It is important too that he had been living several years in Paris when the first of his detective novels was published. Hence Himes may have geared his thrillers, consciously or subconsciously, to a European readership for whom Harlem was an exotic landscape. There exists, one feels, a peculiar sense of distance in these novels, as if the author stands aside from his material and points to it with a long stick for the edification of his readers. Possibly it is this long range perspective, literary as well as literal, that allows Himes the freedom to laugh at the violence of his vision. For it is humor—resigned, bitter, earthy, slapstick, macabre—that protects author, readers and detectives from the gloom of omnipresent evil.[19]

The comedy, of course, does have a serious point: that black life is inherently absurd, "funny" absurd as well as existentially absurd. "My life itself," he writes, "was so absurd I saw everything as absurd." Consequently, what he stores up in his brief stay in Harlem in the mid-fifties is "all the imagination and observations and absurdities which were destined to make my Harlem novels so widely read."[20] Stephen F. Milliken, writing before the publication of *My Life of Absurdity*, says that Himes does have "links with the unfunny existentialist 'absurd'" of Jean-Paul Sartre and Albert Camus, but he is essentially a comic writer who is very angry, an enraged fantasist.[21] The violence of his Harlem novels is comically, not grimly, hallucinatory, and the badman becomes a violent end man.

THE HARLEM NOVELS

John M. Reilly speaks for the critical consensus when he suggests that Himes expresses the "profound absurdity" of Harlem through "sur-real" scenes of exaggerated violence that verge on the "slap-stick."[22] Himes fragments conventional
reality, surreally magnifies it, and shows it from unusual angles. In *The Crazy Kill*
(1959), for example, his ironic narrator speaks with the dry unemotionality of the
police report, finding time to take note of the details of a murdered man's apparel,
the knife that killed him, the design made by his bloody wound:

> The knife protruded from the jacket just beneath the breast pocket, which was
> adorned with a quarter-inch stripe of white handkerchief. It was a stag-handle
> knife with a push-button opener and handguard, such as used by hunters of
> skin game. Blood made irregular patterns over the jacket, shirt and tie.
> Splotches were on the waxed-paper wrappings of the loaves of bread, and on
> one side of the woven rattan basket. (p. 25)

Early in the first novel of the series, *For Love of Imabelle,* a highly cinematic
scene builds from a perfectly sane opening to a Marx Brothers conclusion. A
white policeman has arrested and brought to the station a whore and her trick,
who insist they are merely mother and son out to take the Harlem air. The
woman objects to being called a whore and "slammed the cop in the face with
her pocketbook." All three of them start scuffling. Other policemen join the fray.
The original innocent scuffle turns into a major battle, as confusingly complicated as a Rube Goldberg contraption. Another black arrestee shouts that the
police are "killin' a colored woman!" and he leaps into the maelstrom of fists,
bodies, legs. Into this uproar come Himes's two black detectives, Coffin Ed
Johnson and Grave Digger Jones. They confidently go into action, first shouting
what will become their trademark commands, "Count off!" and "Straighten
up!" and then shooting their enormous pistols into the ceiling. The deafening
roar freezes every combatant and the two detectives get the astonished prisoners
under control (pp. 60–61).

One of Himes's most effective emblems of Harlem's chaotic absurdity is
his scenes of group violence. In *Blind Man with a Pistol* (1969), a roomful of
people attack each other because of jealousy, venality, and fear.

> Viola stabbed him [Dr. Mubuta] in the back. It wasn't enough to hamper him
> and he wheeled on her in a red-eyed rage and clutched the blade with his bleed-
> ing hand as though it were an icicle, and jerked it from her hand. Her gray eyes
> were stretched in fear and outrage and her pink mouth opened for a scream,
> showing a lot of vein-laced throat. But she never got to scream. He stabbed her
> in the heart, and in the same motion turned and stabbed Van Raff in the head,
> breaking the knife blade on his skull. (p. 62)

This is a representative Himes passage. The language reflects the hard-boiled
toughness of the Dashiell Hammett–Raymond Chandler detective novel. The

third-person narrator is more curious than excited or appalled. He has time to notice, with ridiculous incongruity, that the girl has a pink mouth and a "vein-laced throat." Viola's aborted scream grotesquely parodies the low-comic routine in which a pompous poseur gets a pie in the face. The scene is a microcosm of Himes's Harlem. What goes on in it goes on in Harlem all the time. Greed and brutality reign in a lawless world, run by the Syndicate, in which the legal and the illegal join, with gangsters running city hall and respectable businessmen holding high positions in the Syndicate.

One of the key incidents in the domestic series is a scene of group violence involving the two detectives. In the first domestic novel, *For Love of Imabelle,* Coffin Ed and Grave Digger, out to make an arrest, stumble into an apartment rented by the con men they are after, but they lose control when one of the criminals attacks Coffin Ed. Grave Digger starts shooting, and, in an act that determines his temperament for the rest of the series, someone throws acid in Coffin Ed's face. He does not lose his sight, but his face is conspicuously scarred.

Himes stresses the sheer crazy *commonness* of violence. When Imabelle slashes a man with her knife on a busy Saturday night near the 125th Street subway station, a small crowd gathers to gape at the bleeding man. But "Nobody thought it was unusual. It happened once or twice every night in that station." It differed from other such occasions only in the fact that "no one was dead" (p. 139). The universality of Harlem violence induces in its older inhabitants the same kind of stoicism that southern blacks felt in the face of lynching and Klan raids. "It looks like one death always calls for another," sighs old Mamie Pullen in *Crazy Kill,* when her husband has just died and a young man been murdered. "Been that way ever since I could remember. I guess that's the way God planned it" (p. 34). Harlem's attention does not linger long on any specific violent act, even the most sensational ones. The papers play up a white man's murder for a few days, but before readers can get bored, "Someone else has already been murdered somewhere else."[23] The NYPD Harlem precinct station's reports in *Cotton Comes to Harlem* reflect a normal day in the ghetto:

> Man kills wife with an ax for burning his breakfast pork chop . . . man shoots other man demonstrating a recent shooting he has witnessed . . . man stabs another man for spilling beer on his new suit . . . man kills self in a bar playing Russian roulette with a .32 revolver . . . woman stabs man in stomach fourteen times, no reason given . . . woman scalds neighboring woman with a pot of boiling water for speaking to her husband . . . man arrested for threatening to blow up subway train because he entered wrong station and couldn't get his token back. (p. 20)

Much of the violence that gets on the police report results from impulse—anger, jealousy, spite. The violence committed by con men, dope dealers, or Syndicate thugs for money and power is much more vicious. In *The Big Gold Dream* (1960) three men are involved in a deadly struggle for what turns out to be Confederate money. The fight takes place completely in the dark, the adversaries ignorant of each other's identity. Assailant B attacks assailant A with a hammer, first breaking his arm, then battering his head with the same weapon, leaving him a "bundle of bloody rags" (p. 34). But before he can escape with the money, he himself is attacked by knife-wielding assailant C. The two men fling about insanely in the dark, bedsprings and furniture as much their enemy as each other, until finally assailant B escapes from the room, sobbing with exhaustion and nausea, and makes his getaway, only to die of his wounds later. It is an example of Himes's unsurpassed ability to make his statement through metaphors of action.

Himes's Harlem does not behave according to normal expectations. Its governing physical laws, however, are enforced with the most macabre rigor. In *All Shot Up* (1960), Ed and Digger chase a man on a motorcycle. He is decapitated in traffic by a pane of metal sticking out from a small truck. His body, hostage to the laws of momentum, goes right on riding past a driver who is astounded to see "a man without a head passing on a motorcycle with a sidecar and a stream of steaming red blood flowing back in the wind" (p. 84). The truck driver passes out. Later in the same novel a man is stabbed in the head and the dagger emerges on the other side. All but dead, the wounded man wanders about blindly, grisly evidence that, as Ed and Digger keep pointing out, "Anything can happen in Harlem." If it can happen, it will; even if it can't happen, it will.[24]

One of Himes's favorite metaphors of absurdity is the quasi-comic chase that ends in death, a projection of life in Harlem, an example of the black comic utterance: Life is hell, and then you die. In the opening of *The Real Cool Killers* (1959), a white man runs through Harlem pursued by an ever growing crowd, a Max Sennet chase that ends when the man is felled by a gunshot. Chases are in cars and on foot, right out of the Keystone Kops and Buster Keaton, but etched with a sharp blade of satiric violence, the blues rendered with a saturnine belly laugh. *All Shot Up* starts with a combination of comic brutality and the pursuit of an unruly automobile tire. A tire thief witnesses a scam in which a man dressed as a woman pretends to get run down by a car. The disguised man laughingly picks himself up only to get struck for real by a carload of gangsters. The tire thief, frightened and bewildered, lets go of his tire and then has to take off after it as it rolls for several blocks, right to the feet of two white cops.[25]

Bodies are driven around Harlem unbeknownst to the driver. Corpses fall out of hearses and careless observers out of windows. It is a camp horror show that makes us laugh and grit our teeth at the same time. It is a world, too, in which puns dilute the blood. After we have seen the man on the motorcycle decapitated in *All Shot Up,* his girlfriend, waiting in an apartment, assures a nervous accomplice that the con man is reliable: "He ain't going to lose his head," she says (p. 86). And the preacher who falls out of the window in the first scenes of *The Crazy Kill* drops by a lower window painted with an advertisement:

Straighten Up and Fly Right
Anoint the Love Apples with Father Cupid's Original. . . . (p. 7)

This vein of the absurd culminates in *Blind Man with a Pistol.* The pre–*Blind Man* novels contain more or less straightforward plots in which the crime and its perpetrator become clear by the end of the action, and the two detectives walk away with the formula solution, sometimes traditionally explained, sometimes demonstrated in the action. Each novel, too, ends with a conventional restoration of reason and order, though Himes never gives us any impression that this state of affairs will last very long. Money is recovered and given to a deserving party, families are reunited, orphans find each other and plan to make a life together. Even *Run Man Run* (1959), a dark narrative about a psychotic white New York detective chasing black Jimmy Johnson, concludes with Jimmy recovering from his wounds and the threatening detective dead. *Blind Man* ends on an unanswered question and a paradox. Throughout the novel, Ed and Digger's boss, Lt. Anderson, has been after them to find out who started the riot that is the centerpiece of the action. Finally, they call in with the information that the riot was started by "a blind man with a pistol." The answer of their perplexed superior is made in the context of the absurd: "That don't make any sense." "Sure don't," Digger answers laconically, making the final comment on the entire line of Harlem novels.

Even our experience as readers of *Blind Man* is absurd. In this world, unexplained details float like scraps of paper in a ghost wind, objects appear and disappear, characters emerge and retreat in different costumes and with different names. It is Alice in Wonderland married to Dashiell Hammett. The detectives never solve the central crime, the murder of a white man who has come to Harlem after homosexual prostitutes. The Syndicate attempts to suppress the murder investigation because a discovery of the murderer "might uncover an interracial homosexual scandal that nobody wishes known" (p. 200). So just as there is no answer to the causes of the riot, there is no answer to the murder. Clues galore surface. A man with a fez materializes with the murdered man's pants and as quickly disappears, then reappears in another context as the murderer of Dr. Mubuta, who has no apparent connection with the Syndicate or the interracial homosexual scandal. The "Jesus Baby" whose name the white man gasps out with his dying breath could be several figures, one of whom is killed by a vicious lesbian for a reason never clarified. Links and networks suggest meaning and logic, but they break down, run out, end in blank walls. Some of this confusion is due to the ability of the Syndicate, the white conspiracy of government, business, and gangland, to hide answers. But most of it grows out of the inherent, existential absurdity of Harlem. The entire structure of the novel is incoherent. Down one track runs the mystery of the white man's murder. Down another one runs the action of the three political marches. Himes intermingles them in alternating chapters, as if they are part of the same story. But, like the dual actions in William Faulkner's *The Wild Palms,* they run on tracks governed by different time lapses and are acted out by different characters. Only Ed and Digger appear in both sequences. Himes quotes in his foreword a "Harlem intellectual": "Motherfucking right, it's confusing; it's a gas, baby, you dig." This is the decade of civil rights, ghetto riots, the assassinations of Malcolm X and Martin Luther King, the explosion of street protests and police brutality. *Blind Man* seems to be an attempt to capture the wild chaos of the scene.[26]

As the metaphor for this confusion and the ultimate Harlem absurdity, the "blind man with the pistol" illustrates the disconnectedness of events and the pointlessness of the sector's violence. He has no relationship with the rest of the novel's action. He erupts from the underworld of the subway like some deus ex machina, blundering violently with his own grievances, but also the crazy center of everyone else's. If he causes an effect, the relationship is not logically determined, but random. In the rational world, one object cannot be two contradictory things at the same time. But in the world of *Blind Man,* that is the standard. The blind man is not innocent, but he is not "guilty" either. He does not "cause" the riot, he only starts it by becoming a "victim." He is both victim and cause, both the result of a long list of injustices and a chooser of irrational behavior, both guiltless and responsible. He is absurdity and confusion, a madness verging on the burlesque, mindless retaliation that kills the guilty and innocent alike. In his half-page preface, Himes writes that when he heard the story of the blind man from a friend, he was reminded of "today's news, riots in the ghettos, war in Vietnam, masochistic doings in the Middle East. And then I thought of some of our loudmouthed leaders urging our vulnerable soul brothers on to getting themselves killed, and thought further that all unorganized violence is like a blind man with a pistol." The key word in this statement, perhaps, is *unorganized.* It suggests that organized, or commando, violence might be more effective. But *Blind Man* contains no such violence, nor does it seem possible in Himes's absurd world.

The statement, though, links the violence of the American detective and police novel with African American socio-political and racial concerns. In that linkage they affect each other and produce a different attitude toward violence and the men who practice it than either by itself can entertain. The violence in *Blind Man*—and by implication in all the rest of the "domestic" novels—is not a terrible injustice inflicted upon powerless and unprotected but essentially good victims by racist bigots. Nor is it the grimly approved act of retaliation in which the violent retaliator is excused by the injustices he and his people have for so long meekly suffered. Violence here is brutal and unfeeling, empty even of the hatred that imbues purely racial violence. It is the result of an aimless rage, whose pointless excess operates in terms of a sort of temporary insanity in the environment of an absurd world.

Blind Man expresses the radical contradictions that characterized the civil rights movement and the nation in 1969. Whoever believed that any kind of reasonable orthodoxy could be applied to the protest movements of the period would surely render a distorted picture of the bewilderingly many-sided reality. Those who looked hard at the truth understood that it yielded no explanation. Out of this vision Himes's version of violence emerges, and it indicates a literary maturing. He refuses the orthodoxy of Black Power even though he seems to sympathize with its position. In Himes's world, violence is not a weapon in the hands of noble revolutionaries. It is a wild, untameable power that bespeaks a mordantly comic work of moral and social chaos.

THE BADMEN

No other African American novelist produces so wide a range of violent badmen as Chester Himes. His fertility of invention in this genre is Dickensian. His most conventional badman is probably Johnny Perry, in *The Crazy Kill:* conventional, that is, in the Rudolph Fisher sense. In a crisis he is "hard, strong, tough and unafraid" (p. 29), but he is also man enough to show a "tenderness" to his wife "that seemed startling in a man of his appearance" (p. 30). He wears his Harlem fame well, and is gentle and generous to the small fry who gather around him excitedly, as if he is a celebrity, when he gets out of his shiny Cadillac. He is not bloodthirsty or callous. Gamblers can expect a fair game at his Tia Juana Club. For his tough sensibleness and his deep knowledge of the ways of the ghetto, he is respected by everyone whose respect is valuable. Johnny Perry is a man of principle, "as honest as the day is long" (p. 38). But like all of his kind, he is "hot-headed" by nature, which for Johnny is a good quality rather than a defect. The scar on his rugged forehead comes from a vicious fight with another Georgia chain-gang con, who accused him of cheating at cards. He was sent to the chain gang for killing his mother's common-law husband when the drunkard began to abuse her dangerously. This was the protective reaction of a good son, though, not the brutality of a criminal (p. 38). The thanks he gets for it is his "no good" ma's running off with another man while Johnny is doing his time. When a killing occurs in his neighborhood, appearances require that Johnny be booked, but it is clear that he is not a murderer in the moral sense. Such is his élan, moreover, that he can cooperate with the police, telling them the full truth, without seeming to be a snitch.

We know, too, that we have a good badman when we observe his filial relationship with the novel's moral center, one of the few in the Himes canon. Mamie Pullen is the old southern lady who, with her much-revered husband Joe, brought Johnny from Georgia with them when he needed a solid family foundation. Joe was a Pullman cook for twenty years, and in Harlem became a respectable lodge man, a member of the First Holy Roller Church of Harlem, but also a gambler and the ghetto version of a Mafia don (p. 18). Mamie's devotion to Joe is solidly founded on the old southern values that even Johnny idealizes, and she acts as a source of wisdom and self-control for the erratic and sometimes selfish younger generations. Even Himes's two black detectives defer to her as the carrier of tradition, the voice of respected adult authority from the old neighborhood where the two detectives lived as boys. Mamie's presence draws attention to the contrast between the more stable old days and the morally disintegrating present, in which young men and women on the make, who know and care little about love or loyalty, fight out their jealous rivalries and blackmail and double-cross each other. The conflict between the old and new values in *The Crazy Kill* makes it unusual among the domestic Harlem novels. Money does enter into the plot, but the crime which Coffin Ed Johnson and Grave Digger Jones seek to solve is a murder committed not for money but for the religious values of a loopy zealot, the Reverend Short. The Reverend talks to God, and it is from God that he gets the order to kill Val Haines for "living in sin." The Reverend is crazy, but he is not venal. The novel is thus as much about personal relationships as about crime, as much about feelings as about violence. Besides the question of who killed Val Haines, the plot has to solve the conflict between Johnny Perry and his young wife Dulcy. And just as we finally understand how Val was killed, we watch Johnny and his wife finally acknowledge that they love each other, that they can make their own loving peace, and that Johnny can overcome his jealousy and, like a good gambler, trust his luck.[27]

Those in Himes's other Harlem novels more often rip and tear at each other in filthy streets and broken-down tenements and hotels than, like Johnny Perry and his wife, live in fancy apartments and lovingly make up. His more typical Harlem is surreally rapacious. He vivifies it exultantly, using his writing like a camera that takes in the worst neighborhoods with a single telling shot. The Roger Morris apartments up on Coogan's Bluff may be flashy and provide places for the successful underworld chiefs to live, but down lower live the rest:

> Looking eastward from the towers of Riverside Church, perched among the university buildings on the high banks of the Hudson River, in a valley far below, waves of gray rooftops distort the perspective like the surface of a sea. Below the surface, in the murky waters of fetid tenements, a city of black people who are convulsed in desperate living, like the voracious churning of millions of hungry cannibal fish. Blind mouths eating their own guts. Stick in a hand and draw back a nub.[28]

In other words, the criminal low-life interests Himes more than Harlem's criminal aristocracy, and most of his badmen come from this class. In *For Love of Imabelle* (1957), Himes shows the environment he plans to tap. The Braddock Bar, located in Himes's favorite Harlem neighborhood at 126th Street and 8th Avenue, is crowded with "pinched-faced petty hustlers, sneak thieves, pickpockets, muggers, dope pushers, big rough workingmen in overalls and leather jackets. Everyone looked mean or dangerous" (p. 64). The majority of Himes's badmen do not fit into the classic tradition. For example, most of them are not loners. Like the "cannibal fish" of his description, they come together to carry out their scams. Among the Braddock Bar's dramatis personae, for example, is a gang of petty con men who cut and shoot their way around Harlem, searching for a trunk they think holds some valuable pieces of gold ore. In *The Big Gold Dream* various combinations maneuver to steal the lottery winnings of faith-driven Alberta Wright, including falsely pious Sweet Prophet Brown, who uses his Temple of Wonderful Prayer to cheat her of the money. Another phony preacher, Deke O'Malley, employs a whole cast of accomplices to swindle innocent Harlemites in a "back to Africa" scam in *Cotton Comes to Harlem,* and then to recover a bale of cotton he believes contains the money.

The members of these small and large gangs are mutually distrustful and consistently disloyal. They kill each other at the least sign of a double-cross. Their violence is always driven by venality, which is the most powerful emotion most of them experience. Loyalty, love, and confederacy can never draw them like the magnetism of money. They lack the swagger and arrogance of the classic badman type, the preoccupation with style and rep. These men do not kill each other for honor, status, or dominance. They are after the money. It is capitalism at the lowest common denominator, competition boiled down to its most simply brutal form.[29] Deke O'Malley's two gunmen turn on him when they take over the search for the bale of cotton they think contains money. Slick Jensen kills "Susie" Green when he believes the younger man is trying to cheat him. Jodie and Hank, in *Imabelle,* first kill one of their partners for getting too pushy, then neatly slit the throat of an outsider who interferes with their scam.

These men carry on their relentless pursuit of illicit money with unfeeling savagery. In comparison, Stagolee's killing of Billy Lyon pales. Slick Jenkins and "Susie" Green (*The Big Gold Dream*) beat Alberta Wright and torture her with lighted marijuana butts for information about her money. They leave her painfully bound in a closet, her mouth tightly taped and full of blood. In the same novel, Rufus Wright, Alberta's long-lost husband, wields a hammer against a Jewish used-furniture dealer he thinks has Alberta's money. The Jew goes down and Rufus keeps at him with the hammer until there are only "the soft meaty sounds" of the hammer landing "on the Jew's face and head," which "appeared to be a bundle of bloody rags" (p. 33). Like Bigger Thomas, who is almost overcome with horror as he saws off Mary Dalton's head with his knife in order to shove her into the furnace, Rufus here drops the hammer, and "sat down and put his face in his hands. Inhuman sounds spewed from his mouth. He sounded as though he were crying with uncontrollable terror." Then he quickly recovers, efficiently searches the Jew's body, and, finding nothing, descends some stairs to the Jew's workshop to continue his search. His horror is thus balanced by a cold rationality and all-absorbing avarice, for when he finds in the glimmer of his cigarette lighter the Jew's money, "His body was bent forward. His eyes were focused. His face held an expression of savage greed" (p. 34).

There are plenty of "wannabe" badmen who lack the courage necessary for authentic badness, like the arrogant young punks who fancy themselves tough revolutionaries. They challenge Coffin Ed and Grave Digger in *Blind Man with a Pistol* in the backwashes of the riot. They express their courage in their anti-white rhetoric, calling another youngster "chicken" for refusing to throw rocks at the white police trying to control the riot. When Himes's authentically tough detectives confront them, they sullenly skulk off into the darkened doorways, apparently at the all but imperceptible command of a figure in the shadows. Sheik, in *The Real Cool Killers,* is a somewhat more complex and well-developed "wannabe." He leads a band of youths who masquerade in fake beards and white sheets as "Moslems," fantasizing owning big guns and picking off important people from the fire escape where they smoke courage-inducing marijuana (p. 49). Sheik in particular is a Himesian version of Bigger Thomas. Enraged by the disadvantage at which his race puts him, he takes his anger out on his buddies, dominating them by fear and force, and dreaming of founding a gang like that of Roaring Twenties gangster Dutch Schultz. Sheik is ready to commit violence, but only when it seems safe for him. He works it so that others take the risk, using first his close buddy Choo Choo, then a girl, as shields when the police come for him. And while he does possess a kind of feral courage, it is hard not to feel that Himes shares the police chief's scornful summing up of Sheik's badness: "you call yourself the Sheik, the big gang leader. You're just a cheap tinhorn punk, yellow to the core," hiding "behind an innocent little girl" (p. 137).

Himes specializes in "cheap tinhorn punk[s]." Ready Belcher, also in *The Real Cool Killers,* is, according to the old janitor of the brothel out of which Ready works, "just a halfass pimp" (p. 83). But he carries a knife, and "An old razor scar cut a purple ridge from the lobe of his left ear to the tip of his chin," indicating his involvement in conventional street violence. "[W]ith pockmarked skin a dirty shade of black" and only one good "reddish brown" eye (p. 81), Ready seems intrinsically unsavory, just the type to supply a white pervert with young black schoolgirls for s/m sex. But Ready is a creampuff badman who is (understandably) frightened by Grave Digger Jones. "You got that big pistol," he tells Digger, "and you mad at everybody and talkin' 'bout killin' me and all that. Enough to make anybody scared" (p. 101). Chink Charlie, in *The Crazy Kill,* also pretends to toughness, that of the coward who resents those who are stronger, braver, and more successful. A cheaply handsome man, he extracts money from women, blackmailing the attractive wife of Johnny Perry. His fatuous weakness is expressed when he believes he is going to get $10,000 in the blackmail scheme. "All his life he'd wanted to be a big shot, and now was his chance if he played his cards right" (p. 139). But his vanity makes him vulnerable to the woman he has blackmailed. She traps and Johnny kills him.

That violent blacks are little different from violent whites in the pursuit of illicit money Himes makes clear by incorporating several white thugs in his novels. In *All Shot Up,* a white man leads the effort to steal the sizeable campaign stash of a Harlem politician. He has both black and white confederates. They pointlessly hit a black man—engaged in his own con—with their car, impaling him on a protrusion from a wall, and the white leader, as much given to brutality as Slick Jensen, tortures the politician they kidnap in an unsuccessful effort to force him to reveal the whereabouts of the money. Unlike the "tinhorn punks," the black politico, shot painfully in the knee in the course of his capture, refuses to give in. "He was like a wounded tiger, silent, crippled, but still as dangerous a killer as the jungle ever saw" (p. 149). Less fierce and without the nobility of the wounded tiger, one of the white gunmen in *The Heat's On* is a mindless hophead with a loose pistol. In his search for a packet of illegal drugs, he shoots Grave Digger Jones from ambush, sending the detective to the hospital and removing him from the action. In the end, he is killed by Digger's partner, Coffin Ed.

The violence blacks commit in Himes's novels, and their viciousness, disqualifies them for the "poor victim" role seen in the work of so many black protest writers, a role that excused blacks "all their sins and major faults." Himes saw his first novel, *For Love of Imabelle,* and by extrapolation those that followed, as perhaps "an unconscious protest against soul brothers" who claimed such an excuse. "Black victims of crime and criminals might be foolish and harebrained, but the soul brother criminals were as vicious, cruel and dangerous as any other criminals."[30] In other words, he avoids the "psychoanalytical" interpretation of his badmen's violence as displaced rage, anger the violent man takes out on easier black targets when he is frustrated by racist oppression. This was the explanation given for the high incidence of black violence a couple of decades earlier by such sociologists as John Dollard and Hortense Powdermaker. Violent criminals, Himes contends, are all responsible for their actions, blacks as well as whites.[31]

Indeed, at times a reader could be forgiven for thinking that Himes has established a metaphysics of punishment for these violent people, for they are caught in an ineluctable round of death. They kill and are killed, as if the one causes the other. In *Imabelle,* Jodie kills both his confederate and another man in pursuit of a trunk they think contains money, then he himself gets his arm chopped off by a whorehouse madam and, with Hank, is shot dead by Ed and Grave Digger. It is as if some hidden force for justice is at work. But the total picture suggests merely chance and chaos and the assumption that violent acts bring violent ends rather than a system of moral retribution. Gus Parsons, Jodie's partner in crime, commits his own share of violence, but he is killed by a stray bullet in the same melee in which Coffin Ed is hit with the acid. Indeed, most of the time, the killing is like a tennis game, each death a lob over the net that is returned. In *The Heat's On,* for example, Sister Heavenly has, like most of the other characters, gone after the heroin that is the object of all the killing in the novel. As Ginny approaches mobster Benny Mason to give him a bag holding the drugs she has collected for him, Sister Heavenly calls her into a dark doorway and casually and smoothly stabs her, takes the bag, and continues walking in the same direction. When Benny's chauffeur confronts her for the dope, "Without turning her body or slackening her pace, she raised the pistol and pumped four dumdum bullets into the chauffeur's body." With the ball in his court, so to speak, Benny in turn puts a bullet into her brain. Her last thought shows an ironic, fatalistic gallantry: "Well now, ain't this lovely?" (pp. 197–99). In a climate of death, even those who commit no violence themselves get caught in the wildfires that periodically sweep the terrain.

COFFIN ED AND GRAVE DIGGER

Such wildfires are all but unpreventable in the social and economic conditions that prevail in Harlem, and, once alight, they are nearly impossible to contain. This is where Himes's two black detectives come into the picture, Coffin Ed Johnson and Grave Digger Jones, whose presence in all eight novels contributes to the series's coherence. Coffin Ed and Grave Digger, working out of the Harlem precinct station of the NYPD, fight the violence that puts all Harlemites in jeopardy with violence of their own. Every one of the eight novels demonstrates their investigative methods: pistol-whipping suspects or witnesses, knocking them around, socking them in the stomach, slapping them off bar stools, or even shooting them. Himes manipulates his criminal cast of characters so that we side with the two detectives, though we may be shocked by their tactics. Most of those on the short end of their strategies of persuasion are guilty of nefarious doings, slimy behavior, fraud, theft, or violence of their own. There is a certain justice in giving them what we know they deserve without having to consider their civil rights, since our sense of fairness tells us they are not worthy of such protection. More importantly, if Ed and Digger are to deal with the Harlem underworld, their authority needs to come from themselves as well as the institution of the NYPD. Their effectiveness as cops in black Harlem depends upon their keeping the respect of the community they protect, and keeping that respect requires the violence for which they are renowned. "These colored hoodlums," thinks Grave Digger in *Cotton Comes to Harlem,* "had no respect for colored cops unless you beat it into them or blew them away" (p. 43).

The letter of the law is perhaps not safe in the hands of two such cops, but justice is. Knowing they are on the "right side," Ed and Digger can sidestep the law in order to make justice prevail. They let people go who are guilty and make sure with extra-legal means that other guilty parties are apprehended and punished. They dispense sentences and executions in the name of fairness to the small and powerless. In *The Real Cool Killers* they set free the real murderer of a white man because (1) the white man deserved to be killed; (2) the police already have the man they believe was the killer, but he is dead; and (3) the girl who really did the killing deserves a new start in life.[32] In *Cotton Comes to Harlem,* they threaten a guilty white man with newspaper publicity that could ruin him: "When we get through, no jury would dare acquit you; and no governor would dare pardon you" (p. 214). In the same novel, Ed and Digger steal back the money stolen from the Back to Africa movement and return it to the small contributors. And in *All Shot Up* (1960), they appropriate stolen money and donate it to a Harlem boys' club. The detectives dispense homespun justice, bypass the rules of civil rights that too often protect the criminal, and "protect the downtrodden poor of Harlem from their worst exploiters, black and white."[33] They are, in a sense, what Tony Hilfer calls a Jim Thompson character, the superego "running wild, having appropriated the anarchic comic energy of the id."[34]

Morally, of course, this is a dangerous position to take, and the two detectives understand its danger. They continually tell themselves and each other that they are not gods to sit in judgment of others. "We're cops . . . not judges," says Grave Digger in *Cotton Comes to Harlem* (p. 136). But their theory of crime-fighting calls for them to be judges, to take upon themselves the authority to decide who the criminals are and what treatment they deserve. And they often feel unjustly and mistakenly restrained by the strong 1960s current of sympathy for "victims" of police violence as opposed to the victims of criminals. When they fatally injure a slimy small-time hood who pushes dope to the youngsters on the street in *The Heat's On,* negative newspaper publicity forces their temporary suspension. It is the politics of appearance, and their lieutenant says by way of apology that the newspapers "are on one of their periodic humanitarian kicks," with the implication that not only is this public humanitarianism phony, but it goes the wrong way. "Yeah," says Digger bitterly, "humanitarian. . . . It's all right to kill a few colored people for trying to get their children an education [referring to the violence against civil rights protesters], but don't hurt a motherraping white punk for selling dope" (pp. 72–73). Higher-ups in the NYPD see the detectives' violence as a public relations problem. Often, in an intentionally ironic reversal of the frequent complaints of white "police brutality" by young black and white revolutionaries during the sixties, they suspend these black policemen for going beyond the limits of political correctness and evoking public ire. But the white police officers nearest the street action understand Ed and Digger, knowing "that colored cops had to be tough in Harlem to get the respect of colored hoodlums."[35]

Himes sets forth the paradox of the good cop who does bad things. Ed and Digger could turn into racist thugs like Matt Walker, the sinister white cop in *Run Man Run,* for their violence paradoxically lies close to fascism and racism, of which, indeed, one character accuses them. Himes even suggests in *The Heat's On* that his two black detectives are little different from the criminals they set out to bring to justice: They are scarred like any other "colored street fighter. Grave Digger's [face] was full of lumps where felons had hit him from time to time with various weapons; while Coffin Ed's was a patchwork of scars where skin had been grafted over the burns left by acid thrown into his face" (p. 32). Like Dashiell Hammett's Continental Op and Chandler's Philip Marlowe, Ed and Digger are physically and temperamentally tainted by the job they do. Morally incorruptible they may be,[36] but their inclination to pistol-whip confessions out of unarmed men and shoot upon the least provocation links them with the American vigilante who cannot wait for the court. In one sense, they are aligned with the conservative right, whose cry for "law and order" urged summary punishment of the accused rather than a judicious use of the courts. At the same time, "law and order" struck many as code words for dealing with those minorities challenging accepted values and seeking to upset the sanctions that protected whites from blacks. From the "law and order" viewpoint, the arrest of a black man or woman was tantamount to proof of guilt, and rough physical treatment by law officers was justified by the nature of the criminal. In his detective stories, Himes seems to confirm the right's perception of the black community as a place permeated with violence and verging on anarchy. But he differs on the reasons for it. The right hinted that blacks as a group lacked the moral fiber to live peaceably with each other. Ed and Digger claim that economic conditions deliberately created by whites warp black personalities, and violence is blacks' means of adaptation.

Their violence is at the core of the two cops' ambiguous characters. A black cop confronts the racially abused Harlemite with a contradiction, a black man supporting white law; not only supporting it, but beating black heads for it. But that is just the point for Himes. His stated aim was "to make the detectives the heroes" of the domestic novels. He says they are not traitors to their community for working for the "establishment," because they are not "reactionary, fascistminded, and very unlikeable," like "Most genuine black detectives are." They "represent the kind of detectives that should exist, living in the community, knowing the people, enforcing the law, dealing humanely with everyone."[37] They more than anyone understand the extent of criminality in Harlem and know that white law enforcement cannot be trusted to do what is good for the community. Himes never takes the race position or puts forward the extreme cultural nationalist or black aesthetic view that whatever is black is good. Harlem produces black criminals who are cruel, greedy, and self-interested, resorting to the most grotesque violence for the worst aims. Due process and over-fastidious observance of individual rights do not work with these types. Coffin Ed and Grave Digger bring the kind of tough love to the ghetto that white law withholds, a concern for a people beset by destructive forces from within their community as well as from without. Himes brings us back to the old thesis that the good sometimes requires the deployment of the bad, that violence sometimes requires violence to quell it. Blacks have struggled with this moral conflict for generations.

Ed and Digger's conviction that they must use violence against the violent in order to retain the respect of Harlem is often reinforced by Himes's references to the awe felt by the entire black community for the two detectives. Not only that, what blacks would object to in a white cop they approve of in black Ed and Digger, admire to the point of mythologizing. In the eyes of black Harlem, Ed and Digger are almost bigger than life. They "had pistols, and everyone in Harlem knew them as the 'Mens.'"[38] They have learned to use the power of the white man, have shown themselves to be "men," who can terrify even the most manly Harlemite and not only get away with it, but be regarded as heroes while doing it. The myth that surrounds them resembles the myth of the great ballad badmen. It emphasizes their demandingness, not their justice, and it is phrased in hyperbole befitting a stand-up comedian, the sort of language used by straitened people with each other when they are proud of the difficulties they survive: "Coffin Ed had killed a man for breaking wind. Grave Digger had shot both eyes out of a man who was holding a loaded automatic. The story was in Harlem that these two black detectives would kill a dead man in his coffin if he so much as moved."[39] The two men behave like drill instructors at a Marine boot camp— "Count off!" Ed shouts to a crowd gathered on the street. "Straighten up!" says Digger. And they pull their huge .38 pistols and fire into the air or ceiling. That is one of Himes's most amusing gambits: to picture the ceiling of the Harlem precinct station as full of bullet holes made by their .38s. When Ed and Digger apply their no-nonsense power to incorrigible groups of Harlemites determined to march or fight on the streets, white policemen regard them with the same awe as do their own black people.

The violence with which Ed and Digger pursue their version of justice, finally, links them to the whole black badman tradition. Raymond Nelson makes a case for Coffin Ed and Grave Digger being updated versions of the "bad nigger." Cast in the mold of the "bad nigger," Nelson argues, their behavior is ratified by culture and tradition, which gives them "the moral authority they exercise." "They are Nat Turners or Stackalees brought up to date and moved to the city, contemporary avatars of one of the stubbornly pervasive motifs in Black American culture." Coffin Ed and Grave Digger exude the "raw personal power" traditionally associated with this figure, the personal power with which he "defies his world." Since the two detectives are as likely to beat up on the innocent as the guilty in their role as "bad niggers," they may seem "improbable (or undesirable) models for humanity." But the figure to which Nelson says they are related "is valuable as a symbol of defiance, strength, and masculinity to a community that has been forced to learn, or at least to sham, weakness and compliance. As 'bad niggers' Coffin Ed and Grave Digger are part of the continuing evolution of a black hero, and are thus studies in cultural lore rather than examples of individual character."[40]

Himes does make explicit that he sees his cops as heroes. That he may have borrowed from the badman/"bad nigger" tradition seems more than plausible. If he has tapped into the collective black mind of the sixties, he reflects an extension from the Harlem Renaissance in the way the "bad nigger" is regarded in the African American community. Like Fisher's "Shine" Jones, this figure can be tough but he can also be on the side of the law, and this changes profoundly the whole badman equation. That is why I would modify Nelson's otherwise useful and insightful generalization. One of the defining features of the black badman, whether we call him a "bad nigger" or something else, has always been his defiance of the white law. The label "bad nigger" or badman denotes a lawbreaker. Ed and Digger do not break the law in the same way the badman breaks the law. Indeed, they find in the white law a source of protection for the weak from the real, predatory "bad niggers" that threaten them. What Himes does show through his two detectives is a basis upon which white law can be used to protect blacks in ways that would have been impossible before the onset of the civil rights movement. The concept of a black detective would have been a sort of oxymoron. From his vantage point in the French *Série Noire,* the French detective series for which Marcel Duhamel recruited Himes to write his Harlem novels, he makes possible the African American detective.[41]

If Coffin Ed and Grave Digger have an element of the violent badman in them, it is anger, uniquely Himesian anger. Indeed, Himes seems in part to use the domestic novels not only as a study in "cultural lore," as Raymond Nelson suggests, but also as a vehicle for exploring and perhaps exorcising his own excessive rage. Johnny Perry, the sympathetic badman of *The Crazy Kill,* is, as I say above, "hot-headed." The principal cause of his hair-trigger temper, though, is not his natural temperament but the injury he received in his chain-gang fight. A silver plate had to be set into his skull, and the narrator regularly attributes Johnny's violent temper to the pressure of the plate when he is in crisis. This injury figures prominently in his killing Chink Charlie when he thinks Charlie has been making love to Johnny's wife. In an almost psychotic rage, Johnny blacks out while he empties his pistol into Charlie and then beats him bloody (pp. 142–43). Nearly all Himes's characters, not just those in the domestic novels, black out in this way at a point of high rage. It is worth repeating, with respect to his Harlem stories, that this rage is often existential as well as racial, perhaps more the former than the latter. Johnny's metal plate is as much a metaphor for anger as a literal cause of it.

Johnny's temper, with its exogenous origin, runs parallel to that of Coffin Ed. The defining experience of Ed's life as one of Himes's detectives is getting his face burned with acid in the first novel of the series. The incident is mentioned in every subsequent novel, usually in connection with Ed's violent reactions to threatening gestures, however small, from detainees. "Ever since the hoodlum had thrown acid into his face, Coffin Ed had had no tolerance for crooks. He was too quick to blow up and too dangerous for safety in his sudden rages."⁴² In *The Real Cool Killers,* one of the young punks the detectives have detained farts at Ed. Ed kicks him. Simultaneously, another one throws perfume at Ed in contempt. Ed thinks it is acid and in a reflex action, with the "roar of blood in his head," shoots the youngster dead (p. 19). The story circulates and becomes a legend that Ed shoots people merely for farting. White cops use it to needle him; Harlemites use it as an illustration of his touchiness. Himes says that the acid-throwing is what turns Ed "into a psychopath. People should understand about that."⁴³ Digger, as Stephen Milliken points out, "often has to restrain him," feeling guilty for not having protected Ed in that fateful skirmish.⁴⁴

Digger, too, is given to rages that block his reason. When, in *The Real Cool Killers,* he learns that a small-time pimp has withheld crucial information from him, he strikes the man viciously on the head with his pistol. "The muscles were corded in his rage-swollen neck and his face was distorted with violence" (p. 130). But he is more often the one who stays in control, and the timbre of his voice shows it. When he is angered, in situation after situation, he speaks in a "thick, cotton-dry voice," always a symptom that he is restraining great rage.⁴⁵ It is mainly the criminals who hurt the little people that drive the two men to uncontrollable wrath. They have infinite patience with and deep understanding for the innocents who get caught up in the tangles of callous violence. Digger claims that Ed "was never rough on anybody in the right."⁴⁶ There is thus a kind of clinical as well as cultural element in Himes's treatment of the violent man in the Harlem of the fifties and sixties. His figures are both intensely personal and broadly cultural, linked not only with the traditional badman of the turn-of-the-century ballad and the toast narratives of the decades after World War I but also with the literary badmen of Rudolph Fisher or the ghetto escapees of the bildungsroman. In the end, they are unique creations of a mind that was more receptive to the culture of the ghetto, and freer of the politics of the period, than were many of his contemporaries.

8

A 'Toast' Novel

Pimps, Hoodlums, and Hit Men

THE STRUGGLE BETWEEN THE "HIP" AND THE "LAME"

In the late sixties and early seventies, a cohort of black novelists seems to have deliberately set out to write the "toast" into a new form of fiction. It was a genre not destined for either mainstream popularity or critical acclaim. But it took on the world of the street player with gusto. The novels that make up this genre are virtually long prose toasts, with literary and thematic ties to the old badman ballad as well. They cross the ghetto of Chester Himes with that of Toledo Slim and Broadway Sam, depicting an inner city in which crime is everyday business and the most violent men are the most effective at carrying out business. They fuse the middle-class literate tradition and the oral folk tradition, mixing the two sets of values, simultaneously romanticizing and criticizing the man of violence. He is sometimes a tragic figure, stoically resigned to his fall, other times an instrument of protest, insisting that his violent behavior is caused by the unfairness of an oppressive system.

The characters in this genre struggle not for mental growth or identity but for power and status, simplified primitive versions of the values by which respectable society lives. In this world those values are not softened by the courtesies of business protocol or social civility that keep mainstream strivers from doing overt physical harm to their competitors. The toast novel characters never pretend that humanity is more important than power. Yet their struggles are set against a backdrop of mainstream morality. They are aware that their violent activities, like those of the old ballad badmen, lead either to jail or to death, and that those activities mark them as pariahs in the larger society outside the ghetto. These are the people who stay in the ghetto and take up its ways rather than try to get out. They take us into the folkways of the system that mainstream culture regards with distaste and alarm.

Nathan C. Heard's *Howard Street* (1968) is essentially the first such novel. In fact, Heard demonstrates his closeness to the toast genre with his epigraph:

A man can't fool with the golden rule
in a game that don't play fair.

The phrase occurs in a toast called "The Tropics."[1] Heard avoids the "toast" label, preferring to call it "a doggerel hip poem." Heard had himself been a street player of sorts, spending time in the New Jersey State Prison at Trenton, and he brings the toast explicitly into his last novel, *House of Slammers* (1983), in which an inmate recites "Honky Tonk Bud" to an appreciative prison audience and promises to give them "Mexicali Rose" later.[2] In *Howard Street,* Heard fashions Lonnie "Hip" Ritchwood as a kind of Honky Tonk Bud small-time hustler, a violent junkie, but with a cool style. It is less his badness at issue, though, than a conflict involving the code of the ghetto and the possibility of escaping to the suburbs and law-abiding respectability. Like some of the bildungsroman writers, Heard can envision a character who prefers the player's life of the ghetto to the uneventful life of the respectable suburbs, in which case the ghetto can be the honorable choice. Heard views the violence of the ghetto, not necessarily as a symptom of decay and degeneracy, but as a means of survival and success, legitimated by the conditions of The Life. Not that, as a novelist, he condones violence. He simply projects it as his characters see it, dispassionately, amorally. He gives us glimpses of that other life, where families reside securely in nonviolent neighborhoods, pursuing attainable goals, their minds undistorted by fear, their bodies unscarred by drugs or physical abuse, moving freely in their world without harassment by police. Hints of resentment that the ghetto dweller is denied such a life show through. And there is always the background dream that some day the street player will hit it big and forever insulate himself from the street's hazards. But staying can also mean holding on to an honor and beauty that one abandons when leaving to abide by the straight conventions of the middle class.

Heard compresses the essence of the black ghetto into two blocks of Howard Street in Newark, New Jersey. There the violent struggle for power and status goes on at all levels. Youngsters mug drunks and rape women for fun. Police beat up their prisoners and suspects. Hip Ritchwood achieves his reputation by "pulling" the beauteous whore Gypsy Pearl Dupree from her boyfriend, defeating him in an epic public brawl. This means, though, that he must maintain his reputation by showing himself as a consistently credible threat to any competitor or balky trick refusing to pay Gypsy for her services. His success also depends upon dominating his whore, at first with the handsome attractiveness that makes her love him, then by forcing her submission with his fists, beating her for embarrassing him in front of friends, and violently forcing her into sex when his anger shifts to lust.

Those who most effectively employ violence dominate those who are too weak or frightened to resist. Success, measured in dollars, is conspicuously displayed. On Howard Street "anything that ain't showing" makes no impression. Howard Streeters wear themselves out—"hard, hard living, all passion, no love, not for each other and not for themselves."[3] In the struggle on Howard Street, there is no clear virtue or vice, and no clear victory, only overlapping and competitive moral systems. Heard does not suggest that the ghetto, even at its best, can compete equally with the straight world of clean dwellings, safe neighborhoods, legal and regular incomes, and genuine concern for each other. He does show that the ghetto has its own mysterious pull and moral code.

The issue is played out between Hip Ritchwood, Gypsy Pearl, and Hip's brother Franchot, who resides in the ghetto but holds down a responsible job, pays his bills, and contemplates marriage. With the evangelistic fervor of the respectable straight, Franchot tries to persuade Hip and Gypsy Pearl to give up their street-life ways, begging Gypsy to abandon prostitution, leave Hip, and marry him. Gypsy herself is receptive to that proposition, feeling that, married to Franchot, she could, for the first time, "become a woman, full-grown and complete" (p. 200). But the magnet of Howard Street and the mutual repulsion of the two moral systems are too powerful. Not only does Hip prefer his dope habit, he regards himself as a rebel, exposing the hypocrisy of the straight world with his own behavior, which, though it may be illegal, at least does not pretend a pious superiority. Indeed, Heard suggests that Franchot is at least partially blind to his own phoniness. Thinking he can "save" Gypsy Pearl, he fails to see he is really trying to "pull" her from Hip, attempting the same power play that Hip used on Gypsy's former boyfriend. Similarly, he demands from Gypsy a submission every bit as total as the pimp requires of the whore, though he is less brutal in his manner. Thus, when Gypsy tries to protect Hip from the consequences of a drug arrest, Franchot makes the situation a test of her love for him. He demands that she renounce Hip and the world he represents by withdrawing her help, replacing the street code with Franchot's. But that would compel her to betray her own integrity, the values on which she was raised. Heard makes clear that he admires Gypsy Pearl, that Franchot behaves both hypocritically and childishly. The ghetto whore rises above the self-righteousness of straight respectability. That self-righteousness holds "no forgiveness for her." But she has no regrets. More tolerant than Franchot, she reflects that "He had his values and she had hers." "She couldn't live his life, but she could appreciate it, perhaps even more than he himself" (p. 256). "We can't fool around in their league and they ain't got no business in ours" (p. 165), as a Howard Street bartender puts it. There can be no fusion of these two worlds. They have no language in common, no shared viewpoint. The Howard Streeters seem to understand this more clearly than the "lames." This moral expansiveness radiates from Gypsy Pearl as, in the last image of the book, she leaves Franchot and walks "beautifully into the bar" (p. 256).

THE "HIP" VICTORIOUS

In the late sixties and early seventies, the issue of escaping from the ghetto disappears from the toast novel and the ghetto becomes a focus of attention in its own right. It is not simply that it is the site of aberrant behavior or of impossible conditions that need to be addressed by our entire society, but that for all its squalor and violence, it holds a certain kind of glamor, embodying what white *Wall Street Journal* reporter Ron Suskind calls the "imprimatur of coolness."[4] The toast novels I discuss in this chapter have made their contribution to this imprimatur, turning what might be called the "cool of badness" into a literary cult that coincides with the end of the civil rights movement and the emergence of Black Power at the end of the sixties. This is also the period when the escape to a straight life becomes, for those left behind, all but impossible. Calling the sometimes brutish ghetto world cool, these novelists make a virtue of necessity, switching attention from the struggle to join middle-class prosperity to making it in the ghetto on ghetto terms. When escape to the middle-class neighborhood is closed off, and the ghetto dwellers find themselves limited to the resources of the street for self-fulfillment, the violence increases in volume and viciousness, the novelists depict it more unfeelingly and in greater and bloodier detail, and the man of violence takes center stage. Violence is natural to the habitat, and the black male employs it as one of the tools of his work as a man. If, though, it is a feature of ghetto cool, it is also a source of ghetto squalor, and the toast novelists make an effort to dramatize this conflict.

The novels that begin to appear in the late 1960s are largely about the northern inner city that President Lyndon Johnson's mid-sixties "war on poverty" was designed to reach. The "war" Johnson envisioned sought, as Nicholas Lemann describes it, to "empower" the ghetto dweller to become more like white Americans of the middle class through education and employment. Johnson's program was intended to clear the ghettos of poverty and crime and to arrest their physical deterioration. The actual outcome was quite different. The "war" created jobs in administering the various new programs, and those jobs were filled with already-educated African Americans. This "empowered" a new black middle class. But instead of remaining in the ghetto and strengthening its tax base and its social infrastructure, these government employees moved out. This occurred, says Lemann, "in black city slums all over the country: the messy racial transition [from southern rural sharecropper to northern urban unemployed], the overcrowding, the deterioration of education, law enforcement, and other essential institutions, and then the exodus of the black middle class and the descent into real disorganization." The war on poverty inadvertently intensified this process, and while it helped create a whole new group of economically solvent African Americans, it also helped accelerate the disintegration of the ghetto. Between 1966 and 1974, the black unemployment rate rose, school enrollment stayed flat, the number of single mothers on welfare increased, and "the arrest rate for black males between the ages of thirteen and thirty-nine rose by 49 per cent."[5]

The ghetto riots that erupted in the sixties and the increasing rate of violent crime were the result of the social, political, and economic powerlessness of the ghetto dweller that Lemann speaks of. The violence became a social problem to be solved and the psychological establishment weighed in with explanations and solutions. The human being, wrote Erich Fromm, "can escape the unbearable sense of vital impotence and nothingness only by affirming himself in the act of destruction of the life that he is unable to create."[6] Rollo May brings the argument more specifically to bear upon African Americans in the ghetto: "violence has its breeding ground in impotence and apathy. . . . Deeds of violence in our society are performed largely by those trying to establish their self-esteem, to defend their self-image, and to demonstrate that they, too, are significant." African Americans, May insists, are "the most ready illustration" of a whole people "placed in a situation where significance becomes almost impossible to achieve." First in economic, then in psychological slavery, they were permitted to become only servants or entertainers. "If the other phases of behavior are blocked, then explosion into violence may be the only way individuals or groups can get release from unbearable tension and achieve a sense of significance."[7]

But like most commentators on ghetto violence in these years, especially white ones, May and Fromm are as much concerned about the epidemic of riots in the ghetto during the decade of the sixties as about the culture of violence that black writers perceive as a way of life. Black psychologist Kenneth B. Clark best captures the sensibility driving the toast novelist. Most ghetto blacks, he says, live powerlessly on the fringes of white affluence. They want the same things as whites—the prestige and material goods that come with money. Deprived of the status symbols paraded before them on television, in the movies, on radio, in newspapers and magazines, they create their own forms in "the empty status, bombast, and show of the ghetto world" and engage in a "desperate struggle" to acquire them.[8] The toast novelists dramatize this struggle, updating into the seventies the inner city described by Chester Himes, by Wright, Ellison, Baldwin, and the rest of the bildungsroman novelists. They capture the images through which the ghetto player feels himself fulfilled, and in those images they create a kind of counter-system mythology.

The myth in which the collective ghetto badman participates is not a success story. It is a tale of violence and crime, and its hero has courage and stamina, and meets the exigencies of his world on its own harsh terms. He is an unbridled individual carrying on a lonely but flamboyant struggle for ascendancy within an unforgiving system. The dominant image is of the "black renegade," "walking tall" and striving against a perilous world. As Greg Goode puts it, this figure goes for a starring role, seeks to master the dangerous games of betrayal, vengeance, and dominance.[9] The hero plays his role out from a script that predetermines his fate: death, prison, replacement by a younger and stronger player. The hero's experience is painted with a brush of moral ambiguity. We are asked to admire and disapprove of these aggressive men at the same time, to be impressed by their willingness to commit violence but not to condone it. We are troubled by how they degrade the weak and hold them in contempt, but are struck by their own resigned acceptance of ghetto justice when they are its victims. It is a classic American dilemma: our fascination with the unprincipled titan, the antisocial Gargantua.

Most of the toast novels come from Holloway House, a Los Angeles publishing company whose list is made up largely of ethnic fiction, with works by African American writers in the majority. Holloway House, a Euro-American rather than an African American enterprise, started business in the early sixties. It provided then—and provides still—an outlet for aspiring black writers who could not get a reading in the mainstream commercial publishing world, especially those writers who turned out exploitative narratives made up of violence, sex, and action. In the late sixties Holloway began dubbing some of its publications "black experience" works. The label covered a wide variety of stories—about ghetto dope rings and the growth of drug addiction among blacks, revolts against white dominance in small southern towns, hugely wealthy black studs with fortified mansions in the desert outside Las Vegas, groups of men who hang around bars and remember their past.[10] Holloway novels belonging to the badman genre also fall within its more inclusive label, and these are the ones that are relevant to my discussion. Robert Beck (writing as Iceberg Slim), Donald Goines, Joseph (sometimes "Joe") Nazel, Odie Hawkins, James-Howard Readus, Charlie Avery Harris, Laurie Miles, Cole Riley, and Jerome Dyson Wright—these writers by no means exhaust the Holloway roster, but they are responsible for the large majority of the works I discuss. They are not "mainstream" writers, but they have acquired a wide black readership and can be seen as the purveyors of one side of the popular African American perception of the ghetto. They constitute a kind of cultural underground, well known to their fans, but not part of the pop domain that belongs to eighties and nineties rap groups like Run-DMC, Kool G Rap, or 2 Live Crew, whose lyrics bear many resemblances to the language and world these novelists depict.

Robert Beck inaugurated the Holloway version of the toast novel with *Trick Baby* in 1967, and became one of the first popular black authors made successful by a nearly exclusively African American readership.[11] Donald Goines, who was himself stimulated to write after reading Beck's work, and whose first novel, *Dopefiend*, appeared in 1971, has been even more popular. His sixteen titles, all still in print, have sold in the millions. Both Beck and Goines write from personal experience, Beck as a successful Chicago pimp before he went straight and began to write about the South Side ghetto; Goines as a denizen of the Detroit inner city where he ran the streets as a youngster, served time in jail for various crimes, and became a dope addict when he was in the army in Korea. Even after he acquired some respectability with his writing, married, and had children, he maintained his connections with his old environment. Nor could he ever break the dope habit. Perhaps that habit led to his death, for he was shot mysteriously by two white men as he worked on *Inner City Hoodlum* (1975) in his own home. His murderers have never been found.[12]

ANGER OVER WHITE RACISM

The dramatis personae of this genre are the pimps and prostitutes, the dope addicts and drug pushers, the hit men, the syndicate dealers, the macking (pimping) gangsters that people the mythic streets. Black cops join with white cops in investigating crime, and occasional private investigators take center stage. But whoever takes the leading role, the action focuses upon the black "players" who rise and fall in the violent contest for status, power, and wealth. The sides in this struggle have nothing to do with morality or the traditional conventions of racial propaganda, in which blacks are depicted as innocent victims of white crimes that justify violent retaliation. Chester Himes made it possible for black police, as well as white, to shoot or pistol-whip a black suspect. In these toast novels, white police are shown feeling as much sympathy for ghetto victims as black police do. The most vicious violence goes on between the criminals themselves—white and black, Hispanic and black, black and black. But for those novelists who consider the reasons behind the violence, racial awareness and social protest do sometimes play a part. The ghetto is what it is, they say, because of white racism, and they show blacks as victims of that racism, even though the point is not central to their plots. Reflecting much of the official opinion of those who studied the ghettoes and the poor in America, they blame the system—the white establishment—for the lack of jobs, the filthy neighborhoods, and the proliferation of crime.

This critique is expressed partly in a growing hostility toward white liberals. In *Trick Baby* (1967), Iceberg Slim suggests that the whites who pretend to help and to be concerned for ghetto blacks in reality are pursuing a broader plan to keep blacks down, trying to make America look free by admitting a few blacks to a few low-order privileges. Those blacks who are admitted to the club thus betray their race out of fear of being thrown back down into the ghetto.[13] Beck attacks the capitalist class across the board, saving a special venom for the spoiled children of the grasping industrialists who, he says, are responsible for the limits within which blacks are forced to live. They heartlessly confine the powerless black laborer in dangerous low-level jobs whites refuse to do themselves.[14] Similarly, James-Howard Readus has one of his narrators angrily describe how white judges and politicians come into the ghetto and promise improvements during the elections, then disappear when they have won with black votes. The result is the inner city, "typical of all big cities in the North; bordered, surrounded, or within the mi[d]st of black poverty, despair, and the cold corruption of hopeless souls."[15] Nearly every toast novelist includes at least one propagandistic description of the ghetto. Charlie Avery Harris's portrait of his Baltimore ghetto is typical: "a rat-and-garbage-infested alley" whose "back yards were cluttered with rags, paper, glass, wood, junk cars, dead cats and hungry dogs." The children who live in this filth have "but one chance in life; to follow in their father's footsteps" as hopeless street dwellers, petty gamblers, con men, and thieves.[16]

Protagonists of these novels often express a conviction that whites manipulate black men with almost universal success, exclaiming against the system in which a white judge and jury can determine the "destiny" of blacks,[17] expressing frustration at having to do "slave labor for *the man,* nine-to-five, then pumping whitey's money right back into his pocket through guzzling cheap booze."[18] Even ghetto crime is controlled and exploited by the white bosses, "the men upstairs, the syndicate people," who walk "around stone free" while blacks go to jail.[19] Moreover, living in the ghetto severely limits blacks' job opportunities. James Baldwin contended that the black men and women caught in the ghetto had only two choices for employment, the women domestic service or prostitution, the men the church or crime. Charlie Avery Harris's "macking gangster" Junius has only contempt for the weaker ghetto black who fails "to get his" by any means available from the "world he was compelled to live in" (p. 100).[20] As for the professions, such as law, blacks need not apply.[21]

Ghetto violence and white oppression are explicitly connected. A hit man in Readus's *The Death Merchants,* for example, reflects that the criminal violence that is his profession is an "illness," the result of his "sub-social environment." Society, he muses, is "diseased. Genocide surrounded me. Once my ancestors had been proud warriors who knew no limits. . . . Now, we were civilized, with strings on our minds. Products resulting from the bonds of slavery." Abandoned by his father in the classic black family syndrome, he had no protection as a youngster "from the vicious magnetism of vice, and the honkie world" (p. 170). In some cases, the protagonist has gone into crime because of a traumatic experience at the hands of whites. Robert Beck's successful pimp Sweet Jones went into pimping out of a personal hatred, acquired when a southern white mob gang-raped his mother and lynched his father. And in Omar Fletcher's *Walking Black and Tall,* ever since the protagonist saw a white policeman carelessly, almost deliberately, shoot a black man's wife and children during a riot, "Violence was the only thing that made him feel alive" (p. 23). The inclination to violence, the implication goes, derives from frustration at the social prison they live in, an explanation that has been propounded by white, as well as black, sociologists and psychologists since the 1920s.

THE VIOLENT STYLE

But the shootings, the garrotings, the stabbings, the beatings seem to derive as much from the criminal code and the necessities of business as from any displaced rage. Characters are killed because they willingly join the struggle for status and wealth, and that struggle entails ruthless competitors for whom doing in an enemy is nothing personal. The literary consequence of the pervasive violence is a coarsening of attitude, an increase in the volume of brutality, degradation, and depravity, more detailed and exploitative depictions of gore and blood. Donald Goines's *Never Die Alone* (1974) exemplifies the style. Three gunmen surround a car in which fifteen-year-old Edna sits, terrified, while her boyfriend, Blue, slowly bleeds to death in the back seat from a stab wound. Edna's brother

Mike, having gone to the toilet, returns to see the gunmen fire into the car, finishing Blue off. As they open the door to Edna's side, she screams.

> But she was cut off when the man raised a small handgun and fired twice. The heavy slugs plowed into the young girl's face, spattering blood all over the car seat. The force of the bullets knocked her completely over. She slid down the car seat and out the open passenger door. Her body fell on top of Blue's blood-soaked body.[22]

For the next ten pages of well-detailed gunshots and bloodshed, Mike wages a counterattack against the killers of his sister and friend. He himself is wounded, but he kills the three gunmen and the driver of their car, running his last victim over repeatedly with the killers' own car. Mike has been set up by Moon, an influential gangster who pretended to be Mike's friend. Shaking with rage and blood loss, Mike goes after Moon and opens fire on him and his two bodyguards as he enters Moon's luxurious apartment:

> Moon let out a scream of pure panic and tried to run around the bar. The first shot from Mike's gun took him right between the shoulder blades. A second shot shattered his spine. As he slumped forward, knocking a tray of glasses down, Rockie [a bodyguard] rushed toward the panel. He managed to push the button, but the sliding door was too slow. Mike's next shot took Rockie in the forehead, knocking him backward against the panel. Before Mike could fire again, Alvin [the other bodyguard] had squeezed off two shots, both of them taking Mike high in the chest. He bounced back off the wall and tried to raise his pistol again, but another bullet smashed into his mouth and he was dead before he hit the floor. (p. 142)

In the typical rendering of the violent encounter, the narrator assumes a voice of unflinching toughness. He dwells with necrophiliac obsessiveness upon the scatology of oozing body waste, uncontrolled after death, and inventories every detail of the dead or dying figures' rent flesh. He uses unemotional—even clinical—language that separates him from the victims and muffles any empathy or feeling. In part, these passages are baldly concocted to exploit a crude taste for violence in the same way stag movies do sex. But they also reflect a pattern of relatively new conditions and attitudes. They derive from the tough-guy school of fiction, and recall Mickey Spillane's comic-book oversimplifications as well as those of Chester Himes himself. But the single most powerful and immediate influence upon the toast novelist was the Italian American Mario Puzo. His *The Godfather*, as first a novel and then a movie (1969 and 1972, respectively), helped create a tone, an attitude toward crime and violence that many of the toast novelists sought to imitate.[23] *The Godfather* contains some twenty violent incidents, most of them described with the noncommittal, disinterested attention to anatomical detail that characterizes the violent passages in the toast novel. The garrote, the gun, the knife, the brass knuckles—these are not the weapons of a bunch of crude thugs who track mud into the house. They are the instruments of shrewd monarchs of "business," who, like Don Vito Corleone, the revered and respected "godfather" and leader of a Mafia "family," regard themselves as equal to "those great men like Presidents and Prime Ministers and Supreme Court Justices and Governors of the States."[24] These are, Puzo tells us without undue subtlety, giants among men. They awe us with their immense self-certainty and utter ruthlessness. They make their own law. The blood they draw from each other reflects their great male courage and the intensity with which they live their dangerous lives. Their apparent brutality is really a justice they enforce with scrupulous fairness and a consistency far more impressive than that of the small-thinking society that would weaken them out of envy. The greatest of them respect the marriage bond, love their wives and children, observe sexual monogamy. But they never allow that to interfere with business. Business is serious. Business is men's work.

THE FANTASY OF SEXUAL DOMINANCE

Puzo provided a literary model for a ghetto hero, a man with his own code of honor, alienated from an Anglo-Saxon society which demeans him and calls him criminal, but powerful within his limited world. The toast novelists adapt this model to the black street player. Unlike Puzo, however, they illustrate their heroes' dauntlessness partly through their relations with women, with whom they are always tough and dominant. Occasionally, it is true, they show a hero capable of gentleness and love. Readus in particular likes to dramatize his hero's tenderness permeated by strength. J.J., for instance, in *The Big Hit,* lies next to his girlfriend, Peaches. She places "a gentle hand on his cheek. His eyes met hers briefly, then his lips found her hand with a tender kiss."[25] But no matter what the intensity of love, the man retains authority and independence, and his male honor always supersedes his feeling for and his relationships with his women. Knowing that he must return to a dangerous territory, J.J. makes a token gesture toward getting Peaches's permission, but she knows she cannot stop him. "You'll do it anyway, won't you?" she asks. "He looked in her eyes and nodded slowly" (p. 170). These men become angry and cold when their women ask about their business. That, says Max Nolan in *The Death Merchants,* "belongs to me, and *no one* touches it! Not you, or anyone!" (p. 9). The not-so-hidden premise here is that black male power rests on the total submission of women of all races. *Ho* and *bitch* as names for women, popularized in the rap songs of the late eighties and early nineties, are regularly used in these novels, and they imply both a dislike of women and the need to dominate, even degrade them.

The genitalia of the leading men is the never-failing proof of this dominance, and, as in the toasts, they seldom employ it for mere pleasure. Their special sexual powers depend on the size of their penis, the key to effective male performance and the single feature that most satisfies women. "Let me tell you something about big dick niggers," Junius tells the male-emasculating Whore Daughter. "'[V]ery few will use their big dicks as an art of final love-making as I do,' he said smoothly, purposely hipping her that he had a big dick as women prefer and that he was a wizard with its operation. 'Most big dick niggers get their kicks behind hurting dames with it; making them scream. This inflicts [*sic*] the manhood they ordinarily feel without.'"[26] Black masculinity is tested in bed. One group of black women discuss their men in a gossip session. They may fail as fathers or husbands, "But there was one area where the black men always excelled: in bed."[27] As Junius suggests, such hyperbolical sexual dominance seems to compensate for the historical emasculation of the black male, traditionally forbidden relations with white women and kept from declaring black women his own.

This compensation is emphasized on every side. The black man possesses sexual abilities so potent that he makes women his slaves, especially white women. The beautiful married daughter of the Godfather of the Chicago Mafia in *The Death Merchants* finally cannot resist black Max Nolan any longer. "I'm yours," she tells Max. "I can survive any tests. I'll be your slave. . . . I'll wash and iron your clothes if that's a test. I just want to love you, Max, and take what you give me in return" (p. 138). Another protagonist is told by several experienced women that he has a natural genius for sex. Once he has loved them, they never forget. He seems virtually superhuman, making love several times a day and night, tirelessly, gently, superbly. Not only does he unfailingly move heterosexual women to unprecedented climaxes, he overcomes a self-professed lesbian's alleged preference for women. "[E]very woman," he tells her, "really needs a *man*," and after a night of stupendous lovemaking, she agrees: "Even though I may never find another like you, I will never be what I was before."[28]

It is an easy step from the imagery of sexual dominance to the imagery of sadomasochism and violence. As Junius contends, making love with the black man often both punishes women and affords them forbidden pleasure, for women, in these male fantasies, like rough treatment. Sometimes, however, the novelist represents sex as sadistic torture rather than rough enjoyment, approaching the level of snuff films. James-Howard Readus specializes in death at the height of fellatio. In one instance in *The Big Hit* a gangster kidnaps the vain, cheating, well-bred (high-yellow) wife of a mobster he and his partner have been hired to kill. His sexual arousal is heightened by his power over her, and after she brings him to climax, he first smashes her face with his pistol and then shoots her, spraying blood and flesh against the car door. Later on, the hit man surprises his victim in a similar act, but before killing him, he shoots the white girl servicing him just as the man achieves orgasm, and we get more horror-stricken eyes, exploding heads, and flying body parts (pp. 113–14, 214).

The sadistic combination of submissiveness, sex, and violence also often involves light-skinned African American and white women, reinforcing the two male fantasies served: male power and the humiliation of women who symbolize white hegemony over black males. Omar Fletcher's protagonist in *Walking Black and Tall* says this explicitly. He makes love to an attractive white woman he picks up in a bar as she has never been made love to before. Then, as she begins fellatio at his command, he feels "in spite of himself that he was, through the girl's willing submission, getting back at every white bastard that had ever fucked over him" (p. 177). The very use of "fucked over" suggests the relationship between sex and black male rage, black men's feeling they have been raped like women. Women become one way in which they can retaliate.

The relationship between the black man and woman is formalized into a business relationship in the whore-pimp association. The use of "ho" to refer to any woman suggests the role the black man assigns to women. Above all they are submissive, and the whore-pimp stories deal in large part with the techniques for keeping working whores that way. No pimp shoots the source of his income, but he does slap her around, bloody her up, heap verbal abuse upon her, and humiliate her sexually. These novelists compose a kind of collective handbook on the care and feeding of whores.[29] In some cases, their male characters often grow up in the ghetto believing that all women are potential "ho's." In their mythology, whores—and by extension, all women—*like* discipline, *want* to be ordered around. And because, as women and whores, they are naturally fickle and deceptive, they need always to be kept in fear of a good beating. According to these novels, a prostitute receives sexual satisfaction only from being dominated. When Sweet Peter Deeder's whore Toshika shirks her work, he administers "three or four right hand smacks to her jaw," then loses control of himself and blacks out as if intoxicated with excitement. When he comes to, Toshika, weeping with pleasure from the punishment and unbearably aroused, is "pressing her face up against the front of my pants." Both are excited and Toshika performs gentle fellatio until Peter "pulled her up and gave her a long kiss."[30]

At the bottom of the pimp's rough control of his "bitches" is the fear of being turned into a "pussy" by a women who "can make a man sacrifice himself for the sake of that thing between their legs."[31] In many cases, though certainly not all, this fear leads men to avoid all emotional commitments. One of Goines's small-time hoods in *Never Die Alone* hates the idea of being uncontrollably in love with a beautiful, seductive black coquette and attempts to resist the "feeling of concern" he has for her. It makes him feel "weak" (p. 159). There are, of course, exceptions to this—like the macking gangster Junius. As a young man he anonymously rapes a black woman he has never seen before. He satisfies her so completely that he renders her unfit for any other man. Years later, after discovering his children on the streets and undertaking to protect and educate them, he returns to their mother with the implication that the two will live happily thereafter as man and wife.

But the core of the toast novel's sexual drama remains in the psychology of the implicit rage the black man feels against the black woman, and his fear of being dominated by her. This psychology is not subtle. Robert Beck suggests that it all starts with the mother. Significantly, several presidential administrations in the 1960s and 1970s approached black poverty with the assumption that most poor black families were headed by a single mother. In the thematically titled *Mama Black Widow* (1969), Beck's narrator, Soldier, describes how he was driven into homosexuality by a smothering mother and a father who loses his manhood when he cannot pay his bills and is ridiculed by his wife. Men turn into homosexuals when they lack a male model and are subjected to female authority as children. Wives and girlfriends also reduce men to nonmen. Soldier can find no support from his girlfriend. "Stop dreaming," she says when he excitedly mentions an invention he has in mind. "Don't you know that if one of your silly ideas was worth a good goddamn, a white man would have thought of it already." This is what Soldier calls the "negative black woman." Instead of inspiring him and helping him to "achieve the glory of manhood in this hellish white man's world," she sneers at him. The negative black woman is thus allied with the white man, mentally maiming and crippling "the lowly masses of black men." The positive black woman, on the other hand, "uses her glory and strength and power to inspire her man toward self improvement and leadership so that her children might have a strong pattern image."[32] Soldier illustrates what can happen when things go wrong. Most of the respected male characters never shrink before the contempt of the "negative black woman." They maintain dominance through ritualized beatings and forced sex.

INSTINCT, JUSTICE, AND THE ALLURE OF THE LIFE

The toast hero conquers the ghetto the same way he conquers his women, with a combination of force and shrewdness. Everyone knows and fears Junius, the "macking gangster."[33] He handles his whores and his competitors with consummate psychological skill, and when the situation calls for more than psychology, he uses a baseball bat. Harris admires Junius, representing him without irony as a philosopher of ghetto metaphysics and ethics, who can both teach his illegitimate children the wisdom of the streets and smash the skulls of those who oppose him. He would be far less admirable, though, if wisdom were his only strength. It is the baseball bat that sets him above the herd.

Those who want to be men must be ruthless and courageous enough to use the bat or its equivalent. The connection between manhood and violence lies so deep in the toast novelists' characters, and goes so far back in the historical psyche, that it seems part of an unconscious mechanism, a second self or doppelganger. James-Howard Readus is particularly intrigued by this connection. His true men become almost automatons if their self-esteem is threatened. When the protagonist of *Black Renegades* challenges an opponent, he handles his gun with dreamy instinctiveness: "Almost unconsciously he squeeze[s] the trigger" and rips open the other man's chest and throat with several shots (pp. 16–17). This same reflexive impulse takes over Max Nolan in *The Death Merchants,* like another personality, during his first kill as a hit man. As he chokes his victim with a garrote, "something very strange happened," says Max. "I was actually smiling. This wasn't me, I kept screaming to myself. This was some alien that had taken over, but I was drunk with this sensation" (p. 111). Some street players are driven by that sensation into a way of life, becoming shadowy hunters who live with death. Kalchide, for example, one of the hit men in *The Big Hit,* is a "professional assassin" who "enjoyed the work he'd chosen, and he did his work well." Kalchide, perhaps, is an overblown character, a kind of musical comedy Bill Sikes: "People cowered in fear at the mere mention of his name." But at the same time, we feel a sneaking admiration for a man who, indifferent to his victims, enjoys living on the edge and revels in danger (pp. 121, 122). Even women are moved by something indefinable in themselves that leads them to enjoy killing, as when hit woman Laurie Miles shoots another gangster's bodyguard: "I know it sounds strange," she says exultantly, "but I felt a warmth come over me. I actually enjoyed what I was doing there. And, I knew I was good at it."[34]

But overwhelmingly this is a male world, an emphatically *black* male world, in which men go up against each other for control and possession, unregulated by any conventional law. The only authority in this world is power, and whoever controls the most violence wields the most power and enjoys the highest status. Many of the titles suggest a strong vein of black nationalism: Omar Fletcher's *Walking Black and Tall* (1977), James-Howard Readus's *Black Renegades* (1976), Donald Goines's *Black Gangster* (1972). When Kalchide departs from a meeting with his boss, he gives him a "Black Power" handshake. The violent transactions these men take part in may be destructive of themselves and the larger social order in which they live, but the novelists clearly take a certain pride in their characters' ruthless courage and violent style. It is a demonstration of strength that makes black men admirable and successful competitors in the harshest of worlds. They are the essential "bad niggers" brought to a point of unprecedented knowledge and sophistication, renegades against a stultifying culture.

As rebels, they have their own law, a Black Power morality combined with the Italian tradition of blood vengeance and a kind of classic Homeric justice. The gods kill those who kill. What order the toast novel's criminal world has comes from the stringent austerity of this system. Ghetto law is founded on the principle of vengeance, and personal and organizational vendettas take up much of the action. Though he is dying from his wounds, one hit man goes after the man who had set him up. "He merely wanted to exist now for vengeance. Pain meant nothing, he told himself over and over again."[35] Joe Nazel's Turtle, in *Death for Hire,* tracks down his buddy Tracy and kills him for running out on him during a hit. Hit men like Vern Smith's T. C. Thomas in *The Jones Men* (1974) and Readus's Kalchide serve their bosses solely as instruments of vengeance, killing those who double-cross them. This system is the basis of a rough and merciless justice. A syndicate head believes that only when he kills those responsible for offing two of his friends "will justice be exact."[36] In a never-ending cycle, violence brings more violence in turn. The leader of a gang of brutal rapists gets "his throat cut the week after" he drives his victim into the insane asylum.[37] And when Johnny O'Brien goes after the white mob boss who had his best friend killed, he learns that the mobster has himself been killed in a vendetta and "his body stuffed into the trunk of his car."[38]

Thus, though no statutory laws limit these figures, their own system imposes appropriate punishment for violations of the code. Most understand the code and submit to its rigors. They can, within its framework, distinguish between "good" and "bad." Nor do they shrink from passing judgment on people they kill or deciding who should be killed by others. A Vietnam veteran, reflecting a sentiment throughout these novels, becomes a hit man for more money than he was making killing innocent Vietnamese for racist America: "I do away with only those who need to be done away with, helping to clean up the world by getting rid of undesirable characters."[39] Unlike the hit men who take pleasure in their work and who make no pretense to be meting out justice, some are crusaders, private investigators or policemen who, like Himes's detectives, use violence in their jobs only because there is no other way to stop ghetto crime. This is the case with Joe Nazel's ironically named Terence Malcolm Slaughter, in *Street Wars* (1987), who comes up against young punks in Watts and is forced to shoot and kill to defend himself and the law and order he is determined to preserve. In these cases, ghetto violence is mainly negative, and the streets are full of toughs without honor or courage who hit their targets by cowardly stealth or indifferent randomness. They need to be placed under the control of the principled strong man.

Ghetto "justice" reaches everyone, big and small. Loyalty does not help, for one cannot protect one's friends—or oneself—from a planned hit, or a crooked cop's gun butt, or a mistake in a casual hustle. No one is well enough guarded or slick enough to evade the violence inherent in the ghetto experience. The street is ruthless, unforgiving, but this hardness gives the men who live it a kind of mythical glow. Whether on the side of duly constituted law enforcement or part of the ghetto criminal life, they must never let their guard down. "[W]hen you out here dealin' with dog-ass street niggers on a day-to-day basis," says a character in Readus's *Black Renegades*, "you gotta be hard, man" (p. 170). Hardness becomes an ideal, celebrated with grim pride.

The reader feels little sympathy for those who receive deserved punishment: the sneaking backstabbers who get their brains blown out, the arrogant mulatto women who look down on streetmen, the once victorious players who turn coward. But the defeat of the protagonist who faces up to his opponents, understands the rules of the game, and even half regrets the life he has chosen—this arouses in us something like the awe and pity of classical tragedy. The emotion comes from the collective impact of these novels rather than their individual literary merit. They command our attention by their cumulative power, not by their individual esthetic success. They convince us that their badmen feel more intensely than ordinary people, play the dangerous games knowingly, and fatalistically accept the danger and its consequences. They live on a higher plane than the rest of us, and as victims they die with greater flair, for higher stakes, with greater rage or courage. They are larger than life in their appetites; often cruel, ruthless, self-indulgent, but large-minded, hyperbolic.

They accept the system stoically, knowing that the hit they make on an opponent will someday be made on them, and that they are simply part of a round of action and reaction, a relentless process in which they will be displaced by an aspirant who in turn will be displaced by yet another. In *The Jones Men,* to take one of many examples, the assassin observes that "We all here on borrowed time anyway, so if you die, you just die, you know."[40] This is the same fatalism that informed the structure of so many ballads and toasts—crime, flight, pursuit, capture, and punishment, updated in these narratives. Their hero has, like Richard III, set his life "upon a cast" and stands "the hazard of the die." His world, like Richard's, is governed by chance and its players are gamblers.

The street player as gambler chooses this life because he cannot resist its promise. The toast novelist is very clear about this. "The slum I grew up in," says

Whoreson Jones, "seemed to me the most wonderful place in the world."[41] Donald Goines was writing from his own experience. When he returned from Korea, a seventeen-year-old with a dope habit, his family rallied around him. But his "bond" with his old friends drew him back to the street. The action was there, the money, the show.[42] The "inner city hoodlum," the "black renegade," the "pimp," the "street player," the "black gangster": they all possess an appetite for crime and the ostentation it makes possible, the statement to the world of the black man's achievement in a largely black world. "When I was a kid growing up in Baltimore," says Junius, "I used to envy a flock of flamboyant hustlers who hung out on Pennsylvania Avenue. They had flashy cars like hogs and Lincolns, real jewelry, choice broads with commercial asses, and they drew admirers from near and far. . . . I set my goal, patterning after them."[43] The young feel the "tug" of the street, for it has everything: "talent, good and evil." Those who work the street are a special breed, involved in "illegal moneymaking of any variety, violence, and bad reputations."[44] There is money to be had by the quick and the daring. And for the mature streetmen, there is the tribute paid to the star when he enters a tavern and all talk stops and all eyes turn toward him.

The dynamics of the street's allure are simple. If you make it, you are a king. As Iceberg Slim starts his career as a pimp in Chicago, he feels "powerful and beautiful." True, he thinks, "I was still black in the white man's world. [But] my hope to be important and admired could be realized even behind this black stockade." All it takes is flash and front.[45] As Junius puts it, "flash" is a pimp's "way of rapping, dressing, his car, jewelry, crib, his style of living and his reputation."[46] Readus fills his novels with the details of black gangster style. The high-stakes players constitute a social set, whose rites include extravagant balls at expensive country clubs, festivals of conspicuous consumption, and spectacular displays of ghetto fashion: "The women wore sequins, gowns, super-micro-minis, feathers, and minks. The men were immaculate in leather, silk, mohair, and mink." His hero dresses in "a bright, tangerine-colored suit, matching silk shirt, and a pair of expensive, hand-made snakeskin boots. His brown mink coat was draped casually over his shoulders, and his matching hat pulled down rakishly over his eyes." His girlfriend looks "like a beautiful Egyptian goddess in a skin-tight leather pant suit of the same color, matching knee-length boots, and a striking white mink coat."[47] Readus appears to be drawn to the sheer spectacle of the street, the names of its types becoming a kind of poetry for him: "The Avenue is abundant with jive-men, dips, pimps, murphy-men, whores, junkies, informants, leaches, winos, beggars, procurers, card and dice sharks, shoplifters and strongarm artists, all out to beat the inevitable sucker who is careless with his money." The hustlers talk dazzling language, with "their lofty conversations . . . enunciating everything that burned inside of" the younger men.[48]

The young streetman on the rise views his world as a virtual carnival, full of action, color, light. It is filled with illimitable possibilities, offering, right there in the neighborhood to which he is confined, an escape from the humiliation of cockroach-ridden kitchens, peeling wallpaper, toilets that don't flush.

A SPECIAL KIND OF SQUALOR, A SPECIAL KIND OF GUILT

Neither the violence of the badman, however, nor the glitter of the street is consistently heroic or dramatic. One of the things that makes the toast novelist so much worth our attention is his honesty, his readiness to view the life he writes about without softening its rough contours or leaving the reader with an image of untrammeled heroism. Without undercutting the courage of his characters, he also shows us the other side, giving his novel the plausibility of ambiguity, projecting a conflict between the glory of strong violent men in splendid control and the squalidness of mere ghetto brutality. Life is cheap and usually demeaned. If we are not witnessing a vengeful gang killing, we see street brawls, stabbings, shootings, broken limbs, bloodied heads, glazed eyes. These are part of the street's spectacle, always drawing an appreciative, curious, and unfeeling audience. The crowds that gather for a good fight are a staple in this fiction, watching men, and sometimes women, kill each other as if in a movie. The spectators have "an inbred passion for violence," cheering the winners, ignoring the defeated, and "happily" watching the winner lose to the whites in court. If sometimes the hit man displays an awesome second nature in his use of violence, a street fighter often seems "like a robotized executioner."[49] And the audience that takes pleasure in such displays seems as robotized as the fighters. The novelist thus ambivalently elevates the violence of his characters to a mythic level and at the same time mocks the sidewalk crowds for enjoying the mayhem. He might even be carrying the mockery further, to himself for writing and the reader for reading. Both the reader and the sidewalk audience are voyeurs, attracted to the display of bloody catastrophe but remaining uninvolved.

This attitude updates the traditional, long-felt frustration that African Americans cannot unify for their own good. Like crabs in a barrel, the old story went, those below would reach up to those about to get out and pull them back down. The metaphor was relatively benign. Now, though, this backbiting has become malicious and destructive. Tainting the engaging strength of the fatalistic gangster is a tendency toward communal suicide in the inner city's violence, even a love of death, a passion to destroy—or see destroyed—what is alive. In these novels, such passion is not limited to men. Cole Riley's *Rough Trade,* appearing as it does at the end of the eighties, shows the continuance of these themes in a woman's description of a shootout when a Latino gang breaks into the headquarters of rival black drug dealers:

> Shit, just barged in and shot everybody, even Evelyn and she was pregnant. They shot the dudes in the back of the head and Evelyn got it in the back. They shot Kenny in the heart. They blew Carl's nuts off and threw him out the window. (p. 307)

What is notable is not simply the barbarity of the Latinos' actions, but the indifferent, even admiring, tone in which the woman recounts it, "matter-of-factly, puffing on the joint which smelled a lot like angel dust" (p. 307). Her disengagement has the quality of a necrophiliac urge, as Erich Fromm puts it, "to tear apart living structures."[50]

In this vision of the ghetto, dignity is the elusive and fleeting prerogative of only a few, though all pursue it. But the ghetto kills and degrades. The most destructive element in the ghetto is heroin, and the toast novel, echoing its poetic predecessors, takes it as a frequent topic. From Clarence L. Cooper's *The Scene* (1960) to Cole Riley's *Rough Trade* (1987), drug addiction, pushing, turf wars make up major action lines. And a substantial number of these novels deal specifically and primarily with the business, such as Terry Robinson's *White Horse in Harlem* (1965), Nathan Heard's *Howard Street* (1968), Donald Goines's *Dopefiend* (1971), Vern E. Smith's *The Jones Men* (1974). These novels vary in the sharpness with which they represent heroin as a satanic force. Clarence Cooper ends *The Scene,* for example, with an ironically humorous illustration of the inevitability of dope addiction, in which two men, one black and one white, decide to shoot up again after a rehabilitation program because there is no "reason not to."[51] And Nathan Heard's Hip Ritchwood, in *Howard Street,* defends his habit as a revolutionary act that affords him more pleasure than any other activity.

But even in these two early novels, the conclusion is unmistakable that heroin eats away at even the strongest men. Hip Ritchwood, once a vibrant, handsome stud with shining eyes, has become seedy and frayed, his eyes dull, his walk increasingly leaden. And Terry Robinson and Donald Goines write moral fables that show the awful consequences that befall those young innocents caught in the vortex of a dope habit. In *Dopefiend* Goines tells a story of how heroin leads to gangland killings, suicide, madness, and the degeneracy of even middle-class kids. Even in the novels which do not focus on addiction and the drug business, heroin leaks into the characters' lives like the polluted fluids of a chemical dump. Readus's Robert Jackson thinks of all his friends who have been destroyed, "sacrificed at the altar of the Scag God." He, too, before he determines to quit, knows he is "microscopically dying daily," and he hates himself for it.[52] Junius teaches his daughter about the "dreadful histories" of the broken-down whores chasing after slowing automobiles, all in irreversible decay from "tragic-magic."[53] Cole Riley's heroine jeers to her addicted boyfriend that he is no longer human. And virtually all of these novels' gang violence arises from the wars for control of the drug trade. This violence is the ultimate moral degradation. It measures the degree to which the black competitors have fallen in their readiness to destroy their race brothers and sisters with dope and kill each other for the opportunity to do it, and often for a white organization that carries off much of the money.

At the core of the world imagined by the toast novelist lies a special squalor of danger, incarceration, death. No mink is thrown over the shoulder of a male hustler untainted by betrayal, revenge, violence. If the ghetto is a sparkling surface of tempting refractions, beneath it is a murky world of predators, described in extended analogies between the jungle and the ghetto that are combinations of moral warnings and expressions of awe and irresistible attraction. "Predators came in all sizes and colors. Predators, armed with sharp fangs and claws, owned the night, feeding off the innocents who strayed out of their caves seeking relief from the heat, the boredom more deadly than the smothering heat."[54] The worst thing about the underworld is its degradation of black integrity and racial solidarity. When Max Nolan tells his wife he has killed a policeman, she becomes angry. "The thing you tried to escape," she cries, "you became. You became an animal. . . . Don't you know you're the white Mafia's most valuable tool in oppressing other Blacks?"[55] Her accusation tells critically against the romance of the badman. Blacks who kill other blacks—as Max is hired to do—violate a brotherhood necessary to the race. Even the pimps and hustlers should have a sense of racial identity; all oppressed minorities should avoid destroying their own community. Black police commander Thom Uncer, for instance, in Joseph Nazel's *Street Wars*, worries about the "series of gang wars and revenge killings" in Watts. "Blacks slaughtering blacks. Mexicans killing Mexicans. None of it made any sense."[56] This does not mean that the gun-toting black gangsters should turn their weapons against the white system. But killing each other is no good, either. The two young hoodlums in Goines's *Inner City Hoodlum* sense this, and feel uneasy about killing two other young black hustlers. They hope to rise in the street world by such acts, to ride "in a Cadillac, with the top man in the city." But they wonder whether shooting the black men, "who might under other conditions have been friends of theirs," fits their code (pp. 108, 109, 126).

Such sentiments do not express conventional social protest but suggest that the ghetto, unfairly oppressed by a racist white world though it may be, must be seen as responsible for the death of its young. Joseph Nazel's Spider Armstrong, a reporter for a black newspaper, witnesses a bloodbath in which several young people shoot each other. He knows that the killings solve nothing. After the firing stops, the "curious residents" come out of their houses like "vultures" to view the "corpses." They are another form of those bloodthirsty but uninvolved spectators of sidewalk mayhem, and Spider becomes enraged at them, wants to "scream out their blame and shame. They were as guilty as anyone else. They were all guilty."[57]

ICEBERG SLIM AND DONALD GOINES

Robert Beck and Donald Goines, two of Holloway House's best and most popular writers, give this negative dimension to the violence of their street players its most effectively complex shape. They do have a didactic aim, protesting the conditions created by white racism. Beck, as Iceberg Slim, the protagonist of his autobiographical *Pimp*, attributes his life of crime to "the stark reality that black people in my lifetime had little chance to escape the barbed-wire stockade in the white man's world" (p. 309). Goines's Whoreson Jones, also a pimp, demands the reader's sympathy for the hard and unfair lot that imbued him with "the bitterness and loneliness" that made him an unfeeling streetman (p. 278). But when they are writing at their most natural, they disregard politics and protest, look hard at their harsh world, and render its bleak outlines sharply and without sentimentality. For them, gunfire and murder reflect not heroic revolt against a racist system or manly control of a chaotic world, but the squalor of the ineluctable boundaries of ghetto life.

Beck fills his books with brutal street criminals who use violence with no more passion than a plumber wields a pipe wrench, but we can recognize and empathize with his protagonists. Seedy and dishonest to the marrow, perhaps, they are also energetic and clever, and thrive on the daring their con games require. They celebrate when they win and, with the familiar ghetto fatalism, shrug off their losses. We like them also for their great capacity for friendship. Johnny "White Folks" O'Brien, who appears in both *Trick Baby* and *The Long White Con,* in particular moves his companions to affection. Blue Leon Howard, old enough to be Johnny's father, becomes his mentor, trains him in the street life, gets him through dangerous scrapes, nurses him through a life-threatening bout of alcoholism. Speedy Jackson becomes Johnny's companion, contrives elaborate cons, and puts his life on the line with Johnny. They are like infantry soldiers in a ground war, drawn into intimacy by their mutual vulnerability to conditions that will, in the nature of things, inevitably destroy them.

These men trust each other, depend on each other. But they are prisoners of their limits. Johnny loses both these friends in brutal, unfeeling slayings that result from deceit and betrayal. Blue Howard's vain little wife, who is half his age, conspires with her flashy lover to shoot Blue for a few dollars of hit money. Before they abandon his body, they coolly rifle his pockets. When the intended marks of a con Speedy and Johnny are running discover the game, they crush Speedy under the tires of their big Buick and then casually shoot him. The killers in these murders are simply playing the game, and the game rules decree that they allow no feeling to keep them from doing what must be done to win. Johnny understands the game, and we feel his hurt. In his ghetto-tattered humanity he has been deeply wounded. Yet even Johnny must curb his feelings. After each killing, he is forced to acknowledge he is powerless. Even grief is pointless in this squalid world in which killing is as natural as sleeping. After each death Johnny refuses to give way to mourning. He picks up what he has left and goes on.

Beck makes his angriest and most didactic comments on ghetto violence in *Death Wish* (1977). It is a grim tale of the enmity between a black man and an Italian, expressed first in the gang wars of their adolescent years and continued as they become adult leaders of more formal and dangerous crime organizations. Their adult vendetta is simply an extension of those early adolescent power plays, unworthy of grownups. The two men steep Chicago in shootings, stabbings, bombings. Nearly every episode works up to a killing. The soldiers in each army in this battle live behind bunker walls, prisoners and victims of a war they themselves create: Jessie and his black Warriors in the "zone," at whose center is a forty-room mansion turned into an armored fortress; Jimmy Collucci and his Italian Mafiosi in bullet-proof apartments atop high buildings. Both sides live by the code of a distorted machismo.

Beck serves up no heroes in this novel. Jimmy Collucci and Jessie Taylor are arrested adolescents, continuing their old animosities with an insane puerility. Beck ridicules their fatuous gang mentality, their absurd code of vengeance. In bloody burlesques of the supremely efficient hit men of *The Godfather* and its Holloway imitators, both men botch their attempts to get each other, but shoot each other apart in their bungled efforts, like a vicious version of the Three Stooges. Jessie loses both his legs, and, in a travesty of the epic gangland battle, enters the final face-off in a motorized wheelchair incredibly mounted with an automatic weapon. As these grownup juveniles blast away at each other, the air is percussive with the din. Then suddenly there is silence. Everyone is dead. The bodies lie quietly, torn and bloody, and the frightened and the curious come out from cover in classic Holloway style.

Beck does not trivialize this slaughter; he is disgusted by it. Whatever integrity these men might once have possessed dissipates in their lust for power and revenge, to which they subordinate their wives, their children, their honor. In a final burst of anger, Beck ends with the hyperbolical imagery of sexual perversion and grimy scatology:

> The sex-fiend squealing of city death wagons sodomized infant day. Chicago, the gaudy bitch, had banged another carnal night away. Now the fake grand lady lay uglied in her neon ball gown. Sleazed in the merciless light. Her bleak drawers hung foul with new and ancient death.[58]

Death Wish seems to be a deliberate take-off on the new "black experience" narrative introduced into the Holloway camp by Donald Goines. As I have said, Goines was inspired to write when he read a copy of *Pimp* at Jackson State Prison in Michigan. But he turned the lively and amusing ironic realism of Beck's novelistic autobiography into a realism whose irony is humorless and relentlessly bleak. Beck's Iceberg Slim is a raconteur, a rough and more dangerous Jesse B. Semple, who gives us the feeling that he enjoys sitting around swapping stories with his friends. Goines was a novelist, a bit crude and unpolished, but a novelist nevertheless, with a faculty for invention and insight into motive which any writer would be glad to have. Goines is to the novel what Leadbelly is to music, a genius in his own métier. If Leadbelly had one of the two best musical memories of the twentieth century, as has been claimed (Stravinsky had the other), Goines had as many stories in his imagination, and as many different kinds of characters, as Dickens. Greg Goode is correct when he says that Goines, in his sixteen novels, "provided perhaps the most sustained, multifaceted, realistic fictional picture ever created by one author of the lives, choices, and frustrations of underworld ghetto blacks."[59]

Goines's world is even bloodier than Beck's, and more heartless. Goines's badmen feel no friendship for each other. They use the sentiment for gaining advantage. "[K]indness," thinks his character Prince, "was the sweetest con of all."[60] And indeed, he cynically manipulates those who believe in him and exploits the black community's support of the black revolution by creating a revolutionary organization to front for his extortion racket. He thinks of the ghetto as a permanent condition in which the strong and ruthless make their own way, indifferent to those who cannot. "The people that lived there either learned how to get out, or died in the small confines of their prison" (p. 118). Prince congratulates himself for knowing "how to get out," for being "a taker" rather than one "who got took" (p. 119). When he dies, Goines assures us, "there was nothing heroic in his death" (p. 278).

These characters lack even the passion of Jimmy Collucci and Jessie Taylor, who at least felt hatred. Goines's players feel nothing. The adverb Goines uses most often to describe his characters' manner with each other is "coldly." In *Street Players,* the tension of competitiveness edges his men's talk, nervous alertness against insult and theft of their game. Earl the Black Pearl, a premier pimp in Detroit's inner city, talks without bitterness of "so-called friends [who] have but one thought in mind, and that's how to steal one of them whores from" the pimp who "lets his game get funny."[61] He makes this observation with the same shrewd objectivity with which an experienced hunter might describe the behavior of the wild animals he pursues. In the occasional instances of loyalty that Goines does depict in his novels, the emotion flows in only one direction, from woman to man. There is no more faithful woman than Prince's girlfriend Ruby. She stands by the black gangster on his way up, and remains firmly by his side as his empire collapses and he is killed by a hired hit man's bullet. Earl the Black Pearl wins loyalty from beautiful young Vicki, who, as she lies dying from an attack by an insane white trick, proudly hands over to him the money she has clung to in the struggle. Connie, too, loves Earl, sticking with him even when his glamorous success turns to seed, and then going insane when he dies.

The heartlessness of Goines's men fits the bloodiness of their world. Violence always dominates the atmosphere, coming as the inevitable conclusion to the tense relations between men, and overpowering the human feelings that sometimes grow between a few of the women and men. Occasionally, a fragile piece of poetry or a tentative flower of hope struggles to take root in this desolate landscape. But such passages are overwhelmed by the awfulness of the ghetto. Normal ties cannot grow in this life. Birth, renewal, hope—all are foreign to it. When women do get pregnant, they abort, horribly. A pregnant junkie hangs herself, and in her death throes goes into labor. In an appalling symbol of the deadness of the ghetto, the baby dies half-caught in the dead mother's womb, its own head "covered with afterbirth," the floor beneath slimy with involuntarily emitted excrement.[62]

Writing for the *Village Voice,* Michael Corvino places Goines in the context of social criticism and protest. Goines's message, says Corvino, "if he can be said to have one, perhaps lies in the very relentlessness, the magnitude, the savagery, the fury, the luminous power of his pessimism. Any life that can inspire such pessimism cries out to be changed."[63] This is an eloquent and insightful summing up. To be sure, when judged from outside the ghetto, Goines's books do seem to demand some kind of social action. Yet the more convincing conclusion seems even bleaker. Goines's novels are like photographs of a desert: a dry, stony, wide expanse of cracked earth that sprouts no green, its inhabitants engaged in an amoral struggle for the limited food and water, the sun pitiless in its unremitting heat. No social action can transform the desolation of this landscape. Similarly, Goines seems to make no such appeal in the panorama he depicts. We look futilely for a successful protagonist. His characters are shot as they compete for the street's few prizes, or they are caught by the police and put in jail. In *Cry Revenge,* the protagonist is one of the only figures in all of Goines's work capable of love and possessing a strong sense of family. These human attributes do him little good, though. At the end of a vicious vendetta the innocent and the guilty have died, and the hero is himself disabled in a last gun battle in a vacant house on the edge of a small desert town. Dusk falls, the abandoned house is emptied of light, and hundreds of rats come out of their hiding places. As the wounded man falls into "a dark oblivion," he does not "see the small furry creatures as they began their cautious approach."[64] He dies, we assume, hideously, eaten alive by the hungry rodents, who have as little sense of moral restraint as those with whom he struggled in the vendetta. The scene epitomizes Goines's brutal and amoral world.

Goines may be the most pessimistic of these novelists, but he captures much of their essence. We bring our own moral sense to his narratives, but feel it confirmed, if at all, only indirectly and ironically. The heroes of the ghetto myth seem like demons and furies, tearing methodically at each other's flesh, facing their fate in parched, poisoned soil. Crime and violence are the media for their bleak fulfillment, and they assure a Hobbesian life: nasty, brutish, and short. Only the sometimes awkward art that forges these details into stories seems to transcend this world.

9

Walter Mosley and the Violent Men of Watts

In the last three decades of the twentieth century, African American crime writers transformed the work of Chester Himes and the Holloway "black experience" writers. Some twenty-three black novelists in more than sixty novels have joined the all but numberless membership of the crime writers' fraternity. Starting with the conventions laid down by Dashiell Hammett, Raymond Chandler, and Ross MacDonald, they have gone off in the directions pursued by hordes of their white fellows, creating investigative figures that are male and female, gay and straight, official police detectives and freelancers, residents of big cities like New York and Los Angeles and small cities like fictitious Brookport, Massachusetts. All but one or two of these authors work with a signature character around whom the action circulates. Clifford Mason, one of the earliest of the crowd, names his private dick Joe Cinquez after the famous African slave who led his comrades in a mutiny aboard the *Amistad*. Eleanor Taylor Bland's Marti MacAlister is a detective for the Lincoln Prairie (Waukegan, Illinois) Police Department. Gar Anthony Haywood's Aaron Gunner, a veteran of Vietnam, is a castoff of the LAPD police academy who became a private investigator so he could carry a gun. Barbara Neely's Blanche White, of whose ironic name Neely makes a great deal, is a professional domestic who finds herself investigating a murder in the home of her most recent (and wealthy) employers. In the sixty-four novels I have read, there is some very good writing, and also some very bad. By and large the stories do not lack excitement. Often, black lingo is plausibly caught. Smart-aleck dialogue is more often entertaining than tedious. The nineties especially saw an eruption of black crime writers, and they have joined the genre's recent trend toward giving their main character a personal life, usually based on sexual relationships whose stories run parallel to the crime under investigation.[1]

The world the detectives work in seems only superficially black; its figures and surroundings, like those in a coloring book, are not black until they are colored so. This is no criticism. Indeed, it seems to me a good sign, suggesting that fewer and fewer black writers believe that black authenticity resides only in the inner city or lies in a narrow set of stereotypes or conventions. That quality of colorlessness, though, tends to distance many of them from my interest in the badman. Of the twenty-plus crime writers I have looked at, only Walter Mosley incorporates in any substantial way the characteristics of the traditional man of violence. It is not this, necessarily, that makes him the most read and most respected of this group, but it is what makes him appropriate for my study and forces me to disregard a number of good writers in an interesting genre.

Mosley demonstrates that the violent man as a literary figure is still alive and well in current African American fiction. The site of his badmen's action is the largely black area of South Central Los Angeles known as Watts, where he has located his three most successful literary characters. Ezekiel "Easy" Rawlins is a freelance investigator of shady occurrences who, with his homicidal friend, Raymond "Mouse" Alexander, has appeared, to date, in five novels. The first novel, *Devil in a Blue Dress* (1990), was set in 1948; the most recent, *Bad Boy Brawly Brown* (2002), in 1964. Socrates Fortlow, the protagonist of two other books, is an ex-con who has relocated to L.A. from the Indiana prison where he served his time, trying to live down his violent past and take up a quiet, orderly life. His stories are set around 1988.[2] All of these characters are streetwise and tough, immersed, sometimes in spite of themselves, in a wide range of mayhem and violence. That we are in the country of the badman is signaled in the first scene of the first Rawlins novel, *Devil in a Blue Dress.* Easy enters Ricardo's Pool Room on Slauson Boulevard, in the heart of Watts. It "was a serious kind of place peopled with jaundice-eyed bad men who smoked and drank heavily while they waited for a crime they could commit" (p. 129). Easy, Mouse, and Socrates, together with customers of dives like Ricardo's, furnish Mosley with various angles from which to observe and reflect on the man of violence as he still exists in the African American section of sprawling Los Angeles.[3]

Mosley was born and raised in Watts, the only child of a black father and a white Jewish mother. At eighteen he went east to attend college in New England, and moved to New York City in 1981. He has lived there ever since. "L.A. is not my city," he says. "It's not for living."[4] Like the well-educated Rudolph Fisher during the Harlem Renaissance, Mosley shapes his characters with a strong middle-class hand. He sees them not from the street-level viewpoint of the balladeer and toaster—or of Chester Himes, for that matter—but from the perspective of the stories he heard his father and his friends tell, relying on maps and childhood memories for other details.[5] This does not mean he lacks plausibility. His Los Angeles, the streets of Watts, and the interiors of bars and houses all have an authentic look. He does not write as a chronicler or celebrator of his violent men but as an investigative moralist who is interested in mind and motive as event and spectacle, and who wishes to make an African American contribution to the American detective tradition.

Mosley deeply implicates his three characters in violence and the moral questions it raises. Easy and Socrates in particular struggle with their inclination to violence. Unlike the man of violence in folk expression, they see their violent side as a problem. Mosley feels constrained to explain that only extreme conditions made them that way. Their violence is caused by experience, not nature, and there are usually mitigating circumstances.

SOCRATES FORTLOW

Socrates' case is problematical. When he was a young man, he killed two of his friends, a man and a woman, during a drunken orgy. Not only were his life and his honor never in danger, he virtually raped the woman, an act forbidden under Mosley's code. This is the deed of a ballad badman or a toast hero. Stagolee or Dolomite might receive ribald praise for such a feat from the toasters whooping it up at the Bucket of Blood. For Socrates Fortlow, who once belonged to the same class as Dolomite and his toast chroniclers, it is the source of ineffaceable shame and guilt. In the stories collected in *Always Outnumbered, Always Outgunned* (1998) and *Walkin' the Dog* (1999), these murders loom permanently in the background of Socrates' conscience. The badman of the folk ballad and toast and, to some extent, the badman of the "black experience" novel are "ba-ad" in the traditional double sense. They are vicious and hurtful and usually feel no guilt, as well as being admirably frightening to their peers. Mosley gives Socrates a certain degree of "bad niggerness," but only to the extent that Socrates can handle himself on the mean streets and alleys of Watts, while deploying that rough skill with restraint and gaining the sympathy of the reader. We are made to like Socrates because he is not, by temperament, hurtful of others and because he has a well-developed sense of guilt. This is why his original crime must be at least partially mitigated, first by the degree of his drunkenness, then by his deep contrition. In *Walkin' the Dog*, he recalls the event. When he awakens from his drunk to realize "I had killed my friends," he does not try to escape. He is too full of remorse. "I ain't no gangster, man," he says to a couple of cops who have to come to his L.A. home threatening to arrest him on phony charges. "I ain't no thief or hired muscle. I'm just mad, mothahfuckah" (p. 60).

He is "mad" for two very plausible reasons, as he suggests in *Walkin' the Dog*. He is angry with himself for so fatally losing control of his own prodigious strength. And he is angry about the twenty-seven years he had to spend in prison because of that loss of control. His time in prison trains him to use violence to deal with the world, to vent the steamy pressure of rage. "[W]hen the shit come down I only know one way to be," he tells a Watts friend after the latter almost provokes a fight between them, one in which the friend surely "wouldn't have been able to prevail over twenty-seven years of studied violence" (p. 64).

It is hard to imagine a reader feeling such sympathetic identification with the ballad or toast badmen. Their otherness is too palpable, too basic, their values too alien and repulsive. For Socrates, though, our sympathy is great, for Mosley gives him the same values that drive the most genuine and the most sincere middle-class humanitarian. True, in *Walkin' the Dog* Socrates does commit a murder in the alley behind the tiny shack he lives in. But his victim, Ronald Logan, is himself one of the many in these novels who "deserve" death, an arrogant young tough just out of prison and plaguing the neighborhood with his bullying behavior. By killing him, Socrates frees his neighbors of a threat to their lives as well as their peace and quiet. The dead man's own mother, in fact, is "Relieved that the evil she released on this world was gone," a sentiment that releases Socrates from any moral guilt (p. 115). Besides, he was provoked beyond endurance when the strutting youth, referring contemptuously to Socrates as an "old man," tried to rob him of the money he had just legitimately earned. Socrates considers doing the absolutely legal thing, turning himself in. But other values take precedence over the letter of the law, especially his two dependents: a poor old crippled dog, Killer, and a boy of the streets, Darryl, whom he has undertaken to tutor. Socrates wants "to make amends" but "still meet his obligations" (p. 120).

Socrates' encounter with Ronald Logan is one of his first turning points. After the funeral, which he attends, he realizes "that some time in the last week the violence had drained out of his hands. He didn't want to hurt anybody" (p. 124). This is the beginning of the profound change Socrates undergoes over the course of the connected but independent stories that make up *Walkin' the Dog*. The change is completed when Matthew G. Cardwell, Jr., a rogue cop in the Watts precinct, pointlessly kills a young black, reinforcing his reputation for brutality. Socrates, deciding on his own that Cardwell must be brought to justice, stalks him for revenge. At the last minute, he pulls back and, instead of killing the cop, decides to demonstrate nonviolently in front of the station house. His courage evokes the support of the neighborhood and soon he has gained TV fame and brought out the best in the locals. Even the police turn cooperative and sympathetic, getting rid of Cardwell. In the process Socrates' own heart settles into nonviolence, and he seems to have found a way "to make amends" for his long-ago crime:

> . . . he had to stand up without killing. Because killing, even killing someone like Cardwell, was a mark on your soul. And not only on you but on all the black men and women who were alive, and those who were to come after, and those who were to come after that too.
> But there was power in his standing up. Power in words and pictures. . . . And he had swung that power like a baseball bat. (p. 254)

Socrates has become a reformed badman. He is like a character from a Frank Capra movie of the late thirties and forties in which the little guy stands up against institutional corruption, empowering the masses with his own common-man courage. Socrates is more violent and streetwise than James Stewart and Gary Cooper in their roles as Mr. Smith and Mr. Deeds, but though he is no paragon, he comes off, in the words of one of the book's insightful reviewers, as "a man whose soul is tuned to the pain of others. Socrates acts decently not because he hews to a code of right action, but because decency follows from this susceptibility."[6]

RAYMOND "MOUSE" ALEXANDER

"Mouse wasn't a large man," Easy tells us in *Black Betty.* "I could have picked him up and thrown him across the room. But he was a killer. If he had any chance to put out your eye or sever a tendon, he did it." In illustration, Easy recounts one of Mouse's encounters with "a white sheriff in west Texas." The law officer arrests Mouse for vagrancy, puts him in jail with his hands chained behind him, and that night comes to his cell. Mouse knows the white man is set to kill him, so what he does is purely self-defense. When the sheriff strikes him the first time, Mouse pretends to lose consciousness. He falls forward, knowing the other man will reflexively grab him. In this position, Mouse goes for more than the jugular. "I didn't bite his arm," Mouse tells Easy with satisfaction. "Uh-uh. . . . I clamped down on his windpipe an' I didn't pull back until my teefs was touchin'." Easy finishes the story: "Mouse ripped out the sheriff's throat and then took his keys. I always thought of him stopping at the sink to wash the blood from his mouth and clothes" (pp. 76–77). In his fight to survive, Mouse has the fierceness of a wild animal, but the serene imperturbability of a streetman holding a loaded .41.

Mouse is the sort of "bad nigger" people tell stories about, as, perhaps, Mosley's father and his father's friends did. But he is a philosophical badman who has taken the measure of black identity in a white world. He proclaims that "a poor man" cannot "live wit'out blood." This is the logic of the streetman. When it comes to living or dying, Mouse has only one code: survival, whatever it takes. This is the reality of being a "nigger," and to acknowledge it is to replace conventional morality with one's own black one.[7] "Most violent and desperate men have a kind of haunted look in their eyes," says Easy. "But never Mouse. He could smile in your face and shoot you dead. He didn't feel guilt or remorse." This is because he kills by his own "set of rules," a moral code that helps him choose his victims from only those who "deserve to die."[8]

Mouse enjoys distributing his own brand of retributive justice. "Want me t'kill 'im, Ease?" It is a question he asks at least once in every novel. His violent appetite is as natural to Mouse as his mouse-like features and his phenomenal sexual success with the ladies. He has a flair for it, turning the cat-and-mouse image on its head to play with his victims and then dispassionately kill them. Indeed, Mouse never does anything in the heat of passion. He calculates the image he projects, building his own security from the respect he instills in others. The toughest thugs in the game call him "Mr. Alexander."[9] He may have been "small" and "rodent-featured," but, as Easy puts it in *Red Death,* he is a "man who believed in himself without question" (p. 27).

Mosley clearly wants us to think of Mouse as part of the old-fashioned badman tradition. In *Gone Fishin'*, the first novel in which Mouse and Easy appear, the two walk through a bug-infested Texas field and Mouse answers Easy's complaining with his usual aplomb: "All I gotta do is wave my hand in front my face once or twice and the bugs leave me be. An' if anything bite me he ain't never gonna bite nuthin' else" (p. 40), recalling the badman's boast that he is superior to the elements and so bad that even rattlesnakes leave him alone. Like several of the ballad badmen, who see ghosts of their victims and hear voices, Mouse is superstitious. He is afraid that his son LaMarque "done give me the eye," put a curse on him by telling Mouse he hates him.[10] Following the principles of the toast novelists, he tells LaMarque in *Black Betty*, "don't you never kill a man don't deserve to die," then, as insurance, adds, "An' don't you never kill your father or your mother either" (73). The most literal badman allusion appears in the episode that begins this novel. Easy has a recurrent dream of an actual murder Mouse committed, for which he got a jail sentence: Big Hand Bruno Ingram, a swaggering bookmaker, "large and powerful" (p. 1), refuses to pay up the twenty-five cents that Mouse claims he won in a bet on the Dodgers. When Mouse shoots the arrogant bully with his enormous trademark .41 caliber pistol, we have a fleeting feeling that the big man deserved what he got. The prototype of this episode is "John Hardy." For the rest of the book, with Mouse just freed from jail, he is guided by the badman's code of vengeance to pursue the man who turned him in to the police for the killing. Easy finally sends him to the home of Martin Smith, who is dying of cancer. Mouse has his mind on only one possible outcome—that he will kill "somebody." So he shoots Martin and walks out of the house without regret or guilt (pp. 255, 344).

Mosley implies that if any character in his writings is like his own father, it is Mouse. When his father died in 1993, it was "the worst thing" that had ever happened to him. He remembers his father for two things in particular. He told wonderful stories, whose "technique" Mosley copies, and he always gave Mosley "the feeling, when I was a kid, that nothing bad would ever happen to me," that he would always be there for him.[11] Similarly, Mouse is not only a badman but a kind of balladeer who makes himself the subject of his material. "Mouse was a master storyteller," Easy tells us in *A Red Death*, one who could hold an audience with stories that were true though his audience thought they were "well-told lies." But more than that, Mouse is Easy's backup, the strength that always appears when it is needed to prevent anything "bad" from happening to Easy (p. 56).

Many of Easy's friends ask him how he can be so close to "a cold-blooded killer." He "never tried to explain" to them how "In the hard life of the streets you needed somebody like Mouse at your back." Indeed, Easy makes their relationship much more intimate than merely backup. "I didn't have a mother or father, or close family or church. All I had was my friends. And among them Mouse packed the largest caliber and the hardest of rock-hard wills."[12] "I knew Mouse better than any brother I could have ever had," says Easy in *White Butterfly*, "and he'd saved my life more times than a man should need saving" (p. 77).

Moreover, Mouse does have a certain capacity for love and loyalty. He loves his mother, his wife EttaMae and son LaMarque, and Easy. Yet Easy knows that Mouse is an explosive aggregation of opposites and will kill even Easy if he stands in the way of what for Mouse is a higher purpose, like getting revenge, recovering his wife EttaMae, or making money. Easy captures Mouse's essence knowingly. He is, says Easy, "the darkness on the other side of the moon."[13] Mouse might even be Easy's own "secret sharer."

For us to like Mouse, though, the deck must be stacked in his favor. Consistently, the people Mouse kills are never souls we would wish to preserve. His nose for slime is all but infallible. His victims *do,* it seems, deserve to die. Or if not, they beg to, as Martin Smith does. Mouse's bullet, we are sure, releases him from pain and sends him to paradise.

But Mosley's badmen are subject to moral conflict and reform. In the last novel but one of the series, *A Little Yellow Dog,* set in the early sixties of Mosley's fictive world, a "change" comes over Mouse, as it did over Socrates Fortlow. Mouse kills an old friend in a fit of pique during an argument, and for the first time in Easy's acquaintance with him, Mouse regrets something he has done. He renounces violence, becomes a mediator of arguments that come up (to comic effect), and changes into a new person who goes so far as to consult preachers (pp. 23–24).

As usual with Mouse, though, this is not a basic change of mind. Mouse the philosopher does not transform himself so much as reject the principle of violence. Mosley uses this rejection to comment ironically on all violence, especially that which authoritative institutions claim the moral authority to commit. "I 'on't think it's wrong to kill somebody, Easy," says Mouse reflectively, because life is just killing in order "to survive," nor can it be a sin, because people in the Bible do it. "An' you know it ain't really against the law, 'cause we both know a cop'll snuff yo' ass as easy as he could sneeze. Shit. Government kill more people than a murderin' man could count an' ain't nobody takin' no general to court. Uh-uh. No. It ain't wrong" (p. 256). Mouse again claims to know who deserves to die, walking once more that slippery moral slope upon which he has always seemed so sure-footed. In the end, Mosley has us watch as he seems to lose his footing, when his nonviolence appears to lead, ironically, to his own death. Armed only with a hatchet, Mouse is unable to fend off two double-crossing hoods that he and Easy meet to close a deal. He kills one with the hatchet but is himself shot.

EASY RAWLINS

If Mouse is Easy's dark side, in Jungian terms his "shadow," it is no wonder that Easy worries constantly about the morality of his own actions. He feels relief when Mouse appears as his savior, but apprehensiveness about his friend's proclivity for murder. Mouse is the incarnation of Easy's "voice," his enraged reaction when someone is trying to hurt him, like the German sniper he faced in Normandy during World War II, where the violence he fights to suppress was born.

The confrontation forced an "existential" choice between killing and being killed. He chose the former and it marked him so deeply that its power over him remains. The critical moment occurred in the Battle of the Bulge, he tells us in *Devil in a Blue Dress,* when for the first time in his life he received what Saul Bellow would call "reality instructions" from "the voice."

> I was trapped in the barn. My two buddies . . . were dead and a sniper had the place covered. The voice told me to 'get off yo' butt when the sun comes down an' kill that motherfucker. Kill him an' rip off his fuckin' face with yo' bayonet, man. You cain't let him do that to you. Even if he lets you live you be scared the rest'a yo' life. Kill that motherfucker," he told me. And I did. (pp. 105–106)[14]

These are simplified conditions. When one acts violently against other violence in order to save one's life, the moral balance is weighted. "The voice has no lust. He never told me to rape or steal," to exploit the weak and the vulnerable. "He just tells me how it is if I want to survive. Survive like a man" (p. 106). The "voice," in other words, urges violence not as destruction but as survival, and, as here in *Devil in a Blue Dress,* Mosley often avoids circumstances that might reflect dishonorably upon Easy.

This experience has something of the same effect on Easy as Socrates' loss of self-control. Easy often finds himself in similar situations in Watts, and then his fury boils up, the badman in him rattles his cage, and he wants to reach for his gun. "The voice is hard," says Easy. "It never cares if I'm scared or in danger." But it "gives me the best advice I ever get." Like Mouse, the voice can judge if a man needs killing. "He ain't worf living," the voice whispers to Easy about a coward Easy ultimately sends to his death (pp. 104, 172). By the second novel, *A Red Death,* Easy's ambivalence about violence has deepened. True, when he realizes that IRS agent Reginald Lawrence is trying to frame him for a back tax bill, Easy's voice bursts out, "kill the mothahfuckah" (p. 42). That is what Mouse would have done. But the voice troubles Easy. Entering the building for an evening meeting with Lawrence, Easy is in such "a state" over what he feels he has to do that he even considers shooting the old Negro janitor who lets him in. "It's just that sometimes I get carried away," he says. "When the pressure gets to me this voice comes out. It saved my life more than once during the war. But those were hard times where life-and-death decisions were simple" (p. 43). To Mouse, such decisions are still simple. But Easy is bedeviled by a middle-class, law-abiding conscience. This is why he is so apprehensive not only of Mouse but of his own violent side. Throughout *A Red Death,* Easy lacerates himself guiltily for being the cause of the deaths of several people he comes to like a great deal, though he never kills with his own hand.

Easy fits Raymond Chandler's well-known formula for the literary private eye. He does walk down "mean streets" and "is not himself mean," though perhaps a bit tarnished and sometimes afraid. Most of the time he is indeed "the best man in his world and a good enough man for any world." He does talk like his Watts contemporaries and shows a disgust for sham and pettiness.[15] But

Mosley is less romantic about Easy than Chandler is about Philip Marlowe, and he is more conscious of Easy's ironically *un*easy state of mind about his chosen line of work and deliberate in his efforts to clarify all of Easy's flaws. Easy is Mosley's existential hero. Not only does he get subjected to Job-like beatings and stabbings and unjust arrests in the course of his investigations into a world of limitless evil, corruption, and violence, he is the anguished asker of ultimate questions in situations where there are no ultimate answers. When Mosley writes about himself and his work, as well as when he gives interviews, he comes back repeatedly to the same theme. Easy is "trying to do what is right in an imperfect world." "[I]f people respect Easy," says Mosley, it is "because he has taken on a tough job in the real world: he's trying to define himself in spite of the world, to live by his own system of values. . . . The genre may be mystery, but the underlying questions are moral and ethical, even existential."[16] Gilbert Muller takes this a little farther: Easy, he says, "carries with him the burden of his own human failings and ethical uncertainties. Crime is not for him a simple matter of locating a murderer or saving a potential victim but rather an intricate problem in moral perception—a problem that often must be approached from several critical perspectives."[17]

The philosophical irony is that until *A Little Yellow Dog,* Easy actually kills no one. He gets into life-and-death situations, is threatened himself, sees people he is fond of killed, threatens to kill villains himself if they will not reform, and is reputed to actually do so. Yet he agonizes over being "the cause of another human being's demise. I had felt that guilt myself." A memory surfacing in his pained conscience "had me back on the front lines. I was choking the life out of a blond teenage boy and crying and laughing, and ready for a woman too."[18] Easy is riddled with guilt, feeling responsibility even for deaths with which he is only remotely connected, seeing himself as the "criminal," the "villain." "At least Mouse and [Easy's Jewish friend] Chaim acted from their natures," says Easy in *A Red Death.* "They were the innocent ones while I was the villain" (pp. 124–25). Easy, the intellectual, sees himself as the fallen man. Mouse and Chaim are still in the Garden before the apple has been bitten into.

This is not puritanism. It is the angst of a streetman caught between a sensitivity to others' pain and the ruthless code of The Life. The contradiction is an old one: the honorable private "dick" trying to do good in a bad world when virtue is useless. By posing this problem, Mosley carries the probe of the violent man by an African American novelist to its furthest point to date. And by dividing the badman mind into two persons, he selects one of the most efficient paradigms available to the novel. The conflict projected in the brotherhood of Easy and Mouse is an attraction-repulsion dialectic in which Mouse is moral Easy's "amoral double," as Roger Berger puts it.[19] Easy constantly struggles against being taken over by his other half, the dark side of his moon. For Mouse, "killing satisfied some nerve he had somewhere. I was growing the same nerve, and I didn't like that idea at all."[20] By the fourth novel, *Black Betty,* Easy's discomfort with a life soaked with death, the deaths of others and the threat of his own, has convinced him to "go out and find a job that would keep me out of the streets forever" (p. 342). By *A Little Yellow Dog,* Easy seems even more preoccupied with the perils of the savage men among whom he finds himself in his investigative work. He has "shared the same sour air" with them his "whole life. One day one of them was bound to kill me—unless I could make the break" (p. 91).

Yet, like the macking gangsters of the toast novel, Easy feels a kind of exhilaration in the street life. It requires constant alertness and the careful maintenance of one's defenses as well as a strange sort of camaraderie, even with the enemy. Whenever he enters an unknown site—a stranger's office, a back alley—he goes in not knowing "what to expect, but that's what street life is all about—you get thrown in the mix and see if you can get your bearings before your head's caved." Easy's encounter with a sneering white tough as he enters the office of a powerful white L.A. mobster has the potential of being a mortal face-off, but before it can explode Easy is called in to see the mobster. The moment has its crazy allure. Easy feels a kind of "comradeship" with the tough; the violence they both threatened seems to be "just an expression between men—rough humor, healthy competition, survival of the fittest" (pp. 279, 278).

Amidst the moral detritus of the streets, idealism and cynicism are in a constant interplay in Easy's mind, touching on race and ethics, history and philosophy. When in *Black Betty* he discovers who turned Mouse in, he thinks, "The truth has to mean something," and he reflects upon the conundrum of freedom: "Truth and Freedom . . . two great things for a poor man, a son of slaves and ex-slaves . . . [but] there was no escaping Fate. Fate hauls back and laughs his ass off at Truth and Freedom. Those are minor deities compared to Fate and Death" (p. 296). Easy links the violence he experiences and that suffered by African Americans with the great Christian themes of suffering and martyrdom. "I'd seen lynchings and burnings, shootings and stonings. . . . Part of that powerful feeling that black people have for Jesus comes from understanding his plight. He was innocent and they crucified him; he lifted his head to tell the truth and he died" (p. 136). At the heart of *A Red Death* are victimization and moral contradiction. Because he is suspected of having links with Communism, the FBI victimizes Chaim Wenzler, a humane Jew who, having escaped the evil of the death camps, has come to the United States and is trying to help the poor blacks in Watts. Easy is torn between his affectionate admiration for this generous and gentle Jew and helping the FBI as a way of avoiding his own indictment for income tax evasion. He is pained and frustrated by this paradoxical mesh of good and bad, especially when he believes he is the cause of Chaim's death. "Like most men," he says, "I wanted a war I could go down shooting in. Not this useless confusion of blood and innocence" (pp. 136, 203). Fate and Death frustrate him by undermining the protection that goodness might bring a man.

It is hard for decency to survive in the stony soil of Watts's streets. But Easy's cynicism, that of a man who has seen the worst in human nature and extremes of racist violence, does not overwhelm his better instincts. Indeed, it is his cynicism that supports those instincts. Only as a bona fide member of the street community, as one utterly respected by the very worst of the Watts hard-men, as one who understands at the core the mean streets down which he goes—only so can he make a credible choice for decency. And Mosley does make Easy's choice credible. Easy has opted unabashedly and without apology for the very best of middle-class values.[21] He is not greedy, though he believes in capitalism and tries his hand at dealing real estate. He is not sexually prudish, in fact has himself committed adultery with other men's wives, though he believes in fidelity between people who have children. Above all, like Socrates Fortlow, Easy wants to do what is "right," and rightness for him, as for Socrates, is determined not by the code of the badman or the street, but by what is highest in mainstream morality. The code that Easy tries to live by derives from his sense of responsibility to help atone for his own—and others'—contributions to the sum of the world's hurts, to give some bit of assistance, love, and understanding to the innocent who are caught in the roiling depredations of the streets through no fault of their own. His own attempt at marriage doesn't work out. His wife leaves him for another man in *White Butterfly,* taking his only blood child with her. But in *A Red Death* he gives a home to and then adopts a little Mexican boy who, in the previous novel, *Devil in a Blue Dress,* had been sexually abused by a prominent L.A. politician. Then in *White Butterfly,* he gives the boy a sister when he adopts a mulatto girl whose mother was the daughter of a wealthy white family. The little girl is forgotten by everyone but Easy when her mother is murdered. The children give him a personal life unknown to Philip Marlowe and Sam Spade.

In *A Little Yellow Dog,* Mosley places Easy into one of his typical moral dilemmas. "I had spent most of my adult years of hanging on by a shoestring among gangsters and gamblers, prostitutes and killers," says Easy. "But I never liked it. I always wanted a well-ordered working life" (p. 11). No one who consorts with thieves and murderers can be accused of hypocrisy or sentimentality in valuing a life of order and security. What sets Easy apart is that he seeks such stability for others as well as himself, especially when it is a matter of family ties. He provides a home for Jesus and Feather, his adopted children. He forces Ronald White to return to his long-suffering wife and family of nine boys in *Devil in a Blue Dress.* He delivers young Alfred Bontemps from the ruthless bookkeeper Slydell in *A Red Death,* sending him back to his sick mother. "We settled it without bloodshed," says a satisfied Easy. "Alfred got a good job with the Parks Department, paid Slydell, and got his mother on his health insurance" (p. 36). In the same book, he plays divorce court adjudicator, allowing Linda Hughes, who hates her abusive husband, to get away from him, but depriving her of her new lover, André Lavender, whom he sends back to his young wife and infant. In *Black Betty* he helps one of his close friends bury a corpse in his basement in order to protect the family from a dangerous police investigation. And in *A Little Yellow Dog,* Easy's inclination to help people put things straight in their lives by going outside normal channels is at least partly responsible for getting him into trouble over a throaty-voiced schoolteacher's "little yellow dog." Most of these extra-legal maneuvers, in which he surreptitiously puts his own thumb on the scales of justice, make strong contributions to the "family values" of the bourgeoisie and remind us of Coffin Ed Johnson and Grave Digger Jones.

As well as, and usually better than, any other novelist, Mosley brings out the latent aspects of the African American man of violence, a longing for calm, order, and stability, a sense that this man contains not only badness but a potential for less socially disruptive behavior as well. This is a potential, though, that appears in the badman's personality only when the middle-class novelist joins in making his image. Calm, order, and stability are conditions that no badman of the folk would have on his behavioral horizon. But with only a few exceptions, the fictional, as opposed to the folkloristic, badman dreams pretty much in middle-class terms, finding violence a behavior to be reformed and corrected rather than flaunted for the sake of a personal rep. From the Harlem badmen of Rudolph Fisher, to the bildungsroman street kids of the fifties and sixties, through the crazy antics of Chester Himes's rogues and detectives and the blaxploitation pieces of Donald Goines and his Holloway House colleagues, up through the highly literary stylization of the figure by John Edgar Wideman and Toni Morrison, which I take up in chapters 11 and 12, the black novel writer is concerned about the anti-social effects of badman violence and seeks ways of ameliorating them. But the world for Mosley remains an incorrigible mix of violence and peace. Only when Mouse renounces his own violence does he remove himself from its protection, and the result is his putative death. In *Bad Boy Brawly Brown* (2002), Mosley's most recent Rawlins novel, Easy mourns for his apparently dead friend. But so strong is Mouse's character that he continues to exert an influence, not only on Easy himself, who repeatedly dreams of him, but upon other characters when Mouse's mere reputation persuades them to befriend Easy.[22]

With considerable skill Mosley projects this concern into the external forms of Easy's environment. It is as morally and socially polyglot as Easy's own mind, full of cowards who act bad, badmen who are as self-confidently bad as Mouse, and families, couples, and single people who are kind, good, and morally straight. Eloquent black ministers, scam artists with brilliant, encyclopedic minds, prizefighters and ex-prizefighters acting as bodyguards, bookies, card sharps, bartenders not to be messed with, beautiful flight attendants, school janitors, manipulative church deacons, real estate speculators, lady schoolteachers with very hot pants, educators with selfless concern for the young—Mosley's panoramic Watts contains a huge cast of black actors, which he ably juggles, recording their extensive range of idiomatic black speech with masterful confidence and effect. Within this circus of wheeling appetites and conflicts he plants Easy as its solid ethical center, anchored by his moral and mental struggle. From there, from the pit of the street's deep corruption, he sends a message. Faith in human goodness, hope, and charity remain in play. Violent men may continue among us, but some are ready to struggle against their violence, reduce the shock of its effects, and think of a better world.

chapter 10

Rap

Going Commercial

Perhaps the most strident, certainly the most self-promoting, badman of all explodes in "gangsta" rap, a complex social development wrapped in a poetry that, like the toasts, is sometimes doggerel, sometimes cleverly original. It marks the triumphal "crossing-over" of a black badman sensibility into mainstream entertainment, a creative extension of the toast into a new style of expression that also draws on Caribbean forms. As a dozen books and countless articles show, the hip hop style that spawned rap had, by the mid-eighties, taken a powerful place in mass taste in music, clothes, dance, language, and "attitude." The traditional badman of the ballad and the toast reemerges in rap only slightly changed from his folk origins, settling into the world of sports, entertainment, leisure, and fashion, bringing with him his most calculatedly defiant, in-your-face manner.

In the last decade and a half young black street poets from all over the country, some still in high school, have modulated the traditional man of violence into a more commercial form of badness. To the surprise and consternation of many, these young "gangstas" have acquired a huge audience, especially a cohort of equally young white males who have been buying their records, making them rich, and propelling them out of ghetto anonymity into the celebrity ranks of pop stars. These rap poets have given the black badman a vast, new, totally unprecedented notoriety. To a pounding, or sometimes merely rattling, beat, they pour forth avalanches of rhythmically uttered words, boasting of their rapping prowess, mocking other rappers, recounting generic sexual conquests, gunfights between "niggas," fantasies of cop-killing. And they take us on grimly realistic journeys through the devastated neighborhoods that they celebrate as home turf and complain about as results of years of racial prejudice and municipal neglect.

Rap is neither fully folklore (it is far too commercialized and widely known) nor completely fiction (i.e., it is not a novel or short story). So, technically, it falls outside the scope of my study. But so many of its manifestations directly engage the traditional badman type that I feel obliged to take note of the form that has, over the past couple of decades, become a powerful cultural phenomenon. It is important at this point, though, to remember that rap is not all of a piece. It has an "old style" and a "new style." Women as well as men rap, whites as well as blacks. Some talk to animals, some summarize the cracks in the ghetto's social fabric, and some outline their own philosophies of life.[1] Rap may have started in the Bronx, but virtually every major city in America, and some not so major, has its own school of rappers with their own subjects and style. There is a plethora of information about rap. The originators of genuine folk forms like the badman ballad and the toast lie shrouded in anonymity, but rap had a huge audience at its birth, and everyone who was near seems eager to testify to what he or she saw, heard, and did. Books on rap's "history" began appearing even before it really had a history, and proliferated in the 1990s.[2] There is no need to return to this well-trod ground, so I intend to examine rap's youth only in its broadest outlines and as it applies to the badman tradition.

Early rap was utterly benign, more like the scat of Cab Calloway and Ella Fitzgerald than anything else, finger-snapping nonsense words designed only to stimulate the young to dance. The first recorded rap to hit the mainstream, the Sugar Hill Gang's "Rapper's Delight" (1979), begins,

> I said a hip hop the hippie the hippie
> To the hip hip hop, a you don't stop
> The rock it to the bang bang boogie say up jumped the boogie
> To the rhythm of the boogie, the beat.

Their aim is "to move your feet," to "bang bang the boogie to the boogie." "I'm gonna rock the mike till you can't resist," says Big Bank Hank. It was another five years before rap took a turn toward social awareness. In 1982, Grandmaster Flash, one of the founders of hip hop music, recorded "The Message," a mournful recitation of ghetto conditions that destroy the young:

> Broken glass everywhere
> People pissing on the stairs, you know they just don't care
> I can't take the smell, I can't take the noise
> Got no money to move out, I guess I got no choice
> Rats in the front room, roaches in the back
> Junkie's in the alley with a baseball bat
> I tried to get away, but I couldn't get far
> 'Cause the man with the tow-truck repossessed my car.[3]

These are definitely not in the badman style, although they echo many of the toast novels. Another early rap theme, though, was in the old badman tradition and it, too, was introduced by the Sugar Hill Gang in "Rapper's Delight." It was the widespread practice of most black street (and folk) artists, boasting. In "Rapper's Delight," the MCs boast about their rapping prowess:

> . . . I'm a helluva man when I'm on the mike
> I am the definite feast delight.

> I'm goin' down in history
> As the baddest rapper there could ever be;

about their cool duds, their flashy possessions, their money:

> . . . I dress to a T

> Ya see I got more clothes than Muhammad Ali and I dress so viciously
> I got bodyguards, I got two big cars
> That definitely ain't wack
> I got a Lincoln Continental and a sunroof Cadillac
> . . .
> I got . . . more money than a sucker could ever spend.

One does not hide one's light under a bushel in the 'hood. These are the traditional hustler's tactics, advertising one's flash, style, show. While they are part of the long American tradition of boasting, they come most directly from the "macking gangsters" of James-Howard Readus and Charlie Avery Harris, the pimps of Iceberg Slim,[4] and especially from a long toast-poem called *The Hustlers Convention,* written and performed by ex-convict Jalal Nurridin, a member of the proto-rap group The Last Poets. In this piece a couple of ambitious street gamblers go to the Hustlers Convention and suavely triumph over the big-time professional hustlers in all the games of chance, proving "which one of us was really the boss."[5]

Like the characters toasters celebrate and some rappers come to imitate, the Sugar Hill Gang also boast about their virility and their way with women. But they carry off their bragging with amusing appropriations of mass popular culture, as when Big Bank Hank meets ace reporter Lois Lane. Lois tells Hank that she will ditch her boyfriend Superman for him. Not overwhelmed by the concession, he maligns the universally admired comic-book hero with a devastating homophobic put-down and a hyperbolic claim of his own overpowering heterosexual vigor:

> . . . he's a fairy I do suppose
> Flyin' through the air in pantyhose
> He may be able to fly all through the night
> But can he rock a party till the early light
> He can't satisfy you with his little worm
> But I can bust you out with my super sperm.

Hyperbole is the essence of any boasting tradition, and rap both early and late takes its place in the honored tradition that can be traced back to Elephant, Lion, and Bear in the slave tales.

Boasting remains a central theme of rap, as do its objects: personal wealth and success, sex (usually non-erotic and misogynistic), the rap skills of the rapper, and the inferiority of competitors. As the rap tone becomes blunter, more swaggering, and more profane, it approaches more and more closely the character of the badman and a determination, as Bad-Lan' Stone says, to "break up this jamberee." The "jamboree" was anywhere respectable people gathered, where prevailing morality was observed and rules followed.[6] The "bad nigger" and his friends attend these social gatherings looking for trouble.

The Miami rap group 2 Live Crew gained attention by behaving something like Howard Odum's Black Ulysses, singing sexually oriented lyrics that deliberately affronted public morality. Their first record, *2 Live Crew Is What We Are* (1986), contains a song titled "We Want Some Pussy." In his segment of the number, Fresh Kid Ice raps,

> I'm the Peter Piper of the 1980s
> Got a long hard dick for all of the ladies
> I don't care if you got three babies
> You can work the stick in my Mercedes.[7]

This is pretty clever rhyming, and Fresh takes pains to stick a finger in the eye of two large moral constituencies: the anti-obscenity and the anti–teenage pregnancy activists. But 2 Live Crew's real jamboree-breaker was their 1989 album *As Nasty As They Wanna Be,* in which they finally succeeded in knocking over a few tables and breaking a few windows at the church social. Starting with its title, for example, "The Fuck Shop" has the kind of deliberate shock value with which children in particular love to bait their elders, dwelling with affected casualness on details that never find their way into polite company. Brother Marquis raps,

> Please come inside, make yourself at home
> I want to fuck, 'cause my dick's on bone
> You little whore behind closed doors
> You would drink my cum and nothing more
> Now spread your wings open for the flight
> Let me fill you with something milky and white.
>   . . .
> I'll fuck you 'till you sleep like a baby
> And in your dreams, you'll say I'm crazy
> In the fuck shop.

This album succeeded perhaps beyond the group's wildest dreams, for in June 1990, a Florida state court ruled it obscene and its performers subject to arrest. Ultimately, the group had it both ways. They gained much notoriety but were finally acquitted and spared punishment. In what must have been one of rap's most disingenuous albums, *Banned in the U.S.A.,* the rappers presented themselves as martyrs to free speech and seized upon rap's boasting tradition to declare their heroism, claiming to "stand tall from beginning to end" and vowing to continue the struggle against censorship in which their "ancestors [had] died."

Aside from the forbidden language and sexual details they flaunted, 2 Live Crew also helped sustain the theme of male dominance of women that is expressed and implied in so much of the language of late rap. They do this by referring to women, when they do, as objects to be penetrated with the rappers' universally outsized penises. But their unimaginative sexual bluntness comes off as a kind of adolescent act, their mechanical and essentially joyless sex with their ho's and bitches reaching for the same deliberate shock value as their taboo vocabulary. Ice-T, once a member of N.W.A. (Niggaz with Attitude) before they broke up, throws some light upon the question by tackling the issue, with greater slyness, from another angle. In "L.G.B.N.A.F." (Let's Get Buck Naked and Fuck), on his 1988 album *Power,* he insists that the young women are not simply passive victims of predatory males, but voluntarily, nay eagerly, complicit in the sex act, together with the male. "Come on," he raps, "you know you wanta do it, too. / It's good to me, and it's good to you." In fact, he even gets a bit romantic: "Come on up to my room," he urges his girlfriend. "We'll undress by the light of the moon."

The real jamboree breakers, though, are those gangstas who come "straight outta Compton," N.W.A. and their imitators. Their album *Straight outta Compton,* appearing in 1988, did indeed fling an "attitude" into the faces of respectable society and, particularly, the South Central L.A. police. The track "Fuck tha Police" is a not very subtle challenge to hated authority. When rapper Ice Cube says in this piece that "when I'm finished, it's gonna be a bloodbath / of cops, dyin' in L.A.," he does not muffle his message. These lines are inflections of "bad nigger" sentiments. They differ from a badman ballad like "Duncan and Brady" in their unapologetic anger at the police in general. Duncan shoots Brady because Brady violated their agreement to let the "game" go on without interference. But Duncan expresses no social animosity toward Brady. Ice Cube is out for general vengeance against an entire class, complaining about what has come to be called racial profiling, police stopping blacks without probable cause because they expect blacks to be breaking the law. The typical ballad badman, moreover, has to go on the lam because he has actually committed a crime, and his flight is almost always in vain. In the gangsta raps the speaker describes neither crime nor flight, referring to generic, not specific, acts. The raps focus on the typical, the abstract, rather than the particular. They are salted with boasts of standing up to the police, threatening and frightening them. Such boasting appears, for example, in MC Ren's segment of "Fuck tha Police":

> "Fuck the police" and Ren said it with authority
> Because the niggaz on the street is a majority.
> A gang is with whoever I'm steppin'
> And the motherfuckin' weapon is kept in
> A stasha box, for the so-called law
> Wishin' Ren was a nigga that they never saw.

Lights start flashin' behind me
But they're scared of a nigga so they mace me to blind me
But that shit don't work, I just laugh
Because it gives 'em a hint not to step in my path.
For police I'm sayin', "Fuck you punk!"

This has some of the trappings of narrative, but is more like a position statement than an account of an event with a climax and an end. And Ren's confidence in his ability to take out the police is of a piece with other rappers' certainty about their sexual power and rapping superiority. But there is a genuineness of feeling in these anti-cop raps that is absent from other kinds of braggadocio. One senses the desperate rage in the strut of the rapper who affects to be more of a danger to the police than they are to him.

The feeling comes out especially strongly in one of the best-known (and to my mind best) anti-cop raps, Ice-T's 1991 "Cop Killer." Backed by the banging and clanking heavy metal sound of his group, Body Count, Ice-T (Tracy Marrow) shouts, as if over the cacophony of nightmarish Compton streets, his opening line: "Cop killer!" It is a high-decibel, almost hysterical challenge to a violent authoritarianism. The rap, which Ice-T has called "a 'protest record' as well as a 'revenge fantasy' of those who have suffered harassment or brutality at the hands of the police,"[8] suggests the setting and tone of Stagolee's exuberant descent into hell to confront the Devil. "Cop Killer," though, exceeds the old ballad in its somber menace and highly effective rendering of the physical sensations experienced by a young man on the verge of killing a representative of overwhelming authority. Few other raps so potently capture the controlled violence about to be let loose, or the iconography of the man of violence in dress, action, and feeling. After the opening explosion of "Cop killer!" the Body Count heavy metal clangs away and Ice-T starts with a hissed "Yeah!" Then come two verses of highly evocative details in a snarling, insinuating voice that also manages a kind of musicality:

I got my black shirt on
I got my black gloves on
I got my ski mask on
This shit's been too long
I got my twelve gauge sawed-off
I got my headlights turned off
I'm 'bout to bust some shots off
I'm 'bout to dust some cops off
. . .
I got my brain on hype
Tonight'll be your night
I got this long-assed knife
And your neck looks just right
My adrenaline's pumpin'
I got my stereo bumpin'
I'm 'bout to kill me somethin'
A pig stopped me for nuthin'.

It is hard to believe that Ice-T meant it when he claimed he did not expect this to be "a controversial record." He certainly managed to ruffle feathers with it. The L.A. police and a number of politicians were so offended by "Cop Killer" that in the summer of 1992 they forced its removal from the album it originally appeared on, *Body Count.*[9]

The public reaction to rap has focused almost solely on rap's angry defiance, its callow, calculated violations of mainstream manners and values. But numerous pop music critics and journalists have pointed out the more socially "responsible" aspects of the genre, what some call "political" as opposed to "gangsta" rap.[10] Generally acknowledging the puerility and shallowness of albums like *As Nasty As They Wanna Be,* they cite rappers such as Grandmaster Flash ("The Message") and Boogie Down Productions ("Stop the Violence"). Many rappers see their role as double. Like Horace in the *Ars Poetica,* they teach while they delight, coat their tough profane sermons with the pleasures of hard rhythms and fast rhymes. Their young fans can thus be improved as they dance to the beat. For example, KRS-One comments on rap's reputation for violence in Boogie Down Productions's best-known cautionary track:

> Now here is the message that we bring today:
> Hip-hop will surely decay
> If we as a people don't stand up and say:
> "Stop the violence!"

Nothing in rap's antecedents, such as the toast or the ballad, ever displayed such social consciousness, or such a cool beat. Perhaps even more explicitly political, the aim of the L.A. group Da Lench Mob, as one of its members puts it, is "Gettin' all our homies together, gettin' 'em out of the negativity and gettin' them into something positive. Like coming out on the road, seein' places, learning to work the drum, and experience a lot of different things, you know so they can say 'I'd rather do this shit than sell dope.'"[11]

These rappers do not advocate any radical ideology, from either the right or the left. They see no reason to overthrow the capitalist economy, only to take it over, reform it, and make it more equitable and inviting to blacks and other excluded ethnic minorities. Ice-T advises his audiences, "Go to school, gain capital, infiltrate the system, and take it over," become "urban, capitalist guerrillas." As one member of EPMD says, young African Americans also want to be part of something "positive," "gettin' what you want out of life, you know, and helpin' each other."[12] It is a sentiment no self-respecting early badman ever permitted to enter his mind.

The most activist group, though, has been Public Enemy, which was one of the influential rap groups of its era. Led by Chuck D (Carlton Ridenhour), Public Enemy became a kind of Black Power conduit for the 1980s and 1990s. Aggressively protesting the way blacks are treated in white America, Chuck D wrote raps urging African Americans to rejoice in their blackness and to "fight the power." The group's rap of that name appeared as the theme music of *Do the Right Thing,* the 1989 film by black movie director Spike Lee. Later it was included in their album *Fear of a Black Planet* (1990), whose title expresses Chuck D's take on American racism, irrational white fear of the very class it suppresses. "Fight the Power" is an imaginative statement not only of blacks' need to fight for their equality, but of the way rap music itself is partly a weapon in that fight and partly a sign of triumph.

> While the black bands sweatin'
> And the rhythm rhymes rollin'
> Gotta give us what we want
> Gotta give us what we need
> Our freedom of speech is freedom or death
> We got to fight the powers that be
> Lemme hear you say,
> "Fight the power!"

In what is probably the best known, and most criticized, passage of the piece, Chuck D heaps scorn upon two icons of white pop culture, Elvis Presley and John Wayne, neither of whom means anything to blacks. Indeed, they are symbols designed to stultify the black community. "Simple and plain," he says, "Motherfuck him [Elvis] and John Wayne," and follows up by resurrecting the great James Brown number from the 1970s, "'Cause I'm black and I'm proud." With these lyrics, Chuck D churns up a heightened excitement just as Ice-T does in "Cop Killer": "I'm ready and hyped plus I'm amped / Most of my heroes don't appear on no stamps." The title track on the album, "Fear of a Black Planet," is an ironic attempt to calm the fears of whites:

> I've been wonderin' why
> People livin' in fear
> Of my shade
> (or my hi top fade)
> I'm not the one that's runnin'
> But they got me on the run
> Treat me like I have a gun
> All I got is genes and chromosomes
> Consider me black to the bone
> All I want is peace and love
> On this planet
> (Ain't that how God planned it?)

How, asks Chuck D ironically in his book *Fight the Power* (1997), can anyone be afraid of someone like me? He complains that the media, especially Hollywood films, convey images of blacks that demean and mock them, that show them merely as joke-tellers or touchdown-scorers rather than as serious citizens seeking a place in serious social discourse.[13] Even the black TV network, WB, caricatures blacks on its sitcoms. And adding insult to injury, the powerful music industry profits from black anguish. Public Enemy took that name because the U.S. Constitution, defining blacks as three-fifths human in enumerations for proportional representation, made blacks an "enemy," establishing their "sociopolitical meaning. . . . [Public Enemy, says Chuck D] represented a combination of self-empowerment, nationalism, and militancy from the combined influences of the Black Panther Party and the Nation of Islam" (p. 86). He wants blacks to take control of and organize the rap industry, but in order to do that, they have to discipline themselves, behave according to the standard rules. They must avoid blowing up on the road, pitching temper tantrums in hotels, and "smoking weed in the middle of public places," which bring negative media attention (p. 107).

Public Enemy and the rap groups that imitate it are, insists Chuck D, ready to embrace mainstream American values, to push for self-discipline, industry, thrift, and restraint. They pose no threat to the American culture that most cultural watchdogs believe rap is laying siege to. To be sure, the violent figure often seems to overwhelm the more conciliatory one. Rappers Tupac Shakur and Biggie Smalls both met violent deaths in what some say was a bitter clash between the East Coast and West Coast rap factions. The press sometimes made it look as if two old-fashioned badmen had taken to the contemporary streets. Place the raps of Shakur and Smalls next to the political work of Public Enemy, and we see in little the history of the black man of violence and the opposition of his two warring aspects: on the one hand, enslaved, exploited, stultified, and frustrated to the point of angry violence; on the other, perpetually hopeful that one day the lofty promises of the Declaration of Independence would also apply to him. This opposition is the sign and symbol of African Americans' historical status in the New World.

As it appears in rap, however, this opposition lacks historical genuineness. I come to this conclusion as a superannuated, not quite dead, white European male. I of all people should reject what so many in the mainstream have called vile trash.[14] Oddly, I happen to *like* rap, at least much of it that I have heard, its insistent rhythms and the strong, often powerful voices of its young performers. I find much of its musical and poetic style highly imaginative and innovative and am amazed that so many untrained youngsters can produce so much that is inventive, new, and worthwhile. But as participants in the historical stream of badman literature, both oral and written, these young men have to be placed where it seems to me they belong. Let me start with the self-evident premise that the person of the rapper is a fictional creation. Even their names have a fictive quality: Ice-T (after the Holloway writer Iceberg Slim), KRS-One, Grandmaster Flash, Snoop Dogg. The fictional figures who speak in iconographic raps like "Cop Killer" and "Fuck tha Police" represent themselves as badmen, rebels against the social authority the police embody. Many observers complain that such figures and their raps exploit blacks and the conditions they live in, in order to buy into the materialist culture and corporate power that the police protect. These observers assume that raps about violence, attacks on police, and male sexual dominance spur record sales, from which the large music companies profit. Indeed, the rappers do seem to be as much concerned about financial statements as statements of principle. Dr. Dre, who produced *Straight outta Compton* and is a rapper in his own right, sought to escape the violence and

misogyny that made his early rap songs popular. But when his sale
half by the change, he says, "I had to come back to the real. Back to
to recover his popularity in the charts.[15]

Bakari Kitwana, in *The Rap on Gangsta Rap* (1995), speak
ics as well as other rappers when he argues that corporate commercia.
drive the rap artists away from their authentic grass roots, because "most artists
if they want to be deemed 'successful' are forced to maintain a style and image
which often compromises the rap artists' values or their attempt to elevate the
artform." Precisely how much commercial interests compromise their artistic integrity is hard to say. Kitwana does go on to claim that rappers, at least in the nineties, could not get recorded unless they hewed to the corporate line of hardcore
gangsta rap. By focusing on guns, violence, sex, misogyny, and materialism, rappers
distort the reality of the inner city. Most of its residents are hard-working, law-
abiding citizens, constantly struggling against prejudice and injustice. They are
more concerned about the community than are the rappers who assert "extreme
individualism" as the way out for poor blacks, stressing the accumulation of
wealth and its symbols.[16]

However true this all might be, my point is that, paradoxically, the badman rebel personas with which the rappers identify gain them admission into the
very culture against which they purport to revolt. These personas combine the
folk figure of the authentic "bad nigger," who is a danger to society because he
insists on living by his own rules, and the novelistic badman, who either demonstrated that he could rise above his mutinous anger or used his badness to succeed in the mainstream. The rapper clothes himself in the identity of one who refuses to accept racist affronts any more. But he transcends those affronts by
succeeding through his own defiance and on the terms set by the rules he claims
to defy. His defiance is not a mark of his fundamental integrity but a strategy for
a subtle capitulation.

The same can be said about the rap version of the boasting tradition. We
might see the rappers' crowing over their expensive cars, their valuable jewelry,
and their style-setting clothes as a rebellious flaunting of mainstream values and
read every boast about their wealth as an act of revolt. To be sure, such boasting
embodies the greed culture, satirically stripping it of all its softening abstractions
and professed ideals of individual striving and achievement. And every beat
smashes through some historical restraint and thrusts forward some symbol of
material success, blasting away social, educational, economic barriers that have
smothered the ambitious black for so long. "This is what I have done," say these
lines, "and I have done it over your objections, displeasure, and disapproval."
These are badmen who have moved the racial battle into plain sight and have
taken aim at their true enemy, a white socio-economic structure that would keep
blacks in virtual helotry. But here again, rappers are reaping the system's rewards
for *professing* revolt. At the sites of true power, in the executive suites, they and
their defiance are exploited to make money for others.

In chapter 5, I reviewed the transcendence Bigger Thomas achieved by his
transgressive murder of white Mary Dalton. He illustrates the weak spot in the

.apper's badman persona.[17] Bigger accepts that the society whose mores he has violated has the right to punish him for what it deems a crime. But he refuses to internalize the morality of that society and so damns himself irretrievably in its eyes. It is that damnation that delivers him into transcendence and so frightens his attorney, Mr. Max. Mr. Max, a Communist and a critic of American capitalist society, understands how radically Bigger has revolted by refusing to let society make him feel guilt, for "Max's eyes were full of terror" and as he leaves Bigger's cell, he "groped for his hat like a blind man." And as Max leaves the cell and the door clangs shut on the doomed Bigger, Wright conveys the distinct sense that it is Bigger, not Max, who is free. Bigger's bedrock integrity lies in his refusing to be co-opted by a society that has never played him fair.

This is where one must doubt the authenticity of the gangsta rapper's "badness." Once again Ice-T presents us with a suggestive symbol of the problem. On the cover of his 1991 album *Original Gangster* appear two photos. In one, the inset, Ice-T stands erect, a ski hat pulled halfway over his ears, wearing dark glasses, his mouth set in suffering determination, his muscular torso half covered with a sleeveless undershirt, and his hands shackled. He is an icon of the oppressed black male, unbowed, defiant. In the main picture he stands impeccably and insouciantly dressed in a tuxedo, utterly at ease in this symbol of the American upper class, his head tilted just so, his hands playing elegantly with his cuff links, his shades lending precisely the touch of menace that a badman must exude. Behind him sits one of his homies in dark top and trousers, posing, again, just the right hint of a threat. The background is a statement of tasteful, conservative expensiveness, a glistening but understated marble floor, a decorous potted palm, and a white geometrical entrance to a tree-filled atrium, something one might expect in the nouveau riche mansions of L.A.'s modish Brentwood. The picture tells us that Ice-T has, against all odds, made it into the power class, but that he retains his credentials with the trammeled. But the message is so commercially calculated as to falsify both symbols. The implication, to be sure, is that the oppressed black male has defied all the social gatekeepers and encroached upon previously forbidden territory. But Ice-T helps make clear, as well, that he values that territory, that he has internalized its merits, found it worthwhile to don that symbolic tuxedo to demonstrate that he, too, can wear with ease the garments of the socially powerful. Defiance is the single most effective weapon of the true rebel. It is Ice-T's defiance, however, that has gained him entrance into that world he previously defied. A mass white audience has made his defiance fashionable and promoted him from the streets of Compton to the mansions of Brentwood. His defiance, far from terrifying corporate executives, reminds them of the satisfying ring of cash registers.

We can evaluate the ultimate submission of the badman figure in the hip hop culture in two ways. On the one hand, it bodes well for our society and the materialist values that hold it together. If the rappers speak for the angriest element of the African American minority, mainstream culture can rest assured that no real threat will come from that quarter. Even the angriest have retained their faith in American materialism and their eagerness to partake of it. On the other hand, it is sad to see the proud badman, even if only an imagined figure, de-meaned as the ticket of admission into a culture he was invented to flout. As a realist I welcome the potential that lies in the rappers' readiness to blend, when possible, into the broader mainstream. But as a romantic I claim the right to con-tinue to pay homage to a spirit who remained irrepressible even when doomed by his own actions. As we near the end of the badman journey, the figure we started with no longer exists. But neither does the culture that produced him. And in the end it may be that the loss of that robust figure in the African Ameri-can imagination is not too great a price to pay, for it may hint at changes that are not now visible but will ultimately improve conditions for us all.

chapter **11**

The Badman and
the Storyteller

John Edgar Wideman's Homewood Trilogy

BROTHERS AND KEEPERS: A FAMILY MATTER

John Edgar Wideman and Toni Morrison bring a whole new esthetic stature to
the treatment of the African American man of violence. Let me take Wideman
first. He does not set out to deal specifically with the traditional badman figure.
In his Homewood trilogy, made up of the novels *Hiding Place* (1981) and *Sent
for You Yesterday* (1983) and the story collection *Damballah* (1981), he explores the implications of a murder committed by two young black men in the
process of carrying out a minor hustle. But in doing so he presents us with a
splendid compressed history of the black man of violence, showing us how this
figure both reflects and helps create the environment in which he operates, here
the streets of the Homewood neighborhood of Pittsburgh, Pennsylvania. Wideman's young Tommy Lawson, who aspires to high status in these streets, stumbles into his violence and brings sorrow to the family members he betrays by his
foolishness. Tommy commits his crime against the backdrop not only of the
streets of Homewood, but also of the neighborhood's history and the generations of family and close friends that grew up and died in the section of Pittsburgh they helped to create. It is in Wideman's imaginative history that we see
the appearance of the traditional badman in a once stable and close-knit community and how his type changes under the pressures of new and destructive
conditions that shatter families and communities alike.

Wideman, like Claude Brown and other writers of the earlier bildungs-roman generation, escaped the street life of the ghetto and became a quasi member of the American middle class, "quasi" because he has never seemed to feel comfortable with his escape, continuing to brood moodily, and often brilliantly, over the people he left behind. At least part of his darkness comes from the encounter between the values of the straight world in which Wideman has made his life and those of the inner-city streets. Respectable people are grieved and embarrassed by criminal acts, and see them as elements of a chaotic environment that must be corrected and restored to normal. And indeed, one of the main issues that Tommy Lawson's crime raises for Wideman is the degree of guilt which must be assigned to Tommy and the part played by the artist in assessing it. These are not just sociological or esthetic questions for Wideman. They arise from his own experience. In 1975, Wideman's brother Robby, operating with two other men in the Homewood area, attempted a hustle like the one Tommy Lawson tries. Like that one, it went wrong, and one of the group shot and killed a man. The crime put Robby Wideman on the run and confronted the Wideman family, respectable residents of Homewood for several generations, with an unprecedented moral problem. Wideman had already escaped the ghetto through a basketball scholarship to the University of Pennsylvania. He was a top student and received a Rhodes scholarship for a year's study at Oxford. By 1975, he was a respected novelist (*A Glance Away* [1967], *Hurry Home* [1970], and *The Lynchers* [1973]) and a teacher at the University of Wyoming in Laramie. His brother's crime activated Wideman's latent feelings of guilt, though at the same time he became determined, as a writer, to understand his brother's behavior, to explain where the violence had come from, how Robby had become connected with it. To do that he had to return to Homewood, his family, and the past. The result was some of the best writing of his career, and the most searching novelistic treatment yet of the present ghetto world, its relationship with African American history, and the way the man of violence is shaped. First there was the Homewood trilogy. Then there was *Brothers and Keepers* (1984), a meditative documentary on his brother and his brother's experience.

In the center of the picture Wideman draws in these books stands Robby, a real person, and the real act of violence in which he was involved. Robby's crime does not make him a community legend. He becomes instead a source of grief to his proud and respectable family and a sad burden to Wideman himself. In *Brothers and Keepers,* both Robby and Wideman have a voice in examining the robbery and shooting, as well as the conditions out of which they grew and the consequences that followed from them. Robby tells the direct story and reflects upon his life in the Homewood streets and the Pittsburgh prison where he was sent for life. Wideman the writer records, comments, and wonders, shaping the material that comes from his own memory and his long, intense talks with Robby. *Brothers and Keepers* pursues the crooked ways of cause and effect. "You never know exactly when something begins," Wideman writes. "[P]eople and events take shape not in orderly, chronological sequence but in relation to other forces and events, tangled skeins of necessity and interdependence and chance that after all could have produced only one result: what is."[1] He attempts to untangle those skeins to get at the significance of Robby's act.

In describing his preparation for the scam, Robby tells us a great deal about the thinking of the ghetto "player." "Robbing people. Waving guns in people's face. Serious shit. But it was like playing too. A game. A big game and we was just big kids having fun" (p. 145). That's what Robby wanted to do, not thinking he would ever be hurt or physically hurt anyone else. Fun was what Robby was always after. Robby and his friends are also ambitious and impatient with the slow route to wealth and the trifling goal of the suburban house with a lawn and a picket fence. They go after the crass heart of the mainstream dream of success. Like the conspicuously consuming billionaires of today, they want power and "port." "We the show people," says Robby, "The glamour people. Come on the set with the finest car, the finest woman, the finest vines. Hear people talking about you. Hear the bar get quiet when you walk in the door. Throw down a yard and tell everybody drink up. See. It's rep. It's glamour." Robby understands that these goals reflect the limitations the ghetto imposes upon aspiration, but he accepts the limitations with the same kind of fatalism with which he describes his life on the street: "What else a dude gon do in this fucked-up world. You make something out of nothing" (p. 131). Such a mix of limits and appetites guarantees violent results.

So just how responsible is Robby? Wideman does not challenge the general standards of law and social discipline, but he does find many reasons outside Robby's control that explain his ending up as a convict doing life. For example, Robby had abandoned his wife and son and the straight jobs at which he hardly managed to support them. But Wideman believes he had plenty of help from society in his failure: Robby's chance for a normal life was as illusory as most citizens' chances to be elected to office or run a corporation, at least if "normal" implies a decent job, an opportunity to receive at least minimal pay-off for years of drudgery and delayed gratification. For Robby, and 75 percent of young black males growing up in the 1960s, "normal" was poverty, drugs, street crime, Vietnam, or prison (p. 220).

Even Bette Wideman, their mother, who worries about Robby's "wildness," is slow to "blame" Robby and his friends. "No jobs, no money in their pockets. How they supposed to feel like men?" (p. 68). She had already become "uncompromisingly bitter" when the Homewood clinic refused to take a friend's illness seriously and, without treatment, he died. She sees Robby's trouble partly as a result of the same unforgivable callousness with which the white doctors treated her friend (pp. 68–69). Where once she had faith in the municipal superstructure of the area in which she has always lived, she now deeply distrusts it. Homewood is fundamentally different from what it was when she was growing up. Wideman's perception of that difference controls his Homewood trilogy and gives the reader the tools for understanding what has happened to black ghetto attitudes since the end of the civil rights era. The Homewood in which Bette Wideman grew up was a "close-knit, homogeneous community," in which relations "were based on trust, mutual respect, common spiritual and material concerns" (p. 73). That old Homewood was certainly constrained by white prejudice, but it maintained its "strong personality," and guaranteed moral and social as well as physical nourishment for its young. But slowly the net of "racial discrimination, economic exploitation, white hate and fear" was drawn tighter and tighter around the ghetto, until the people of Homewood could no longer ignore it. Its signs were everywhere: in the decaying buildings, the unstocked grocery store shelves, the increasing population of junkies nodding on the corner. For Bette Wideman, these are all of a piece with the death of her friend and the trouble her son has got into. The system, she believes, wants more from Robby than simple punishment, to which he is willing to submit. It wants "not only his humanity but the very existence of the world that had nurtured him" (p. 72). She concludes that the life sentence that Robby receives is no accident, that what is happening to Robby and the ugly things happening to African Americans in all the ghettos are "not accidental but the predictable results of the working of the plan" (p. 72).

In his concluding reflections on the experience he has been through with his brother, Wideman brings the reader back to his thesis, that within a confusion of causes there is a deliberate plan that means no good for the African American caught in the ghetto. The prison holding Robby exists in parallel to that of the ghetto. As Robby says, it degrades and corrupts, sending convicted felons back into society angrier and more dangerous than when they entered. "And," says Robby, "it's spozed to be that way, far as I can tell"; it's deliberate. The prison and the ghetto are metaphors for each other.[2] Each is inhabited mostly by blacks, each produces desperate men and women, and each is the creation of a society that blames the victim. The ghetto and the prison are kept hidden from a prosperous straight world that does not want to be bothered. That is the world that Robby contends with, and Wideman tries to make sense of. Wideman ends the book without a clear-cut victory or defeat for either side. The prison remains as rigid and reactionary as before, and Robby's pleas for clemency and an early release have failed, but he has earned an associate of arts degree, which proclaims he is ready to try to submit himself to mainstream expectations. No horizon reveals itself to him, but he continues to march in what he thinks is the right direction: "it is now time to take our lives and our world into our own hands and shape it for the better," he tells the sad-hopeful audience at his graduation, showing "the world that all you needed was a skill and with that skill [you could] become a productive member of society and never its burden again" (pp. 241–42). Wideman regards this confirmation of the best values of the majority culture as an expression of Robby's heroism, his survival against all odds.

HIDING PLACE: LOOKING FOR MANHOOD

Brothers and Keepers was published a year after the last volume of the trilogy, and so stands as a kind of summary and explanation of the earlier books. It is especially useful for getting at *Hiding Place,* the first installment of the trilogy, for *Hiding Place* deals directly with Robby's crime. Tommy Lawson, a fictional version of Robby, participates in a scam during which his partner kills a man, and he has to go on the run. The action of the novel deals with the crime and Tommy's attempt to hide from the police in the days after the shooting.

The entire Homewood trilogy can be seen as a rumination upon Tommy's crime and the degree of his responsibility. Tommy believes that part of the blame for his crime rests on the ramshackle ghetto and its theft of the young's self-esteem. Standing in the midst of the stench and rubble of Homewood, Tommy wonders, "And what that make me? What it make all these niggers?" Those who try to play by the morality of the straight world, obey the law, work reliably in regular jobs, do without—they have nothing but threadbare lives of threadbare respectability. His case, he insists, is even worse. When he tried going straight, working, raising a family, he could find no work sufficient to support his wife and child. As Tommy sees it, the world blames him for conditions for which he is not responsible but which determine his fate. When those conditions drive him to "do what you have to do," he becomes an "outlaw."[3]

Tommy's brother, John, Wideman's alter ego, says that he, too, realizes "it's not all Tommy's fault. I know he's a victim in a way too" (p. 102). John acknowledges the power of the ghetto culture and the damage it inflicts upon its young. Comparing Tommy with a runaway slave offers another way to evaluate Tommy's act. In the concluding story of *Damballah,* which looks at the characters in *Hiding Place* from another angle, Lawson ancestor Sybela Owens escapes from slavery and comes north to settle in Homewood. The system from which she runs interprets her running as a crime, and had she been caught and returned, she would have been punished. Has anything changed, wonders John in telling Robby about her, "in the years between her crime and yours"? What, really, was Tommy's choice? The ghetto requires Tommy to be either a slave or a criminal. With slavery the only alternative, Tommy has no choice. Thinking of the ghetto as an extension of the "peculiar institution," John can see that there might be other "words than 'crime' to define [Tommy's] choice" of action, that Tommy's behavior was forced upon him by circumstances.[4] Judgment depends on the standards by which we decide to judge behavior.

Yet the question remains incompletely answered. What set of standards can be honored that permits stealing, murder, hurting others; that is so permissive, so "understanding," that it denies any connection between will and act, so nihilistic that it sees the will as totally subservient to its environment? Is not this merely the love of a brother who would equate Sybela's escape from slavery with Tommy's flight from a crime in which an unnecessary murder was committed? Even the two people who love him most cannot entirely acquit Tommy. His brother, who is perhaps more tolerant of him than anyone else, finally comes to believe that even when the damage of the ghetto is considered, Tommy cannot look for relief from responsibility. "[H]e's hurt people and done wrong," John thinks, "and he can't expect to just walk away" (p. 102). Harder on Tommy than anyone, though, is old Mother Bess, the ancient matriarch of the neighborhood, who represents several generations of Homewood living. She refers scornfully to Tommy's thievery, his drug dealing, his violence. Many people there in Homewood are poor, she insists, but "They ain't outlaws" (p. 149).

That is the dilemma of assigning responsibility to a ghetto player like Tommy. If we hold him to the same standards of behavior to which we hold young men growing up outside the ghetto, the inequality is palpable. Not only does Tommy start far behind, but he starts with a different set of values. The world reacts to him differently, helps him and impedes him with different expectations and different tools. On the other hand, John grows up in the same environment and escapes the sense of constriction that turns Tommy to crime. In fact, the law-abiding Johns make up the majority of ghetto dwellers. So why should Tommy be treated with greater leniency and have less expected of him than they?

Tommy's irresponsibility appears in its most damaging form in his relationship with his wife and son. Tommy yearns to be important, and there are "times when he screamed for freedom . . . needed to get out of the house and be free" (p. 121). He cannot explain this even to himself, and it undercuts his ability to help his family. He knows he has been a "wrong nigger," but the "Life" on the street is an addiction, even when he is a minor player, even when he knows his pool hall importance is meaningless. As Tommy sees it, he has no choice. "Do what I have to do to get by," says Tommy, and if that puts him outside the law, so be it; it is the only life offered (p. 149). Wideman does not solve the question of Tommy's responsibility. Only a true believer on one side or the other can do that. What is important for Tommy in *Hiding Place* is whether he will emerge from his "hiding place" a man. His literal hiding place is Mother Bess's shed, but according to the African American spiritual that Wideman quotes as an epigraph, that shed can only be a temporary sanctuary:

Went to the Rock to hide my face
Rock cried out, No hiding place.

The world as it is must be faced, and Tommy does come to understand the message of the spiritual, to grasp that no help can save him. After wandering Homewood, remembering his childhood, visiting his wife, assessing the conditions of the ghetto that he angrily blames for his predicament, Tommy matures, arrives at what for him is a new reality. Above all, he loses his fear of death, declaring that death is the worst the authorities can now force upon him. He is not "ready to die," to be sure, but if the police do kill him, he knows who he is. This prepares him for any exigency, death as well as life. He is now "ready to live and do the best I can cause I ain't scared" (p. 151). Like Robby, Tommy accepts the limits of his world, unfair perhaps, but ineluctable, and any affirmation he makes of his only life in his only world must be an affirmation of those limits. The seeds he plants in Mother Bess's back yard while he is hiding show his hope for the future and his new belief in "resurrection."

ROT AND RENEWAL

Tommy's disastrous scam takes place in an environment of crime and petty violence typical of the inner city in the seventies. The first scene of *Hiding Place* establishes a framework not only of shootings and death but of police injustice;

cops kill a black man by mistake and blame it on the dead man's partner. But police have been forcibly asserting white supremacy, and Homewood has been expressing its helpless resentment, since slave times. Much of the violence that Wideman finds in the ghetto does not come from the police, at least directly. It comes from a new mentality, and rises out of deteriorating conditions. It is mindless and purposeless, generally transpires between blacks, stays within the black community, and serves no revolutionary ideology or personal goal. Lives go for ridiculously low prices. Tommy's partner, Ruchell, "wastes" a man named Chubby during their attempted scam. Indeed, Chubby *is* wasted. Ruchell, who has no reason to kill Chubby, is not a John Hardy or a Railroad Bill, putting down an antagonist with legendary coolness. He fumbles the job and looks more ridiculous than cool. But Chubby is not innocent either. He has been in trouble all his life, "Tomming for the dagos," spending time in jail (where he killed a man), and involving himself in various Pittsburgh killings. "It was just a matter of time," says one of the barbershop loungers. "Somebody bound to blow his head off sooner or later" (p. 143).

The greatest change in the nature of Homewood violence comes from the youngsters, the preteen group. They are far more casually and thoughtlessly violent than the adults. Even Tommy Lawson is struck by their brutality. "Those kids was stone crazy," Tommy reflects. "Kill you for a dime and think nothing of it." Nor does anyone's reputation for strength or toughness frighten them. Indifferent to the lives of others, they are also indifferent to their own. "They come at you in packs. Like wild dogs" (pp. 58–59). These are kids who kill, not in the folk tradition of the strutting badman, but in the reality of the streets of the contemporary inner city. Stagolee at least had a reason to shoot Billy Lyon. The violence of the children is without drama, pathos, even anger. It is violence of a new sort, striking enough for sociologists and psychologists to begin to regard it as important. Charles E. Silberman cites statistics showing an increase in violence from 1960 to the mid-seventies, especially street crime and rape by aggressors who do not know their victims. He concludes, though, that the "most disturbing aspect" of this increase

> is the turn toward viciousness, as well as violence, on the part of many young criminals. A lawyer who was a public defender noted for her devotion to her clients' interests, as well as for her legal ability, speaks of "a terrifying generation of kids" that emerged during the late 1960s and early '70s. When she began practicing, she told me, adolescents and young men charged with robbery had, at worst, pushed or shoved a pedestrian or storekeeper to steal money or merchandise; members of the new generation kill, maim and injure without reason or remorse.[5]

Such violence was never connected with the traditional man of violence. He fought, shot, stabbed, killed for reputation and status. In many representations, he understood the significance of his extreme act, and sometimes even felt guilty, hearing voices in his jail cell or converting to religion in atonement. These youngsters do not kill in anger or passion. They simply point and shoot, acting out a moral code bereft of feeling that places no value on life, either their victims' or their own.[6]

It is the violence of the youngsters, more than police brutality, that symptomizes the rot and decay eating out the center of Homewood life. It signals what Wideman in another context calls "cultural collapse."[7] The roving gangs of vicious youngsters and violent men like Chubby embody a moral deterioration which Wideman represents in the physical deterioration of the Homewood neighborhood. "Kelley Street is a wasteland for two blocks after Braddock. Like it's been bombed. All the houses knocked down, snow-cluttered piles of plaster, bricks and lathe boards. Rotten beams jutting from basement cavities into which houses were bulldozed" (p. 116). Tommy Lawson reflects angrily upon the "filth and germs and rot" (p. 58). Carl French speaks ruefully of "garbage in the streets" and "junkies going through your mail box" (p. 100). The ugliness of the ghetto world affects its residents as drastically as violence, while it serves as the culture out of which violence inevitably grows.

But if Wideman hammers away at the forces of disintegration, he is also sensitive to many signs of renewal. Big Bob, the barber, gives shelter and work to the retarded Clement. If one part of Kelley Street looks like the victim of aerial bombing, in the next block the owners keep their homes "freshly painted" (p. 116). Tommy's brother John has escaped the ghetto streets and gone out west, where "It's a good place to raise children." Families try to maintain stability. Brothers and sisters, aunts and uncles, sons and daughters all lend moral support to Tommy's mother Lizabeth, who fears he will be killed. Concern for Tommy extends throughout the community in a kind of civic connectedness. And above all there is Mother Bess. She not only gives Tommy his temporary hiding place, she represents the unifying power that works as an antidote to Tommy's destructive behavior. Between her and Tommy we can see the ghetto as a dynamic organism in which opposing forces produce an anguished but vital tension. Mother Bess has no use for the kind of irresponsible law-breaking that forced Tommy into hiding. Hers are the conservative values that Wideman sees as typical of the "folk."[8] She loves Tommy as she loves all the young people she has mothered, and whom she calls her "children." But her love is prickly, demanding. She holds herself and her children to the standards that promote the survival and continuity of Homewood. Bess is the memory of the place, older than anyone, ironic, stoical, above all realistic. She knows she is no "mother," as the younger people call her, nor does she have curative powers. Over her long life, she has seen things that tell her the world is hard, relentless, and unfair, a killer of the good as well as the bad, the innocent as well as the guilty, and totally irrational. But Mother Bess aims to survive with dignity, never to give in, and this is the lesson she would teach Tommy (p. 53).

Mother Bess's determination provides examples of survival through fortitude and tenacity. The message she sends from the past to the present is "I will never give in," "I won't back down." It makes transcendence of the violence possible. In "The Beginning of Homewood," the concluding story of *Damballah,* Wideman describes how Homewood's present is fortified by its past. Sybela

Owens, the founder of the central Homewood line, mystically looks forward to her unborn progeny, the "shadowy generations" yet to come. They are, like Walt Whitman's "men and women . . . ever so many generations hence,"[9] bound to her and each other by her "memory" and her "pain," the "filaments" of which are "thinly stretched" but "unbreakable" (p. 205). We carry the past with us, and the "spirits" of our past depend upon us for their continued "existence" just as we depend upon them "to live our lives to the fullest."[10] We are strengthened by the past as concrete is reinforced by steel rods.

But the past cannot exist separate from the present, and as Bess helps Tommy emerge from his hiding place, Tommy helps Bess emerge from hers. Years ago, when her husband died, Bess moved out of the present back to the past of Bruston Hill, where the Homewood line originated but where now only an old half-burned shack stands. Bess spent her life among the dead, the memories of her old life, until "she was dead herself" (p. 154). The uninvited arrival of Tommy forces her out of her coffin. Tommy gives her someone to take responsibility for. Tommy, in a way the wolf-pack twelve-year-olds do not, activates the best of the Homewood process.

After waspish resistance, Bess comes to respond to Tommy's need. He becomes her "progeny," a descendant of Sybela Owens, so to speak, part of the community in which the past is constantly reborn. They quarrel like "kin." Each claims the other is at fault, not doing enough, or doing too much, causing discomfort to the other. It is the bristly intimacy of deep family ties. Bess confirms those ties in what Wideman sees as her victory in the book's last moments. As the police arrive on her dark hillside searching for Tommy, Bess takes the final step of her own liberation. She burns down her little shack, in "her special triumphant moment," effectively renouncing her hiding place and announcing that she, like Tommy, is "not scared, not frightened." As she determines to "go down there and tell the truth," to help Tommy, she brings into play Homewood's main strength, the indissoluble bonds between the old and the young, the past and the present (p. 158). Her reemergence strengthens her sense of belonging to Tommy's world, redeems it from the violence with which his run began.

SENT FOR YOU YESTERDAY: THE SKEINS OF HISTORY AND THE SACRAMENT OF STORYTELLING

In *Damballah* and *Sent for You Yesterday* Wideman reconstructs the past out of which the present of *Hiding Place* grew. Homewood is not altogether the "close-knit, homogeneous community" of *Brothers and Keepers,* nor the stable, secure neighborhood that Bette Wideman grew up in. *Sent for You Yesterday* traces the changes in the Homewood community from the twenties to 1970. Homewood has its own problem with violence that comes, interestingly enough, with a character who could be called an old-style badman. Albert Wilkes is a jazz pianist, white-ladies' man, and general bon vivant. He is not vicious, but he does relish his reputation, and his recklessness gets him into bad scrapes. In 1927, in an episode that could have become material for a ballad, he shoots a white policeman over the latter's wife. Like Tommy Lawson, he has to flee. Then, in a typical Wideman coloration, seven years later, when he returns, the waiting police catch him in the home of a law-abiding citizen, playing the piano for the children, and "blow him away" as the youngsters watch. One of the children remembers "The white men smiling as they pulled off [Wilkes's] bloody clothes" (p. 193).

Wideman's characterization of Albert Wilkes suggests that it is not the badman figure *per se* he doubts in his critique of violence, only the tawdry point-lessness of the Chubbys and Ruchells of Homewood and the scary amorality of the kids who kill. Wideman's Wilkes is very much a man of the streets as well as a man of his time. He finds real pleasure in the streets and satisfaction in his rep-utation, not only as a genial fellow, but as a mercurial character not to be fooled with. He defines his historical moment, and exudes a buoyancy and good humor missing in the more passionless, crime-prone atmosphere of the seventies and eighties. In Wilkes and his close friend John French, Wideman sees the arche-typal clash between the streets and the home that he had earlier depicted be-tween Tommy and his brother John, even between himself and his own brother Robby. In the old days, Wilkes and French "owned the streets," but French got married and willingly gave up The Life. There are no easy alternatives to the di-lemma: John French is pulled in both directions. In the end, Wilkes suffers the fate of his kind. He is cut down at a relatively young age. French stays alive by acceding to his wife's wishes. He stays in instead of going out with Wilkes on the night he is killed. In his survival he provides a sense of stability and security to his children and grandchildren, but the conflict between home and the streets is never fully resolved because it is not resolvable. Through Wilkes, though, Wide-man suggests that only in pre–World War II Homewood were the conditions right for his hearty type. By the sixties, the new, and considerably less attractive, breed of violent man was being produced by an environment whose possibilities for black men had narrowed dramatically.

Much of that environment, in Wideman's view, can be explained by the patterns of immigration that have transformed the old Homewood. The old resi-dents complain of the "black tide" from the South, which flooded Homewood and other northern cities during the Depression, changing the community "for-ever." The immigrants from the South undermine the ordered, regulated society established by old Sybela Owen and her children, and in which streetmen like Albert Wilkes appeared as normal parts of the neighborhood's sturdy class pat-terns. As these residents and their descendants see it, with each wave of newcom-ers, the community moral fiber disintegrates further. The immigrants' own southern values are weakened and their self-control sapped by transplantation. Having sent down no roots yet, they feel no sense of obligation to the neighbor-hood. Whole families crowd into single rooms, send their rude and undisciplined children into the streets. The women shamelessly expose their bodies, filling the air with loud and, as the older residents say, "nasty" talk.

These tensions between the old and the new are part of the process leading to the "cultural collapse" in the Homewood of the seventies, to the disappearance of colorful figures like Albert Wilkes and John French, to Tommy's crime, to the wild packs of roving twelve-year-olds, to junkies who will do anything for a fix, to hoods like Chubby so free with their guns. Like his wife Freeda, John French is already wondering in 1934 whether Homewood has "really gone down as bad as he thinks," whether it is "falling apart" (p. 68). Homewood's deterioration advances with each generation. The Second World War means the end of Homewood as Lucy Tate knows it. Wideman excels in connecting specific historical events with demographic and cultural changes driven by racism, as he does in Lucy Tate's ruminations upon these relationships. The beginning of the end of Homewood, she thinks, comes with the bombing of Pearl Harbor and the four years of a white man's war. From the way people leaned toward their radios when the news came out, Lucy knew that "everybody in Homewood . . . was going to war. She knew that and the walls of the house on Cassina [Street] started tumbling" (p. 201).[11] After the war, veteran Carl French contends that it was a holocaust in which Caucasians blasted thirty-caliber machine gun bullets into ragged waves of desperate Japanese, piling dead bodies up "like cords of wood," which were then pushed into the sea by the blade of Carl's bulldozer. Hallucinating Japanese soldiers' screams and dead bodies as he walks toward his own suicide in 1962, Brother Tate, who has been irreversibly changed by Carl's stories, "smells death in the air" and knows that "another war is coming," the Vietnam war. Since it supplies the human fodder for them, Homewood's health is affected by these wars; the odor of death that comes from them may be, thinks Brother, "just Homewood dying" (p. 177).

Homewood's decline results partly from the natural process of decay. But in the black community, Wideman contends, the extra ingredient in that process is racism. The wars that trouble Lucy and Brother Tate are simply another form of white violence, not direct, like lynching or race riots, but indirect. Wars disrupt fragile living patterns and destroy preservative order with their industrial and manpower needs. More directly, racism gnaws constantly at Homewood, as whites continue to exploit the community like an old slave plantation. The white police may have shot Albert Wilkes in 1934, "But what counted," Carl French suggests from the perspective of 1970, "wasn't the murdering puppets in uniforms so much as it was the ones who pulled their strings," the absentee owners, who "held Homewood like a lemon and squeezed pennies out drop by drop and every drop bitter as tears, sour as sweat when you work all day and ain't got nothing to show for it" (p. 80).

In these images, Wideman shows how the "close-knit, homogeneous community" that Bette Wideman remembers in *Brothers and Keepers* slowly deteriorated under the pressure of racial discrimination, economic exploitation, white hate and fear, as well as its own inner turmoil and conflict. If this is the "cross" that being black in the ghetto is, that same blackness contains its own "celebration,"[12] the secret of its endurance, and the Homewood trilogy gives utterance to the dynamic tension between the two. The force for continuity that countervails the impulse to disorder and disintegration is the perpetuation of the past. In *Hiding Place,* Mother Bess embodies this force. In *Sent for You Yesterday,* the transaction between past and present is more explicit. Wideman returns us to the Homewood of the twenties and thirties, then brings us back to the present, where we hear the younger generation comment on those decades, see the way in which material and perceptual changes take place.

Lucy Tate in particular looks back upon "All the good old people and good old times" (p. 194). Many others in the Homewood trilogy also regard the past as superior to the present. For Lucy, the old Homewood people "were special." They "took up space and didn't change just because white folks wanted them different" (p. 199). They taught her that, like Mother Bess, "you don't have to give up." Those were the days when the old people made Homewood "real" by "singing and loving and getting where they needed to get." But along the way, their descendants "gave it all up." They became frightened, and now have nothing to pass on to the next generation except "empty hands and sad stories" (p. 198). In *Hiding Place,* Wideman puts the same sentiment into the mind of Tommy Lawson, a member of the generation to whom Lucy and Carl have nothing to pass on. Tommy was brought up by John and Freeda French, the people who Lucy says made Homewood "real."[13] Tommy remembers John with great affection. He broke or bent the rules of propriety but was a powerful force for family cohesion. Those years were "the best time of his life," and it "all went to pieces" when the strength-giving older generation died (p. 119). As Lucy would have it, she and Tommy's mother and father and uncles failed to carry John French's strength over into their present.

Wideman makes it clear, however, that Lucy suffers from tunnel vision. We must take her nostalgia with a large pinch of salt, as we take the grumbling about the ways of the immigrants. The deterioration of Homewood may be incremental, overcoming the counterforce of conservation and continuity. But the dynamic tension of the ghetto remains, the force of decay and the force of renewal. The decay, ironically, rises from the new, and the renewal, just as ironically, rises from the past. Lucy, like Mother Bess, carries more of the past into the present than she is aware of. Irascible and argumentative, Lucy scorns her old friend and lover Carl French for dwelling on the past, blind to her own inclination in that direction. But that dwelling on the past is the substance of *Sent for You Yesterday.* It is a tough fabric of memories and stories which Lucy and Carl tell one evening to John Lawson, Carl's nephew and Tommy Lawson's college-educated brother from *Hiding Place.* As Wideman's alter ego, John seeks to recover his membership in the Homewood community after his apostasy to the world outside, where he attempted to erase all signs of his ghetto upbringing. Through the stories of old times Carl and Lucy take John back into the past, and by the end of the evening, when they return to the old Tate house where Lucy has lived nearly her whole life, John is prepared to engage in the rite of his own rebirth. As "Black music" plays on the FM radio, the atmosphere becomes charged with all the old sounds that John "remembers," and the ghosts of Brother Tate and old Albert Wilkes appear in the doorway and take their seat at the piano. And John gets up to respond to the music, part of the past, part of his Uncle Carl and Lucy. "I'm on my feet," he tells us. "Learning to stand, to walk, learning to dance" (p. 208). If the past triumphs through Mother Bess at the end of *Hiding Place* when she burns her shack and starts down Bruston Hill to assert herself against the police, it is victorious through John Lawson in *Sent for You Yesterday* as he renews himself in the Tate kitchen. He becomes the reader's key to the past because he is the one who embodies the community and family memory in the stories that make up his narrative. In this moment of John Lawson's renewal, Wideman updates John Grimes's similarly worded triumph at the end of Baldwin's *Go Tell It on the Mountain*: "I'm coming. I'm on my way."

Wideman adds a dimension that Baldwin would have approved of. His storyteller has an almost sacramental function in the Homewood trilogy, and in his other fiction as well. In the title story of *Damballah*, Orion, who refuses to give up his African heritage for the slave values the whites would impose upon him and the other slaves, regards a "boy" watching him fish in the African style. Orion thinks, "This boy could learn the story and tell it again," and by telling the story of his people truthfully, he could correct the lies told about the Africans by the whites (p. 18). In another tale, an old woman needs a story to make the old times real, to open the door to the past and illuminate it. The younger family members listen to the story and relive the past through it. "Past lives live in us, through us," Wideman writes in his brief epigraph to *Sent for You Yesterday*. "Each of us harbors the spirits of people who walked the earth before we did, and those spirits depend on us for continuing existence, just as we depend on their presence to live our lives to the fullest" (p. 3). In "The Beginning of Homestead," John Lawson remembers his Aunt May telling stories, with their various parts and digressions, each one "worth telling." If she seems to ramble, the listener must understand that beneath it all is a fundamental coherence that embraces "everything," and that "the listener is not passive but lives like everything else within the story."[14] The storyteller is thus a mediator in the mystical transaction, and the Homewood trilogy is the mediation. The story, though, does not explain or "unravel the mysteries." Like "authentic black music," says Wideman, the story "recalls" the past, what is ultimately unexplainable, "gives [memories] a particular form, a specific setting, attaches the mysteries to familiar words and ideas."[15] As Shakespeare's Theseus says, he "gives to airy nothing a place and name."

John Lawson, the storyteller of the Homewood trilogy, is linked to the past through the stories he hears and the stories he tells, and becomes the mediator not only between past and present but between "guilty" Tommy and a judging society. Wideman, in a move bound to impress any admirer of the longstanding figure of the "bad nigger," replaces Lawson with the storyteller. He might have used the badman's opposite, the respectable, law-abiding wage-earner of the middle class. By bringing the artist-storyteller to the forefront, Wideman avoids giving victory to one or the other or passing final judgment against the Chubbys, the Ruchells, the Tommy Lawsons, the kids who kill, the Albert Wilkeses. Instead, he reserves to the mediating artist, be he balladeer, poet, toaster, or novelist, the power of giving this vital figure a right and proper place among the generations living and dead.

chapter **12**

Toni Morrison

Ulysses, Badmen, and Archetypes—Abandoning Violence

They are the misunderstood people in the world. There's a wildness that they have, a nice wildness. It has bad effects in society such as the one in which we live. It's pre-Christ in the best sense. It's Eve. When I see this wildness gone in a person, it's sad. This special lack of restraint, which is a part of human life and is best typified in certain black males, is of particular interest to me. It's in black men despite the reasons society says they're not supposed to have it. Everybody knows who "that man" is, and they may give him bad names and call him a "street nigger" but when you take away the vocabulary of denigration, what you have is somebody who is fearless and who is comfortable with that fearlessness. It's not about meanness. It's a kind of self-flagellant resistance to certain kinds of control, which is fascinating. Opposed to accepted notions of progress, the lock-step life, they live in the world unreconstructed and that's it.

Toni Morrison[1]

OUTLAWS

It is amazing to me that it is Toni Morrison, among living black novelists, who brings the most probing and insightful eye to the tradition of the violent man and provides the most fitting conclusion to my study. Perhaps that is what makes her a worthy Nobel laureate. She speaks as a member of a black intellectual elite that desires to preserve the uniqueness of the African American sensibility, establish a sense of communal independence, and participate in the American mainstream on its own terms. No discussion of any aspect of black literary history would be complete without taking her contributions into account. It is not only her international reputation that makes her one of the dominant voices in current black writing, but also her range of reference, her readiness to experiment, and her devotion to the themes and conventions of the African American tradition. "I think long and carefully about what my novels ought to do," she says in a 1981 interview. "They should clarify the roles that have become obscured; they ought to identify those things in the past that are useful and those things that are not; and they ought to give nourishment."

It is what she says next, though, that makes her one of the most significant spokespersons on the badman and brings her explicitly within the purview of my discussion. "My work bears witness and suggests who the outlaws were, who survived under what circumstances and why, what was legal in the community as opposed to what was legal outside it."[2] These make up one of the "archetypes" which Morrison feels herself called to explore.

Many men who are outlaws, not so much contemporary type outlaws but the outlaws that I knew in my youth (laughter), were those kinds of people. They were, oh, I don't know, episodic; they were adventurers. They felt they had been dealt a bad hand, and they just made up other rules. They couldn't win with the house deck and that was a part of their daring. They looked at and that was solution to them [*sic*], whereas other Black people—they were horrified by all that "bad" behavior. That's all a part of the range of what goes on among us, you know. And until we understand in our own terms what our rites of passage are, what we need in order to nourish ourselves, what happens when we don't get that nourishment, then what looks like erratic behavior but isn't will frighten and confuse us. Life becomes comprehensible when we know what rules we are playing by.[3]

Outlaws, in other words, can be a source of nourishment and liberation for the African American community, leading the more timid into new modes of consciousness, toward otherwise inconceivable choices and identities. In Morrison's view, paying attention to and respecting such "outlaws" and their behavior lies at the core of her art. The African American sensibility is complete only when it embraces the lawbreaker. It does this through "irony," and irony is the basis of the "Black style." She does not purport to explain this style in technical terms but describes it as a form of black laughter, a peculiar sense of humor which "has nothing to do with what's funny at all," but rather "with taking that which is peripheral, or violent or doomed," what other cultures would see no "value" in, and conferring importance upon it, like the "duress" under which the outlaw suffers. This is "part of what made us stay alive and fairly coherent, and irony is a part of that—being able to see the underside of something, as well."[4]

With these comments, Morrison places the entire history of the African American badman, the man of violence, the "bad nigger," into a new perspective. The type becomes an important aspect of identity in the cultural code of an ostracized race, a way of thumbing one's nose at the values of the powerful. The chronicles of Railroad Bill, Dupree, Devil Winston may be seen, from Morrison's viewpoint, as injections of energy into the folk psyche, nourishing boosts of controlled hyperbole, part laugh, part frightened thrill, part rebellion. The celebrations of Stagolee and Dolomite in the crude urban toasts are, in this view, sly and deliberately overly vulgar appreciations of the legendary "street niggers" who jeer at respectability. Even the gangsta heroes of rap find shelter under this umbrella, which sees them as offering a kind of camp sensibility, a wry revolt against the demands of social as well as literary convention.

LAYING THE FOUNDATION: *THE BLUEST EYE* AND *SULA*

Morrison's "outlaws" are not immediately recognizable as evolved forms of the traditional man of violence. As a novelist, employing written rather than oral expression, she is much more conscious of how this type functions for her art than were her folk predecessors. Her men are for the most part engaged in an archetypal search for a life lived "intensely and well," a search that leads them, inevitably, beyond the limits of accepted behavior. For Morrison, it is the black man rather than the black woman who usually refuses to submit and violates official and unofficial social "legalities." His is an enterprise both daring and dangerous, and it takes courage—or sheer recklessness—to brave the consequences of acting like a man. It is a theme she has addressed from the very beginning of her career. Cholly Breed-love, who impregnates his own daughter in *The Bluest Eye* (1970), is, in Morrison's words, a "'free man,' not free in the legal sense, but free in his head."

> [He] could do a lot of things; and I think it's a way of talking about what some people call the "bad nigger." Not in the sense of one who is so carousing, but the adjective "bad" meaning, you know, bad and good. This is a man who is stretching, you know, he's stretching, he's going all the way within his own mind and within whatever his outline might be. Now that's the tremendous possibility for masculinity among black men. And you see it a lot. Sometimes you see it when they do art things, sometimes just in personality and so on. And it's very, very deep and very, very complex and such men as that are not very busy. They may end up in sort of twentieth-century, contemporary terms being also unemployed. They may be in prison. They may be doing all sorts of things. But they are adventuresome in that regard.[5]

With characters like Cholly, Morrison articulates the change in attitudes toward traditional types that the African American community, in all its diversity, has been undergoing for the past half century. To call Cholly Breedlove "free," for example, is a leap of understanding that only a Morrisonian imagination could make. She perceives such freedom as dangerous because Cholly, abandoned by his mother and rejected by his father, has "nothing more to lose," and only "his own perceptions and appetites" to interest him. Indeed, having "already killed three white men," he is indifferent, even superior, to the prison he serves time in and its furtive-eyed guards.[6] He refuses in his mind to be "an extension of another's will,"[7] rejects the expectations of both the black and the white community. In Cholly she lays out one of the principal elements of her version of black masculinity: the determination to be oneself, refusing to submit to the will of any person or society. This resoluteness is the catalyst of the Morrisonian male's search.

I must make a disclaimer at this point. Morrison's novels are not necessarily "about" the male characters I discuss here. In many cases I focus upon those characters at the expense of what, in the general consideration, are more important female characters in each novel. I give my main attention to Cholly Breed-love and Ajax, for instance, in *The Bluest Eye* (1970) and *Sula* (1974), when Pecola Breedlove and Sula herself are the central subjects of the narratives. My aim, though, is to examine Morrison's treatment of her men, and that is what guides my close attention to them at the expense of her women.

It is intriguing that Morrison admires such men as Cholly Breedlove, or rather that she understands them. She sees beneath their violence and their irresponsibility, their dangerous outlawry, and feels an affinity for them. They are promiscuous sexual companions and bad fathers. Their inclination is to wander rather than to settle into domestic responsibility, to explode at trifles, to beat up on their women and even rape their own children. Like Cholly before he marries, they follow their "whims" and enjoy a "kind of absence of control." Such "lawless" types "interest" Morrison. They refuse to stay put, insisting upon following the next road around the mountain just to see what is there: this is, says Morrison, "the Ulysses theme, the leaving home." It is "one of the monumental themes in black literature about men." Morrison perceives this urge to wander as part of the "magic that men possess."[8] Such men are what Morrison calls "the salt tasters,"[9] men who make choices and take risks that lead to others' misunderstanding them.

Take away that magic and what is left is a defeated ghost of a man. This is what happens to Cholly when he marries Pauline and fathers Pecola. Once he submits to the bourgeois demands of marriage, he is smothered by its sameness and bewildered by the demands of parenthood, for it is the life of impulse and violence that feels natural to him. The proper matrons who form the moral chorus of Loraine, the small town in Ohio in which the action of *The Bluest Eye* takes place, do not see Cholly as a once-free man caught in the choking tangle of domestic life. Instead he is a "crazy nigger" not quite right in the head, who not only tried to burn down his own house with his wife and child in it, but who did nasty things to his own daughter. Indeed, Cholly is the destructive force that ruins an innocent child, then abandons her and her mother. He lets Pecola bear her child and lose her mind, a dead flower that never properly blooms. It is, of course, not Cholly alone that brings tragedy to this bereft family but the whole environment of a society whose tight rules of behavior and standards of beauty work such painful effects upon the blamelessly ugly. But by the time the baby of his own seed dies, Cholly is long gone, doing, as Morrison suggests, what black men do.

If Morrison does not condone what Cholly does, she does not judge him either. And in the end, she sympathizes with a man who was once free and who was stronger than the jails that would imprison him. In prying open the soul that makes him human, Morrison exposes the pathos of his nature. She may see Cholly as a figure in the "bad nigger" tradition, but by the time he disappears from the story, he is a man whose flight is less adventurous than desperate. But then the whole premise of *The Bluest Eye* is that the blighted Breedlove family has no hope: because Pauline was never wanted as a child, because Pecola is unredeemably "ugly," because Cholly had no childhood, because the straitlaced community of Lorain refuses to accord these wasted people any charity, because of *everything*. Cholly's character is the keynote by which the small family tunes its pitiful instruments.

Morrison's versions of the traditional badman do tend to be socially "lawless," like Stagolee and John Hardy, but without their violence or brutality. Reputation is not something Morrison's "badmen" worry about. Manliness does not depend upon the degree of fear a man can strike in an opponent or his readiness to use a gun. It is finding a way of being oneself, achieving a self-confident identity that balances a reverence for the past with the ability to love in the present. Morrison's "badmen" are thus either literally or by implication questers, whose quest sends them beyond accepted norms. This—and I want to push the point strongly—is what makes them "ba-ad," not violence, and this is their link to tradition. It suits Morrison's own temperament and signals a willingness in the African American sensibility to abandon violence as the test of strength and masculinity. In its place, self-esteem and self-confidence become the basis of masculine strength.

Sula's lover Ajax is a case in point. He is "very much like" Cholly in the years before he married Pauline. Like Cholly, he follows his whims, moving about a world that appears to be quite under his control—the streets, the crap games, the honky-tonks—but is disapproved of by the rigidly respectable custodians of public morality. Unlike Cholly, though, Ajax is utterly comfortable in his own identity. Calm, quiet, a man among men, in control of his own urges and appetites, superior to racist anger, he is also capable of healthy, though uncommitted, passion. Not only does he give Sula a sexual satisfaction she has never known, he treats her as an equal. But when she displays a possessiveness she is astonished to find in herself, he flees to the road, taking with him a self he never allowed Sula to know. She is dismayed to find, after he leaves, that his name was not Ajax, but A. Jacks, or Albert Jacks.[10] Ajax's sense of self requires freedom from all emotional involvements. When faced with Sula's sudden desire to own him, Ajax refuses to be possessed and departs, keeping his masculinity intact. Sula grows sick and dies.

Like Cholly Breedlove's flaws, Ajax's retreat from intimacy is not necessarily to be either applauded or condemned. It is what certain men do. What manly men do *not* do is illustrated in *Sula* by Jude Green. The husband of Sula's best friend, Nel, he whines trivial complaints about whites, his boss, his customers, in order to elicit pity and commiseration from Nel. He begs for a woman's understanding and support, her motherly sympathy, her uncritical admiration. Ultimately, he allows himself to be broken and his marriage destroyed because he is too weak to resist Sula's seductive sexuality. She conquers him. He flees, because he fears having broken the rigid sexual rules by which Nel lives.

The women in Morrison's first two novels do not fare well at the hands of their men. The problem is not male violence but the men's insistence upon their personal freedom. This, says Morrison, puts "an incredible amount of magic and feistiness in black men that nobody has been able to wipe out. But everybody has tried."[11] Such feistiness makes for interesting characters, characters whose energy can propel events and energize narrative action. Such men are seekers who, like Ulysses, brave ocean storms to find a way "to live this life intensely and well." "If there is any consistent theme in my fiction," says Morrison, this is it, and as often as not, it is the feisty man who carries this theme.[12]

Morrison's first two novels were published in the early seventies, and they coincide with the first rush of the black woman's movement, the decaying tradition of the toast, and the surging popularity of the super-macho hero in the toast novel and blaxploitation films like *Superfly* (1972) and *Three the Hard Way* (1974).[13] Many black feminists, energized by the peaking momentum of the civil rights movement and resentful of the exclusive maleness of Black Power, bombarded black men in general with bitter complaints about their brutality, their unreliableness, their self-centered posturing. This black man exulted in violence. It was his stock in trade, the basis of his claim to manhood. And as he clapped it to his bosom, he claimed entitlement to his black woman's body, subduing her with his never-failing sex and disciplining her with a hard fist as necessary.

Morrison sails serenely above the stereotypes of the feminists and the rage of the makers of the macho superhero. She expresses, instead, genuine respect for the powerful tradition of the violent man. She acknowledges its long history as a salutary outlet for the frustrations of the suffocated male, the reality of whose anguish Morrison respectfully acknowledges. But she pulls from the traditional image her own understanding of what in it is important and relevant to a new age. The result is a fairly coherent figure whose central features appear in her main male protagonists, who are built on the minor players Cholly and Ajax. He contains much that is heroic. She shows this in how he overcomes cultural, historical, and political obstacles to a life in which he can respect himself. As an explorer, a cultural trailblazer, a wanderer, he seeks a stability that, like Gatsby's "orgastic future," too often recedes before him. His identity, not surprisingly, seems to lie in the seeking, not the finding. Beneath his veneer of toughness Morrison discovers vulnerabilities, confusions, indecisiveness, despair. They are often more obstacles of self, though, than environment, and it is the drama of overcoming these obstacles that makes up the intensity of his life and attracts Morrison's attention.

INTO THE LIMELIGHT: *SONG OF SOLOMON* AND *TAR BABY*

In her next two novels, Morrison brings her Ulysses figure to center stage, in part through her introduction of a male chorus. In *Song of Solomon* (1977) Tommy's barber shop is the public forum where the local notion of manhood is communally hammered out. With this as her instrument, Morrison shows how testy men can get when their manhood is questioned. In a discussion of Emmett Till, the black youngster who was murdered in Mississippi in 1955, Guitar Baines calls Till a man, but the more cautious Freddie says the boy simply got himself killed, and

> "A dead man ain't no man. A dead man is a corpse. That's all. A corpse."
> "A living coward ain't a man either," said Porter.
> "Who you talking to?" Freddie was quick to get the personal insult.
> "Calm down, you two," said Hospital Tommy.
> "You!" shouted Porter.
> "You calling me a coward?" Freddie wanted to get the facts first.
> "If the shoe fits, put your rusty foot in it."[14]

The discussion also functions to demonstrate the violent qualities of Guitar. He is especially animated by the argument because, we learn, as a youngster he loved to fight. He prides himself, too, on being "a natural born hunter." And, as a member of a secret group of seven black men, he turns his fascination with killing into a quasi-religious campaign against whites. "Seven Days" members kill a white person, randomly picked, whenever they learn that whites, anywhere in the country, have killed a black person. In Guitar some of the traits of the traditional badman remain, but while no pure badman would ever join a black nationalist moral crusade, Morrison suggests that Guitar illustrates how, by the late sixties and early seventies, the Black Power movement might plausibly legitimize "bad niggers." "If you believe," says Morrison, like Guitar does, "that the revolution means some action, some violent action, and you follow that all the way through, if killing is part of it, this is the logical consequence of it. You can become just a killer, a torpedo, with the best intentions in the world."[15] Defending the Seven Days, Guitar moves with the same driven mercilessness as a hit man in a toast crime novel. When he comes to believe that his boyhood friend, Milkman Dead, has stolen money that rightfully belongs to his group, Guitar makes several attempts on his life.

Milkman and Guitar are, in a sense, two sides of Morrison's type, Guitar the violent, Milkman the questing. Impelled partly by Guitar and partly by his own sudden longing to find his family roots, Milkman becomes the wanderer, a successful one, as it turns out, breaking through the bonds of his own middle-class ennui to confirm the heroism of his ancestors and find love in a lower class. In a slight departure from her usual ambiguous conclusions to quests, Morrison has Milkman mystically fulfill his search when he hurls himself from a Virginia cliff "into the killing arms of his brother," Guitar.[16] This is the only such mutually reinforcing male encounter in all Morrison's novels to date. It is fitting that the fractured relationship between Milkman and Guitar be mended in a consummation of violence.[17] Milkman Dead and Guitar Baines are reconfigurations of the traditional badman, each preoccupied with one of the major issues of the seventies: Guitar with Black Power and Milkman with the black search for self.

William "Son" Green in *Tar Baby* (1981) is much more explicitly the wanderer and more clearly connected with the mythic badman. Son is the first character in the novel to step on stage, when he jumps ship off a small Caribbean island and wades ashore, already a fugitive, still incomplete after years of wandering. An outlaw of sorts, he becomes a secret nocturnal observer in the expensive island home of American candy-manufacturing millionaire Valerian Street. While the household is asleep, he moves silently about the bedrooms, watching the residents in their slumber, stealing food when he can, and growing more and more ragged by the day. Only when he is finally discovered does he realize that he has stumbled into a bourgeois household full of suppressed tensions, racial, marital, and generational. His outlaw qualities make him the perfect catalyst for bringing these tensions to the surface.[18] He is a special shock to this household of sheltered respectables, the slop bucket brought into the parlor. Each member of this isolated cast reacts differently to Son's strangeness: Valerian, for example, with studied insouciance; his aging ex–beauty queen wife, Margaret, with paralyzed fear.

Sydney and Ondine Childs, Valerian's live-in black servants of many years, see in Son a perfect representation of the "bad nigger," a shiftless ne'er-do-well who shuns work and runs away from the trouble he inevitably gets into. They dislike and distrust him as a threat to their own class status, servants made proper by their upbringing and their ties with a wealthy white man.[19] Jadine, the Childses' niece, vividly reinforces this view of Son. Reflecting her own anxiety about this type, she warns him against trying to rape her. Refined by the first-class education paid for by Valerian and working as a model in the high couture of Paris, Jadine is sure that she, too, correctly labels Son a traditional "bad nigger." His hair especially transfixes her. It

> looked overpowering—physically overpowering, like bundles of long whips or lashes that could grab her and beat her to jelly. And would. Wild, aggressive, vicious hair that needed to be put in jail. Uncivilized, reform-school hair. Mau Mau, Attica, chain-gang hair. (p. 97)[20]

But in spite of the class differences evoked by his wild appearance, Jadine finds him irresistible, and eventually their struggle is a clash not between the crudities of the "street nigger" and the refinements of a cover girl for *Elle* magazine, but between Son's reverence for his rural folk past and Jadine's determination to be a new black woman: educated, sophisticated, liberated from the restrictions black culture has always placed upon its women.

Son is Morrison's improvisation upon Cholly Breedlove, Albert (Ajax) Jacks, and both Guitar Baines and Milkman Dead. Explicitly linking him to her Ulysses-style wanderer, she calls him a member of "that great underclass of undocumented men." These are the uncounted of the world, "an international legion of day laborers and musclemen, gamblers, sidewalk merchants, migrants, unlicensed crewmen on ships with volatile cargo, part-time mercenaries, full-time gigolos, or curbside musicians." For Morrison, this is not merely a black typology. It is universal. These men are disaffected with the mainstream, rebels against convention, "[a]narchic, wandering." White and black American writers are interested in them because they challenge things as they are and evoke drama, conflict, and a sense of the heroic. "Some were Huck Finns; some Nigger Jims. Others were Calibans, Staggerlees and John Henrys" (pp. 142–43).[21]

By linking the traditional Stagolee with other, less aggressively belligerent figures, Morrison highlights in Son not his violent nature but his quest for growth and discovery. He has fled the Florida town that he loves after unintentionally killing his young wife, not because he is shiftless or irresponsible. He is an identity in the making, in eight years on the run having gone through "seven documented identities and before that a few undocumented ones," all "fabrications of the moment" (p. 119). His shaky foundations make him a perfect subject for the other characters to do their own improvising on, finding in Son what they want to find and making up stories about him, fantasizing about his nature. Moreover, Son may be a version of the Stagolee figure, but he puts the powers of that badman boaster to the service of his love for Jadine rather than using them to dominate. For example, one toaster swaggerer brags that

> I've hoboed with lightning and wrestled with the thunder.
> I'm the motherfucker that put this world on the wonder. . . .[22]

In other toasts and the earlier boasting songs, the boaster often claims to have control of the elements as well as of wild animals and dangerous snakes. Son realizes that beneath Jadine's all-confident surface lies a crystalline fragility, "So it would be his duty to keep the climate mild for her, to hold back with his hands if need be thunder, drought and all manner of winterkill, and he would blow with his own lips a gentle enough breeze for her to tinkle in" (p. 189). Morrison goes further afield, too, to illustrate the depth and the complexity of Son's type. His disaffection with accepted society gives him a lucidity of vision that permits him to see through the fraud of the culture represented by Jadine, Valerian, and the Childses. He has become, like a Hemingway hero, "suspicious of all knowledge he could not witness or feel in his bones" (p. 143).

In the conflict between Son and Jadine, we finally come to a direct struggle between the two diametrically opposed cultures that has been implicit in the novelistic treatment of the badman since the twenties. Son comes from the folk past, in whose male-centered culture the older women pamper their men and grant them dominion.[23] He wants Jadine to understand and appreciate that culture. Jadine has devoted her young life to escaping this racial past, taking over the values of western European civilization, declaring her right to like "'Ave Maria' better than gospel music" and believe that "Picasso *is* better than an Itumba mask" (p. 62) without being thought to have surrendered her integrity.

As Son urges her to join him in respecting the rural folk values of Eloe, Florida, Jadine demands that Son begin a formal education that would fit him to take his place beside her. Both balk at the other's expectations. The narrator, with scrupulous neutrality, comments, "One had a past, the other a future and each one bore the culture to save the race in his hands. Mama-spoiled black man, will you mature with me? Culture-bearing black woman, whose culture are you bearing?" (p. 232). Each is the tar baby for the other. Jadine thinks of Son as a pillar of strength she might lean upon, dreaming of "safety," but her new-found maturity rejects that tar baby. She breaks with Son. Son likewise sees Jadine as a trap and makes the connection explicitly, calling her, among other things, a "tar baby side-of-the-road whore trap" (p. 189). Each accuses the other of refusing to give up the old slave ways.

The very qualities that Jadine and Son are drawn to in the other (the old folk and the new middle class) are precisely the qualities that keep them apart. The end of their relationship coincides with the end of the narrative, and each finds some sort of resolution in an intensification of their own position. Jadine returns to Paris resolving to challenge the images of black women that have dogged her and to become the self she has set out to be, a modern black woman who can be strong outside of the ancestral past. Son's resolution is folk-mythic rather than realistic. He retreats to the company of the "chevaliers," legendary black horsemen who, as slaves escaping a foundering ship, were blinded by their first sight of the beautiful Caribbean island where their ship went down. Gaining freedom from their French masters, and taking possession of the horses that also got ashore, they now spend their time riding blindly through the rain forest, magically guiding themselves through the trees and vegetation. It is suggested more than once that Son is somehow linked to these mythic horsemen, and that in them lies a tremendous power and his own salvation.[24] Son imagines them blind and naked, their blindness signifying true knowledge, their nakedness suggesting their primal identity. Blindness is the environment here, for Son is rowed to the magic forest by a nearly blind old woman who believes in the chevaliers. When she deposits him on the rocky shore in a symbolic fog that prevents physical sight, he becomes, not one of the chevaliers, but a Brer Rabbit thrown into the briar patch. With increasing confidence, assisted by the natural world itself, he runs "Lickety-split. Lickety-split" into the forest where the horsemen are blind but their world is bright with inner vision. Ulysses' journey ends as his return to his legendary origins sets him on a new life.

Morrison clearly wished to represent this final move as positive, which would suggest that he can best develop his consciousness by freeing himself from Jadine. And while he is a rabbit as he runs lickety split, the implication is that he will soon become one of the chevaliers, a quite amazing transformation that might strike some readers as not only surprising but amusing. But Morrison is serious. In an interview with Nellie Y. McKay, she says that there is

> a strong possibility that [Son] joins or is captured by the horsemen—captured by the past, by the wish, by the prehistoric times. The suggestion in the end, when the trees step back to make way for a certain kind of man, is that Nature is urging him to join them. First he crawls, then he stands up, he stumbles, then he walks, and last, he runs, and his run is lickety-split, lickety-split, which has a movement of some confidence, and also suggests the beat of a rabbit running.[25]

Son seems to have chosen the past, while Jadine has chosen the future. Each sacrifices something of the life rejected.

Morrison tends to bring her novels to highly ambiguous, if not incomprehensible, conclusions. But she maintains that her endings come from the stories she remembers friends and relatives telling. Those stories were intended, she says, to teach some sort of lesson, to create a new state of consciousness through their events. Similarly, she wants her novels to effect a "catharsis in the sense" that "order is restored at the end—and the character [achieves] a glimmering of some knowledge that he didn't have when the book began." Thus "at the end of *Tar Baby* I wanted the choice to be there, where it's possible for [Son] to make a choice and only to hint at the choice that he makes because the deed is done. It can't be undone." I take her to mean that she wants to suggest that Son is on the verge of "some realization," which he arrives at through the action of the story. This realization, as yet unformed, embodies a resolution of his long journey toward self-understanding, first in his travels, then in his intense experiment with Jadine. The pain and anxiety he has suffered is the "information" which informs his realization and procures the story's cathartic resolution.[26] Ulysses dons the identity of a blind chevalier.

TRILOGY: THREE STAGES OF THE BADMAN LOVING

Morrison's last three books make up a trilogy dealing with different sorts of "excessive love." "In *Beloved*" (1987), says Deirdre Donahue, Morrison "wrote about the love of a mother for her child, in *Jazz* [1992], she examined romantic love." In *Paradise* (1998), as Morrison herself puts it, "it's the love of God, or some version of a moral life. The passionate, even excessive devotion to God as is manifested in how we construct paradises."[27] What is there about this theme that gives it a three-novel urgency and that convinces Morrison it is worth a decade of her creative life? In *Beloved,* Sethe kills her baby daughter because she loves her too much to give her up to pursuing slave-hunters. In *Jazz,* middle-aged Joe Trace kills his teenage girlfriend because he cannot bear to lose her to Harlem's superficial allure. In *Paradise,* Steward and Deacon Morgan lead several men to attack a group of women to preserve the purity of their all-black town of Ruby, Oklahoma. There are several common threads here that suggest an answer to the question. The excessive love that Morrison explores leads to violence. The characters believe they are serving a moral purpose higher than the prohibition against killing. And their violence results from a condition that is uniquely African American, posing uniquely African American problems. In each case, good intentions are fated to go very wrong, not because failure is the African American destiny but because this is the way with human passion. But also, in each case, a desired resolution is achieved and a certain closure is reached. In *Beloved,* Paul D is on the verge of saving Sethe from her grief and starting a happier future with her. Joe Trace reconciles with his grieving wife Violet. And we are told by Richard Misner, Ruby's young minister, that regardless of the attack on the women (of whom all but one escape death) he will stay in the town, "because there was no better battle to fight, no better place to be than among these outrageously beautiful, flawed and proud people."[28] This may come as a surprise to the reader who has observed him gnash his teeth at the rigid narrow-mindedness of Ruby's town fathers. But Morrison's intent is clear, in *Paradise* as well as *Jazz* and *Beloved:* out of turmoil and death comes awareness, and the exhausted but resilient system renews itself. It is a pattern that Morrison sees in the African American experience, and each of the novels in the trilogy develops an aspect of that experience. Efforts to meet difficult contingencies are, in their excess, doomed, but they demonstrate the irrepressibility of the black spirit and can eventually lead to spiritual peace.

It seems to me that this peace, rather than identity and awareness, is the goal of the Morrisonian badman-adventurer in the trilogy. The adventurer makes the journey and passes through his (usually) seven identities, searching for awareness and a belief in his own manhood. The pattern of exhaustion and renewal is embodied in those journeys. But the state that he comes to at the end of the novel is one of quiet and contentment rather than, for instance, the "lickety split" galloping of Son Green at the end of *Tar Baby* or the strenuous unpredictability of Milkman's death leap in *Song of Solomon.*

Paul D begins his journey in the minus column. As a slave, he is accorded less manhood than the strutting barnyard fowl named "Mister," an honorific with which no white man ever addresses a black man, slave or free. Mister, as Paul D complains, is "allowed to be and stay what he was. But I wasn't allowed to be and stay what I was" (p. 72). Paul D is forced to wear a spiked iron collar, is sold to a cruel slave dealer whom he tries to kill, is locked like an animal in a submerged barred cage on a southern chain gang, escapes, and makes his way to sanctuary with a helpful lady in Delaware, at each stage putting on and taking off a new identity, dying and being born again in a seven-cycle search for some finality. Joe Trace also goes through seven different identities. Like Paul D, though a generation later, Joe travels archetypally through the black history of the post-Reconstruction years. He encompasses a defining socio-historical background just before, during, and after World War I, recapitulating key black experiences: his own birth and orphaning in Virginia, his childhood as a foster son without a mother or last name, his training to be a hunter, violence in the South, his marriage and migration to New York, his move from Lower Manhattan to Harlem, race riots, white prejudice and anger against blacks in the war plants, and finally the end of the war.

But these journeys are only background for the struggle that the novels recount, for the men's eighth identity and a hoped-for closure. Paul D's final struggle is with Beloved, the daughter Sethe killed some eighteen years earlier, who has returned as a vindictive poltergeist to make Sethe's life miserable. As Susan Bowers nicely puts it, Beloved is "much more than Sethe's resurrected daughter. She is the embodiment of the collective pain and rage of the millions of slaves who died on the Middle Passage and suffered the tortures of slavery."[29] Very much like Son's in the Street mansion, Paul D's arrival brings the affairs of Sethe's Cincinnati household to their climax. He forces Beloved out of her bedeviling poltergeist form into that of a mysterious human being and then indirectly causes the exorcism of her destructive spirit. Finally, in the act that brings the narrative to its tentative, ambiguous, and typically Morrisonian "resolution," Paul D undertakes to restore Sethe's will to live, which she lost with the disappearance of Beloved.

As well as loving Sethe, Paul D owes her a debt of gratitude for granting him his manhood back in slavery. She also wrenches open the "tobacco tin" heart in which Paul D has self-protectively stuffed his feelings all the years he has been on the road. His effort to imbue Sethe with the strength to live comes after battling his own unhealthy sexual attraction to the destructive Beloved. He needs to gain for himself emotional repose and for Sethe redemption for her act of excessive love. Kneeling by the bed to which she has retired in paralyzing grief after losing Beloved, he attempts to give her back her sense of womanhood in the same way that she gave him his manhood. When she laments that Beloved had been her "best thing," Paul D insists that "You your best thing, Sethe. You are." Sethe is incredulous but hopeful, and the implication is that he and Sethe together may ward off a slave past so voracious that it would swallow the present and the future whole. Now that there is hope, they can look forward to "some kind of tomorrow" (pp. 272–73).

Joe Trace's journey through his various identities leaves him incomplete, as Paul D was when he arrived at Sethe's home in Cincinnati. He has lost his love for his wife, Violet, who is incapable of communicating with him but coddles the doll she wishes were the baby she never had. His feeling for Violet was his only connection with the past which still holds the secret of his identity. And he merely goes through the motions of living at a time, the mid-1920s, when Harlem is booming with jazz music and speakeasies. In this state of mind, he is not "prepared," even by the odyssey of his seven identities, for the teenage girl he suddenly and unexpectedly falls in love with, much as Paul D is unprepared for Beloved.[30] But Dorcas Manfred is Joe's Eve, the woman who introduces him to the ecstasies of the first apple. He can talk to her, tell her about the emptiness he feels, and believe she understands. She fulfills the role of Joe's absent mother. She closes the circuit broken when Joe lost his blood mother and infuses energy into Joe's life in a way he has always yearned for. Joe has spent his life searching for such a completeness. As a youngster he took the name "Trace" because his parents disappeared "without a trace," leaving him disconnected and estranged, and ever seeking reconnection. He longs for a response to his extended hand, wishing to be created, like Michelangelo's Adam on the ceiling of the Sistine Chapel in the electric originating moment of human history. Dorcas becomes Joe's Eve, leading his Adam *into* paradise (pp. 133–34). It is a new beginning, to be sure, but not with Dorcas. What is the regenerative spark for Joe is the click of the prison door for Dorcas, who, suffocated by Joe's passion, throws him over for a boy her age. Grieving over this new abandonment, Joe reenacts the central scene of the old "betrayal" ballads. He kills the unfaithful lover.

Joe claims, laconically, that he kills Dorcas because he "Didn't know how to love anybody" (p. 213). His problem, though, like Sethe's, is that he loved too much. Such a state of mind is explained at the novel's beginning: if you don't know "When to love something and when to quit . . . you can end up out of control or controlled by some outside thing" (p. 9). That is precisely what happens to Joe on the day he tracks Dorcas down like the trained hunter he once was. "Something else" takes him over, "excessive love," and he becomes a murderer (p. 130). In this state he confuses an instrument of death, his gun, with one of birth and renewal, his outstretched hand.

But the act Joe committed in a state of excessive emotion sets the stage for his reconciliation with Violet and a more fundamental connection with his past than his affair with Dorcas provided. The bridge is Dorcas's teenage friend Felice, who after the murder visits Joe and Violet to "listen" to their "stories." One of Morrison's agents of life, as Paul D is for Sethe, Felice becomes the means for Joe and Violet to arrive at their point of emotional rest. Young, practical, and independent, Felice exhibits a sympathy and understanding for Joe and Violet's generation that Dorcas, in her youthful selfishness and self-absorption, missed. Holding within herself the future after the Jazz Age wears itself out, she is the link between the past and the present and midwifes the new intimacy between Joe and Violet. The old circuit is rejoined and their present closeness recalls a scene of their intimate early love. In that moment, as Joe now relives it, a youthful, vibrant Violet comes in from the field and falls asleep on her bed, one of her men's work shoes off, the other on. Joe returns from a two-month absence, undoes her other shoe and removes it, and muses that the laugh she utters in her sleep is "a light happy laugh that he had never heard before, but which seemed to belong to her." Outside, "women in the houses nearby" sing "'Go down, go down, way down in Egypt land. . . .' Answering each other from yard to yard with a verse or its variation." Their call and response, telling and reacting to a story, is a token of the completeness that begets in Violet "a safe sleep. Deep, trustworthy, feathered in colored dreams" (p. 226). At the end of the feverish action recounted in the novel, Joe and Violet find in their bed a sense of the old satisfaction, a comfort in

> their whispering, old-time love. They are under the covers because they don't have to look at themselves anymore; there is no stud's eye, no chippie glance to undo them. They are inward toward each other, bound and joined by carnival dolls and the steamers that sailed from ports they never saw. That is what is beneath their undercover whispers. (p. 228)

The circle is closed, and here in the present of the novel Joe resolves at last his relationship to his problematic past and discovers tranquility.

In a reprise of one of the old ballad paradigms, Joe kills Dorcas in 1926 because he loves her too much to let her go. In *Paradise,* the men of all-black Ruby, Oklahoma, go on a rampage in 1976 against the women of a secular "Convent" outside of town because they are too devoted to their vision of Ruby's racial integrity, which they believe is threatened by the Convent's residents. "[V]iolent conflict," says Morrison, can indeed "happen as a result of efforts to establish a Paradise. Our view of Paradise is so limited: it requires you to think of yourself as the chosen people—chosen by God, that is. Which means that your job is to isolate yourself from other people. That's the nature of Paradise: it's really defined by who is *not* there as well as who is." The book is thus "an interrogation about the very idea of Paradise," and its title has "a sort of question mark implied behind it."[31] That blacks built all-black towns both before and after slavery is part of the historical record. As she has done before, Morrison takes this bit of history and makes it the basis of her "interrogation" of the exclusivity required by paradises, the "excessive love" for what amounts to a religious principle. Inevitably, that exclusivity will eventually result in the kind of violence that is expressed in what is probably Morrison's best-known opening sentence: "They shoot the white girl first."

The Morgan twins, Steward and Deacon (Deek), who lead the attack on the Convent, are particularly related to Morrison's previous outlaw questers like Cholly Breedlove, Son Green, Paul D, and even Joe Trace, the "bad nigger" rover, carrying a search for identity and freedom beyond the bounds of convention. But it is a negative relationship. The only quest with which Steward and Deek are connected is the one pursued by their revered parents and grandparents in their journey from Mississippi to Oklahoma to found the all-black town of Haven, of which Ruby is only a copy. True, Deek and Steward, as World War II veterans, lead the remnants of the original town to Ruby in an attempt to revitalize the community, but the conditions are considerably easier in the late 1940s than they were in the late nineteenth century, when their ancestors made their trek. Indeed, the most heroic aspect of the trip from old Haven to new Ruby is the transport of Haven's great oven (by automobile) piece by piece, an accomplishment in which the men feel a childish pride, while their women hide their disdain for their excessive efforts for a merely symbolic appliance.

Haven and the great oven that was used by its citizens before they could afford stoves were anything but symbolic. In 1889 the ex-slave "Founding Fathers," discouraged by the growth of virulent race prejudice in the South after Reconstruction, had undertaken the epic journey from Mississippi to Oklahoma. There they founded their all-black town on the noblest of principles, common effort and communal love; and for the noblest of purposes, the freedom and safety of a victimized people. They called it Haven, and for a generation, it is all its founders hoped for. But it is based on a fatal flaw. Having been rejected by a town of prideful mulattos during their arduous trek, Haven's founders think of their settlement not only as protection against white prejudice, but also as an exclusive "haven" for dark-skinned Negroes. They are permanently scarred by the "Disallowing," the central searing memory that draws them tightly together and vulcanizes their sense of community. But instead of pledging never to engage in such inhumane exclusivity themselves, they determine to gain revenge and seal themselves off from any repeat of such humiliation. In an inversion of the usual direction of prejudice in America, dark, rather than light, skin is established as the test of admittance into their paradise. From such actions, Morrison tells more than one interviewer, bad things can result, even when done "with the best intentions."[32]

As for the "New Fathers," when they reach the site for Ruby, they turn into reactionaries rather than adventurers, bent upon preserving the orthodoxy of their ancestors and denying all post–World War II change. Conformity replaces freedom in their moral code. Legend becomes their guide, their nostalgic perception of the old ways their model, and "blood rule" (p. 195) their dark and sacred shibboleth. They take the economic prosperity they enjoy through the fifties and sixties as a sign of God's approval and intensify their insistence upon the faith of their fathers, turning noble endurance into dogma, puritanism, self-approval, intolerance, spiritual stagnation. The New Fathers fail to adapt culturally and politically to the profound changes taking place: the liberalization of general social attitudes and behavior, the voting rights won by the civil rights movement, the growth of black self-esteem and identification with Africa and the values of "negritude."

By 1976, the pressures both outside and inside their "paradise" begin to threaten everything the New Fathers stand for. Serious rifts develop between the townspeople; the young are alienated from the old, and men from women; the town's two churches are competing; and resentment is simmering among those who have been ostracized because of their light skin or their liberal expressions of their sexuality. The New Fathers are deeply troubled by these dislocations in their paradise. Since they cannot blame themselves, Deek and Steward find in these troubles "evidence" of the noxious influence of the Convent. It was, in fact, once a real convent but now is the temporary dwelling of a group of five women who represent everything these men hate and fear, the rejection of men for women and a flourishing like a verdant but unpruned garden. The women become convenient scapegoats for Ruby's frictions. The New Fathers' righteous rage is biblical in its intensity, Old South in its fanaticism. They, the men, are the priests of the old religion and must take action against the anti-Christ.

And no wonder. The Convent's moral success highlights Ruby's failure, for it is a counterparadise to Ruby. It is inclusive where Ruby is exclusive. But some of its strengths are also weaknesses. If Ruby has too much discipline, the Convent has too little. It may accept without test anyone who needs help, but it lacks purpose. In the eyes of the Ruby men, it is a sink of sin and sexual excess, a witch's coven that threatens the godly and the innocent. And so the New Fathers arrive at the Convent in the early morning and attack, shooting "the white girl first." From here the novel circles back around through various stages of the past to explain the "they," the implications of "the white girl," and the reason for the shooting. Morrison deliberately never explicitly identifies the white girl, in order to emphasize the unimportance of color in a book whose main crimes are justified by the "blood rule," that is, the use of skin color as the ground for deciding who is to be allowed into paradise.[33]

This is surely one of the most profound dividing lines in American culture, more profound than class, region, religion, even, perhaps, than gender. When we say "color" in America we nearly always mean black. Very early on in our history, blackness became attached to slaves. To be black was to be a slave. To be a slave was to be black. There are plenty of other divisions in this land, to be sure, but none so tenacious or emotional as that between white and black. In *Paradise,* Morrison attacks that division with an unusual obliqueness. Whatever the weaknesses of this novel, she has never probed deeper nor with greater universality. She shows how color poisons all those along its spectrum, in particular, perhaps, those classified as "black" by the majority culture.

The men who attack the Convent have never had their mettle tested, have known heroism only through the stories of their fathers and grandfathers. Their whole identity is wrapped up in the Old Fathers' struggle against poverty, racism, and rugged frontier conditions. Those older generations hunted and fished to put food on the table. They worked sixteen to twenty hours a day because they could hire no one else to build the barns, plough the fields, plant the seed, and harvest the crops. The women, while working by their side, submitted meekly to their dominance, preparing food, making preserves, sewing clothes. None of these strong women, so far as Steward could see, thought of herself as oppressed or exploited. For Deek and Steward Morgan, and others of their generation, this was the biblical trying time for their bloodline, when prophets strode the land with giant steps and the seed people planted their roots deep into the soil, living a pious life supported by divine approval. Now, the land has been tamed. The Morgan twins display the clean fingernails of the banker rather than the dirt-encrusted ones of the man of the soil. Meat and vegetables come from the store rather than from the field and forest. Hunting is now a game rather than a necessity. The great oven, once the indispensable "utility" for baking the town's flour and warming the wet and newly baptized, has turned into a "shrine" (p. 103). Modern appliances make the women's role irrelevant. Their most cherished efforts have been reduced to ritual and symbol rather than heroic reality.

On first glance, *Paradise* appears to be a conventional criticism of the blustering male seeking to dominate his women. More than one woman in the novel criticizes the Morgans for their sexism. Moreover, the women in the Convent turn out to be considerably more than these masculine leaders of Ruby can handle. To be sure, they do "shoot the white girl first," but they do not kill her. The only woman they do kill is Consolata, the aging Convent "mother" who has been wanting to die anyway. The rest of the women turn their familiar kitchen tools into weapons in fending off these bungling males: boiling soup, a cast-iron fry pan, a wicked butcher knife. Five Convent women successfully resist nine big men and return to life outside utterly changed. This could have been slapstick comedy in the hands of a bitter critic of black men. But Morrison refuses to be drawn into the feminist attack. She sees in the Morgans not only their intolerant sexism but the whole past that they long for but have lost. The New Fathers are the descendants of the American pioneer, living an easy life but chafing at their loss of hardiness, seeking their old masculinity in guns and hunting and the enforcement of women's submission. As blacks, they are a domesticated version of the wandering badman. Instead of refusing the discipline of conventional society in their search for identity, they grimly enforce that discipline, desperately trying to impose a certainty they do not feel.

In making the women of the Convent more than equal to the Ruby men, Morrison does not set out to demean the New Fathers' masculinity. Instead, she shows the pathos in the futility of their effort to preserve an irretrievable past, the desperation in their attempt to cling to a tradition they have already lost. They are not just black men who, like the Stagolee of the urban toast, insist upon bending their women and their children to their will. They are American men whose traditional notions of masculinity have been placed under siege by a new world they have lost control of. Besides, there can be no true pathos unless the subject is worthy of our sympathy. And even in their defeat, there seems, ultimately, something worthy in Deek and Steward and the other Ruby men who go after the women. Certainly the new reverend, Richard Misner, who probably as much as any character speaks for Morrison, sees a reason for not abandoning Ruby, a town in which the "exquisitely human" struggle for a paradise is carried on with an exasperating but admirable persistence.

The resolution to which the Morgan twins are brought is stated only indirectly. It is identified with the town itself and so brings the trilogy, and Morrison's thought at the end of the twentieth century, to a communal close. The Reverend Misner decides to stay, seeing the death of young Save-Marie, at whose funeral he preaches in the closing moments of the novel, as a sign of the town's having passed through its last convulsive phase. A new cycle seems to be panting "at the gate," and while Steward shows few signs of regret, Deek has sought out Misner to express a promising contrition. It is Misner, too, who suggests the more positive function of religious faith, the solace it can bring, its assistance in catharsis.

The story of the African American badman, the man of violence, is one of blood, noise, and death. But like the other two novels in her trilogy, *Paradise* drifts toward its conclusion, after the clamor of the fight at the Convent, in a pensive, meditative mood, the commemorative quiet of Save-Marie's funeral. In what might be an epitaph for Morrison's version of the badman tradition, she ends on a coda of great lyrical beauty. The figures in the center of her final image are, ironically for us, not men but women; and not two black women but a black and a white one, survivors, perhaps, of the Convent, but not necessarily so. They are like two spirits who descended some time ago from a world of perfection and now, their work done, they lie upon a beach in that moment of rest between the conclusion of an arduous task and the start of a new one. The ocean is the central metaphor, the booming repetitiveness of the great waves, cyclical, rhythmic, accompanying the words of Piedade's song. These two unidentified women take solace in each other's presence and their long history of love for one another.

The beach on which these two conciliatory figures recline gleams with the evidence of imperfect humanity, "[d]iscarded bottlecaps," "a broken sandal," "[a] small dead radio." These are the subjects of Piedade's song, and it is full of the sense of "solace," the satisfaction of "speech shared" and of having a place where one belongs that characterizes the endings of *Beloved* and *Jazz*. Like the waves and the tide, her characters move between sadness and joy, disconsolation and hopefulness, coming at last to rest, not in an ideal situation, but in the only one they have access to, the humanly flawed. Thus Morrison concludes,

> When the ocean heaves sending rhythms of water ashore, Piedade looks to see what has come. Another ship, perhaps, but different, heading to port, crew and passengers, lost and saved, atremble, for they have been disconsolate for some time. Now they will rest before shouldering the endless work they were created to do down here in Paradise. (p. 318)

On this beach, resting between each crash of the breakers on the wet sand—this is where, we feel, the citizens of Ruby are right now, and the women of the Convent who have gone on with their lives. It is where, maybe, all of Morrison's characters have settled, just off of, or waiting to get on, their boat to wherever the next current may take them.

Morrison leaves her Ulysses, that very much revised "badman," in the hands of two female spirits. If they speak for the entire trilogy, they bring his restless spirit to rest and imply that his destructive violence can be cathartic. The figure they regard with a feminine eye is a descendant of the badman that has preceded them in so many different forms, the early ballad, the Renaissance novel, the bildungsroman of the fifties and sixties, the streetman's toast, the Holloway "black experience" novel. They are not critics of this figure, these women, but affectionately humane revisionists who can understand without scorn the irresistible wandering and violent habits of the African American man of violence. With them this journey through badman territory can come to a peaceful, respectful close.

APPENDIX
Analysis of Thirty Prototype Ballads

I have divided these prototypes into four groups based on the kind of violence their eponymous character is involved with. In this analysis, I list the number of prototypes in each group, the nature of the act the prototype's variants deal with, the name of the central character (which is also usually the title of the piece), and a collection in which a prominently cited and oft-collected variant appears.[1]

1. The "Police" Ballads

Four in which a black man kills a white law officer: Danny Major in "Bugger Burns" (Lomax and Lomax, *Our Singing Country*, p. 331); Duncan in "Duncan and Brady" (Leadbelly's version from Folkways Records, Huddie Ledbetter Memorial, Vol. 2, FA 2014B); "Railroad Bill" (Lomax and Lomax, *American Ballads and Folk Songs*, p. 119); and "Dupree" (Odum and Johnson, *Negro Workaday Songs*, p. 56).

2. The "Fugitive" Ballads (including Po' Laz'us)

Six in which a black man kills or is killed (or shot) by another black man: an unnamed black badman hunts another and kills him in "Lookin' for that Bully" (Odum and Johnson, *The Negro and His Songs*, p. 204); "John Hardy" kills a man over a card game (Cox, pp. 175 ff.); "Stagolee" shoots Billy Lyons (Hughes and Bontemps, p. 359); "Eddy Jones" is killed on a train (Odum and Johnson, *The Negro and His Songs*, p. 205); "Poor John" is stabbed by an unnamed assailant (Odum and Johnson, *The Negro and His Songs*, p. 155); badman Bill Bailey shoots the unnamed narrator in "I Went to the Hop-Joint" (Scarborough, p. 90). I also include in this group "Po' Laz'us" or "Bad Man Lazarus," who is the archetype of all the fugitives. But rather than killing or being killed by another black badman, badman Laz'us is pursued and killed by the sheriff after he steals from the company commissary (Odum and Johnson, *Negro Workaday Songs*, p. 50).

3. The "Betrayal" Ballads

Ten in which a black man or woman kills a spouse or lover: "Devil Winston" kills Vinie (Wheeler, p. 109); Bill Martin kills Ella Speed in "Bill Martin and Ella Speed" (Lomax and Lomax, *American Ballads and Folk Songs*, p. 117); an unnamed narrator kills an unnamed girlfriend in "The Coon-Can Game" (Scarborough, p. 88); an unnamed man kills Delia in "Delia" (White, p. 215); Jim Strange kills Lulu "on a Saturday night" in "Jim Strange Killed Lulu" (Work, p. 246); an unnamed narrator kills his girlfriend in "I Went to the Hop-Joint" (Scarborough, pp. 90–91; this is a different ballad from the one of the same title listed in Group 2); Bad Lee Brown kills his unnamed woman in "Bad Lee Brown" (the Lomaxes call it "Bad Man Ballad" in *American Ballads and Folk Songs*, p. 80; Wheeler calls it "Late One Night," p. 109; and Laws calls it "Little Sadie," p. 250); Frankie kills Albert in "Frankie and Albert," sometimes called "Frankie and Johnnie" (Lomax and Lomax, *American Ballads and Folk Songs*, p. 103), with a variant titled "Pauly" and sometimes "Lilly" in which Lilly kills Paul (Odum and Johnson, *The Negro and His Songs*, p. 229); an unnamed black woman kills "Big Jim" (Lomax and Lomax, *American Ballads and Songs*, p. 111). I also include in this group "Eliza Stone," whose eponymous heroine kills no one but is a "bad" woman (Odum and Johnson, *Negro Workaday Songs*, p. 12).

4. The Boasting Songs

Nine in which the badman-bully boasts of toughness and threatens death to other blacks but kills no one: "Bolin Jones," "Roscoe Bill," "Don't Fool wid Me," "Shootin' Bill," "I'm de Hot Stuff Man," "Buffalo Bill" (Odum and Johnson, *Negro Workaday Songs*, pp. 62, 63, 65, 67); "Joe Turner," "Bad-Lan' Stone," "Wild Negro Bill" (Odum and Johnson, *The Negro and His Songs*, pp. 206, 212, 213).

The Collections

Cox, John Harrington. *Folk-Songs of the South.* 1925. Reprint, New York: Dover Publications, 1967.

Hughes, Langston, and Arna Bontemps, ed. *The Book of Negro Folklore.* New York: Dodd, Mead, 1958.

Laws, G. Malcolm, Jr. *Native American Balladry: A Descriptive Study and a Bibliographical Syllabus.* Rev. ed. Philadelphia: American Folklore Society, 1964.

Lomax, John A., and Alan Lomax. *American Ballads and Folk Songs.* New York: Macmillan, 1934.

——. *Our Singing Country: A Second Volume of American Ballads and Folk Songs.* New York: Macmillan, 1949.

Odum, Howard W., and Guy B. Johnson. *The Negro and His Songs: A Study of Typical Negro Songs in the South.* 1925. Reprint, Hatboro, Penn.: Folklore Associates, 1964.

——. *Negro Workaday Songs.* 1926. Reprint, New York: Negro Universities Press, 1969.

Scarborough, Dorothy. *On the Trail of Negro Folk-Songs.* 1925. Reprint, Hatboro, Penn.: Folklore Associates, 1963.

Wheeler, Mary. *Steamboatin' Days: Folk Songs of the River Packet Era.* 1944. Reprint, Freeport, N.Y.: Books for Libraries Press, 1969.

White, Newman I. *American Negro Folk-Songs.* 1928. Reprint, Hatboro, Penn.: Folklore Associates, 1965.

Work, John Wesley. *American Negro Songs and Spirituals.* New York: Bonanza, 1940.

NOTES

Introduction

1. L. D. Reddick, "The Negro as Southerner and American," in *The Southerner as American*, ed. Charles Grier Sellers, Jr. (Chapel Hill: University of North Carolina Press, 1960), 133.

2. Samuel M. Strong, "Negro-White Relations as Reflected in Social Types," *American Journal of Sociology* 52 (1946–47): 23, 24.

3. H. Nigel Thomas, *From Folklore to Fiction: A Study of Folk Heroes and Rituals in the Black American Novel* (New York: Greenwood, 1988), 56. Alan Dundes argues in *Mother Wit from the Laughing Barrel: Readings in the Interpretation of Afro-American Folklore* (New York and London: Garland, 1981) that Brer Rabbit and Trickster John "are rarely, if ever, mean or bad," and therefore cannot be thought of in the same way as the "bad nigger" (578). See also Cecil Morris Brown's discussion of the phrase in his "Stagolee: From Shack Bully to Culture Hero" (Ph.D. diss., University of California, Berkeley, 1993), chapter 6.

4. Charles H. Smith, "Have American Negroes Too Much Liberty?" *The Forum* 16 (October 1893): 181.

5. Robert E. Hemenway, *Zora Neale Hurston: A Literary Biography* (1977; reprint, Urbana and Chicago: University of Illinois Press, 1980), 224.

6. Lawrence W. Levine, *Black Culture and Black Consciousness: Afro-American Thought from Slavery to Freedom* (New York: Oxford University Press, 1977), 420. For one of the earliest discussions of this meaning and pronunciation, see H. C. Brearley, "'Baad Nigger,'" in Dundes, *Mother Wit,* reprinted from the *South Atlantic Quarterly* 38, no. 1 (January 1939): 75–81.

7. Levine, *Black Culture and Black Consciousness,* 420.

8. Ibid. Emphasis added.

9. Roger D. Abrahams, "Some Varieties of Heroes in America," *Journal of the Folklore Institute* 3, no. 3 (December 1966): 347. The term is widely used in accounts of desperadoes of all stripes. For instance, in *The Story of the Outlaw* (New York: Outing, 1907), Emerson Hough writes of the "hard men" led by Jim McCandlas (or McCanles) in Wild Bill Hickock's territory (172).

10. For further discussion of the badman types see Robert G. O'Meally, "'Game to the Heart': Sterling Brown and the Badman," *Callaloo: A Black South Journal of Arts and Letters* 14 (February–May 1982): 43–54. O'Meally further reconfigures the terms used by Abrahams and Levine, settling on the "good badman" and the "bad badman" to correspond, more or less, with Levine's "moral hard man" and Abrahams's "hard-man."

11. Price M. Cobbs and William H. Grier, *Black Rage* (New York: Basic, 1968), 65–66.

12. Ibid., 66.

13. Ralph Ellison, "Richard Wright's Blues," in *Shadow and Act* (1964; reprint, New York: Signet, 1966), 100; James Baldwin, "Many Thousands Gone," in *Notes of a Native Son* (1955; reprint, Boston: Beacon, 1984), 42.

14. Baldwin, "Many Thousands Gone," 42.

15. Howard W. Odum and Guy B. Johnson include "Eliza Stone" in their *Negro Workaday Songs* (1926; reprint, New York: Negro Universities Press, 1969), 12. She kills no one but is a "bad" woman. In *The Negro and His Songs: A Study of Typical Negro Songs in the South* (1925; reprint, Hatboro, Penn.: Folklore Associates, 1964), 229, the same authors print a ballad variously called "Lilly" or "Pauly," in which Lilly kills Pauly, but we get little helpful information in the song. And there are plenty of references to black women who carry razors and ice picks, which they can wield as dangerously as any man. But they never acquire a legendary identity, as Frankie does, or Stagolee, Railroad Bill, and John Hardy.

At the same time, Trudier Harris, writing the "Bad Woman" article for the *Oxford Companion to African American Literature* (ed. William L. Andrews, Frances Smith Foster, and Trudier Harris [New York: Oxford University Press, 1997], 42–43), is correct to point out that Sula Peace, in Toni Morrison's *Sula* (1974), and women characters like her might be called "ba-ad." They revolt against conventional expectations of the black female. She also cogently cites Eva Canada in Gayl Jones's *Eva's Man* (1976), who, as she remarks, "not only kills her lover but bites off his penis." But all Professor Harris's citations refer to novels written in the last thirty years, reinforcing my point that there is really no tradition of a violent "badwoman" similar to that of the badman.

16. Hazel V. Carby, introduction to *Race Men* (Cambridge, Mass.: Harvard University Press, 1998).

17. Joshua Wolf Shenk, "Guns and Roses," review essay, *The Nation* 268, no. 22 (June 14, 1999): 15.

1. The Classic Badman and the Ballad

1. For an analysis of these thirty prototypes that groups them according to the kind of violence their protagonists committed, see the appendix.

2. I take most of my examples from ballad samples collected from 1905 to 1925, largely by Howard W. Odum, John Wesley Work, Dorothy Scarborough, and others. John and Alan Lomax, though they did much collecting of their own in the late twenties and the thirties, usually borrowed their ballad examples from these earlier collectors.

3. John Wesley Work, *American Negro Songs and Spirituals* (New York: Bonanza, 1940), 43.

4. G. Malcolm Laws, Jr., *Native American Balladry: A Descriptive Study and a Bibliographical Syllabus,* rev. ed. (Philadelphia: American Folklore Society, 1964), 17, 22, 86, 92. The five nonmurder ballads are "Boll Weevil," "Joseph Mica," "Dese Bones Gwine Rise Again," "The Blue Tail Fly," and "John Henry," with "John Henry" as the only "perfectly authentic" one. Of course, a number of pre-1920s blues songs also dealt with violence, usually involving a man going after a "creeper" who has stolen his girlfriend or a woman attacking a "Lizzie" who has stolen her man. But these are expressions of emotion and feeling rather than narrative accounts of an event. See, for example, Howard W. Odum and Guy B. Johnson, *Negro Workaday Songs* (1926; reprint, New York: Negro Universities Press, 1969), "Dere's a Lizzie after My Man," 163; and "A Creeper's Been 'roun' Dis Do'," 149.

5. Howard W. Odum and Guy B. Johnson, *The Negro and His Songs: A Study of Typical Negro Songs in the South* (1925; reprint, Hatboro, Penn.: Folklore Associates, 1964), 212. Sterling A. Brown thought Professor Johnson to be "one of the most sympathetic and informed students of Negro folklore." See his essay "Folk Literature," in *A Son's Return: Selected Essays of Sterling A. Brown* (Boston: Northeastern University Press, 1996), 210.

6. Alan Dundes, *Mother Wit from the Laughing Barrel: Readings in the Interpretation of Afro-American Folklore* (New York and London: Garland, 1981), 267. Dundes's

helpful, succinct statement appears as the headnote to Mimi Clar Melnick's essay "'I Can Peep through Muddy Water and Spy Dry Land': Boasts in the Blues," which was written in 1967. Her thesis is that the blues boaster seeks "status" above all, and he achieves it through flashy clothes, "fancy cars, women (pretty and in large quantity), and in some instances liquor and weapons." His most powerful possession, though, is money, without which none of these tokens of status is available. Her analysis is valid enough, but bears little relevance to my discussion of the boasting badman, as I will show. The badman gains status through his badness, his violent (or potentially violent) behavior, not through the superficies of clothes, jewelry, or money. The blues boaster is a dandy; the badman boaster is a "ba-ad nigger."

7. Odum and Johnson, *Negro Workaday Songs*, 62.

8. Roger D. Abrahams, "Some Varieties of Heroes in America," *Journal of the Folklore Institute* 3, no. 3 (December 1966): 347.

9. Lawrence W. Levine, *Black Culture and Black Consciousness: Afro-American Folk Thought from Slavery to Freedom* (New York: Oxford University Press, 1977), 417–18, 410.

10. Dickson D. Bruce, Jr., *Violence and Culture in the Antebellum South* (Austin: University of Texas Press, 1979), 151.

11. Greil Marcus, *Mystery Train: Images of America in Rock 'n' Roll Music* (1975; reprint, New York: Dutton, 1976), 76–77.

12. Alan Lomax, *The Folk Songs of North America in the English Language* (Garden City, N.Y.: Doubleday, 1960), 572.

13. Ibid.

14. John A. Lomax and Alan Lomax, *American Ballads and Folk Songs* (New York: Macmillan, 1934), 99.

15. B. A. Botkin, ed., *A Treasury of American Folklore* (New York: Crown, 1944), 122, 123.

16. Commerce with the devil is widespread in African American folklore from the spirituals to the blues, and the Faust motif appears frequently as well, though more often in the form of selling one's soul in return for special musical talent. David Evans, in *Tommy Johnson* (London: Studio Vista, 1971), 22–23, tells the story of how blues singer Tommy Johnson claimed to have learned his music from the devil in return for his soul. "Learning music from the devil," says Evans, "is a common motif in negro folklore." Skip James explains his blues song "Devil Got My Woman" as an example of the devil's constant presence in life. See Stefan Grossman, ed., *The Country Blues Songbook* (New York: Oak Publications, 1973), 51. Zora Neale Hurston, in *Mules and Men* (1935; reprint, N.Y.: Harper Perennial, 1990), 3, remembers that in the tales she heard as a child "even the Bible was made over to suit our vivid imagination. How the devil always outsmarted God and how that over-noble hero Jack or John . . . outsmarted the devil." And John W. Roberts, in *From Trickster to Badman: The Black Folk Hero in Slavery and Freedom* (Philadelphia: University of Pennsylvania Press, 1989), 200, claims that most badmen are connected with the devil, having received their powers from him.

17. Robert Winslow Gordon, *Folk-Songs of America* (New York: National Service Bureau, 1938, publication no. 73-s), 46. The famous opening line comes from Edward Bulwer Lytton, *Paul Clifford*, vol. 3 of *The Works of Edward Bulwer Lytton* (New York: P. F. Collier, n.d.), 235: "It was a dark and stormy night. . . ."

18. John Russell David, *Tragedy in Ragtime: Black Folktales from St. Louis* (Ann Arbor, Mich.: University Microfilms, 1976), 278.

19. Josh Dunson and Ethel Raim, ed., *Anthology of American Folk Music* (New York: Oak Publications, 1973), 54.

20. Langston Hughes and Arna Bontemps, ed., *The Book of Negro Folklore* (New York: Dodd, Mead, 1958), 361.

21. Christopher Marlowe, *Dr. Faustus,* in *The Complete Plays of Christopher Marlowe,* ed. Irving Ribner (New York: Odyssey, 1963), 5.2.168.

22. Henry M. Belden and Arthur Palmer Hudson, ed., *The Frank C. Brown Collection of North Carolina Folklore,* vol. 2 (Durham, N.C.: Duke University Press, 1952), 564.

23. Vance Randolph, ed., *Ozark Folksongs,* rev. ed., vol. 2 (Columbia: University of Missouri Press, 1980), 146.

24. Odum and Johnson, *Negro Workaday Songs,* 56.

25. See the appendix.

26. John A. Lomax and Alan Lomax, *Our Singing Country: A Second Volume of American Ballads and Folk Songs* (New York: Macmillan, 1949), 309. The Lomaxes title this version of the ballad "As I Set Down to Play Tin Can."

27. See Orlando Patterson, *Slavery and Social Death: A Comparative Study* (Cambridge, Mass.: Harvard University Press, 1982), 38–45.

2. Postbellum Violence and Its Causes

1. For discussions of nineteenth-century black violence in the North, see Roger Lane, *Violent Death in the City: Suicide, Accident, and Murder in Nineteenth-Century Philadelphia* (Cambridge, Mass.: Harvard University Press, 1979), *The Roots of Violence in Black Philadelphia, 1860–1900* (Cambridge, Mass.: Harvard University Press, 1986), and *Murder in America: A History* (Columbus: Ohio State University Press, 1997); also David M. Katzman, *Before the Ghetto: Black Detroit in the Nineteenth Century* (Urbana: University of Illinois Press, 1973); and Kenneth L. Kusmer, *A Ghetto Takes Shape: Black Cleveland, 1870–1930* (Urbana: University of Illinois Press, 1976).

2. David M. Oshinsky, *"Worse Than Slavery": Parchman Farm and the Ordeal of Jim Crow Justice* (New York: The Free Press, 1996), 128.

3. Quoted by Edward L. Ayers, *Vengeance and Justice: Crime and Punishment in the Nineteenth-Century American South* (New York: Oxford University Press, 1984), 231.

4. William D. Miller, *Memphis during the Progressive Era, 1900–1917* (Memphis: Memphis State University Press, 1957), 92, 211 n. 10.

5. Tera W. Hunter, *To 'Joy My Freedom: Southern Black Women's Lives and Labors after the Civil War* (Cambridge, Mass.: Harvard University Press, 1997), 162. Atlanta's Decatur Street, according to Hunter, was the heart of the lower-class entertainment section. It teemed with bordellos, gambling dens, and saloons, as well as more legitimate businesses like laundries, cinemas, restaurants, and portrait studios. Respectable blacks tried to keep their young adult children from going there, and usually failed. Hunter emphasizes, too, the intermingling of the races along Decatur Street. "Chinese laundrymen, Jewish and Greek shopowners, Yankee spielers, Italian chorus men, and moonshine mountaineers" all did business along the street. Jazz, ragtime, blues flourished along with prostitution, drinking, and gambling (152).

6. Stephen Ward Angell, *Bishop Henry McNeal Turner and African-American Religion in the South* (Knoxville: University of Tennessee Press, 1992), 165.

7. W. E. B. Du Bois, *Some Notes on Negro Crime, Particularly in Georgia. Report of a Social Study Made under the Direction of Atlanta University; Together with the Proceedings of the Ninth Conference for the Study of the Negro Problems, Held at Atlanta University, May 24, 1904* (Atlanta: Atlanta University Press, 1904), 13, 16, 18–31.

8. W. E. B. Du Bois, *The Souls of Black Folk,* in *Three Negro Classics,* ed. John Hope Franklin (New York: Avon, 1965), 329.

9. See, for example, Paul Oliver, *Blues Fell This Morning,* 2nd ed. (New York and Cambridge: Cambridge University Press, 1990), 203, and Miller, *Memphis,* 93. See also Robert C. Toll, *Blacking Up: The Minstrel Show in Nineteenth-Century America* (New York: Oxford University Press, 1974), 5, who says that the urban migration contributing to the violence separated the rural workers from their folklore and "the verbal arts—stories, songs, tales and jokes," taking out of their lives "much more than amusements, because in folk societies verbal arts taught values and norms, invoked sanctions against transgressors, and provided vehicles for fantasy and outlets for social criticism. They were central to group identity. They told people who they were and how to live with their neighbors."

People needed a substitute for what was lost, something "that could establish a new sense of community and identity for them and their neighbors."

10. E. B. Reuter, *The American Race Problem* (New York: Crowell, 1927), 363; quoted also by H. C. Brearley in *Homicide in the United States* (1932; Montclair, N.J.: Patterson Smith, 1969), 115.

11. Lane, *Violent Death in the City,* 122. See his review of the same discussion in *Murder in America,* 184–88, where he adds the proposition that much of the violence among blacks, as well as whites, was due to the "bachelor subculture," in which young unmarried men had little else to protect but their honor and did that with hair-trigger reactions to any personal affront. White men, too, failed to control themselves in undisciplined environments where state authority was weak and conflicts were settled by the participants themselves. In *The Legend of Joaquín Murrieta: California's Gold Rush Bandit* (Twin Falls, Idaho: Big Lost River, 1995), 6, John F. Varley describes the combustible Gold Rush environment in the California Mother Lode, where undisciplined younger men made up most of the population and tempers were highly combustible. "Everyone carried arms," says Varley, "and, at the least quarrel, out came the revolvers. Someone would yell, 'Don't shoot,' the crowd would surge back, and the combatants would blaze away. 'A man's life is but little thought of,'" Varley quotes Marysville businessman Franklin Buck as saying.

12. Jacqueline Jones, *The Dispossessed: America's Underclasses from the Civil War to the Present* (New York: Basic, 1992), 132–35, 137, 138.

13. See also Jacqueline Jones, *Labor of Love, Labor of Sorrow: Black Women, Work, and the Family from Slavery to the Present* (New York: Basic, 1985), 6, in which she points out that black women, like black men, did not participate in the industrial work force at the end of the nineteenth and the beginning of the twentieth centuries. They labored in the fields and worked as household domestics, producing raw cotton for the mills and freeing their white employers to enter the higher-paying industrial work force and become consumers.

14. Herbert G. Gutman, *Work, Culture, and Society in Industrializing America: Essays in American Working-Class and Social History* (New York: Knopf, 1976), 20, 59.

15. Lane, *Violent Death in the City,* 122–24, 131. There is much evidence that blacks in large numbers in both the North and the South were relegated to unskilled, low-paying jobs outside of the new industrial economy. Kenneth L. Kusmer reports in *A Ghetto Takes Shape,* 66, that "In Cleveland in 1890, only three blacks were employed in the city's rapidly expanding steel industry, and virtually no black males worked as semiskilled operatives in factories." See also Katzman, *Before the Ghetto,* 105:

> In 1890 there were no blacks in the brass and ship industries, and only twenty-one blacks were found among the 5,839 male employees in the tobacco, stove, iron, machine, and shoe industries. Ten years later only thirteen Negroes worked in Detroit's book, shoe, brass, chemical, furniture, gas, iron and steel, machine, stove, tin, tobacco, and wire factories—industries employing 10,498 males. Of the 36,598 men reported in the 1900 census to have been engaged in manufacturing and mechanical pursuits, only 139 were Negro, and of these, forty-seven were in the building industry. In 1910 only twenty-five Afro-Americans were recorded among the 10,000 mostly foreign-born, semiskilled operatives and laborers who worked in Detroit's automotive factories. . . . Black women fared no better than the men. In 1910, 87% of the employed black women were employed in domestic and personal service. There was not a single black among the 1,186 telephone operators in the city; among the 2,081 saleswomen in stores in Detroit, only 1 was black; among 1,474 women clerks, 3 were Negro; and of 7,106 office clerical workers, only 10 were black.

16. David Gordon Nielson, *Black Ethos: Northern Urban Negro Life and Thought, 1890–1930* (Westport, Conn.: Greenwood, 1977), updates Dollard's notion that the segregation of African Americans drove them deeper and deeper into their own group until it created within them all a "black ethos," a way of meeting the world that was conditioned by their color and their assumptions about themselves because of it.

17. John Dollard, *Caste and Class in a Southern Town*, 3rd ed. (New York: Doubleday Anchor, 1957), 267–70. The first edition of this work appeared in 1937. For his book-length presentation of this "frustration-aggression" thesis and its Freudian bases, see John Dollard et al., *Frustration and Aggression* (New Haven: Yale University Press, 1939). It is worth noting that the Martinique student of psychiatry Frantz Fanon, in his study of the native population of Algeria during its war of liberation from France, sees the native Algerians as "niggers," whose colonization by the French is analogous to the oppression of African Americans. "The native," he writes, "is a being hemmed in," forced to "stay in his place, and not to go beyond certain limits. This is why the dreams of the native are always of muscular prowess" and aggression. "The colonized man will first manifest this aggressiveness which has been deposited in his bones against his own people. This is the period when the niggers beat each other up, and the police and magistrates do not know which way to turn when faced with the astonishing waves of crime in North Africa." See Frantz Fanon, *The Wretched of the Earth,* trans. Constance Farrington (New York: Grove, 1968), 52.

18. H. Nigel Thomas, *From Folklore to Fiction: A Study of Folk Heroes and Rituals in the Black American Novel* (New York: Greenwood, 1988), 158.

19. See especially Kenneth M. Stampp, *The Peculiar Institution: Slavery in the Antebellum South* (1956; reprint, New York: Vintage, n.d.), 335: "Having to submit to the superior power of their masters, many slaves were extremely aggressive toward each other"; Dickson D. Bruce, *Violence and Culture in the Antebellum South* (Austin: University of Texas Press, 1979), 150: violence among slaves may have arisen from "a deflection inward of hostility toward whites and white presumptions," as well as from mistrust of others and from "the unpredictable conditions of plantation life"; and Alan Lomax, *The Land Where the Blues Began* (New York: Pantheon, 1993). Lomax finds that the violence used by the "planter class" to keep emancipated blacks in line in the 1890s later led to conflict within the black community: "As always, such cynical violence imposed from the top led to violence within the exploited group—a very ugly emotional safety valve" (xv).

20. Hortense Powdermaker, *After Freedom: A Cultural Study of the Deep South* (New York: Viking, 1939), 174.

21. Du Bois, *The Souls of Black Folk,* 330, 331. Drawing on this passage, Gunnar Myrdal makes the same point in *An American Dilemma: The Negro Problem and Modern Democracy,* vol. 2 (1944; reprint, New York: Harper and Row, 1962), 525–26. The persistence of this insight to the present day can be seen in Randall Kennedy's *Race, Crime, and the Law* (New York: Pantheon, 1997), 26–27, in which Kennedy acknowledges that African Americans commit crimes at rates disproportionate to their numbers in the population of the U.S. but argues that this very disproportion leads them to an "inversion of values," a certainty that the law is the black man's enemy and that all arrests and convictions are evidence of racism, prejudice, and unfairness. Were American whites more aware of this belief, they would not have been so shocked at the general African American approval of O. J. Simpson's acquittal of the murder of his wife, Nicole Brown Simpson, and her friend Ron Goldman in 1996.

22. H. C. Brearley, "The Pattern of Violence," in *The Culture of the South,* ed. William T. Couch (Chapel Hill: University of North Carolina Press, 1935), 690. For more recent discussions that make the same point, see Fox Butterfield, *All God's Children: The Bosket Family and the American Tradition of Violence* (New York: Alfred A. Knopf, 1995), 61, 63; and Oshinsky, *"Worse Than Slavery,"* 132. Martha Grace Duncan, in *Romantic Outlaws, Beloved Prisons: The Unconscious Meanings of Crime and Punishment* (New York and London: New York University Press, 1996), 78, points out that some observers trace the use of violence rather than the courts in settling personal disputes to the weakness of the state. Since state institutions could provide no protection, bandits and badmen inspired "fear and respect," because they employed violence without restraint. Similarly, David T. Courtwright says that men who make defending their honor with violence a center of their lives "typically flourish in remote rural areas where the state is

weak or its rationalizing minions are held in contempt." Courtwright, *Violent Land: Single Men and Social Disorder from the Frontier to the Inner City* (Cambridge, Mass.: Harvard University Press, 1996), 29.

23. Powdermaker, *After Freedom,* 174.

24. Ibid., 170, 169.

25. Marvin E. Wolfgang and Franco Ferracutti, *The Subculture of Violence: Towards an Integrated Theory in Criminology* (1967; reprint, New York: Tavistock, 1969), 153, 263. Edward L. Ayers suggests in *Vengeance and Justice,* 234, that southern males, both black and white, are more prone to violence as a way of asserting and defending their self-esteem than men in other regions of the country: "Honor, not dignity, shaped character and bred violence." In *Violence and Culture in the Antebellum South* (Austin: University of Texas Press, 1979), 97, Dickson D. Bruce argues that for the "plain-folk" in the South, violence was a practical matter. "It is not," says Bruce, that the plain-folk saw violence "as a meaningful form of manly action. It was rather that violence was one of several available forms of action in society." And Roger Lane writes in *Murder in America,* 351, that "with little else to protect, the need to maintain personal respect, even personal safety, through fighting at the slightest provocation became for many [blacks] the kind of cultural trait it was among the white elite."

26. David Oshinsky devotes approximately the first third of his book *"Worse Than Slavery"* to reviewing the details of and the scholarship on the convict lease system. See also Mathew J. Mancini's book-length study *One Dies, Get Another: Convict Leasing in the American South, 1866–1928* (Columbia: University of South Carolina Press, 1996).

27. For such views see also Howard W. Odum, "Negro Folk-Song and Folk Poetry," *Journal of American Folklore* 24, no. 94 (October–December 1911): 351; David Cohn, *Where I Was Born and Raised* (Boston: Houghton Mifflin, 1948), 111; and Butterfield, *All God's Children,* 61. Things have changed very little. In *Street Kingdom: Five Years inside the Franklin Street Posse* (New York: Warner, 1999), 119, Douglas Century remarks about ghetto badman Big K's release from juvenile detention that "Back in those days [the mid- to late eighties], coming home from a long juvenile bid up north, you were treated like a returning war hero," and he describes how Big K is treated "like The Man" by the youths still on the street.

3. Between the Wars

1. William Wells Brown, *Clotel,* in *Three Classic African-American Novels,* ed. Henry Louis Gates, Jr. (New York: Vintage, 1990), 192. See also my discussion of this passage in Bryant, *Victims and Heroes: Racial Violence in the African American Novel* (Amherst: University of Massachusetts Press, 1997), 34–35.

2. Martin R. Delany, *Blake; or, the Huts of America,* ed. Floyd J. Miller (1859–62; Boston: Beacon, 1970).

3. See David Bakish and Edward Margolies, *Afro-American Fiction, 1853–1976* (Detroit: Gale Research, 1979). The three novels I am thinking of are James D. Corrothers, *The Black Cat Club: Negro Humor and Folk-Lore* (1902; reprint, New York: AMS Press, 1972); Paul Laurence Dunbar, *The Sport of the Gods* (1902; reprint, New York: Collier, 1970); and James Weldon Johnson, *The Autobiography of an Ex-Colored Man* (1912; reprint, New York: Knopf, 1927). Subsequent page references to each of these novels are given in the text.

4. See Evelyn Brooks Higginbotham's very useful discussion of Mrs. Johnson in *Righteous Discontent: The Women's Movement in the Black Church* (Cambridge, Mass.: Harvard University Press, 1993), 66–67.

5. Both *Megda* and *Four Girls at Cottage City* have been reprinted recently by Oxford University Press, the former with an introduction by Molly Hite and the latter with one by Deborah E. McDowell. In her chapter on these two writers in her *The Coupling Convention: Sex, Text, and Tradition in Black Women's Fiction* (New York: Oxford University Press, 1993), 48, Ann duCille writes that their "primary concern is not race or ro-

mance but religion and female moral authority." By far the fullest account of the writers of these years is Blyden Jackson, *The Long Beginning, 1746-1895,* vol. 1 of *A History of Afro-American Literature* (Baton Rouge: Louisiana State University Press, 1989).

6. See especially T. E. D. Nash, *Love and Vengeance; or Little Viola's Victory. A Story of Love and Romance in the South; also Society and Its Effects* (published by the author, 1903).

7. His novels include *The Conquest* (1913), *The Forged Note* (1915), and *The Homesteader* (1917). Another, *The Masquerade,* was plagiarized from Charles W. Chesnutt's story of the tragic mulatto, *The House behind the Cedars* (1900).

8. Arlene A. Elder, *The "Hindered Hand": Cultural Implications of Early African-American Fiction* (Westport, Conn.: Greenwood, 1978), 9, 19. In *Righteous Discontent,* 195, Evelyn Brooks Higginbotham quotes activist Virginia Broughton's call for a "distinctive literature," by which she meant, as Higginbotham puts it, a literature that "declared that blacks must publish their side of history in order to contest racist discourses and instill pride in their people."

9. Walter H. Stowers and William H. Anderson, *Appointed: An American Novel* (1894; reprint, New York: AMS Press, 1977), 258, 272.

10. Charles Waddell Chesnutt, *The Colonel's Dream* (1905; reprint, Upper Saddle River, N.J.: Gregg, 1968). See also *The House behind the Cedars* (Boston: Houghton, Mifflin, 1900) and *The Marrow of Tradition* (1901; reprint, Ann Arbor: University of Michigan Press, 1969).

11. Chesnutt, *The Marrow of Tradition,* 110, 282-83, 296.

12. James Weldon Johnson, *Black Manhattan* (New York: Knopf, 1930), 73.

13. Indeed it is hard not to connect the episode to his own behavior with his wife, Alice Ruth Moore. As Eleanor Alexander makes indisputably clear in *Lyrics of Sunshine and Shadow: The Tragic Courtship and Marriage of Paul Laurence Dunbar and Alice Ruth Moore—A History of Love and Violence among the African American Elite* (New York: New York University Press, 2001), 164-68, Dunbar was not a gentle lover, especially when he was drunk (and that was often). In Alexander's account, Dunbar sexually assaulted his fiancée even before they were married and induced a fear in her that she tried to keep secret out of pride. Dunbar, who took a sexist view of marriage, at first convinced her that it was love that drove him. "Only let my love in some measure condone my weakness," he wrote to Moore after the first "rape." "I was a drunken brute who let his passion obscure his love" (164). Alice "endured" Dunbar's violence from before their marriage in 1899 to January 25, 1902, when, "in a drunken rage, Paul nearly beat her to death. Later he boarded a train to New York, and the Dunbars never saw each other again" (168). *The Sport of the Gods* came out just two or three months later, in April. That this was for Alice a near-death experience, Dunbar makes clear in the tale he writes in *The Sport of the Gods.* This is a connection that bears further exploration.

14. Ibid., 160. Indeed, some have seen in *The Sport of the Gods* a resemblance to the naturalistic novels of Émile Zola, Frank Norris, Stephen Crane, and Theodore Dreiser, "in which," as Hugh M. Gloster says in *Negro Voices in American Fiction* (New York: Russell and Russell, 1948), 50, "man is conceived as a powerless figure in an amoral and careless world." More specifically, Peter Revell suggests in *Paul Laurence Dunbar* (Boston: Twayne, 1977), 159, that Joe's murder of Hattie "strongly recalls the murder scene in *McTeague,* and similarly suggests that the simple-minded antihero has been turned into a monster by the false standards he lives by." But Joe clearly is at fault for his drinking and any careful comparison of the relevant scenes in *McTeague* and *Sport of the Gods* will show that Norris is indeed a naturalist, consciously depicting the human being as an animal driven by instinct and the basest of appetites—sex, food, and money—while Dunbar is a melodramatic moralist. McTeague is emotionally unmarked by his killing of his sweetheart; Joe Hamilton is reduced to a zombie by horror and regret.

15. According to the Chicago Historical Society's *Historical Guide to the Neighborhoods,* by Glen E. Holt and Dominic A. Pacyga (1979), 18, "The name 'Levee' came from

Memphis and New Orleans where levee areas along the river were the principal vice districts." Holt and Pacyga report that this area was bounded by State and Wabash Avenues, which run north and south, and Adams Street on the north and 12th Street on the south. It grew into the vice district as boarding houses appeared to serve the single male "transients," who were generally poor and footloose. On their ground floors they often housed various kinds of businesses, such as "cut-rate stores, cheap restaurants, penny arcades, and later, nickel theatres," which, given the marginal respectability of the area's foot trade, often "engaged in some form of illegal activity." In *Chicago Ragtime: Another Look at Chicago, 1880–1920* (South Bend, Ind.: Icarus, 1985), 119, Richard Lindberg finds the levee district contained in a slightly different configuration of streets. It "existed on the southern tip of the Loop, bounded on the east by Dearborn Street, with Clark on the west and Harrison on the north. This was known as the wicked Custom House Place Levee."

16. Lindberg, *Chicago Ragtime*, 120 n. 2.

17. Allan H. Spear, *Black Chicago: The Making of a Negro Ghetto* (Chicago: University of Chicago Press, 1967), 14–15, map 1, after p. 14, and table 3, p. 15. As Spear points out, in 1900 "the Negro population of the city was still relatively well distributed. Only two wards had a Negro population of more than 10 per cent. In 1898, just over a quarter of Chicago's Negroes lived in precincts that were more than 50 per cent Negro, and over 30 per cent lived in precincts that were at least 90 per cent white. As late as 1910, Negroes were less highly segregated from native whites than were Italian immigrants."

18. Lindberg, *Chicago Ragtime*, 120. See also Lee Coyle, *George Ade* (New York: Twayne, 1964), 26. Coyle describes Chicago in the nineties as "a sprawling, dirty, rough-neck town full of brass knuckles, loud laughter, easy money, and exquisite suffering. Gambling houses, brothels, pool halls, and saloons boomed and multiplied. The levee district was unsafe after dark, and the morgue registered several new guests every day. Streetwalkers, pickpockets, cutthroats, tramps, and country cousins who didn't make the grade infested the night with their poison."

19. Finley Peter Dunne says the same thing of Mr. Dooley's Archer Avenue, that in the Archer Avenue "community you can hear all the various accents of Ireland, from the awkward brogue of the 'far-downer' to the mild and aisy Elizabethan English of the southern Irishman, and all the exquisite variations to be heard between Armagh and Bantry Bay." Dunne, *Mr. Dooley at His Best,* ed. Elmer Ellis (New York: Charles Scribner's Sons, 1938), 3–4.

20. See Henry Louis Gates, Jr., *The Signifying Monkey: A Theory of African-American Literary Criticism* (New York: Oxford University Press, 1988), 176: "by 1895, dialect had come to connote black innate mental inferiority, the linguistic sign both of human bondage (as origin) and of the continued failure of 'improvability' or 'progress,' two turn-of-the-century keywords"; and Elsa Nettel's point that dialect became a conventional put-down of the African American freedman, "a symbol of servitude, reflective of the white's desire, conscious or not, to enslave the Negro through language," quoted by Joanne Braxton in *The Collected Poetry of Paul Laurence Dunbar* (Charlottesville: University Press of Virginia, 1993), xxiv, from Nettel's *Language, Race and Social Class in Howells's America* (Lexington: University of Kentucky Press, 1987), 76. See also Dickson D. Bruce's insightful discussion of Corrothers in *Black American Writing at the Nadir: The Evolution of a Literary Tradition, 1877–1915* (Baton Rouge: Louisiana State University Press, 1989), 123–26.

21. James D. Corrothers, *In Spite of the Handicap* (New York: George H. Doran, 1916), 20, 137.

22. Bruce, *Black American Writing at the Nadir,* 105–107.

23. Corrothers, *In Spite of the Handicap,* 137: "certain thoughts could not be expressed so well in any other way as in dialect."

24. Corrothers, *In Spite of the Handicap,* 136. The first Mr. Dooley article for the *Journal* seems to have appeared on Saturday, February 19, 1898, 4, "Mr. Dooley Discusses the Cuban Question." It appears without fanfare and even without Dunne's name

on the byline, suggesting how well known Mr. Dooley had become to Chicago readers and the coup performed by the *Journal* in luring him away from the *Evening Post.*

25. George Ade, *Fables in Slang, and More Fables in Slang* (1899, 1900; reprint, New York: Dover Publications, 1960), v.

26. Corrothers, *In Spite of the Handicap,* 69–70, 40.

27. William Stanley Braithwaite, Book Reviews, *Colored American Magazine* 5, no. 2 (June 1902): 152.

28. James T. Farrell, in his introduction to *Artie and Pink Marsh,* by George Ade (1897; Chicago: University of Chicago Press, 1963), ix, says the same thing about Ade's and Dunne's characters.

29. J. Saunders Redding, *They Came in Chains: Americans from Africa,* rev. ed. (Philadelphia: J. B. Lippincott, 1973), 217.

4. From the Genteel to the Primitive

1. James Weldon Johnson, ed., *The Book of American Negro Spirituals* (New York: Viking, 1925), 49. Take note, though, of Miss Agatha Cramp in Rudolph Fisher's *The Walls of Jericho.* Fisher portrays her as the typical ignorant white philanthropist who regards the singing of spirituals as a sign of what remains primitive about blacks. She wonders to her maid, Linda, "All Negroes sing spirituals, don't they?" Linda, illustrating by her membership in the Harlem Episcopal Church how far blacks have come in the dignity of their religious ceremonies, reflects for a moment and says that she has gone to a concert of spirituals sung like jazz and to a Methodist church where "the folks get happy and shout," but just to watch them since "I've never heard them at my church in regular service." Rudolph Fisher, *The Walls of Jericho* (1928; reprint, New York: Arno Press and the New York Times, 1969), 65.

2. Robert Hemenway, *Zora Neale Hurston: A Literary Biography* (1977; reprint, Urbana and Chicago: University of Illinois Press, 1980), 54–55.

3. Willard B. Gatewood, *Aristocrats of Color: The Black Elite, 1880–1920* (Bloomington: Indiana University Press, 1990), 338. For Hughes's article, "Our Wonderful Society: Washington," see *Opportunity,* August 1927, 226–27.

4. Langston Hughes, "The Negro Artist and the Racial Mountain," in *On Being Black: Writings by Afro-Americans from Frederick Douglass to the Present,* ed. Charles T. Davis and Daniel Walden (Greenwich, Conn.: Fawcett, 1970), 161.

5. Charles S. Johnson, "The New Frontage on American Life," in *The New Negro,* ed. Alain Locke (1925; reprint, New York: Atheneum, 1974), 297. See also Nathan Huggins, *The Harlem Renaissance* (New York: Oxford University Press, 1971), 72.

6. See John Richardson, *A Life of Picasso,* 2 vols. (New York: Random House, 1991–96), 1:488 n. 24, 2:24. In volume 2, Richardson refers to the "clunky primitivism" of the Iberian heads, their "bulging eyes, mammoth ears, heavy jaws," suggesting that they provided Picasso, in his work on *Les Demoiselles d'Avignon* (1907), "with an ethnic catalyst for stylistic experimentation" (2:23).

7. See Charles Scruggs's useful discussion of how both H. L. Mencken and James Weldon Johnson allude to Synge's *Playboy of the Western World* as a model for using folk vernacular to inject new energy into contemporary literary expression, in "H. L. Mencken and James Weldon Johnson: Two Men Who Helped Shape a Renaissance," in *Critical Essays on H. L. Mencken,* ed. Douglas C. Stenerson (Boston: G. K. Hall, 1987).

8. Jean Toomer (*Cane,* 1923), Langston Hughes (*Not Without Laughter,* 1930), and Countee Cullen (*One Way to Heaven,* 1932) all deal with what might be called "primitivist" subject matter, but not the classic man of violence.

9. Martin Bauml Duberman, in *Paul Robeson* (New York: Knopf, 1988), 98, quotes Hughes in a letter to Robeson after the release of a second batch of Victor Records spirituals: "The great truth and beauty of your art struck me as never before one night this summer down in Georgia when a little group of us played your records for hours there in the very atmosphere from which your songs came." The irony is that the force that con-

tributes to the destruction of the folk form, the phonograph record, is here cited as a purveyor of folk purity.

10. Claude McKay, *A Long Way from Home* (1937; reprint, New York: Arno Press and the New York Times, 1969), 228–29. The "Jakes," of course, refers to Jake Brown, the protagonist of McKay's *Home to Harlem*.

11. Robert Bone, *Down Home: A History of Afro-American Short Fiction from Its Beginnings to the End of the Harlem Renaissance* (New York: G. P. Putnam's Sons, 1975), 153.

12. Hemenway, *Zora Neale Hurston,* 166. Hazel Carby says that in *Their Eyes Were Watching God* (1937) Hurston tries to resolve her own sense of distance between her educated self and the folk of Eatonville even while she seeks to represent them as subjects. And she approaches her village like an "anthropologist" when she returns to collect the material for her book on folklore, *Mules and Men* (1935). She describes the Eatonville folk not as the loud and threadbare immigrants who arrived in the northern cities and embarrassed college Negroes on racially mixed transportation, but as a kind of esthetic principle. See Carby's essay "The Politics of Fiction, Anthropology, and the Folk: Zora Neale Hurston," in *History and Memory in African-American Culture,* ed. Geneviève Fabre and Robert G. O'Meally (New York: Oxford University Press, 1994), 33.

13. Rudolph Fisher, *The Short Fiction of Rudolph Fisher,* ed. Margaret Perry (Westport, Conn.: Greenwood, 1987), 119. Subsequent page references to this volume are given in the text.

14. Rudolph Fisher, *The Conjure-Man Dies: A Mystery Tale of Dark Harlem* (1932; reprint, New York: Arno Press and The New York Times, 1971), 235, 236. Subsequent page references are given in the text.

15. Fisher, *The Walls of Jericho,* 263, 250. Subsequent page references are given in the text.

16. Interestingly, Hazel Carby, in *Race Men* (Cambridge, Mass.: Harvard University Press, 1998), 189, points out the same thing about Danny Glover's character Simon in the film *Grand Canyon* (1991, dir. Lawrence Kasdan): he "can voice the moral codes and ethics of the middle class and be streetwise at the same time."

17. This is the way Professor William H. Robinson, Jr., of Howard University, refers to Jinx and Bubber in his introduction to the reprint of *The Walls of Jericho,* v.

18. These helpfully exact and insightful words are Bernard W. Bell's in *The Afro-American Novel and Its Tradition* (Amherst: University of Massachusetts Press, 1987), 140.

19. Lawrence Otis Graham, in *Our Kind of People: Inside America's Black Upper Class* (New York: HarperCollins, 1999), 13, quotes Episcopal minister Harold T. Lewis as saying that "The black upper class has most often been associated with the Episcopal Church." Graham explains that "The Episcopal faith was attractive because of its formality, and both faiths [Episcopal and Congregational] were appealing because they were known for having well-educated clergy and a small number of members. Well-to-do black Americans with roots in the West Indies had natural historic ties with the Episcopal Church, which had served a major role in Jamaica and other former British colonies for several generations."

20. James R. Giles, in *Claude McKay* (Boston: Twayne, 1976), 73, says that in the beginning Harlem is a kind of Eden, "an oasis of pleasure and sensuousness for Jake; it is the one place in the world in which he can be free and comfortable," and "a haven that is almost 'pure' because it is comparatively uncontaminated by guilt, lust for power, or by materialism." My analysis tends to modify this conclusion. Jake's Harlem from the beginning contains a vein of viciousness and violence.

21. Claude McKay, *Home to Harlem* (1928; reprint, Boston: Northeastern University Press, 1987), 283, 72. Subsequent page references to this volume are given in the text.

22. In *Claude McKay,* Giles points out that many of the major critics of *Home to Harlem* saw Jake as the simple innocent (78). Robert Bone sees him as "pure instinct" (*The Negro Novel in America,* rev. ed. [New Haven: Yale University Press, 1965], 68) and

Nathan Huggins as "a child-man, having the simplicity and innocence of Mark Twain's Nigger Jim, and the childlike openness and spontaneity of E. E. Cummings's Jean Le Negre" (Huggins, *The Harlem Renaissance,* 125). Wayne Cooper, in *Claude McKay: Rebel Sojourner in the Harlem Renaissance* (Baton Rouge: Louisiana State University Press, 1987), is less absolute. Jake "was, in effect, the natural man forever dear to pastoralists and their urban counterparts, the authors of picaresque novels." But Jake's "sense of the real was too firm" for him to be a complete "innocent." "If anything, he embodied traditional black folk sense moved to the city. He was the product of a hard realism that expected and asked no favors" (241).

23. McKay himself once had an experience like Zeddy's. In Nice, in 1925–26, he got into an argument with an officious Italian who goaded him with the comment that since "all Negroes are boxers," McKay would probably want to box with him. "Look here," said McKay in a rage, "I won't defile my hands with your dirty dago skin, but I'll cut your gut out," whereupon he pulled out a knife and chased the Italian. But "In a moment sanity flashed back into me as quickly as it had fled and I put the knife in my pocket. . . . It was the first time I had ever drawn a blade in a fight, and I was ashamed." He tells the story in *A Long Way from Home,* 275.

24. Arna Bontemps, "Why I Returned," in *The Old South: "A Summer Tragedy" and Other Stories of the Thirties* (New York: Dodd, Mead, 1973), 10.

25. Ibid., 10–11, 9. In Arna Bontemps and Langston Hughes, *Letters: 1925–1967,* ed. and selected by Charles H. Nichols (New York: Dodd, Mead, 1980), 2, Nichols makes this same point, that Paul and Buddy, the two principal males in Bontemps's life, represented the typical conflict in the lives of Renaissance writers.

26. Arna Bontemps, *God Sends Sunday* (1932; reprint, New York: AMS Press, 1972), 23, 26, 64. Subsequent page references to this volume are given in the text.

27. In a move that will be picked up by many later writers, Bontemps transfers to the black neighborhood barbershop the choral function of the badman-ballad women who dress in red and publicly mourn or celebrate the death of the badman. See especially Toni Morrison's barber-shop segments in *Song of Solomon* (1977; reprint, New York: Penguin, 1987), 80–83, 99–101.

28. Howard W. Odum, *Rainbow round My Shoulder: The Blue Trail of Black Ulysses* (New York: Grosset and Dunlap, by arrangement with the Bobbs-Merrill Co., 1928), 79.

29. See especially the first chapter of Hemenway, *Zora Neale Hurston,* 9–31. To say that Hemenway's book is indispensable is to understate its value. It is not only the best book on Zora Neale Hurston, but one of the best on the Harlem Renaissance, and an example of the art of biography and of literary criticism and history of the highest sort.

30. Ibid., 99–102.

31. Hazel Carby points out that, with respect to the conflict between folk orality and educated literacy, Hurston did not practice the kind of folk purity she preached during the Renaissance: "Hurston could not entirely escape the intellectual practice which she so despised, a practice which reinterpreted and redefined a folk consciousness in its own elitist terms. Hurston may not have dressed the spirituals in tuxedos, but her attitude toward folk culture was not unmediated: she did have a clear framework of interpretation, a construct which enabled her particular representation of a black, rural consciousness." Carby, "The Politics of Fiction, Anthropology, and the Folk," 32.

32. Zora Neale Hurston, *Moses: Man of the Mountain* (Philadelphia: J. B. Lippincott, 1939), 95. Hurston likes this figure and it leads to one of her more impressive dramatizations of the cowardly and intolerant. In *Their Eyes Were Watching God* (1937; reprint, Harper and Row, 1990), 138–39, Mrs. Turner, the color-prejudiced mulatto who runs a restaurant in Lake Okechobee, Florida, is one of those who, as in the "pecking-order in a chicken yard," delivers "Insensate cruelty to those you can whip, and groveling submission to those you can't. Once having set up her idols and built altars to them it was inevitable that she would worship there. It was inevitable that she should accept any inconsistency and cruelty from her deity as all good worshippers do from theirs. All gods who

receive homage are cruel. All gods dispense suffering without reason. Otherwise they would not be worshipped. Through indiscriminate suffering men know fear and fear is the most divine emotion. It is the stones for altars and the beginning of wisdom. Half gods are worshipped in wine and flowers. Real gods require blood." Subsequent page references to this volume are given in the text.

33. Zora Neale Hurston, *Mules and Men* (1935; reprint, New York: HarperPerennial, 1990), 162. Subsequent page references to this volume are given in the text.

34. Zora Neale Hurston, *Jonah's Gourd Vine* (1934; reprint, Philadelphia: J. B. Lippincott, 1971), 99, 104. Subsequent page references to this volume are given in the text.

35. Zora Neale Hurston, *Dust Tracks on a Road* (1942; reprint, New York: Harper Collins, 1996), 32–33. Subsequent page references to this volume are given in the text.

36. For Sandra Pouchet Paquet, Tea Cake "is the iconoclastic folk hero who takes Janie home to the folk as his bride," a model of "the benevolent, instructive, protective, and wise ancestor." See her essay "The Ancestor as Foundation in *Their Eyes Were Watching God* and *Tar Baby*," in *Toni Morrison's Fiction: Contemporary Criticism*, ed. David L. Middleton (New York and London: Garland, 1997), 185.

37. Addison Gayle, Jr., *The Way of the New World: The Black Novel in America* (Garden City, N.Y.: Anchor, 1976), 177.

38. Hurston, *Dust Tracks*, 154.

39. Hurston, *Mules and Men*, 150; *Dust Tracks*, 155. Big Sweet's attitude recalls the well-known badman anthem: "I've got a tombstone disposition, graveyard mind. / I know I'm a bad motherfucker, that's why I don't mind dying."

40. Hurston, *Dust Tracks*, 145, 146, 150.

41. Ibid., 146.

5. The Ghetto Bildungsroman

1. Kenneth B. Clark, *Dark Ghetto: Dilemmas of Social Power* (New York: Harper and Row, 1965), 11.

2. Richard Wright, *Native Son* (1940; reprint, New York: Harper and Row, 1966), 41–42. Subsequent page references to this volume are given in the text.

3. Wright, "How 'Bigger' Was Born," introduction to *Native Son*, xi, xiii.

4. Accounts of whippings and torture in the antebellum slave narratives and the detailed accounts of lynchings in turn-of-the-century novels present us, perhaps, with even grislier material, but they operate in quite different genres and are meant to make different points. I deal with such violence in *Victims and Heroes: Racial Violence in the African American Novel* (Amherst: University of Massachusetts Press, 1997), chapters 1 and 4 especially.

5. Wright, "How 'Bigger' Was Born," xxvii.

6. Eldridge Cleaver, *Soul on Ice* (1968; reprint, New York: Dell, 1969), 108.

7. St. Clair Drake and Horace Cayton, *Black Metropolis*, with an introduction by Richard Wright (New York: Harcourt, Brace, 1945), xviii, 97, 760.

8. Wright, "How 'Bigger' Was Born," xx.

9. Richard Wright, *White Man, Listen!* (1957; reprint, Westport, Conn.: Greenwood, 1978), 147.

10. Bernard W. Bell, *The Afro-American Novel and Its Tradition* (Amherst: University of Massachusetts Press, 1987), 160, 166.

11. Arna Bontemps, "Harlem, the Beautiful Years," *Negro Digest* 14, no. 3 (January 1965): 67–68. Quoted by Betty Taylor Ashe in *A Study of the Fiction of Arna Wendell Bontemps* (Ann Arbor, Mich.: Universal Microfilms International, 1979 [Ph.D. diss., Howard University, 1978]), 19.

12. Wright isn't as mocking about the old tom-tom gambit—which whites during the Renaissance were said to hear in the jazzy music of the Harlem clubs—as Ralph Ellison is in *Invisible Man*. The businessman's wife who seduces Ellison's narrator tells him that he's got a "primitive" attraction, that "tom-toms" beat in his voice, a primitive force that "takes hold of one's emotions as well as one's intellect" (403).

13. James Baldwin, "The Harlem Ghetto," in *Notes of a Native Son* (1955; reprint, Bantam: New York, 1968), 47. The essay first appeared in the February 1948 issue of *Commentary*.

14. Richard Wright, *12,000,000 Black Voices* (1941; reprint, New York: Thunder's Mouth, 1991). The photographs come from the files of the Farm Security Administration, Department of Agriculture, and they include pictures taken by Walker Evans, Dorothea Lange, and Arthur Rothstein. Subsequent page references to this volume are given in the text.

15. Baldwin, "The Harlem Ghetto," 59.

16. As Baldwin says in the title essay of *Notes of a Native Son*, 94–95, reflecting upon the death of his own father, "bitterness is folly. . . . Hatred, which could destroy so much, never failed to destroy the man who hated and this was an immutable law."

17. Baldwin, "Many Thousands Gone," in *Notes of a Native Son*, 33. Robert Bone, in his revised edition of *The Negro Novel in America* (New Haven: Yale University Press, 1965), suggests that Baldwin "attempts to spiritualize his sexual rebellion." The heterosexual belongs to a "laity," the homosexual, along with "Negroes . . . hipsters, and jazzmen," to a "clergy" (238, 228).

18. Ralph Ellison, "Harlem Is Nowhere," in *Shadow and Act* (1964; reprint, New York: Signet, 1966), 283.

19. Ralph Ellison, "Change the Joke and Slip the Yoke," in *Shadow and Act,* 72–73.

20. Ralph Ellison, *Invisible Man* (1952; reprint, New York: Random House, 1972), 354, 357, 360. Subsequent page references to this volume are given in the text.

21. I would not, though, go as far as Stephen B. Bennett and William W. Nichols do in "Violence in Afro-American Fiction: An Hypothesis," *Modern Fiction Studies* 17, no. 2 (summer 1971): 224, saying there is a "beauty in that last symbolic defiance of white oppression" and suggesting that Tod is given "a kind of immortality" when a youthful white witness describes Tod's blow to the policeman with awe: "Biff, bang! One, two, and the cop's on his ass!" (*Invisible Man*, 428).

22. Ellison says that Rinehart is "chaos" and "change," and "has lived so long with chaos that he knows how to manipulate it. It is the old theme of *The Confidence Man*. He is a figure in a country with no solid past or stable class lines; therefore he is able to move about easily from one to the other." See "The Art of Fiction: An Interview," in *Shadow and Act*, 181. Rinehart also might be seen, allegorically, as a trickster, his initials, "B. P.," standing for "Bliss" and "Proteus," the first for "the sheer bliss of impersonation," the second for the changeability of impersonation. And Rinehart is there formally "to suggest a mode of escape from Ras" and another way of applying "his grandfather's cryptic advice" in the earlier part of the novel to "overcome 'em with yeses" ("Change the Joke and Slip the Yoke," in *Shadow and Act*, 71).

23. Claude Brown, *Manchild in the Promised Land* (1965; reprint, New York: New American Library, n.d.), vii. Subsequent page references to this volume are given in the text.

24. Ronald Fair, *We Can't Breathe* (New York: Harper and Row, 1972), vii. Subsequent page references to this volume are given in the text.

25. Geta LeSeur studies this form in greater detail and with a considerably different emphasis than I do in *Ten Is the Age of Darkness: The Black Bildungsroman* (Columbia and London: University of Missouri Press, 1995). Her subject is both the African American and West Indian American novels of change and development and her aim is to show how such narratives as *Invisible Man, Go Tell It on the Mountain, Manchild in the Promised Land* and many others are indeed bildungsromans according to her definition. They are, she says, "novels of initiation, childhood, youth, education, and the various other definitions used for the bildungsroman, with autobiographical components. . . . The heroes and heroines of these novels are not concerned with what is specific to them as artists, but with something more generally shared in the human experience. The artist is concerned with inward problems and struggles, with emotive experiences, moral values, and imaginative ideals" (26).

26. Philip B. Kaye, *Taffy* (New York: Crown 1950). See my discussion of *Taffy* from the perspective of racial violence in *Victims and Heroes,* 217–18.

27. Lewis Yablonsky, "The Violent Gang," in *Violence in the Streets,* ed. Shalom Endelman (Chicago: Quadrangle, 1968), 235.

28. Both of Simmons's novels were republished in 1997 by W. W. Norton in its Old School Books series. Norton's Web site quotes Simmons on the influence upon his writing of the great jazz musicians. "He wrote *Corner Boy* while studying at Washington University and serving in the army," and "He recently retired from a teaching position at California State University, Northridge" (http://www.wwnorton.com/osb/cornerau.htm, accessed July 5, 2002).

29. Herbert Simmons, *Corner Boy* (Boston: Houghton Mifflin, 1957), 47. Subsequent page references to this volume are given in the text.

30. Mark Kennedy, *The Pecking Order* (New York: Appleton-Century-Crofts, 1953), 278.

31. R. Lincoln Keiser, *The Vice Lords: Warriors of the Street* (New York: Holt, Rinehart and Winston, 1969), 74, 76.

32. George Cain, *Blueschild Baby* (1970; reprint, New York: Dell, 1972), 180, 115. Subsequent page references to this volume are given in the text.

33. Keiser, *The Vice Lords,* 71, 77.

34. Elijah Anderson, *Code of the Street: Decency, Violence, and the Moral Life of the Inner City* (New York: Norton, 1999), 9–10. For more commentary on alienation of the sort Anderson speaks of see Jewelle Taylor Gibbs, "Health and Mental Health of Young Black Males," in *Young, Black, and Male in America: An Endangered Species,* ed. Jewelle Taylor Gibbs et al. (New York: Auburn House, 1988), especially 228.

35. Anderson, *Code of the Street,* 66. What Anderson describes, of course, as the bildungsroman suggests, is hardly new. In an exciting passage of *The Autobiography of Malcolm X,* Malcolm X recounts how numbers runner West Indian Archie confronts "Red" Little, Malcolm's pre-Muslim name, over a bet Red claims to have won. Archie the hustler is simply maintaining one of his major business attributes, his reputation. "For a hustler in our sidewalk jungle world, 'face' and 'honor' were important. No hustler could have it known that he'd been 'hyped,' meaning outsmarted or made a fool of. And worse, a hustler could never afford to have it demonstrated that he could be bluffed, that he could be frightened by a threat, that he lacked nerve." But this applies to Red as much as to Archie, and Red knows that he must kill Archie if the argument goes far enough, kill him or be himself devastatingly disgraced. Luckily, some of Archie's friends ease him past the danger zone later in a bar, and Red walks out still in one piece. See *The Autobiography of Malcolm X* (1965; reprint, New York: Grove, 1966), 127–33.

36. Nathan McCall, *Makes Me Wanna Holler: A Young Black Man in America* (New York: Random House, 1994), 115. Subsequent page references to this volume are given in the text.

6. Toasts

1. Quoted from an informant by Bruce Jackson, *"Get Your Ass in the Water and Swim Like Me": Narrative Poetry from Black Oral Tradition* (Cambridge, Mass.: Harvard University Press, 1974), 9.

2. Anthony M. Reynolds, "Urban Negro Toasts: A Hustler's View from L.A.," *Western Folklore* 33, no. 4 (October 1974): 269–70.

3. In *From Folklore to Fiction: A Study of Folk Heroes and Rituals in the Black American Novel* (New York: Greenwood, 1988), H. Nigel Thomas sees the toast as a means for releasing aggressive desires otherwise repressed in a dangerous racist society. They are "signifying" satires on the values of the white bourgeoisie (34). Hence, we are not to take them as serious celebrations of street heroes. His other cogent point, improvising upon a remark of Lawrence W. Levine's in *Black Culture and Black Consciousness: Afro-American Thought from Slavery to Freedom* (New York: Oxford University Press, 1977), 429, is that the toast "Shine" is "a brilliant mockery of the postulates of the American dream" (35). For

a performance of two of the best-known toasts, "Shine" and "The Signifying Monkey," which I discuss below, see black comedian Rudy Ray Moore's movie *Dolemite* (1975). Moore plays a "good" badman who assists the FBI in exposing a crooked mayor. Although he takes the name Dolemite, he is nothing like the toast character of that name, though he performs the toast as part of his regular comedy routine. He deliberately establishes a link with the toast character, and his performance of the two classic toasts is splendid. He also plays Dolemite in *The Human Tornado* (1976). *The Legend of Dolemite* is a 1994 documentary by Foster Corder, featuring testimonials to Moore's influence on rap from rappers such as Ice-T and Eazy-E as well as film stars such as Eddie Murphy and Arsenio Hall.

4. Jackson, *"Get Your Ass in the Water,"* vii, 29. See also Jackson's excellent essay "Worksong and Toast: Two Dead Genres," in *History and the Tradition in Afro-American Culture,* ed. Günter H. Lenz (Frankfurt and New York: Campus Verlag, 1984). Here he provides a useful summary of the problems faced by white collectors of black folklore as well as a sentence or two on the obscurity of the toast's beginnings. In a review of *"Get Your Ass in the Water"* (*CLA Journal* 1, no. 19 [September 1975]: 105–107), Hortense J. Spillers applauds the collection of toasts Jackson prints but delivers a withering attack on his introduction, citing his "oversimplifications" and complaining that "he simply sat down and regurgitated all the old stuff." In her conclusion, Spillers poses a number of excellent questions about the toast that Jackson should have asked and answered but didn't. For example, "In several versions of 'Stagolee' . . . the hero crawls through mud to a town called the 'Bucket of Blood,' and there follows a bar scene with loose gals and armed dudes. Does this narrative, and others like it, reflect influences of cinema or other aspects of technical culture? What explains the pathetic qualities of a tale like 'Toledo Slim' with its patterns of memory and betrayal?" I have no explicit answers for her questions, either, but in discussing the toast versions of the violent man I address the quality of sadness and loss that sometimes appears in toasts like "Toledo Slim."

5. See William Labov, Paul Cohen, Clarence Robins, and John Lewis, "Toasts," in *Mother Wit from the Laughing Barrel: Readings in the Interpretation of Afro-American Folklore,* ed. Alan Dundes (New York and London: Garland, 1981), 330.

6. Roger D. Abrahams, *Deep Down in the Jungle . . . : Negro Narrative Folklore from the Streets of Philadelphia,* rev. ed. (Chicago: Aldine, 1970), 88, 109.

7. Jackson, "Worksong and Toast," 248–50.

8. See Abrahams, *Deep Down in the Jungle* (1970) and *Positively Black* (Englewood Cliffs, N.J.: Prentice-Hall, 1970); Jackson, *"Get Your Ass in the Water"* (1974); Reynolds, "Urban Negro Toasts"; Dennis Wepman, Ronald B. Newman, and Murray B. Binderman, *The Life: The Lore and Folk Poetry of the Black Hustler* (Philadelphia: University of Pennsylvania Press, 1976), expanded from their article "Toasts: The Urban Black Poetry," *Journal of American Folklore* 87, no. 345 (July–September 1974): 208–24; Labov et al., "Toasts"; Seymour Fiddle, *Toasts: Images of a Victim Society* (New York: Exodus House, 1972).

9. In his *Die Nigger Die!* (New York: Dial, 1969), H. Rap Brown, the misbehaving chairman of the radicalized Student Nonviolent Coordinating Committee, speaks affectionately of having gone into bars when he was a youngster and listening to the men tell their tales and "signify." He means toasting. "By the time I was nine, I could talk Shine and the Titanic, Signifying Monkey, three different ways, and Piss-Pot-Peet, for two hours without stopping" (30).

10. For a thorough reading of "The Signifying Monkey," see Abrahams, *Deep Down in the Jungle,* 64–65.

11. Of the seven toast collections I use, only one, that by Anthony Reynolds, contains no Stagolee toast.

12. Julius Lester, *Black Folktales* (1969; reprint, New York: Grove, 1970), 113.

13. Abrahams reports in *Deep Down in the Jungle* (135) that "four [Stagolee] texts from the Kentucky Folklore Archives are very similar to the Camingerly texts, confirming the quite remarkable uniformity among the majority of the collected Stagolee toasts. We

might owe this uniformity to the communities in which the toasts are most consistently kept alive, the prisons where so many black men are herded in the American justice system." "Camingerly" is a conflation of the names of the three small Philadelphia streets in which Abrahams did his field work: Camac, Ismeninger, and Waverly.

14. With respect to Hortense Spillers's suggestion that the mud may have some particular source (see n. 4 above), I confess an ignorance equal to Jackson's of any subtle symbolic significance. My hunch is that the mud is simply a metaphor for the nastiness of the night and the difficult obstacles Stagolee has to surmount in order to get to his watering hole. The image of the great Stagolee crawling through mud also suggests that the street poet does not lose himself in awe of the unrivaled badman. Finally, as I go on to say, it is a sign of nature's disrespect and hence a condition against which Stagolee must react as a badman should, with violence.

15. Jackson, *"Get Your Ass in the Water,"* Stagolee 1A, 46. The number of "rockets" Stag pumps in the many variants ranges from two to nine, and the target varies from the chest to the head.

16. Abrahams, *Deep Down in the Jungle,* 137.

17. In such toasts, Roger Abrahams speculates in *Deep Down in the Jungle,* 31, the young black male's search for a "kind of heroic male environment is in part a reaction to the emotional dominance of the mother or grandmother" in matrifocal households where the boy feels excluded. In defense, says Abrahams, he comes to scorn the women and their soft and sometimes middle-class virtues.

18. Jackson, *"Get Your Ass in the Water,"* 49.

19. Ibid., 45.

20. Abrahams, *Deep Down in the Jungle,* 4, 12, 65–66. In *"Get Your Ass in the Water,"* 33, Jackson agrees, but with a modification: the badman is a rebel, all right, but he engages "in an undirected rebellion against an unspecified opponent."

21. Abrahams, *Deep Down in the Jungle,* 66.

22. Jackson, *"Get Your Ass in the Water,"* Stagolee 1C, 47–49.

23. In *Deep Down in the Jungle,* 84, Abrahams says that most of the toast stories tend toward the comic, so that the tellers and the audience can both accept and reject, permitting "identification and at the same time reservation." This is reflected in the target of the comedy, too, the self and the oppressor, with the derision implicit in the comic tone directed toward both the teller and his audience and the "power figure who is rendered inept."

24. Labov et al., "Toasts," 341.

25. See also Abrahams, *Deep Down in the Jungle,* 54–56.

26. Abrahams stirred up a minor tempest with his suggestion that the trickster is a child and the badman an adolescent. Bruce Jackson understands the trickster as a sly, knowing, and very adult role-player. He acts the role of the child in order to take his stand against forces more powerful than he. Badmen like Stagolee, says Jackson, lack the self-awareness of the trickster and so are nearer to the child level. They are rebellious, to be sure, but against nothing in particular and everything in general. See *"Get Your Ass in the Water,"* 33–36. John W. Roberts claims that neither of these white men is right. The badman, says Roberts, has evolved from the trickster. In the toasts he becomes a revolutionary black power figure and hence must be regarded by the black community as a "hero." See his *From Trickster to Badman: The Black Folk Hero in Slavery and Freedom* (1989; reprint, Philadelphia: University of Pennsylvania Press, 1989), 200, passim.

27. See especially Jackson's excellent, and still relevant, discussion of the whole process of toast collecting in his essay "Worksong and Toast," 248–49, especially his comment that since toasts were "often obscene, violent, misogynistic and vulgar . . . until the mid-1960s they were unpublishable in America."

28. Abrahams, *Deep Down in the Jungle,* 160, 163–64. Jackson also has a Jesse James variant in *"Get Your Ass in the Water,"* 63.

29. Of the seven collections that provide my material, this toast appears only in Jackson's *"Get Your Ass in the Water,"* although Dolomite's reputation is widespread, per-

haps given impetus by black comedian Rudy Ray Moore's adoption of the name in the seventies. Jackson collected Dolomite #4A, 57, from a 1970 recording by James F. Beyers of a performance of it by Rudy Ray Moore, Governor's Inn, Buffalo, New York, June 1970. See n. 3 above.

30. Jackson, *"Get Your Ass in the Water,"* 57–60.

31. Abrahams, *Deep Down in the Jungle,* 175.

32. Labov et al., "Toasts," 335–36.

33. This particular version of this famous badman sentiment comes from "The Great MacDaddy," in Abrahams, *Deep Down in the Jungle,* 163.

34. Ibid., 131.

35. Reynolds, "Urban Negro Toasts," 268, 284–85.

36. Wepman, Newman, and Binderman, *The Life,* 6.

37. Ibid., 96. For a discussion of the inevitable fall of the pimp, see Christina Milner and Richard Milner, *Black Players: The Secret World of Black Pimps* (1972; reprint, New York: Bantam, 1973), 118–22. Their informants, though, are stoical. Forty-five-year old "Harris" puts it this way: "But if I get broke today, man, I look at it like this, I'll say to myself, 'It was good while it lasted,' because I did get a chance to do some of the things that I have wanted to do in life, you know" (119).

38. See Bruce Jackson's discussion of the "homiletic" element in some toasts in *"Get Your Ass in the Water,"* 15–16.

39. Wepman, Newman, and Binderman, *The Life,* 51, 53. See also "Honky Tonk Bud," 54–59, for another player who carelessly sells dope to a narcotic agent. Michael H. Agar records a longer but similar variant of "Bud" in "Folklore of the Heroin Addict: Two Examples," *Journal of American Folklore* 84, no. 332 (April–June 1971): 181–82. His analysis of addicts' familiarity with toasts is useful. He found that the form is not specific to the heroin addicts, whom he studied at the Lexington, Kentucky, Clinical Research Center. He had assistants interview fifty addicts, half black, half white, and found that 86 percent had heard of "King Heroin" and 35 percent of "Honky Tonk Bud," more blacks having heard of "Bud" than whites. Only 6 percent of the interviewees could recite "Bud," but 16 percent could "Heroin." "Sixty-five percent of the sample had never heard of the term 'toasts,' although, of these, 97 percent knew of one or more by title." These two were the best known, though a few mentioned "Morphine, Morphine," "The Fall," "Signifying Monkey," and "Stagger Lee" (176).

40. Abrahams, *Positively Black,* 49.

41. All of these toasts are in Wepman, Newman, and Binderman, *The Life,* 73, 90, 94, 96, except for "Toledo Slim," in Abrahams's *Positively Black,* 49.

42. Ibid., 36–50.

43. Ibid., 79.

44. Ibid., 79, ll. 9–12. Line numbers for all subsequent references to this toast will be given in the text.

45. See especially Milner and Milner, *Black Players,* who discuss the way the best pimps avoid any close relationships in order to tend exclusively to their business and its profits, especially 96.

46. Abrahams, *Positively Black,* 47, 49.

47. Fiddle, *Toasts,* 16.

7. Chester Himes

1. These novels are *For Love of Imabelle* (1957; reprint, Chatham, N.J.: Chatham Bookseller, 1973); *The Crazy Kill* (1959; reprint, New York: Berkeley, 1966); *The Real Cool Killers* (1959; reprint, New York: Berkeley, 1966); *All Shot Up* (1960; reprint, Chatham, N.J.: Chatham Bookseller, 1973); *The Big Gold Dream* (1960; reprint, Chatham, N.J.: Chatham Bookseller, 1973); *Cotton Comes to Harlem* (New York: G. P. Putnam's Sons, 1965); *The Heat's On* (1966; reprint, Chatham, N.J.: Chatham Bookseller, 1975); and *Blind Man with a Pistol* (New York: William Morrow, 1969). Where context

makes the source clear, page references to them are given in the text. All but *Blind Man with a Pistol* were originally published in France, translated into French from Himes's English. For the various French titles under which the novels were published see the excellent "Chronological List of the Works of Chester Himes" in Edward Margolies and Michel Fabre, *The Several Lives of Chester Himes* (Jackson: University Press of Mississippi, 1997), 195–98; and the equally helpful list in James Sallis, *Chester Himes: A Life* (New York: Walker, 2000), 337. *The Heat's On* was reprinted as *Come Back, Charleston Blue* by Berkeley Press in 1972, the new title taken from the unsuccessful movie adaptation.

2. Margolies and Fabre, *The Several Lives of Chester Himes*, 155. The passage comes from a letter to Himes's literary agent Rosalind Targ.

3. Stephen F. Milliken, *Chester Himes: A Critical Appraisal* (Columbia, Mo.: University of Columbia Press, 1976), 198.

4. Chester Himes, *The Quality of Hurt*, vol. 1 of *The Autobiography of Chester Himes* (Garden City, N.Y.: Doubleday, 1972), 19.

5. Himes's biographer, Michel Fabre, questions whether he ever was a pimp—"He boasts a lot." Personal correspondence, February 11, 1991. See also Margolies and Fabre, *The Several Lives of Chester Himes*, 26–30, for a discussion of Himes's years in the Cleveland and Columbus criminal worlds.

6. Himes, *The Quality of Hurt*, 60.

7. Chester Himes, *If He Hollers Let Him Go* (Garden City, N.Y.: Doubleday and Doran, 1945), 107.

8. John A. Williams and Charles F. Harris, ed., *Amistad 1* (New York: Random House, 1970), 60.

9. "So I cite these various revolutions, brothers and sisters, to show you that you don't have a peaceful revolution. You don't have a turn-the-cheek revolution. There's no such thing as a nonviolent revolution." Malcolm X, *Malcolm X Speaks: Selected Speeches and Statements,* ed. George Breitman (New York: Grove, 1965), 9.

10. Williams and Harris, *Amistad 1*, 45. No doubt the novel he refers to is *Plan B,* published by the University Press of Mississippi in 1993 with the instrumental assistance of Michel Fabre. See Margolies and Fabre, *The Several Lives of Chester Himes*, 146, 190 n. 1. Sallis lists it as part of the *Harlem Cycle* published by Payback Press (Edinburgh, 1996–97). Sallis, *Chester Himes*, 337.

11. Himes, *The Quality of Hurt*, 22.

12. Joe taught sociology at the University of North Carolina, Greensboro. See Flontina Miller, "Racism Impetus behind Author's Career," in *Conversations with Chester Himes,* ed. Michel Fabre and Robert E. Skinner (Jackson: The University Press of Mississippi, 1995), 116.

13. Himes, *The Quality of Hurt*, 47.

14. Fabre and Skinner, *Conversations with Chester Himes*, 62.

15. Chester Himes, *My Life of Absurdity*, vol. 2 of *The Autobiography of Chester Himes* (Garden City, N.Y.: Doubleday, 1976), 197. To be sure, it must be said that the woman involved in this fracas probably started it, at least by Himes's account. This was Regine Fischer (Margolies and Fabre, *The Several Lives of Chester Himes*, 93), whom Himes calls "Marlene" in his autobiography. She is as full of rage as Himes himself and, after this violent street encounter, slashes her wrists. Even so, Himes was not gentle with his women, who seemed to enrage him more than men.

16. Chester Himes, *Lonely Crusade* (1947; reprint, Chatham, N.J.: Chatham Bookseller, 1973), 362.

17. Chester Himes, *The Third Generation* (New York: World, 1954), 346.

18. Chester Himes, *The Primitive* (New York: New American Library, 1955), especially 122 and 124. Himes's preferred title was *The End of a Primitive,* and a new uncut edition of the novel under this title was published by W. W. Norton in 1997 in its Old School Books series. A number of explicit sexual references in chapter 10 were cut by the original editors. They have been restored in the new version.

19. Edward Margolies, "The Thrillers of Chester Himes," *Studies in Black Literature* 1, no. 2 (1970): 4–5.

20. Himes, *My Life of Absurdity,* 29. In a 1970 interview with Michel Fabre, Himes remarks that he did not find his writing "therapeutic," as it apparently was for Wright. "It's just an attempt on my part to illustrate the absurdities of life." Fabre and Skinner, *Conversations with Chester Himes,* 89.

21. Milliken, *Chester Himes,* 12. Himes alludes to Albert Camus in the first sentence of *My Life of Absurdity:* "Albert Camus once said that racism is absurd." The absurdity of racism, of course, was not at the center of Camus's thinking about the absurd, but it was for Himes. His is not the philosophical and ontological absurdism of Camus, but the practical comic absurdism of the minstrel tradition or the slave tale.

22. John M. Reilly, "Chester Himes' Harlem Tough Guys," *Journal of Popular Culture* 9, no. 4 (spring 1976): 939.

23. Himes, *The Real Cool Killers,* p. 148.

24. One wonders just how much of his sense of the absurdity of Harlem violence Himes got from his favorite writer, Dashiell Hammett. In Hammett's *Red Harvest,* Dan Rolff stabs Whisper Max Thaler with an ice pick. "He looked funny as hell," says the Continental Op, "standing there with the butt of the sticker sticking out of his side. Then he flashes the rod and puts two pills in Dan just like one, and the both of them go down together, cracking heads, Dan's all bloody through the bandages. . . . I roll them over, and they're a pair of stiffs." *The Dashiell Hammett Omnibus* (1929; reprint, New York: Knopf, 1935), 220.

25. Might Himes have been thinking of the famous episode of the escaping bicycle tire in Jacques Tati's 1953 French film *Mr. Hulot's Holiday?*

26. See also H. Bruce Franklin, *Prison Literature in America* (New York: Oxford University Press, 1989), 227, quoted by Sallis in *Chester Himes,* 100–101. Sallis states Franklin's point "that Himes's novels form a concise social history of the United States from World War II through the black urban rebellions of the 1960s."

27. Margolies and Fabre point out that the working title for *The Crazy Kill* was "A Jealous Man Can't Win," an "inside joke about himself." *The Several Lives of Chester Himes,* 101.

28. Himes, *For Love of Imabelle,* 111.

29. See Gilbert H. Muller's discussion of the analogy in *Chester Himes* (Boston: Twayne, 1989), 86.

30. Himes, *My Life of Absurdity,* 111. See also Fabre and Skinner, *Conversations with Chester Himes,* 134.

31. Sociologist Lonnie H. Athens, in his book *Violent Criminal Acts and Actors,* suggests that people who commit violence are, in the majority of cases, in full control of their actions and must be held responsible for them. They planned "to commit violence, decided consciously to act and felt wholly responsible for what they had done. This was consistent with his childhood observations that violent people rarely seemed crazy (on the contrary, crazy people were nonviolent), and contradicted the prevailing theories that murderers killed in bursts of unconsciously motivated passion and in spite of themselves." Quoted from Christopher Lehmann-Haupt's review of Richard Rhodes, *Why They Kill: The Discoveries of a Maverick Criminologist* (New York: Knopf, 1999), in *The New York Times,* September 27, 1999, B7.

32. Here Himes is closer to Ross Macdonald in *The Drowning Pool* than to Dashiell Hammett, whose Sam Spade, in *The Maltese Falcon,* says that it goes against the grain of the detective to let any murderer go, regardless of the circumstances.

33. Margolies, "The Thrillers of Chester Himes," 3.

34. Tony Hilfer, *The Crime Novel: A Deviant Genre* (Austin: University of Texas Press, 1990), 150, speaking of Thompson's novel *Pop. 1280.*

35. Himes, *Cotton Comes to Harlem,* 163.

36. Raymond Nelson writes that Ed and Digger are "trapped in a hopelessly venal institution [but] remain incorruptibly honest. . . . Burdened with a body of law ludicrously

inappropriate to the conditions of Harlem life, they are lonely dispensers of justice." See Raymond Nelson, "Domestic Harlem: The Detective Fiction of Chester Himes," *Virginia Quarterly Review* 48, no. 2 (spring 1972): 266–67.

37. Fabre and Skinner, *Conversations with Chester Himes,* 85.

38. Himes, *The Heat's On,* 32.

39. Himes, *All Shot Up,* 30.

40. Nelson, "Domestic Harlem," 266–67.

41. See Sallis, *Chester Himes,* 270–71.

42. Himes, *Cotton Comes to Harlem,* 43.

43. Fabre and Skinner, *Conversations with Chester Himes,* 21.

44. Milliken, *Chester Himes: A Critical Appraisal,* 233.

45. Himes, *The Heat's On,* 92.

46. Himes, *The Real Cool Killers,* 149.

8. A "Toast" Novel

1. For versions of this toast, see Anthony Reynolds, "Urban Negro Toasts: A Hustler's View from L.A.," *Western Folklore* 33, no. 4 (October 1974): 267–98, and Seymour Fiddle, *Toasts: Images of a Victim Society* (New York: Exodus House, 1972).

2. Nathan C. Heard, *House of Slammers* (New York: Macmillan, 1983), 86–91.

3. Nathan C. Heard, *Howard Street* (1968; reprint, New York: New American Library, 1970), 193. Where context makes the source clear, page references to this novel and others discussed in this chapter are given in the text after an initial citation.

4. See Sara Mosle's review of Ron Suskind, *A Hope in the Unseen: An American Odyssey from the Inner City to the Ivy League* (New York: Broadway, 1998), in the *New York Times Book Review,* August 2, 1998, 6.

5. Nicholas Lemann, *The Promised Land: The Great Black Migration and How It Changed America* (New York: Knopf, 1991), 149–50, 192–201, 103, 282.

6. Erich Fromm, *The Anatomy of Human Destructiveness* (New York: Holt, Rinehart and Winston, 1973), 366.

7. Rollo May, *Power and Innocence: A Search for the Sources of Violence* (New York: Norton, 1972), 23.

8. Kenneth B. Clark, *Dark Ghetto: Dilemmas of Social Power* (New York: Harper and Row, 1965), 175.

9. Greg Goode, "Donald Goines," in *Afro-American Fiction Writers after 1955,* ed. Thadious M. Davis and Trudier Harris (Detroit: Gale Research, 1984), 96–100; and "From Dope Fiend to Kenyatta's Last Hit: The Angry Black Crime Novels of Donald Goines," *MELUS* 11, no. 3 (fall 1984): 41–48.

10. See for example Donald Goines, *Dopefiend* (1971); Joe Nazel, *Uprising* (1976) and *The Golden Shaft* (1974); and Odie Hawkins, *Men Friends* (1989).

11. Christina and Richard Milner, in *Black Players: The Secret World of Black Pimps* (1972; reprint, New York: Bantam, 1973), 23, report that the pimps they talked to for their study of The Life in San Francisco spoke of writing their own autobiographies, "like Iceberg Slim." They were doing their work in the late sixties, so Beck had already gained wide popularity in the community from which he had come.

12. See Eddie Stone, *Donald Writes No More* (Los Angeles: Holloway House, 1974), 220. I discuss four of Goines's racial violence novels in *Victims and Heroes: Racial Violence in the African American Novel* (Amherst: University of Massachusetts Press, 1997), 268–70.

13. Robert Beck [Iceberg Slim, pseud.], *Trick Baby* (Los Angeles: Holloway House, 1967), 251, 240.

14. See Robert Beck [Iceberg Slim, pseud.], *The Long White Con* (Los Angeles: Holloway House, 1977), 18.

15. James-Howard Readus, *The Death Merchants* (Los Angeles: Holloway House, 1974), 36.

16. Charlie Avery Harris, *Macking Gangster* (Los Angeles: Holloway House, 1976), 9–10.

17. James-Howard Readus, *Black Renegades* (Los Angeles: Holloway House, 1976), 71–72.

18. Omar Fletcher, *Walking Black and Tall* (Los Angeles: Holloway House, 1977), 6.

19. Donald Goines, *Inner City Hoodlum* (Los Angeles: Holloway House, 1975), 23.

20. In *Black Players,* 32, Christina and Richard Milner speculate that the term "mack" or "mack man" for pimp comes from the French *maquereau,* "mackerel, pimp." The connection with "mackerel," they say, lies in the fancied fishy "odor of the female sexual parts." "Probably the evolution of the term occurred in New Orleans, one of the origin cities of Black pimping in America, where French language influences remain strong." John Leland probably uses the Milners for his identification of *maquereau* and "pimp" in his article "Rap and Race," *Newsweek,* June 29, 1992, 49.

21. Joseph Nazel, *Death for Hire* (Los Angeles: Holloway House, 1975), 83.

22. Donald Goines, *Never Die Alone* (Los Angeles: Holloway House, 1974), 141.

23. Sam Peckinpah's film *The Wild Bunch* (1969) and Arthur Penn's *Bonnie and Clyde* (1967) should be paired with *The Godfather* (directed by Francis Ford Coppola) as founders of the new violent style.

24. Mario Puzo, *The Godfather* (New York: G. P. Putnam's Sons, 1969), 363.

25. James-Howard Readus, *The Big Hit* (Los Angeles: Holloway House, 1975), 167.

26. Charlie Avery Harris, *Whore-Daughter* (Los Angeles: Holloway House, 1976), 129.

27. Cole Riley, *Rough Trade* (Los Angeles: Holloway House, 1987), 146.

28. Jerome Dyson Wright, *Poor, Black, and in Real Trouble* (Los Angeles: Holloway House, 1976), 193, 197.

29. See especially Robert Beck [Iceberg Slim, pseud.], *Pimp* (Los Angeles: Holloway House, 1969); Donald Goines, *Whoreson* (Los Angeles: Holloway House, 1971); and Odie Hawkins, *Sweet Peter Deeder* (Los Angeles: Holloway House, 1979).

30. Hawkins, *Sweet Peter Deeder,* 104–105. Cocaine Nell, in the toast of that name, says in the last line that "good treatment ruins a whore." See Bruce Jackson, *"Get Your Ass in the Water and Swim Like Me": Narrative Poetry from Black Oral Tradition* (Cambridge, Mass.: Harvard University Press, 1974), 125.

31. Hawkins, *Sweet Peter Deeder,* 28–29.

32. Robert Beck [Iceberg Slim, pseud.], *Mama Black Widow* (Los Angeles: Holloway House, 1969), 142–43. Ishmael Reed makes the same point in *The Last Days of Louisiana Red* (New York: Random House, 1974), 34–35, attacking the growing black feminist movement in his portrayal of "Minnie the Moocher" as a "strong, glamorous female with hustling powers whose old man is her inferior, a 'cokey' who has a drug problem." She is no victim, as she claims, but "an acolyte of an ugly cause," collaborating with white men in undermining black men. In *Black Macho and the Myth of the Superwoman* (New York: Dial, 1977), 16, Michele Wallace complains that the black woman is getting a bad rap from men like these. She writes that just as the black woman begins to think positively about herself, voices from all sides begin to address her accusingly: "You crippled the black man. You worked against him. You betrayed him. You laughed at him. You scorned. You and the white man." Folklorist Roger D. Abrahams, though, also places much blame upon the black woman in the matrifocal ghetto household. The mother (or grandmother) tends to be the most consistently present adult in the young black male's life, but as she tends to favor the girls in the household and as the young man is too often unable to bring home any money through a decent job, he seeks companionship on the street. He joins a gang, "knowing they [the gangs] are condemned, not only by white man's laws but also by the women in his house. Seeking this kind of heroic male environment is in part a reaction to the emotional dominance of the mother or grandmother." In the gang and later in his criminal activities, he establishes his virility and comes to scorn the women and their soft and sometimes middle-class values. See Abrahams, *Deep Down in the Jungle . . . :*

Negro Narrative Folklore from the Streets of Philadelphia, rev. ed. (Chicago: Aldine, 1970), 31. These books are among the attempts in these years to understand better the precise nature and makeup of the black ghetto family.

33. See n. 20. Most of the Holloway writers use "macking" to mean "pimping," and Clarence Major gives that definition in his *Dictionary of Afro-American Slang* (New York: International, 1970). Charlie Avery Harris, though, seems to intend much more by the term. His Junius is not only a pimp. He is a prince of the streets, playing almost every game and dominating them all.

34. Laurie Miles, *Black Hit Woman* (Los Angeles: Holloway House, 1980), 171.

35. Goines, *Never Die Alone,* 213.

36. Readus, *The Big Hit,* 158.

37. Beck, *The Long White Con,* 165.

38. Beck, *Trick Baby,* 308.

39. Miles, *Black Hit Woman,* 95.

40. Vern E. Smith, *The Jones Men* (Chicago: Regnery, 1974), 9. This is one of the few non-Holloway novels I treat in this chapter.

41. Goines, *Whoreson,* 49. This was Donald Goines's first book. He started it as a prisoner in Michigan's Jackson State Prison.

42. Stone, *Donald Writes No More,* 51.

43. Harris, *Whore-Daughter,* 137–38.

44. Wright, *Poor, Black, and in Real Trouble,* 141, 156.

45. Beck, *Pimp,* 117, 118.

46. Harris, *Macking Gangster,* 147.

47. Chester Himes is one of Readus's predecessors, as is shown in this passage from Himes's *For Love of Imabelle* (1957; reprint, Chatham, N.J.: Chatham Bookseller, 1973): the Palm Café is full of "smooth Harlem hustlers with shiny straightened hair, dressed in lurid elegance, along with their tightly draped queens, chorus girls and models—which meant anything—sparkling with iridescent glass jewelry, rolling dark mascaraed eyes, flashing crimson fingernails, smiling with pearl-white teeth encircled by purple-red lips, exhibiting the hot excitement that money could buy" (72).

48. Readus, *Black Renegades,* 196, 35–36, 116. Not much seems to have changed in the dress codes of the sporting life, except taste, since Little Augie won the unofficial best-dressed-man award for a sensational outfit created for the occasion: "He wore a full dress suit made of leaf-green satin, with a cape and top hat to match. His lapels were gold, as were also his pumps and the knob of his green cane, and his hair was oiled and pressed to his head like patent leather. Della's dress was plum-colored, her petticoats gold; she too wore gold slippers." Arna Bontemps, *God Sends Sunday* (1932; reprint, New York: AMS Press, 1972), 79. The setting is the last years of the nineteenth century.

49. Harris, *Macking Gangster,* 18–19.

50. Fromm, *The Anatomy of Human Destructiveness,* 332.

51. Clarence L. Cooper, *The Scene* (New York: Crown, 1960), 305. Cooper also wrote *The Syndicate* (1956–60), *Weed* (1961), and *The Dark Messenger* (1962), all published by Regency in Evanston, Illinois, and possessing the same qualities as *The Scene. The Scene* was republished in 1998 by W. W. Norton in its Old School Books series. Norton lists Cooper as Clarence Cooper, Jr., and states on its Web site that Cooper was born in Detroit in 1934 and spent much of his life as an addict and a convict. "He died penniless and alone in the 23rd Street YMCA in New York City in 1978." <http://www.wwnorton.com/osb/sceneau.htm>, accessed May 21, 2002.

52. Readus, *Black Renegades,* 60.

53. Harris, *Macking Gangster,* 109.

54. Nazel, *Death for Hire,* 57. For an example of how closely these Holloway novels relate to the toasts of nearly the same period, consider this quatrain from one of the best of the toasts, "The Fall": "It was Saturday night, and the jungle was bright, / And the Game was stalking its prey. / The code was crime in the neon line, / And the weak were

doomed to pay." Dennis Wepman, Ronald B. Newman, and Murray B. Binderman, *The Life: The Lore and Folk Poetry of the Black Hustler* (Philadelphia: University of Pennsylvania Press, 1976), 79.

55. Readus, *The Death Merchants,* 168–69.

56. Joe Nazel, *Street Wars* (Los Angeles: Holloway House, 1987), 34.

57. Nazel, *Death for Hire,* 222.

58. Robert Beck [Iceberg Slim, pseud.], *Death Wish* (Los Angeles: Holloway House, 1977), 288.

59. Goode, "Donald Goines," 91. In *Hip Hop America* (New York: Viking, 1998), 36–37, music critic Nelson George says that Goines writes about "lost, mentally diseased people existing in squalid conditions in blunt, brutal prose that, early in his career, possessed the ugly poetry of bracing pulp fiction."

60. Donald Goines, *Black Gangster* (Los Angeles: Holloway House, 1972), 13.

61. Donald Goines, *Street Players* (Los Angeles: Holloway House, 1973), 15.

62. Goines, *Dopefiend,* 237.

63. Michael Corvino, "Motor City Breakdown: Donald Goines's Tales from Ground Zero," *The Village Voice* 32, no. 31 (1987), 51.

64. Donald Goines, *Cry Revenge* (Los Angeles: Holloway House, 1974), 214.

9. Walter Mosley and the Violent Men of Watts

1. Besides Mosley, the twenty-two novelists I refer to are Nikki Baker, Evelyn Taylor Bland, Charlotte Carter, Christopher Darden (yes, *that* Darden), Nora DeLoach, Grace F. Edwards, Terris McMaham Grimes, Gary Hardwick, Gar Anthony Haywood, Hugh Holton, Clifford Mason, Penny Mickelbury, Barbara Neely, Percy Spurlack Parker, Gary Phillips, John Ridley, Judith Smith-Levin, Pamela Thomas-Graham, Blair S. Walker, Valerie Wilson Wesley, Chassie West, and Paula L. Woods. Of these, only three—Haywood, Mason, and Parker—published novels before 1990.

2. Except for *Bad Boy Brawly Brown* (Boston: Little, Brown, 2002), the Rawlins novels were all published in New York by W. W. Norton. The editions I use in this discussion are *Devil in a Blue Dress* (New York: Norton, 1990); *A Red Death* (1991; reprint, New York: Pocket, 1992); *White Butterfly* (1992: reprint, New York: Pocket, 1993); *Black Betty* (1994; reprint, New York: Pocket, 1995); and *A Little Yellow Dog* (1996; reprint, New York: Pocket, 1997). The first Easy Rawlins book that Mosley wrote was *Gone Fishin'* (1997; reprint, New York: Pocket, 1998). According to Mosley, the manuscript, in which Easy and his friend Mouse take a journey to a small Texas town and make discoveries about themselves on the way, was rejected by a number of publishers before it was finally brought out by Black Classic Press in 1997. Socrates Fortlow has appeared only in two collections of short stories, *Always Outnumbered, Always Outgunned* (1998; reprint, New York: Washington Square, 1998), and *Walkin' the Dog* (Boston and New York: Little, Brown, 1999). Mosley has also written a quasi–science fiction novel heavy in mysticism and philosophy, *Blue Light* (1998; New York: Warner, 1999), and a slight meditation on contemporary morality called *Workin' on the Chain Gang* (New York: Ballantine, 2000). Where context makes the source clear, page references to these books are given in the text.

Mosley plans several more Easy Rawlins mysteries, in which Easy will "get old" and people will "get sick and die." See D. J. R. Bruckner, "Mystery Stories Are Novelist's Route to Moral Questions," *New York Times,* September 4, 1990, C13. But in *Fearless Jones* (2001), he introduces two characters who are improvisations upon Easy and Mouse: Paris Minton, the narrator and main investigator, and Fearless Jones, a World War II hero with a fist of steel and a heart of gold. I am omitting this novel from my discussion because in it Mosley adds nothing of importance to the badmen he has already created.

3. Mary Young, in "Walter Mosley, Detective Fiction, and Black Culture," *Journal of Popular Culture* 32, no. 1 (summer 1998), 141–50, makes the point that the Easy Raw-

lins stories do not follow the model of hard-boiled detective narratives founded by Dashiell Hammett and Raymond Chandler, but rather reflect the African American storytelling tradition. Easy, she says, is the trickster who outwits the white massa' of the plantation, that is, both the police and the corrupt white politicians and businessmen who employ him. Mouse, who never saw a shady criminal he didn't feel like killing, is the badman in the Stagolee tradition. As my discussion will show, both Easy and Mouse carry many of the badman genes, though Young does make her case for aspects of the trickster in Easy. I might add that the character Mouse "Navrochet" to whom Young unaccountably refers is the Raymond "Mouse" *Alexander* who is Easy's murderous best friend at least through *A Little Yellow Dog,* in which he renounces his violent past, becomes converted to an odd kind of religious fundamentalism, and in the end appears to die, unarmed, while trying to protect Easy's life.

4. Sarah Lyall, "Los Angeles Memories and an Unlikely Hero," *New York Times,* June 15, 1994, B4. See also Thulani Davis, "Walter Mosley," *Bomb* 44 (summer 1993): 52–57; Bruckner, "Mystery Stories are Novelist's Route to Moral Questions," C13; and Kristina L. Knotts, "Walter Mosley," in *Contemporary African American Novelists: A Bio-Bibliographical Critical Source Book,* ed. Emmanuel S. Nelson (Westport, Conn.: Greenwood, 1999).

5. Lyall, "Los Angeles Memories," B4.

6. Sven Birkerts, "The Socratic Method," review of *Always Outnumbered, Always Outgunned,* by Walter Mosley, *New York Times Book Review,* November 9, 1997, 11.

7. Mosley, *Devil in a Blue Dress,* 159, 209.

8. Mosley, *A Red Death,* 58, and *A Little Yellow Dog,* 73.

9. Mosley, *A Little Yellow Dog,* 259.

10. Mosley, *A Red Death,* 147.

11. Doña Brown, "Interview: Walter Mosley," *Bookcase* 1, no. 6 (September 1995): 20.

12. Mosley, *A Little Yellow Dog,* 21.

13. Mosley, *White Butterfly,* 63–64, 77.

14. The same syndrome of unconscious violence is dramatized in the toast novels discussed in chapter 8. One wonders if Mosley was paying tribute to another tough-guy writer, Norman Mailer, whose Stephen Rojack, in *An American Dream* (1965; reprint, New York: Dell, 1967), is also seized by the pure instinctual "it" on the battlefield in Italy when he successfully and single-handedly takes out two German machine gun nests (12–13). Stephen Rojack is an embodiment of what Mailer had called in the 1950s the "white Negro," the "existential hipster," who lives on the edge of the abyss and, like the macks and hit men of the toast novel, links sexual dominance and the fulfillment it brings with the essence of maleness. See especially Rojak's subjugation of his wife Deborah in a titanic wrestling match between the evil female who would unnaturally dominate and the heroic male who courageously (and successfully) struggles to maintain the mastery to which nature entitles him (35).

15. Raymond Chandler, *The Simple Art of Murder* (Boston: Houghton Mifflin, 1950), 398.

16. Walter Mosley, "The Black Dick," in *Critical Fictions: The Politics of Imaginative Writing,* ed. Philomena Mariani (Seattle: Bay, 1991), 133. Mosley says, "Mysteries, stories about crime . . . are the ones that really ask the existentialist questions such as 'How do I act in an imperfect world when I really want to be perfect?' I'm not really into clues and that sort of thing, although I do put them into my stories. I like the moral questions." See also Bruckner, "Mystery Stories are Novelist's Route to Moral Questions," C13.

17. Gilbert H. Muller, "Double Agent: The Los Angeles Crime Cycle of Walter Mosley," in *Los Angeles in Fiction: A Collection of Essays,* rev. ed., ed. David Fine (Albuquerque: University of New Mexico Press, 1995), 294.

18. Mosley, *A Red Death,* 86, 75.

19. Roger A. Berger, "'The Black Dick': Race, Sexuality, and Discourse in the L.A. Novels of Walter Mosley," *African American Review* 31, no. 2 (summer 1997), 294.

20. Mosley, *A Red Death,* 225.

21. Mosley says in "The Black Dick," 132, that Easy is "a reluctant detective who is poor and black with middle-class aspirations."

22. Mosley keeps his options open, though. Several times in *Bad Boy Brawly Brown* Easy raises doubts about whether Mouse is truly dead. My guess would be that Mosley will bring him back in a later novel.

10. Rap

1. See, respectively, De La Soul, "Tread Water," on *3 Feet High and Rising* (1989); Grandmaster Flash, "The Message" (1984); and KRS-One (Kris Parker) with Boogie Down Productions, "My Philosophy," on *By All Means Necessary* (1988).

2. David Toop, *The Rap Attack: African Jive to New York Hip Hop* (Boston: South End, 1984), and Steven Hager, *Hip Hop: The Illustrated History of Break Dancing, Rap Music, and Graffiti* (New York: St. Martin's, 1984), are early, nonacademic books containing helpful personal details about the first years of rap. Among the burst of books that appeared in the nineties are Mark Costello and David Foster Wallace, *Signifying Rappers: Rap and Race in the Urban Present* (Hopewell, N.J.: Ecco, 1990); Michael Eric Dyson, *Reflecting Black: African-American Cultural Criticism* (Minneapolis: University of Minnesota Press, 1993) and *Between God and Rap: Bearing Witness to Black Culture* (New York: Oxford University Press, 1996), two analyses of rap by a professor of theology, philosophy, and ethics; Joseph D. Eure and James G. Spady, eds., *Nation Conscious Rap: The Hip Hop Vision* (New York: PC International, 1991); S. H. Fernando, Jr., *The New Beats: Exploring the Music, Culture, and Attitudes of Hip-Hop* (New York: Anchor Doubleday, 1994); Nelson George, *Hip Hop America* (New York: Viking, 1998), a literate, well-informed, and sophisticated exploration of rap from all angles by a novelist and cultural critic; Havelock Nelson and Michael A. Gonzales, *Bring the Noise: A Guide to Rap Music and Hip-Hop Culture* (New York: Harmony, 1991); Tricia Rose, *Black Noise: Rap Music and Black Culture in Contemporary America* (University Press of New England: Hanover, N.H.: 1994); and James G. Spady, Charles G. Lee, and H. Samy Alim, *Street Conscious Rap* (Philadelphia: Black History Museum Umum/Loh Publishers, 1999). University of Chicago literary critic and historian Houston A. Baker has also thrown his formidable critical skills into a reflection on rap in *Black Studies, Rap, and the Academy* (Chicago and London: University of Chicago Press, 1993), declaring that, despite its lowbrow beginnings and mainstream distaste for its more unsavory examples, rap deserves serious esthetic study.

3. I'm indebted to Matthew Chaldecott for these lyrics.

4. In one of the best of the many books on the subject, *Hip Hop America,* 189, Nelson George sees a link between such rappers as KRS-One and Ice Cube and "the authentic pulp fiction tradition of Iceberg Slim and Donald Goines."

5. Lightnin' Rod [Jalal Nurridin], *Hustlers Convention* (New York: Harmony, 1973), 76. See Hager, *Hip Hop: The Illustrated History,* 47, and also Abiodun Oyewole and Umar Bin Hassan with Kim Green, *On a Mission: Selected Poems and a History of the Last Poets* (New York: Henry Holt, 1996) for the Last Poets' more nationalistic poetry, which they recited to background music.

6. See chapter 1. See also Howard W. Odum, *Rainbow round My Shoulder: The Blue Trail of Black Ulysses* (New York: Grosset and Dunlap, by arrangement with the Bobbs-Merrill Co., 1928), 79.

7. I'm indebted to my son, Craig Bryant, for supplying me with these lyrics (which I myself could not understand from the record).

8. Fernando, *The New Beats,* 142.

9. See Brian Cross, *It's Not about a Salary—: Rap, Race, and Resistance in Los Angeles* (London: Verso, 1993), 58; and Rose, *Black Noise,* 130. Rose agrees with Ice-T that this is not really a "rap" song; that, with its heavy metal quality, it more accurately belongs to rock music. I admit to being one of the guilty uninformed. My position is that it

fits better into the rap category, since its main element is the use of a hyper-rhythmic voice without a melody. Not only that, its worldview strikes me as more accurately rap than rock.

10. See, for example, Steven Loza, Milo Alvarez, Josefina Santiago, and Charles Moore, "Los Angeles Gangsta Rap and the Aesthetics of Violence," in *Musical Aesthetics and Multiculturalism in Los Angeles*, ed. Steven Loza, vol. 10 of *Selected Reports in Ethnomusicology* (Los Angeles: UCLA Department of Ethnomusicology, 1994), 150–54.

11. Fernando, *The New Beats*, 126–27.

12. Ibid., 142, 198.

13. Chuck D with Jusuf Jah, *Fight the Power: Rap, Race, and Reality* (New York: Delacorte, 1997), 6–7. The page numbers in the rest of this paragraph refer to this edition.

14. See, as one of many examples, Bob Herbert, "A Musical Betrayal," *New York Times*, National Edition, Op-Ed Page, January 29, 2001, A27.

15. Allison Samuels, N'Gai Croal, and David Gates, "Battle for the Soul of Hip-Hop," *Newsweek*, October 9, 2000, 61.

16. Baraki Kitwana, *The Rap on Gangsta Rap: Who Run It? Gangsta Rap and Visions of Black Violence* (Chicago: Third World, 1995), 23, 57–58.

17. See also my discussion of Bigger in *Victims and Heroes: Racial Violence in the African American Novel* (Amherst: University of Massachusetts Press, 1997), chapter 8.

11. The Badman and the Storyteller

1. John Edgar Wideman, *Brothers and Keepers* (1984; reprint, New York: Viking Penguin, 1985), 19. Subsequent page references are given in the text.

2. Says Wideman, "The prison is the street, the street is prison," in "The Politics of Prison: Doing Time, Marking Race," *The Nation*, October 30, 1995, 505.

3. John Edgar Wideman, *Hiding Place* (1981; reprint, New York: Vintage, 1988), 58, 149. Subsequent page references are given in the text.

4. John Edgar Wideman, *Damballah* (New York: Avon, 1981), 200.

5. Charles E. Silberman, *Criminal Violence, Criminal Justice* (New York: Random House, 1978), 4–5. See also 62–63. From our viewpoint in the twenty-first century, this hardly needs documenting, so widespread has youth violence become, among not just young blacks in the inner city but white children in what whites always deemed the safe and secure schools of the suburbs. William Oliver, though, continues to shine the spotlight on African Americans. In *The Violent Social World of Black Men* (New York: Lexington, 1994), 67, 65–66, he quotes Mac, one of his street informants, who believes that most of the violence on the street occurs when drug sellers try to hold back money from sales to the dealers and the dealers put them down. "There's more violence over drugs [than women]," says Mac. "Half of the guys don't care about girls, they just want drugs. I think most of the fights got something to do with drugs, or somebody getting fast or somebody stealing something." Moreover, the younger men are much more violent than those of, say, twenty-five to thirty. Instead of fighting with fists or talking it out by "woofing," they pull a gun and shoot. "These young boys, they don't want to do nothing—they don't even want to go to school. All they want to do is break in, steal, and do drugs—that's all. The majority of these young boys are raising themselves. Their parents don't care what they do."

6. Wideman is preoccupied with young blacks like these. In *Cattle Killing* (Boston: Houghton Mifflin, 1996), 7, he bitterly suggests a sociological reason for their violence in a passage linking their killing each other to the slaughterhouse: "Shoot. Chute. Black boys shoot each other. Murder themselves. Shoot. Chute. Panicked cattle funneled down the killing chute, nose pressed in the drippy ass of the one ahead. Shitting and pissing all over themselves because finally, too late, they understand. Understand whose skull is split by the ax at the end of the tunnel." Again, in *Two Cities* (Boston: Houghton Mifflin, 1998), a repeated scene has two young gang members enter a crowded post office and saunter arrogantly to the front of the line, knowing no one will challenge them because they carry guns.

7. Quoted in John O'Brien, ed., *Interviews with Black Writers* (New York: Liveright, 1973), 216.

8. Wilfred D. Samuels, "Going Home: A Conversation with John Edgar Wideman," *Callaloo: A Black South Journal of Arts and Letters* 17 (February 1983): 53.

9. Walt Whitman, "Crossing Brooklyn Ferry," section 3, l. 2.

10. John Edgar Wideman, *Sent for You Yesterday* (New York: Avon, 1983), 3. Subsequent page references are given in the text.

11. Later, this street will figure prominently in Wideman's *Two Cities*.

12. Wideman, *Damballah,* dedicatory letter "To Robby," 5.

13. John French and Freeda French are the real names of Wideman's maternal grandparents. John Wideman's father, Edgar, paid tribute to John French as a man of stubborn strength. Freeda French was one of the old Homewood hands who distrusted the southern blacks who came north in the early 1900s, seeing "them as a threat to the live-and-let-live, mellow détente the Frenches and other early, predominately light-skinned Homewood residents had achieved with their Italian neighbors." See John Edgar Wideman, *Fatheralong: A Meditation on Fathers and Sons, Race and Society* (New York: Pantheon, 1994), 118, 121–22.

14. Wideman, *Damballah,* 198.

15. Wideman, *Brothers and Keepers,* 197.

12. Toni Morrison

1. In *Black Women Writers at Work,* ed. Claudia Tate (Harpenden, Herts., England: Oldcastle, 1985), 125–26. One wonders if Morrison might have had in mind for her wandering Ulysses figure Sterling A. Brown's Big Boy in "Odyssey of Big Boy," the first poem in his first collection of poems *Southern Road* (1932) and reprinted in his *Collected Poems,* selected by Michael S. Harper (New York: Harper and Row, 1980), 20–21. Big Boy invokes such ballad heroes as Stagolee and John Henry and describes the "odyssey" of work and women he has pursued north and south like a wandering Ulysses. He follows the archetypal path of the itinerant black laborer, restless, on the move, never settling down, stoically awaiting his own end. Morrison's figures are more sophisticated, but she seems to be thinking of similar odysseys.

2. Thomas LeClair, "'The Language Must Not Sweat': A Conversation with Toni Morrison," in *Toni Morrison: Critical Perspectives Past and Present,* ed. Henry Louis Gates, Jr., and K. A. Appiah (New York: Amistad, 1993), 370, 371. The interview first appeared in *The New Republic,* March 21, 1981.

3. Bessie W. Jones and Audrey Vinson, "An Interview with Toni Morrison," in *Conversations with Toni Morrison,* ed. Danille Taylor-Guthrie (Jackson: University Press of Mississippi, 1994), 179, 182.

4. Henry Louis Gates, Jr., would call this "signifying." See his *The Signifying Monkey: A Theory of African-American Literary Criticism* (New York: Oxford University Press, 1988). As Gates sees it, signifying is a black speech practice that lies at the heart of the system by which blacks communicate, with each other as well as with outsiders. It can consist of stirring up trouble and spreading bad feelings between others, as the Signifying Monkey does between Elephant and Lion in the folktale and toast. It can mean insulting an antagonist in a street contest through subtle slurs on the competitor's mother or other relative. But it can also be "irony," in which the ironist says or does one thing and means another, or "puts one on," as does the folk hero "John de Conqueror," who gets the best of his master or employer by playing to the "superior's" assumption he is stupid.

5. Robert Stepto, "'Intimate Things in Place': A Conversation with Toni Morrison, May 19, 1976," in *Toni Morrison,* ed. Gates and Appiah, 386.

6. Toni Morrison, *The Bluest Eye* (1970; reprint, New York: Washington Square, 1972), 125–26.

7. Eugene D. Genovese uses this phrase to describe Hegel's position on the function of slavery in *Roll, Jordan, Roll: The World the Slaves Made* (New York: Pantheon, 1974), 88.

8. Stepto, "'Intimate Things in Place,'" 391–92.

9. Barbara Hill Rigney, *The Voices of Toni Morrison* (Columbus: Ohio State University Press, 1991), 51.

10. Toni Morrison, *Sula* (1973; reprint, New York: Bantam, 1975), 115, 117.

11. Stepto, "'Intimate Things in Place,'" 384.

12. Mel Watkins, "Talk with Toni Morrison," *New York Times Book Review*, September 11, 1977, 48, 50.

13. The very first experimentations with rap were also appearing at this time, but gangsta rap, which seems like a fusion of the toast tradition, the toast novel, and the early blaxploitation film all compacted into a slick commercial package targeting middle-class youth, both black and white, didn't emerge until the late eighties.

14. Toni Morrison, *Song of Solomon* (1977; reprint, New York: Penguin, 1987), 81. Subsequent page references to this novel are given in the text.

15. Jones and Vinson, "An Interview with Toni Morrison," 178.

16. See my lengthy discussion of this aspect of the novel in *Victims and Heroes: Racial Violence in the African American Novel* (Amherst: University of Massachusetts Press, 1997), chapter 12, "It Ends in Brotherhood."

17. One wonders just how much Morrison might have been thinking, in this final scene, of the climactic struggle between the "old man" and the great fish in Ernest Hemingway's *The Old Man and the Sea* (New York: Charles Scribner's Sons, 1952): "You are killing me, fish, the old man thought. But you have a right to. Never have I seen a greater, or more beautiful, or a calmer or more noble thing than you, brother. Come on and kill me. I do not care who kills who" (92).

18. See also Sandra Pouchet Paquet, "The Ancestor as Foundation in *Their Eyes Were Watching God* and *Tar Baby*," in *Toni Morrison's Fiction: Contemporary Criticism*, ed. David L. Middleton (New York and London: Garland, 1997), 199.

19. Toni Morrison, *Tar Baby* (1981; reprint, New York: New American Library, 1983), 140. Subsequent page references to this novel are given in the text.

20. Terry Otten, "The Crime of Innocence: *Tar Baby* and the Fall Myth," in *Toni Morrison*, ed. Linden Peach (New York: St. Martin's, 1998), 45–46, points out that "Jadine considers Son's hair symbolic of criminality." But this very criminality forces Jadine's own id to appear, her shadow, the black appetites in herself that she abhors, making her frightened of what Otten calls "the 'beast' in the glass."

21. Ralph Ellison agrees with her, remarking in "Change the Joke and Slip the Yoke" that "restlessness of the spirit is an American condition that transcends geography, sociology and past condition of servitude." See *Shadow and Act* (1964; reprint, New York: Signet, 1966), 72.

22. Anthony M. Reynolds, "Urban Negro Toasts: A Hustler's View from L.A.," *Western Folklore* 33, no. 4 (October 1974): 273.

23. See Paquet, "The Ancestor as Foundation," 200, who says that Son's dream of Eloe contains the vision of a male-dominated society, with strong females who nurture and survive, to be sure, but who also submit to male dominion.

24. See *Tar Baby*, 130–31, for the fullest elaboration of the myth. "The essence of the myth," says Paquet ("The Ancestor as Foundation," 197–98), "is freedom as phallic power." Son ultimately emerges "as the embodiment of phallic power and race consciousness."

25. Nellie Y. McKay, "An Interview with Toni Morrison," *Contemporary Literature* 24, no. 4 (winter 1983): 425.

26. See Jones and Vinson, "An Interview with Toni Morrison," 176–77.

27. Anna Mulrine, "This Side of 'Paradise,'" *U.S. News and World Report*, January 19, 1998, 71; Deirdre Donahue, "Morrison's Slice of 'Paradise,'" *USA Today.com*, <http://www. usatoday.com/life/enter/books/b128.htm>, accessed May 25, 2002; "A Conversation with Toni Morrison," formerly on *Borders.com*. Missy Dehn Kubitschek, in *Toni Morrison: A Critical Companion* (Westport, Conn., and London: Greenwood, 1998), 139,

makes a connection I have seen nowhere else: "*Jazz* is the second novel of Morrison's trilogy responding to the three works of Dante's *The Divine Comedy: Inferno, Purgatorio,* and *Paradiso. Beloved* depicts the hell of slavery and its immediate aftermath. Paralleling purgatory rather than hell, *Jazz* depicts much suffering but with a more positive and certain ending." The title of the latest novel "echoes" Dante's *Paradiso.* Kubitschek provides no documentation for this claim, but it does have a certain persuasiveness.

28. Toni Morrison, *Paradise* (New York: Knopf, 1998), 306. Subsequent page references are given in the text.

29. Susan Bowers, "*Beloved* and the New Apocalypse," in *Toni Morrison's Fiction: Contemporary Criticism,* ed. David L. Middleton (New York and London: Garland, 1997), 217.

30. Toni Morrison, *Jazz* (1992; reprint, New York: Penguin Books/Plume, 1993), 129. Subsequent page references are given in the text.

31. See <http://ww.cob.montevallo.edu/student/hatchercl/PARADISE.HTM>, accessed May 25, 2002. Morrison repeats this idea in an interview on *Borders.com:* Those who believe they are chosen to occupy a paradise must ask themselves, she says, "'If you are chosen, does that not also require you to exclude other people?' The basis of being selected is the rejection of others, and paradise itself is a gated place." So while religious piety can be "a solace, a guide, a kind of protection against sin and evil," it can also "freeze and become arrogant and prideful and ungenerous." All religions and beliefs are vulnerable to such thinking. "I was very interested in how that happens with the best intentions in the world." The Ruby elders especially thought "everything outside of themselves" was "an enemy—someone who was that different." See "A Conversation with Toni Morrison," *Borders.com.*

32. "A Conversation with Toni Morrison," *Borders.com.*

33. "I did that [obscured the identity of the white girl killed first] on purpose. I wanted the readers to wonder about the race of those girls until those readers understood that their race didn't matter. I want to dissuade people from reading literature in that way." See Paul Gray, "Paradise Found," *Time,* January 19, 1998, 67.

Analysis of Thirty Prototype Ballads

1. In *Black Culture and Black Consciousness: Afro-American Thought from Slavery to Freedom* (New York: Oxford University Press, 1977), 412, Lawrence W. Levine includes in his list of bad men figures like Billy Bob Russell, Brady, Dolomite, and the Great MacDaddy. They don't fit into my discussion for a number of reasons. Billy Bob Russell is a friend of Lazarus's and has no song about himself, though Odum and Johnson title one of their ballads about Lazarus "Billy Bob Russell" (Odum and Johnson, *Negro Workaday Songs,* 53). Dolomite and the Great MacDaddy are the inventions of the urban toasters of the 1940s and 1950s. And Brady is the white policeman shot down by Duncan for "comin' in while the game was goin' on."

INDEX

Jerry H. Bryant is Emeritus Professor
of English at California State University.